Venetians in Constantinople

THE JOHNS HOPKINS UNIVERSITY STUDIES IN
HISTORICAL AND POLITICAL SCIENCE
124TH SERIES (2006)

1. Benjamin Ehlers, *Between Christians and Moriscos: Juan de Ribera and Religious Reform in Valencia, 1568–1614*

2. Eric R Dursteler, *Venetians in Constantinople: Nation, Identity, and Coexistence in the Early Modern Mediterranean*

Venetians in Constantinople

*Nation, Identity, and Coexistence in
the Early Modern Mediterranean*

ERIC R DURSTELER

The Johns Hopkins University Press
Baltimore

This book was brought to publication with the generous assistance
of the Gladys Krieble Delmas Foundation.

Johns Hopkins Paperback edition, 2008
2 4 6 8 9 7 5 3 1

The Johns Hopkins University Press
2715 North Charles Street
Baltimore, Maryland 21218-4363
www.press.jhu.edu

The Library of Congress has catalogued the hardcover edition of this book as follows:

Dursteler, Eric.
Venetians in Constantinople : nation, identity, and coexistence in
the early modern Mediterranean / Eric R Dursteler.
p. cm.—(The Johns Hopkins University studies in historical and
political science; 124th ser., no. 2)
Includes bibliographical references and index.
ISBN 0-8018-8324-5 (hardcover : alk. paper)
1. Italians—Turkey—Istanbul. 2. Venice (Italy)—Commerce—History.
3. National characteristics. I. Title.
DR435.18D87 2006
949.61′80045104531—dc22   2005019345

ISBN 13: 978-0-8018-9105-2
ISBN 10: 0-8108-9105-1

A catalog record for this book is available from the British Library.

Per Whit

Contents

Acknowledgments

The research and writing of this book have consumed more than half of my adult life. Over the years many individuals and institutions have contributed significantly to its completion. While my name alone appears on the title page, and any errors are of course mine, I would like to recognize those who have played especially significant roles in this project.

I was able to spend a pleasant and profitable year and a half researching in Venice as a result of generous funding from several sources. Without such crucial support, this project could never have been brought to completion. My thanks, then, to the Brown Friends of Italian Studies, the University of Florence, Brigham Young University, the Fulbright Commission, and the Gladys Krieble Delmas Foundation. I am especially grateful to these latter two institutions whose generous support allowed me to spend a wonderful year in Venice accompanied by my wife and children.

As important as financial support is to the completion of any project, even more meaningful to me has been the personal support and encouragement I have received from many individuals both in the United States and in Italy. While a student at Brown University, I was very fortunate to work closely with several members of the faculty. These include Engin Akarli, Philip Benedict, Juergen Schulz, and Amy Remensnyder. I am especially grateful to Anthony Molho. He challenged me greatly during my graduate school years but also encouraged me, helped me to obtain research funding, and suggested outlets where I could present and publish my work. He was an ideal mentor and has become a good friend.

Others who have provided encouragement, constructive criticism, and moral support include Edward Muir, Margaret King, Stanley Chojnacki, Palmira Brummett, Cemal Kadafar, Joanna Drell, Emily O'Brien, Kurt Graham, Frank Christianson, David D'Andrea, Karl Appuhn, Christopher Carlsmith, Bruce Casson, Monique O'Connell, and Marilyn Cooper. In Italy, Giovanni Levi, Francesca Trivellato, Maria Fusaro, Michael Knapton, Paolo Preto, and Rheinhold C. Mueller all provided much appreciated assistance and advice at various stages of my research. In Venice, Gabriele Argenti and his family provided a poor graduate student with room and board and a lasting friendship. Lucio Gabrieli and Mauro Saccardo introduced me to the Venice hidden behind its facades. Vittorio Mandelli explained the intricacies of Venetian institutions and the complexities of the Venetian language and always guarded my seat at *posto numero uno* in the Archivio di stato. Thanks to Daryl and Mary Lee, Shawn and Kelly Miller, John and Melissa Snyder, and Kip Clark for friendship and regular distractions from writing and research. John Snyder also provided artistic and technical assistance with the book's images.

A special mention goes to the archivists and staff members of the archives and libraries in which I worked in Venice. Dr. Maria Pia Pedani-Fabris of the Archivio di stato assisted me both in the archive and with her own work on Veneto-Ottoman relations. Roberto Greggio, formerly of the Archivio di stato, merits special mention. He took the time to explain the barely indexed notarial records at the heart of this study to a slightly bewildered graduate student and generously shared the private indices he had prepared while reorganizing this collection. His personal kindness and interest made my many months of research pleasant and fruitful.

The extensive revisions required to transform a 650-page dissertation into a manageable book manuscript were accomplished against the musical backdrop of *All Soul's Vespers: Requiem Music from Cordoba Cathedral* and *Nova Cantica-Latin Songs of the High Middle Ages,* which served both to put my mind into the appropriate historical context and to drown out the exuberance of my children.

Friends, colleagues, students, and institutions at Brigham Young University have been of great assistance in bringing this project to completion. Craig Harline and Michael Farmer read various versions of the manuscript and provided helpful suggestions on how to improve it. Donald Harreld also read the manuscript and provided key references that greatly shaped my thinking on merchant nations and community. De Lamar Jensen and Douglas Tobler nurtured and inspired my love for history early on. The College of Family, Home, and Social Sciences and the History Department have been consistently supportive with both funds and time, as has the David M. Kennedy Center. Special thanks to Deans Clayne Pope and David Magleby and to Jeffrey Ringer, for their support. Thanks are also due to the staff of the Harold B. Lee Library who tracked down almost every obscure book or article I requested. The maps were produced by Whitney Fae Taylor and Brandon Jones of the Brigham Young University Map Lab. Crystal Moore-Walker, Anaïs Haase, and Daniel Daines took care of all the small things as my research assistants. Finally, without the support and wisdom of a great depart-ment chair, Frank Fox, this book would never have been completed. All young scholars should have such a chair to help them navigate the shoals along the road to tenure.

My most important acknowledgment must go to my family, who have accom-panied, supported, and cheered me along this long road. Without the material and, even more, the moral, support of my parents, Larry and Tamra Dursteler, I would never have switched career paths in midstream. Their unfailing assistance and confidence have been a source of strength to me and my family. This book has evolved against the backdrop of my real career as husband and father. When this odyssey began, Lauren was starting kindergarten and Collin was still in diapers. Now Lauren is ready to leave for college, Collin is starting high school, and another child, Addy Serena, who was named after La Serenissima, the city where she started her life, has rounded out our family. My children have made the trip so much brighter with their enthusiasm for their dad's obsession; they have provided needed distraction and comic relief, and they have helped me always maintain a balanced perspective on life. Finally, this book would never have been started or completed without the support and encouragement of my wife, Whitney. Whenever I was in danger of slipping beneath the waves, she kept me afloat. These pages are dedicated to her.

Portions of this book previously appeared in often significantly different form in several articles. I am grateful to the editors and publications for permission to use portions of these works: "Identity and Coexistence in the Eastern Mediter-ranean, ca. 1600: Venice and the Ottoman Empire," *New Perspectives on Turkey* 18 (1998): 113–30; "The *Bailo* in Constantinople: Crisis and Career in Venice's Early Modern Diplomatic Corps," *Mediterranean Historical Review* 16 (2001): 1–25; "Commerce and Coexistence: Venetian and Ottoman Merchants in the Early Modern Era," *Turcica* 34 (2002): 105–33; "Neighbors: Venetians and Ottomans in Early Modern Galata," in *Multicultural Europe and Cultural Exchange*, ed. James P. Helfers (Turnhout, Belgium: BREPOLS, 2005), 33–47.

Venetians in Constantinople

Introduction

In early June 1614, fleeing a failed love affair, one of the early modern era's most intrepid travelers, Pietro della Valle, set out from the Venetian port of Malamocco. A poet, an orator, and a soldier, the twenty-eight-year-old scion of a noble Roman family sailed on the *Gran Delfino,* a Venetian war galleon armed with forty-five artillery pieces that all but guaranteed a safe passage amid the corsairs that infested the Mediterranean. His objective was one of the most popular and intriguing destinations of early modern travelers, the seat of the sultan of the Ottoman Empire, Constantinople.[1] This departure marked the beginning of an eleven-year "pilgrimage of curiosity" that would take the Roman through Ottoman and Persian lands, and eventually as far as India. During his travels, della Valle actively engaged the cultures he encountered: he "copied ancient inscriptions, collected oriental manuscripts, dug up Egyptian mummies, researched Arabic science, translated or even composed Persian literature," and even mastered several of the region's languages. Because of the breadth and depth of his travels and experiences, he has been recognized as a particularly astute and thoughtful early modern cultural reporter.[2] Della Valle's voyage into the east lasted just over two months, and he landed in Galata,[3] Constantinople's cosmopolitan suburb across the Golden Horn on August 15, 1614.

During the course of his voyage, della Valle composed a detailed and suggestive description of the "men and women, soldiers, sailors, merchants and passengers," some five hundred in total, who accompanied him. He paid particular attention to his fellow travelers, who were a decidedly diverse lot: "There were Catholic Christians, heretics of various sects, Greeks, Armenians, Turks, Persians, Jews, Italians from almost all cities, French, Spanish, Portuguese, English, Germans, Flemings, and to conclude in a few words, [people] of almost all religions, and nations of the world."[4]

Della Valle's taxonomy represents his attempt to both order and describe the people he encountered. It illustrates the complexity of the world in which he traveled, as well as two of the primary markers of early modern identity, religion and nation. The image of the "medley of this company," as della Valle describes it, sharing the limited space of the *Gran Delfino*—eating, drinking, conversing, passing the long days together for more than two months—also hints at unexpected possibilities of cultural exchange in the Mediterranean of the seventeenth century. Della Valle saw nothing unusual or troubling in the diverse mix of his fellow travelers; indeed he described his experience with them as "truly delightful," which suggests the potential for seemingly antagonistic cultures to interact and even coexist.[5] It is this nexus between identity and coexistence, specifically in the context of the relationship between the two great early modern Mediterranean sea powers—the Venetian and the Ottoman empires—that is the focus of this study.

COEXISTENCE

The intersection of cultures has attracted much scholarly attention since at least the anthropological turn that produced the "new cultural history."[6] The most important initial studies were usually within the context of European expansion and encounters with the societies of Asia, Africa, and the Americas.[7] More recently the cultural pluralism of the Mediterranean has been rediscovered: as della Valle's experience suggests, it represents an excellent laboratory in which to pose questions regarding identity, cultures, and the ways in which individuals and groups interacted in times of peace and of conflict.[8] Because of their long and unique shared history, their abundant archival resources for the early modern period, and the richness of their modern historiographical traditions, the relationship between the Venetian and the Ottoman empires represents an ideal case study for examining the nature of cultural contacts in the Mediterranean.[9]

In the case of Venice, scholars in recent years have been drawn to the multicultural character of the city and the possibility of analyzing diverse groups interacting in "relative harmony," both in the city itself and in its expansive eastern empire, the *stato da mar*.[10] In the early modern era, the Venetian Empire was uniquely situated to function as both boundary and cultural middle ground, "a place of transition" in which people from throughout the Mediterranean and from every corner of Europe came together. As Luigi Groto wrote in 1616, Venice was like " 'a tiny dot on a great sphere' towards which all the civilizations of the Mediterranean converge."[11] A culturally diverse group of merchants, travelers, and officials regularly mixed in the cities of the Venetian Empire, and indeed, many travelers felt in entering the lagoon that they had already arrived in the exotic "Orient." This pluralistic milen is vividly depicted in the narrative scenes of painters such as Gentile Bellini and Vittore Carpaccio.[12] As William McNeill evocatively described it, the Venetian Empire represented the frontier of the European world, the hinge between east and west.[13] Similarly, because of the diversity of the cultures that mixed within its borders and the complexity of their convergence over an extended period of time, cultural historians have also increasingly been drawn to the study of the Ottoman Empire.

Because of their lengthy common border and shared engagement in the eastern Mediterranean, for almost five hundred years, the histories of Venice and the Ottoman Empire were tightly intertwined. From its earliest days, Venice's fortunes were directly founded on its Levantine trade, and during the Byzantine Empire's waning centuries the city-state emerged as the dominant European commercial power in the eastern Mediterranean, as well as a significant political and military force, with colonies and outposts in Dalmatia and the Aegean and Ionian Seas. As Byzantium declined, the Ottomans increasingly assumed the role of Venice's partner and rival. Already in the late thirteenth century, because Venice's eastern territories were directly in its path, the Ottoman expansion began to have important political and commercial implications for both states.[14] Well before the conquest of Constantinople in 1453, Venice recognized the changing political and commercial tides, and gradually established closer ties with the Ottoman sultans.

While all major European polities at one time or another maintained diplomatic and commercial relations with the Ottoman Empire, none did so to the extent of the Republic of Venice.[15] Commerce was the initial basis of this relationship: for a time in the fifteenth century, after disposing of the Genoese challenge, Venice nearly monopolized Mediterranean trade. This imbalance of economic power in the region was perceived as a threat by the sultans, who implemented policies to weaken Venice's stranglehold on Levantine commerce. These policies, combined with challenges from commercial competitors both old and new, gradually chipped away at the Venetians' monopoly in the difficult sixteenth century, yet Venice remained among the Ottomans' most important international trading partners well into the seventeenth century.[16] To be sure, Venetian and European

The Eastern Mediterranean

trade, more generally, represented a relatively marginal part of the Ottoman econ-omy, dwarfed by the much larger domestic market. This is not to say that Otto-mans were indifferent to commerce with Venice; indeed Venetian luxury goods remained highly sought after in the Porte.[17] For Venetians, however, even in the changed economic environment of the sixteenth century, the Levant continued to occupy a place of primacy in their collective imagination, and many believed, as did Girolamo Priuli, that their city's fortunes were still inseparably tied to the east.[18]

The Ottomans also affected Venice's political affairs in the Italian peninsula: while it carved out an increasingly powerful *terraferma* state, in part as a response to the Ottoman expansion, that same threat served as a counterweight that kept the city-state from shifting the Italian balance of power decisively in its favor.[19] The disastrous wars with the Ottomans in 1463 and 1499, the near cataclysm of Cambrai in 1509, and the troubled years leading up to the treaty of Bologna in 1530 all made Venice painfully aware of its changed status and led its rulers to pursue a realpolitik policy of neutrality, a tricky balancing act between the French, the Habsburgs, and, most importantly, the Ottomans. As Guicciardini observed, the Venetians' experience with the Ottoman Empire over the half century after the conquest of Constantinople taught them that "knowing well the art of defense" was better "than engaging the enemy in battle."[20] From the first years of the sixteenth century, "the *Serenissima* lived between the anvil of the Habsburgs and the hammer of the Turks," or as described by a papal nuncio, "between two counterweights."[21] The extent to which this stance of neutrality permeated Venetian society is evidenced in the assertion of a young citizen bureaucrat who affirmed that in his official duties he would not favor one prince over another as was required of "everyone who was born in Venice, city of great concord and of great neutrality."[22]

Venice's was not a true neutrality, however; rather, the Signoria was involved in a difficult and sensitive "game of balance" and of "equivocation," trying to play one power off the other. The Venetians used diplomacy, a system of ever-shifting alliances, and control over the dissemination of information to both the Habsburgs and the Ottomans in a sometimes desperate effort to appease and manipulate both states into positions favorable to the weakened republic as it confronted a brave new Mediterranean world.[23] In the final equation, however, Venice's rulers clearly understood that their city's economic and political viability was most closely linked to their ability to maintain good relations with the dominant Mediterranean power of the day, the Sublime Porte. When presented with the possibility of obtaining peace with the Habsburgs, the patrician Lunardo Emo "wept at the speaker's platform" as he warned his fellow senators against angering the Ottomans by choosing Charles V over Süleyman. A similar pro-Ottoman position was also the keystone of Doge Andrea Gritti's diplomatic policy.[24]

Venice's dependence on Ottoman goodwill was everywhere evident: after the discovery of the Cape route, for example, it became clear that only the sultans were powerful enough to challenge Portuguese monopolization of the spice trade; thus Venice pursued "a more subtle, even submissive, policy toward the Ottomans," which led to a resurgence in the trade by 1550.[25] Venice's submission was further encouraged by its reliance on Ottoman grain, which was so significant that one official reported that Venice's Dalmatian subjects would die of famine if the Ottoman trade were ever interrupted.[26] In addition, Venice's military forces often depended on the recruitment of Ottoman subjects, most notably the famed *stradioti,* a reliance that Girolamo Priuli decried as being like a "man cutting off his penis to spite his wife."[27] Politically and economically, then, there is little question that after 1470, Venetian well-being was subject to the favor of the sultans, which earned the city the sobriquet, "the Turk's Courtesan," and much disdain among the corps of Christendom. Of Venice, Pius II said famously, if over-simply, "too much intercourse with the Turks has made you the friends of the Mohammedans and you care no more for religion."[28]

Although circumstances occasionally dictated a momentary shift in this policy, Venice was generally successful in maintaining its neutral stance, evidenced most conspicuously in the rarity after 1503 of open conflict with the Ottomans.[29] Indeed, one of the striking, but often overlooked, features of Veneto-Ottoman relations in the early modern period is the degree to which the two powers' relations were characterized by coexistence rather than conflict. From 1500 to the fall of the Venetian Republic in 1797, Venice and the Ottoman Empire were at peace, save for several relatively brief interludes of open hostility, punctuated by raiding and other corsair activities. These moments of open warfare were generally short-lived (with the exception of the War of Candia from 1645 to 1669) and were distinguished more by attempts on both sides to repair the rupture quickly than by total warfare. Thus, while hostility was certainly one aspect of Veneto-Ottoman relations, in many ways it must be seen as exceptional against this backdrop of peace.

This reality of Ottoman and Venetian coexistence is in many ways at odds with the way the encounter between the major religious cultures of the Mediterranean has been characterized. In these depictions, relations between Europe and the Ottoman Empire, and more broadly between Christianity and Islam, are generally reduced to a shorthand of binary oppositions—East/West, Muslim/Christian, Venetian/Turk, Europe/Other. This dichotomy is readily apparent in the titles of important monographs: *Islam and the West, Europe and the Turk, Venezia e i turchi*.[30] The continued currency and persistence of this "oppositional framework"[31] among the general population as well as scholars is evident in the influential "clash of civilizations" model that Samuel P. Huntington has posited, as well as in many works produced in the wake of the events of September 2001 and the subsequent hostilities in Afghanistan and Iraq.[32]

This bipartite vision of the early modern Mediterranean world is a product of the complex interaction of both historical and historiographical trends. Historically, its roots extend back to biblical representations of Near Eastern foes, but especially to the epic confrontation between classical Greece and the Persian Empire. In the postclassical era this clash metamorphosed into the inheritance struggle between the two great religious offspring of the classical world, Islam and Christendom. Each posed the threat of "conquest and conversion" to the other, though this was especially true in the case of Christendom, which progressively lost ground in Islam's early centuries.[33] In Europe, one product of this political and religious rivalry was an extensive anti-Muslim and anti-Ottoman literature that demonized the other and contrived to inspire crusades to liberate cruelly oppressed lands under the heel of Islam. In the nineteenth and twentieth century, nationalists (both Christian and Muslim) seeking to explain the political and economic retardation and cultural marginalization of their nascent nation-states drew on this polemical literary body to blame their failings on the deadening influence of the repressive Ottoman rule.[34] This vision conveniently ignored centuries of coexistence and the relatively tolerant attitude of the Ottoman state toward its minority populations,[35] and a narrative of subjugation at Ottoman hands became entrenched in western intellectual culture, which resulted in modern political and religious antagonisms being teleologically imprinted onto the past.[36] Likewise, the fissures of the cold war era were reflected onto the past, depicting the Mediterranean as cleanly divided into two civilizational camps, opposed to each other geographically, culturally, and religiously, and each driven to impose its own image on the other in an ideological war of the worlds.[37] The current of anti-Turkish and anti-Islamic opinion persists today, fed by stereotypical depictions of Islam in western media, and by events such as the "war on terror" and the recent debate over Turkey's entry into the European Union, which the papacy has opposed on the grounds that Islam is "in permanent contrast to Europe."[38]

These Manichean historical currents have been mirrored in the historiography of the encounter between Europe and the Ottoman Empire. Since the nineteenth century, significant bodies of historical literature have focused on two fundamental aspects of the millennial engagement of these Mediterranean cultures: image and impact. One of the most common early approaches to the study of the Ottoman Empire by western scholars examined the impact of the "Turks'" presence and expansion on Europe. Foundational early works, such as Johann Wilhelm Zinkeisen's *Geschichte des osmanischen Reiches in Europa* and Nicolae Iorga's *Geschichte des osmanischen Reiches* were supplemented in the mid-twentieth century by Dorothy Vaughan's *Europe and the Turk*, Paul Coles's *The Ottoman Impact on Europe*, and Gibb and Bowen's *Islamic Society and the West*. These scholars focused to a greater or lesser degree on Ottoman history, but they also prominently dealt with the diplomatic and political implications that the Ottoman threat presented to European society and civilization. While significant contributions of historical scholarship, these works were based on a "clash of civilizations" model in their treatment of Ottoman-European relations and insisted on a fundamental opposition between two essentially different and ultimately incompatible cultures.[39]

Parallel to this history of the Ottoman impact, other scholars advanced a cultural-intellectual history, a literature of the image of the "Turk" in European culture. Works such as Clarence Dana Rouillard's pioneering *The Turk in French History, Thought, and Literature,* Samuel Chew's *The Crescent and the Rose,* R. W. Southern's *Western Views of Islam in the Middle Ages,* Norman Daniel's *Islam and the West: The Making of an Image,* Robert Schwoebel's *The Shadow of the Crescent,* and Paolo Preto's *Venezia e i turchi* all were concerned, at their core, with the manner in which Islam and the "Turks" were perceived and depicted as the Christian and European other.[40] A number of recent publications suggest that this fascination with the representations of Islam in European society continues.[41] Generally, this literature of image has unfolded in rich detail the virulent portrayal of Islam and Muslims within European society, and especially within European literature. This historiography is based on the seemingly endless literary output in Christendom devoted to explaining, demonizing, and dismissing Islam throughout their long, shared history.[42] While some of these scholars have been more nuanced in their discussion of the image of the "Turk," acknowledging changes in views over time and diversity in attitudes depending on proximity, in the final analysis, the literature of image most often has painted a synchronic picture of hostility and misunderstanding that varies little from the Middle Ages into the early modern era.[43]

This binary narrative of opposition, misunderstanding, and animosity that has dominated the historiographical discourse has in recent years been questioned by scholars who have argued for the need to approach the encounter between Islam and Christianity with a more nuanced view of the nature of culture and cultural interaction. These scholars maintain that structuralist and essentialist assumptions that reify abstractions such as nation, culture, religion, or civilization, and assume an inherent division and oppositional relationship between metacategories such as East and West, have obscured a more complex and varied reality. The traditional picture assumes a degree of cultural unity and homogeneity within these groups, and an unwavering antagonism between them, which is at odds with both the new cultural historians' more sophisticated understanding of cultures and with the fluidity of borders and identities during the premodern period. Cultural contact and interaction were messier, more contradictory, and variable than this two-dimensional, static pattern allows.[44]

In terms of the literature of image, this revisionist view has challenged the often monotone and static depiction of previous image literature that limned Islam and the Ottoman Empire solely "as a barbarous monster." Maxime Rodinson, for example, argues that "Christian Europe did not, as is commonly assumed, have one, but several images" of Islam.[45] Lucette Valensi shows how in the Venetian *relazioni* there existed alongside the traditional rhetoric an admiration for the strength of the Ottoman state's institutions and the courage of its soldiers.[46] She and other scholars have rightly pointed out the literary rumblings of a break with the medieval dogmas among some early modern observers. Following the conquest of Constantinople, Europe developed closer political and economic ties with the Ottoman Empire, giving rise to a greater curiosity and a need for more accurate information regarding the Ottomans. Growing numbers of travelers between east and west both were a product of and contributed to this demand.[47] Another important element in this evolving picture was the spread of printing. As Rouillard suggests and others have since shown, this surge in information on and interest in the "Turks" led to increasing treatments of the matter in European art and literature, with subtle increases in objectivity and accuracy.[48] Indicative of Europe's fascination and preoccupation with its neighbor is that in France alone, from 1492 to 1630 four times more books were published on the Ottoman Empire than on the New World.[49] Not surprisingly, some of the most nuanced and popular discussions of the Ottomans were contained in the *relazioni* of the Venetian baili who served in Constantinople, charged as they were to provide balanced, accurate information intended to guide the republic's very sensitive Ottoman policies.[50]

In response to the traditional literature of impact, some scholars have begun to question the axiomatic view that emphasizes the fixed nature and adversarial character of Europe and the Ottoman Empire. Instead they have proposed a more complex approach to both identity and cultural interaction. Recent research, particularly by Ottomanists such as Cemal Kafadar, Suraiya Faroqhi, Palmira Brummet—but also Peter Sahlins writing on early modern France, Molly Greene and Sally McKee on Crete, Jeremy Prestholdt on East Africa, and Joan-Pau Rubiés on India[51]—has made meaningful strides toward developing a more sophisticated model of cultural interaction that rejects the essentialization of identity and the reduction of the Mediterranean to a series of oppositional metacategories.[52] Their work has challenged the "totalizing concept of the 'Other'" expressed in Edward Said's influential orientalist model as conceptually limiting and reductionist in interpreting and explaining cultural exchanges. They have argued instead for the need to "disarticulate the notion" that the premodern Mediterranean world "was composed of isolated blocks, secure and content in their foreignness."[53] Indeed, Richard Bulliet in a recent, provocative work contends that far from being diametrically opposed as in Huntington's "clash of civilizations" model, the histories of Christendom and Islam are so closely intertwined that the Mediterranean ought to be envisioned in terms of a shared "Islamo-Christian" civilization.[54] Linda Darling's epitaph on the old view of the encounter between Islam and Christianity suggests the degree to which the paradigm has begun to shift: "The idea that the west is eternally opposed to the east, that the east stood still while the west progressed, should be relegated to the horse-and-buggy era as something once believed but no longer credible, like the flat earth, spontaneous generation, or the medical use of leeches."[55]

IDENTITY

One of the core issues in the emerging discourse on Mediterranean culture focuses on identity. Questions of identity have, of course, permeated much recent discourse, both erudite and popular. Influenced by both the new cultural history and postmodernist reflections on identity, scholars have increasingly abandoned the structuralist-essentialist model for a view of self that emphasizes its fluidity and socially constructed character.[56] This shift has been informed by current events, including mass migrations, the breakup and refashioning of long-standing nation-states, and the breakdown of linguistic, cultural, economic, and political boundaries in the era of globalization.[57] In Europe, the growth and expansion of the European Union has produced a wide-ranging examination of European identity. Because of its religious and ethnic diversity, its status as a Christian and Muslim cultural middle ground, and the degree of geographic mobility in the region, the Mediterranean has become a fashionable focus for discussions of both cultural convergence and identity.

While much has been written on identity in the context of the modern world, we know decidedly less about it in the early modern era. To get some sense of the way in which contemporaries understood both themselves and how they configured their world, we return to Pietro della Valle's intellectual pilgrimage. In his taxonomy della Valle lines up his fellow travelers into two parallel columns: the first includes "Catholic Christians, heretics of various sects, . . . Turks, . . . Jews"; the second "Greeks, Armenians, . . . Persians, . . . Italians from almost all Cities, French, Spanish, Portuguese, English, Germans, Flemings." In short, della Valle concludes, his companions represent "almost all religions, and nations of the world."[58] These two categories—religion and nation—are essential to della Valle's conceptualization, and along with social hierarchies, they are the key categories of identity that contemporaries mobilized to order their world.

The first labels della Valle employs are religious: he divides his fellow travelers into Catholics, heretics, Jews, and Turks. During the early modern period religion remained one of the primary elements of individual and group identity. Where political status had perhaps comparatively minimal significance, religion was a fundamental constituent of identity because of its ability to "penetrate the masses of a population" in a way which pre-modern states were unable.[59] If Europeans no longer realistically harbored hopes for a united Christendom and regularly referred to themselves less by religious than regional and cultural signifiers, and if the Islamic world was rent by its own internal divisions, religion remained at the core a key, even assumed, element in constructions of identity.

In situations in which religious pluralism existed, religious identifiers were particularly common. This is evident in the general tendency among Christian Europeans to group the widely diverse elements of Islam generically under the rubric "Turk." Although an ethnic and linguistic term, "Turk" was widely used in this period as a religious catch-all to describe all Muslims.[60] Curiously, the same term was also employed occasionally to describe Protestants.[61] In the Ottoman Empire, people were usually classified by religion, not language or ethnicity, and Ottomans often referred to Christians "not in territorial or national terms but simply as infidels [kafir]." Indeed the popular view was *"al-Kufr kulluhu milla wāhida* [unbelief constitutes one nation]."[62]

In acknowledging the enduring importance of religion in questions of identity, however, we should not assume that religion was the only determining factor either in constructions of identity or in conceptualizing the world. The ideological clash between Islam and Christianity did not dictate all the actions of every early modern man and woman all the time. Muslims and Christians were not perpetually engaged in a life-and-death struggle: "coexistence and symbiosis were possible" and almost certainly the quotidian norm rather than the exception.[63] While modern observers often attribute an unwavering religiosity to the medieval and early modern periods, the reality was infinitely more tangled. Many individuals moved easily between religious poles, and indeed polities were never averse to allying with a perceived infidel if the stakes were right. Robert Donia and John Fine have shown that Bosnian nobles were generally "indifferent to religious issues. They intermarried and formed alliances across denominational lines; when it suited their worldly aims, they changed faiths easily."[64] Evidence from throughout Venice's *stato da mar* and across the Mediterranean provides innumerable instances of religious migration across seemingly inviolable boundaries and suggests that frontiers of faith were more porous than we have previously believed.[65] This same "confessional ambiguity" of the Mediterranean was also evident in Reformation Europe in relations between Catholics and Protestants.[66] Even when religious boundaries were not violated, a certain religious syncretism existed among Catholic, Orthodox, and Muslim in the Mediterranean who shared popular beliefs in miraculous saints and the efficacy of Christian baptism.[67]

In the political realm too, apparently rigid divisions between Christian and Muslim states, proved much more pliable than is often acknowledged. Venice, of course, had little trouble breaking with Christendom to treat with the Ottoman Empire; indeed the city was famed for the position expressed by the Senate after Lepanto, "*Prima semo veneziani, poi cristiani* [first we are Venetians, then Christians]."[68] Even at this moment of glory following the first major defeat of the Ottomans in memory, Venice clearly recognized the importance of pursuing an independent policy in opposition to the crusading stance advocated by the papacy and Spain, and it soon broke with its Christian allies to sue for a separate peace. Venice was not alone in this openness to the Ottomans: in the same breath European powers could decry Venice and its policies, demonize the "Turks" as infidels, and still attempt to benefit from relations with the sultans themselves.[69] At one time or another, almost every European power, including the papacy, made overtures toward the sultans and even established open alliances with them.[70] Peasants too were generally more interested in the oppressiveness of their sovereigns' rule than in their religion. A sixteenth-century Balkan maxim stated, "better the turban of the Turk than the tiara of the Pope," and peasants throughout the Mediterranean often voted with their feet by fleeing Christian rule for Ottoman or even assisting the sultans' forces in their conquests of Christian lands. This ambiguity was succinctly expressed by Luther: "A smart Turk makes a better ruler than a dumb Christian."[71]

In the case of Islam, the familiar maxim that religion subsumed all and that "unbelief constituted one nation" is generally invalid, but especially so in the case of the Ottomans, who derived from their frontier milieu a cultural mix of classical Islamic legal traditions joined with Byzantine and Inner Asian elements. Ottoman society was particularly open to Christians and Jews, and the cases of non-Muslims or converts to Islam who played leading roles in the Ottoman state are too common to enumerate. In the early modern era, the Ottomans engaged in close economic, political, and cultural relations with many so-called infidel powers and were very open to importing "Western" ideas and specialists. Indeed, while Europeans were narcissistically convinced that the sultans had "as objective the monarchy of all the world and the destruction of Christendom," in reality Ottoman military and political efforts were focused primarily against fellow Muslim rulers in Egypt, Iran, and North Africa.[72] The sultans also recognized and exploited the divisions among Christians after 1517 to their political advantage.[73]

To return to della Valle, it is clear that our intrepid traveler did not conceive of his world solely in religious terms. He divided his companions into a second, nonreligious subset: Greeks, Armenians, Persians, French, Spaniards, Portuguese, English, Dutch, Germans, and Italians from all cities; in short, people from all the "nations of the world."[74] In this he was in no way unique; every early modern traveler utilized this taxonomic category. For example, the sixteenth-century imperial ambassador Ogier Ghiselin de Busbecq wrote of encountering "Ragusans, Florentines, Venetians, and sometimes also Greeks, and men of other nations."[75] The idea of nation is, of course, notoriously imprecise, and its conceptual utility is seriously undermined by the significant variance between its modern and premodern usages. Eric Hobsbawm has argued that the modern concept of nation is "historically very young," dating back at most to the eighteenth century. Such a view of the nation is at the heart of the work of the postmodernist, anti-essentialist views of scholars such as Ernst Gellner and Benedict Anderson who see nations as socially constructed, "imagined communities."[76] While these important works have focused primarily on the modern era, some scholars working on premodern Europe have challenged this view, holding that the roots of the modern concept of nation are firmly situated in the Middle Ages.[77] Although this is not the place to engage this debate, a historically precise understanding of early modern concepts of nation, because of its widespread usage, is crucial to understanding premodern identities.

Etymologically, the word *nation* derives from the Latin *natio,* which shares the same stem as *natus.* In the classical era, *nation* referred to people born in the same city or region, such as Jews or Syrians who resided in Rome or some other city. In medieval and early modern times, *nation* retained this classical, geographical connection with place of birth, origin, or descent.[78] This is particularly evident in Romance languages: Dante used *nazione* to refer to "men who originated in the same province or city," and an early French dictionary's definition cited Froissart's *"je fus retourné au pays de ma nation en la conté de Haynnault* [I returned to the land of my birth in the county of Haynnault]." Machiavelli used the terms province and nation, and often *patria,* interchangeably, as did Guicciardini.[79] The meaning of *nation* in the early modern period, then, remained closely linked to the classical concept of nation as a community of people with a shared place of origin.[80]

Early modern Ottoman and other writers in the Muslim world utilized a concept with some similarities to the premodern European notion of nation. This is evident in the writings of the Ottoman intellectual and bureaucrat Mustafa Ali, the historian Naima, and the seventeenth-century Ottoman poet Nabi who referred to Constantinople as "the nursery of many nations."[81] The Ottomans came to use the term *taife*, which could describe generically any group, in a similar fashion to the premodern European uses of *nation*. While Ottomans referred to Europeans generically as Franks (*Ifrandj* or *Firandj*), they clearly recognized degrees of difference in this general category. Thus they described their own Latin-rite Christian subjects as *"tatlısu frengi,* sweet-water Franks," while other European Christians were designated "salt-water Franks," and were further differentiated into cultural and linguistic groups: *"taife-ya Efrenk-i Ingiliz* or *taife-yi Efrenk-i Filemenk"* (English Franks or Dutch Franks).[82]

The association of nation with geography is evident in the practice of using place of birth as surname among non-nobles.[83] This association is also clear in a Venetian dispatch in which Bailo Almoro Nani refers disparagingly to a certain Mustafa, "who was by nature Greek, and as one partial to the rite of his nation spoke more in that language than in Turkish."[84] His birth identity (his nature or nation) was Greek, and linguistically he was Greek, but in religion he was a "Turk." Nani's observation suggests a second element of identity associated with provenance and birth: language. To nineteenth-century nationalists, language and nation were inseparable; in premodern times the relationship between language and identity was significantly less clear-cut. While often an important piece of the whole, language was rarely "the prime identity criterion."[85] This was evidenced in the unusual linguistic combinations of the nations of medieval universities, as well as the linguistic diversity of many conglomerate states, including the Holy Roman, Venetian, Ottoman, and Spanish empires. In the case of Denmark, one scholar has argued that "as long as language was not considered a vital component of man's identity, the multilingual character of the state raised no problems."[86] In the frontier region between France and Spain, "the Cerdans' chosen languages of expression . . . stood in no necessary relation to their possible identities and chosen loyalties."[87] In the varied world of the Ottoman Empire, with its linguistic diversity and not insignificant body of multilingual individuals and groups, "language was a means of communicating between peoples, not a means of distinguishing among them."[88] The existence of the Italianate *lingua franca* in the European and Mediterranean regions also served to complicate the importance of linguistic boundaries.[89]

If regional provenance was one of the most important elements of "national" identity, it was both expressed and reinforced by language, and by other external markers. These might include dress, foodways, and common customs, as well as more intangible factors such as a sense of some kind of a shared historical past.[90] Costume especially was an important, if easily mutable external signifier of identity.[91] Latin-rite Ottomans, for instance, were recognizable by their luxurious "gownes black, & . . . velvet caps," which stood in contrast to the garb of Greek-Ottomans, who wore violet-colored clothing and bonnets.[92] Books that illustrated and illuminated costume and identity were popular in the latter half of the sixteenth century, particularly among travelers. Peter Mundy carried an illustrated reference book during his Levantine travels, which depicted "the severall habitts used all Constantinople, where most officers and Nationes are distinguished by their habits."[93] While sumptuary laws were common to most polities of the day, they were especially important in the often confusing Mediterranean world, and particularly the Ottoman Empire.[94]

Beyond its integral significance in constructions of identity, the term *nation* was also used to express concepts of community. Nation was commonly applied in a variety of cultural and institutional usages, including divisions of students at university, or religious officials at church councils.[95] For the purposes of this study, one of the most important early modern usages of nation was in reference to communities of merchants and diplomats living abroad under the aegis of a particular city or state. Thus early modern Constantinople was home to Venetian, French, English, and Dutch nations. These trading and diplomatic nations were juridically defined, and membership was limited, at least in theory, to a small cadre of individuals who met certain specific legal requirements. In practice, these communities' borders were much less clearly delineated, and they contained individuals of many different religious, linguistic, political, and geographic backgrounds. For example, the Dutch merchant nation in Constantinople consisted of subjects of the Habsburg emperors from the Southern Provinces, as well as individuals from the Northern Provinces who were subjects of the new Dutch Republic. Other members of the nation were "Dutch by choice, such as some Czech Calvinists." Often Protestants of every persuasion accepted the protection of the Dutch nation, though a number of Catholic priests and monks did as well.[96]

If the nation-state in the nineteenth century was seen as the political expression of the cultural, even biological, *volk,* in premodern times nation did not necessarily correspond to any political entity so much as to a cultural geography that often seems random. This is evident in the accounts of our travelers who referred to Greeks, French, Spaniards, Dutch, English, Germans, and Italians. In some instances—the French and the English, for example—nation did generally correspond to polity. In other cases—the German, the Greek, the Italian—it did not. It is revealing that both della Valle and Busbecq acknowledged the complexity of the category Italian, by further breaking it down to variations based on regional, political, and cultural differences—Venetians, Florentines, and so forth.

Although nation was not necessarily coterminous with political status, this did certainly make up one possible layer of identity. As J. H. Elliott has observed, "loyalty to the home community—the sixteenth century *patria*—was not inherently incompatible with the extension of loyalty to a wider community, so long as the advantages of political union . . . outweigh[ed] the drawbacks."[97] This is evident in the experience of the many Greek subjects of Venice's *stato da mar* who came to Constantinople to trade or work in Ottoman shipyards and galleys, and often married and settled in the city, never to return to their lands of birth. While to outsiders culturally and linguistically quite indistinguishable from the many Greek subjects of the sultan, they differentiated themselves as Venetian subjects by registering annually in the embassy's chancellery in order to avoid paying Ottoman taxes. As Venetian subjects, they were legally under the bailo's jurisdiction, yet they often moved effortlessly between Ottoman and Venetian institutions as circumstances dictated, playing the two systems off each other to their own benefit. Their identity in a sense was hyphenated—while religiously and culturally members of the larger Greek nation that cut across several political boundaries, as well as residents of the Ottoman Empire, which in many cases employed them, politically they continued to identify themselves as Venetian subjects. They were "political amphibians," and they were not unique in their adaptability.[98]

As the experience of Venice's Greek subjects in Constantinople suggests, we should not exaggerate the importance of political factors in early modern identities. Europe in this period was characterized by "vast polyglot and polyethnic" composite states from Vienna, Paris, and Madrid, to Constantinople.[99] Certainly the Venetian Empire qualified as a composite polity, stretching from Bergamo in northern Italy to the islands of Crete and Cyprus in the eastern Mediterranean. The empire's physical space contained a precarious mixture of diversity, including historically antagonistic groups, an "ethnic pluralism," whose relationship to the state was not always clear.[100] There was no natural geographical, religious, linguistic, or cultural coherence to the state's "heterogeneous totality of distinct territories," except that provided politically by Venice's governing institutions.[101] Legislation recognized only a tiny minority of the empire's inhabitants as Venetian, namely the patriciate in Venice and a small number of non-noble citizens.[102] The remainder of the imperial population, and indeed the majority of Venice proper's inhabitants, all fell under the broad rubric of subjects. Subjects from certain *terraferma* cities were accorded Venetian citizenship, but in comparison to the patriciate and the *cittadini originari*, they were second-class citizens. Most of Venice's subjects, however, never even acquired this level of political status and remained part of the mass of generally undifferentiated subjects.[103] Given the

composite nature of so many contemporary polities, as well as the constant variability of political boundaries, it seems clearly unwise to attribute political divisions sketched on maps too weighty a significance in individual or communal
constructions of identity.[104]

Indeed, while Venice coalesced into a reasonably viable political and economic
construction, in many ways the state remained "disorganic and fragmentary."[105]
The often loose ties that bound Venice's expansive empire could fail at times, as
was vividly underscored in the disaster of the War of the League of Cambrai, in
which all Venice's mainland holdings were rapidly lost to an alliance led by the
warrior pope, Julius II.[106] Misgovernment and arrogance on the part of Venetian
officials accentuated latent dissatisfaction among the ruling elites of these conquered territories, who in some ways viewed the *dominante* as an "occupying
force."[107] While these prodigal lands eventually returned somewhat sheepishly to
the fold, the trauma of the experience made manifest the weaknesses of the
Venetian state to the patriciate. The lessons of 1494 and 1509 were clear: in Italy,
governments "could not command enough support or loyalty from [their] subject
communities to have any firm faith in survival. External danger made for internal
threat."[108] If this were true for Venice's *terraferma* state, it was even more the case
for the *stato da mar*. In both Cyprus and Crete, prominent local families openly
encouraged the Ottomans to attack the islands in the hopes of throwing off what
they perceived as oppressive Venetian rule.[109]

Contemporary observers commented on the precariousness of early modern
states. English traveler Henry Blount observed, "the Greeks lived happier under
the Turks, than [the Sicilians] under the Spanish" and that the Sicilians were "not
much averse from the Turkish government."[110] When the Duke of Florence's
corsairs tried to liberate Chios from its Ottoman overlords, the island's inhabitants complained to Clement VIII.[111] At the core of these expressions was the
realization that for the popular majority, the real difference between one sovereign and another, even a Muslim one, was in many ways irrelevant. This realization and the specter of another Cambrai profoundly informed the policies and
politics of Venice's rulers during the sixteenth and seventeenth centuries, particularly in their relationship to the distant and diverse regions of the *stato da
mar*.[112]

In the final analysis, "national" identity—that is, one's sense of association
with region or place of birth—seems to have been, in many instances, stronger
than religious or political identities. This is apparent in the case of the Ottoman
grand vizier, Albanian-born, who was described as "very inclined" to men of his
region and language, regardless of their religion. Such identification often bene-

fited Venice's dragomans from the same region but on the Venetian side of the border, who emphasized their birth and regional over their political and even religious identity in order to facilitate their access to and negotiations with officials at the highest levels of the Ottoman government.[113]

This cursory reflection on identity in the early modern era has not treated a number of other factors such as social estate, occupation, or gender, all of which certainly were important facets of individual and group identities. Nor has it considered the place of family in constructions of identity, which may prove to have been the most important factor of all.[114] In describing the multivalence of identity, my intention has not been simply to replace panoptic labels such as Venetian or Ottoman with inelegant chains of descriptors such as Venetian-Roman Catholic-Greek or Ottoman-Jewish. Rather, I would like to propose a different way of conceptualizing identity which divorces it from static and often convoluted fusions of all its imaginable constituent parts. Identity in the early modern era did not possess "an essential, primordial quality," nor was it "defined by a nuclear component of social or cultural characteristics." It was not an object but rather a process, "a bundle of shifting interactions," a "part of a continuum." It was socially constructed, a process of defining and redefining or, perhaps better, of imagining boundaries. It was then, as it is today, "contingent and relational."[115]

Perhaps overly influenced by the nation-state paradigm, we have often overlooked the intricacies of early modern identity and instead have categorized and systematized the much messier reality of the prenational world into simplistic religious and political blocs. Early modern observers, while utilizing broad organizing categories, acknowledged the possibility of individual and group identities that were more multilayered than simply religion or nation. Busbecq, for example, wrote of encountering a man who was an "an Italian Greek, i.e., both in birth and manners half Greek and half Italian." The English organ builder Thomas Dallam met a man who "was a Turke, but a Cornishe man borne." Another English traveler recorded an encounter with "Mr. Wyllyam Robynsoun, ane Inglyshe man, . . . [whom] tyme hathe so allterred . . . that he ys becom a Slavonyan in natur."[116] This fluidity is also evident in the mobility of merchants, artisans, and others who became citizens of Italian city-states through adopting, and adapting to, the culture of their new homes and being awarded citizenship by privilege.[117] Clearly contemporaries were comfortable, or at least familiar, with ambiguity and multivalence in individual identity.

We have ample evidence of the fluidity of identity in the early modern Mediterranean. A familiar example is that of the Marranos, who were expelled from Spain in 1492 in part for crypto-Judaism. As one scholar has written, the Marranos "used their Jewishness instrumentally, presenting themselves, when occasion called for it, as Jews, but as often as not assuming Christian identities." Evidence also exists of Christians in the Ottoman Empire reconfiguring themselves similarly.[118] Another group that has attracted much attention are the renegades, men and women who crossed over from the Christian to the Muslim sphere and in so doing violated the most elemental boundary in the early modern era.[119] They represent a fascinating collection of individuals, and in some cases whole communities, who adapted not only their political but also their religious identity in response to a range of factors.

One might argue that because Jews and renegades exist on the margins of society they are not representative; however, there is ample evidence of a similar versatility and protean quality of identity among the quintessential Venetians, its merchants. Venetian legislation required that all merchants trading under the city's aegis be Venetian citizens, born or naturalized; by 1550 in practice most were the latter. Many came from the Venetian *terraferma*, but others were not even culturally Venetian or Italian, such as the Helman brothers, who fled the religious troubles of the Low Countries.[120] In some cases even Ottoman subjects traded as Venetian merchants without obtaining citizenship. The archetypal Venetian merchant in Constantinople, then, was Venetian not by birth but as a result of shedding—or rather adapting—cultural, political, and even religious layers of identity in order to participate in the lucrative Levantine trade. As the Marranos, renegades and merchants of Venice suggest, identity in the premodern Mediterranean was more than just a sum total of its parts; it was a dynamic process.

IDENTITY AND COEXISTENCE

This study reconsiders identity in the early modern world in a more fluid and complex fashion in order to both illuminate and explain Veneto-Ottoman cultural interaction and coexistence. To accomplish this, it is necessary to move beyond the "clash of civilizations" model, which surveys the relationship between Islam and Christianity from a geopolitical and rhetorical perch on high, and instead to analyze the lived reality microscopically and on a local, cultural level. Focusing on a localized microcosm such as the Venetian nation reveals the experience of Venetians and Ottomans living side by side and illuminates the complex ways people of diverse religious, cultural, linguistic, and social backgrounds interacted and coexisted on a communal level. By moving from the global to the local, shuttling "between the macroscopic and the molecular levels," a more precise picture of the real rather than the rhetorical character of everyday existence on the frontier materializes.[121] In order to supersede broad generalizations and categorizations that help organize, but may also obscure, the past, we must turn to individuals and small groups and examine their experiences without assuming that their relationship to a state, religion, or culture was paramount.[122]

Venice's merchant and diplomatic nation in Constantinople represents an ideal environment for examining the nature of identity and its place in understanding cross-cultural contacts in the Mediterranean. The Venetian community was one of the largest and most vibrant foreign communities in the Ottoman capital in the late sixteenth and early seventeenth centuries. Located in the interstices of the Mediterranean, it is particularly well situated for studying the character of cultural interaction and identity because of its proximity to and close dealings with the diverse world of the Ottoman capital. Chronologically, the decades from 1573 to 1645 are intriguing because they represent the longest continuous period of peace between the Venetian and Ottoman empires, which permits an examination of Veneto-Ottoman relations in a time not distorted by hostility. Finally, the rich archival records surrounding the Venetian nation—including extensive notarial records, diplomatic reports and correspondence, supplemented by travel literature and French, English, and Ottoman sources—show the physiognomy and experience of this community, as well as its place within the broader networks of early modern Constantinople.[123]

The essence of my argument is really quite straightforward. First, through a detailed study of the microculture of Venetians in Constantinople in the late sixteenth and first half of the seventeenth centuries, I argue that while factors such as religion, culture, and political status all could be integral elements in constructions of self and community, we must avoid the inclination to essentialize identity into any single one of these elements. Early modern identity was multilayered, multivalent, and composite. It was also not an apprehendable object, the sum total of its constituent parts, but rather a dynamic process. This is evidenced both in the Venetian nation, with its multiple layers of official and unofficial elements and its porous boundaries, and in the self-fashioning of Jews, renegades, merchants, and subjects who inhabited the broader world of Constantinople.

Second, I challenge the conflictual model of Veneto-Ottoman relations and suggest instead a more sophisticated understanding of the intersection of cultures. Although dissonance and strife were certainly part of this relationship, coexistence and cooperation were more common. The Orientalist image of a binary Mediterranean is unsatisfactory because it is rooted less in quotidian experience than in the descriptive vituperativeness of the era's rhetoric, which easily lends itself to "generalizations and striking metaphors" that oversimplify in-

finitely more complex realities.[124] Overreliance on certain genres of literary documents, from which broad postulates about Veneto-Ottoman relations have been
drawn, has produced what Stephen Greenblatt calls the "theoretical mistake
and . . . practical blunder [of] collaps[ing] the distinction between representation
and reality."[125] While there clearly is a relationship, the two must not be conflated.
Rhetorical literature allows us to glimpse perceptions of the other from both
Christian and Muslim perspectives, but it leaves open for speculation the question of whether this matched actual experience. Perhaps an Italian saying ex-
presses succinctly the concept I am suggesting: *tra il dire e il fare c'è di mezzo il
mare* (the chasm between words and actions is as large as the sea). Ottomans and
Venetians did find ways to inhabit the same world in relative peace; the challenge
is to explain this reality.

A more complex understanding of both identity and the interaction of cultures in the sixteenth and seventeenth centuries can help us understand Veneto-
Ottoman coexistence. Early modern identity was not "a cultural trap" of totalizing
categories but rather an ongoing process of fashioning and refashioning. Premodern societies were not characterized by rigid, invariable, or inviolable patterns of association and identity; rather barriers that have often been "regarded as
watertight and impassible" were much more permeable and porous than imagined.[126] When viewed in this light, the experience of Venetians in Constantinople
seems less exceptional and may even suggest some broader insights into identity
and cultural interaction in the early modern world.

STRUCTURE

This argument is developed in three stages. The first part examines the struc-
ture and institutions of the Venetian nation in Constantinople and suggests the
need for a more ample, fluid view of community and communal identity. One of
the core questions is who was a Venetian. Chapter 1 looks at what I have termed
the official nation—the bailo, his *famiglia,* and the institutions of the nation.
Chapter 2 examines the other major component of the official nation, the merchants, suggesting that the label of merchant of Venice masked a much more
unstable and intricate reality than this seemingly clear-cut rubric implies. Chapter 3 considers the community on the periphery of the official core, the unofficial
nation. This largest component of the broader Venetian community was made up
of men and women in Constantinople without the express endorsement of the
Venetian state yet who functioned within and were considered an integral part of
the nation.

Chapters 4 and 5 build on the first chapter's problematization of the concepts of community and nation and address the question of identity in the early modern era. Through an examination of Jews, Christian renegades, but also merchants, patricians and the community of Latin-rite Ottomans, these chapters challenge the structuralist, essentialized image of identity as based on religion and/or nation and instead attempt to show that early modern identity was a composite of many factors, as well as a fluid process of definition and redefinition.

Chapter 6 attempts to connect the discussions of nation and identity to the issues of cultural exchange and coexistence. Freed from a fixed model of identity, I argue that Venetians and Ottomans interacted in a more complex and varied fashion than the binary, clash of cultures model permits. Coexistence between Muslim and Christian, Venetian and Ottoman, was possible, and even common on the Mediterranean frontier, and this was facilitated by the fluidity of both individual and collective identity.

NAMES AND DATES

Standardizing dates is a tricky proposition when studying the early modern Mediterranean. In Venice, for example, the year began not on January 1, but on March 1. Thus in most cases, a Venetian document dated "February 23, 1588 (*more veneto*)" would on a modern calendar refer to February 23, 1589. I have elected to record dates as they are indicated in the original documents, with MV following the year to indicate that the date is based on the Venetian calendar year, or the *more veneto*. In the case of the Turkish and Jewish worlds, each of which has its own calendrical traditions, I have simply placed the equivalent Christian year in parentheses.

CHAPTER ONE

The Venetian Nation in Constantinople

The foundations of the Venetian trading and diplomatic nation in Constantinople date to the earliest days of La Serenissima. Initially a minor outpost in Italy, Venice increasingly became a significant political and commercial partner of the Byzantines. In 1082, in recognition of its assistance against the Normans, the Emperor Alexius I Comenus granted Venice special customs privileges, as well as a quarter in the city to facilitate the trade of Venetian merchants who had already long been established in the Byzantine capital. The subsequent centuries, particularly following the fourth crusade, saw the Venetian colony in Constantinople grow to perhaps over ten thousand inhabitants, "a veritable little republic, organized in the image of" the *dominante*. Indeed, its head, the bailo, became one of the most powerful men in the city and the Venetian presence a threat and disruption to the Byzantine emperors' power. From this and other bases in its *stato da mar* empire, Venice by 1400 had significantly weakened its chief competitors and effectively dominated the trade of the eastern Mediterranean.[1]

The expansion of the Ottomans transformed Venice's position and increasingly forced the city to adapt to new realities, particularly in the eastern Mediterranean. At the conquest of Constantinople in 1453, the Venetians were forced to transfer the bulk of their colony from its prime location within the capital city, across the Golden Horn to the international suburb of Galata. Galata was where the Genoese colony had been located historically, and it became the center of the international community under Ottoman rule. Following the fall of the Byzantines, Venice lost its commercial monopoly, but its merchants continued to enjoy the favor of Mehmed the Conqueror, who granted them several lucrative privi-

leges. This patronage came to an end in 1463, when the Republic declared war on
the sultan. Over the next fifteen plus years, the Venetian presence in the Ottoman
capital dwindled to almost nothing, a pattern that would repeat itself to a degree
again in 1499, 1537, and 1570.[2] More significant to the fortunes and status of
Venice than the temporary setbacks of these brief periods of hostility, however,
was the intentional Ottoman policy of weakening the city's dominant position in
Mediterranean trade. Ottoman actions, combined with competition from old and
new commercial rivals, gradually eroded this monopoly after 1500, but Venice
continued to be one of the Ottomans' most important international mercantile
partners well into the seventeenth century.[3]

Though much reduced from its medieval heyday, the early modern Venetian
nation remained a vibrant, dynamic community, among the largest foreign communities in Constantinople. A 1560 estimate reported ten to twelve merchant
houses in Constantinople; fifty years later Simone Contarini reported that where
once there had been eighteen to twenty Venetian merchant houses, in his day
there were only five. An observer around 1625 provides a comparative context: he
put the number of merchant houses at eight or nine for each of the major trading
nations in Constantinople—the French, English, Venetian, and Ragusan.[4] The
Venetian nation was not limited to merchants, however. Its other chief raison
d'être was diplomatic, and to achieve the political objectives of its sponsoring
state, the merchants were supplemented by the members and support staff of the
Venetian diplomatic mission, who might have numbered between fifty and one
hundred at any given time.

While scholars have tended often to focus on merchants and diplomats as the
sole constituent parts of the nation, the Venetian nation in early modern Constantinople was much larger and more varied than this. Indeed, the category of
Venetian in this frontier region comprised a much more diverse collection of
individuals and groups than just traders and diplomats of the official nation. The
unofficial nation included many more men and women who existed on the margins of the official community. These marginal members numbered perhaps
several thousand, with the majority hailing from the islands of Venice's *stato da
mar* empire. During the early modern era, then, the Venetian trading nation in
the Ottoman capital was a complex composite of individuals from widely varied
socioeconomic and cultural backgrounds. It was not a static community, consist-
ing of precisely delineated individuals and groups; rather it was a dynamic entity,
a community that drew together a much wider range of persons than has been
traditionally suggested. This and the next two chapters are devoted to developing a
detailed snapshot of this variegated Venetian nation: Chapters 1 and 2 examine

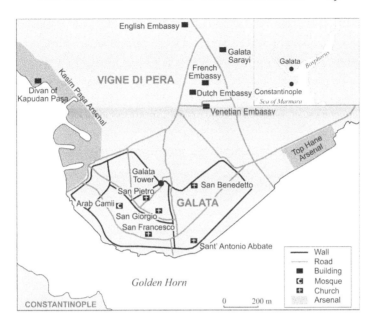

Galata/Pera

the core of the official nation—the merchants and diplomats who were sanctioned to reside in the Ottoman capital. Chapter 3 looks at the more numerous marginal members of the community who composed the unofficial nation. The present chapter considers the core institutions and individuals of the official, diplomatic nation, the baili and their household.

The geographical center of the Venetian community in Constantinople was the embassy, referred to by contemporaries as the bailate. Some time between the fall of Constantinople in 1453 and the outbreak of the war of 1499, the baili relocated to the center of the thriving port suburb of Galata. Following the war of 1537–40, the baili established a second household, outside the city walls in the hills above Galata/Pera, called the Vigne di Pera, where they generally resided during the summer months because it was cooler and a somewhat safer refuge from the plague.[5] Following the war of Cyprus, the baili abandoned the residence in Galata and moved to the Vigne di Pera property permanently; gradually the embassies of other European powers followed.[6] While Girolamo Trevisan described the house as "old, uncomfortable, [and] disordered," it was, according to Leonardo Donà, "an excellent house compared to the others in the land."[7] The summer home was also preferable because the suburb was more tranquil and healthier than crowded Galata, and it provided the baili greater liberty to move about at all hours, as Galata closed its gates at night. Another attraction of the Vigne di Pera location, according to one observer, was that it permitted the baili "to be more free, and to have more ease to smuggle escaped slaves and similar."[8] Indeed, as a result of such abuses, in 1612–13 a grand vizier threatened to move all European embassies to Constantinople to keep them under closer surveillance.[9]

If by the end of the sixteenth century the baili had transferred permanently to the Vigne di Pera, most Venetian merchants continued to live within the city limits of Galata, in close proximity to Ottoman Greek, Muslim, and Jewish merchants, as well as the merchants of other European nations.[10] The reason the merchants did not generally move to the suburb was that Galata was the center of commercial life of the international merchant community, and it was closer to the port. This was where most trade took place, as goods were bought and sold in the loggia of Galata,[11] similar, as one traveler reported, to the Bourse in Antwerp or the Exchange in London. Merchants gathered here at least twice daily. Beyond this, there was no formal merchant house, or *fondaco*, for the nation such as existed in many other Mediterranean and northern European ports.[12] This lack of a commercial center was another reason the bailate functioned as the focal point of the nation. The physical separation between the commercial and political branches of the nation was the source of some dismay among the merchants, who felt that the official residence was "in a place inaccessible to everyone" except the bailo. They complained, "whoever wants to nourish his children needs to be near them, because being distant one can only poorly nourish and watch over them."[13]

The embassy complex in the Vigne di Pera was composed of several different buildings, surrounded by a wall. The enclosed space was large enough that the inhabitants often gathered to "play ball" in the courtyard.[14] In the sixteenth and seventeenth centuries, the main house was constructed of wood, as were most buildings in Constantinople.[15] The bailate was divided into public and private areas; the latter included numerous bedrooms in which the various members of the bailo's entourage lived, a room for the embassy's janissaries, and a large room for the bailo himself. The public rooms were devoted to the various functions of the embassy. These included the chancellery, a large meeting room in which the bailo received supplicants and guests in his official capacities, a banquet hall, and the rooms where the so-called *giovani della lingua* studied to become Venetian dragomans. The bailo's numerous postal couriers lived apart, in a rundown house in the courtyard, because of fears that they might introduce disease into the complex.[16] The house had a small chapel, which Alvise Contarini described in

1636 as "collapsing in numerous places, without an altarpiece, [and] indecorous." It also held a prison, had several secret passages, and was surrounded by a balcony built in the 1590s.[17]

The bailate was the center of the life of the nation, the institutional and administrative focus of the community. As a result, anyone resident in or passing through Constantinople who had any link with Venice, no matter how tenuous, came into the ambit of the bailate. Though they lived in Galata, Venice's merchant Council of XII convened its regular meetings in the embassy to treat the myriad issues that affected their trade. Greek-Venetian subjects from throughout the *stato da mar* appeared at least annually to register their political status. Men and women enslaved in Constantinople or exiled from Venetian lands appeared daily in large numbers to entreat the intervention of the baili in their behalf. In addition, the bailate was a center of the international community's lively interactions, and it was regularly frequented by many Ottomans of diverse cultural and religious derivations. The bailo's table was always full of guests, and the rooms of the embassy often overflowed with overnight visitors.[18] Frequent banquets, complete with party games, also attracted a large and diverse group of participants.[19]

The coherence and continuity of Venetian institutions, particularly those associated with the chancellery, made them the most authoritative foreign institutions in Constantinople. When significant transactions or documents of importance had to be registered, particularly when they dealt with intercourse across religious or political boundaries, the participants had them recorded in the bailo's notarial volumes. When other ambassadors borrowed money, or sold goods of great value, the affair was registered at the Venetian chancellery. When disagreements arose between merchants, diplomats or other elements of the international community, the bailo often served as arbitrator. Ottoman subjects, too, regularly utilized the services of the Venetian chancellery.

The embassy accommodated only the bailo and his *famiglia*. None of the merchants or other members of the broader Venetian community lived in the complex, or even necessarily nearby. In some parts of the Levant, merchants lived together in a shared space, such as the two large, walled *fondaci* in Alexandria. These contained storerooms and shops on the ground floor, baths, an oven, and lodgings on the second floor, all surrounding a courtyard with pleasant gardens.[20] The situation in Constantinople was quite different: there was no large, common commercial complex to house merchants and their goods. Rather, merchants lived in individual houses spread throughout Galata and maintained shops and warehouses in the *bedestan* and the caravansary.[21] Often these houses were rented, but some merchants also owned houses and other immobile properties in Galata and the Vigne di Pera.[22] The merchant Marcantonio Vidali, for example, owned a piece of land contiguous to the bailate and rented it to the baili as pasture for their horses; another merchant, Edoardo da Gagliano, owned a house he rented to a fellow trader.[23] Some of the houses had gardens where the merchants would meet with members of the nation, as well as other European merchants and Ottoman associates and friends.[24]

If the embassy was at the geographical center of the Venetian community, its human focus was the bailo. Among contemporaries, there was certainly no question that the office of bailo in Constantinople ranked as the most important and sensitive position in the storied Venetian diplomatic corps.[25] Because of the importance of Venice's relations with the Ottoman Empire, the office of bailo in Constantinople garnered much renown for its holder and could bear significant fruits for the career of a Venetian patrician.[26] Conversely, a failure could snuff out a promising career and end in disgrace, even death, as in the case of Girolamo Lippomano. When the Signoria suspected him of passing sensitive information to the Spanish, he was recalled and killed himself (or was killed, as some alleged) as he came into sight of Venice's campanile.[27]

The origins of the office of bailo date to the eleventh century, and the title *bailos* was derived from the holders' primary function as Venice's representatives before the Byzantine emperor, the Basileus.[28] While initially their responsibilities centered primarily on the commercial affairs of Venetian merchants throughout the Byzantine Empire,[29] over time the baili came to be charged with political and diplomatic duties as well, and eventually they became de facto ambassadors.[30] By the end of the Byzantine era, the bailo had become one of the most powerful men in Constantinople, second perhaps only to the emperor; indeed, he too wore the imperial purple.[31]

With the irruption of the Ottomans into the capital city, this status was irreversibly changed: no longer would Venice enjoy the dominant commercial and political position it had during Byzantine times, and the reality of treating with the much more powerful Ottomans created a much changed circumstance, to which the Venetians only slowly adapted. The fiasco of the League of Cambrai in 1509 and subsequent events in the troubled first decades of the sixteenth century further served notice to Venice that the situation it faced in the Italian peninsula and in the Mediterranean had altered significantly, and probably permanently. Venice had clearly slipped into the second tier of European states, something that Venetian contemporaries increasingly realized and pragmatically accepted after the end of the second Veneto-Ottoman war in 1503.[32] As a result, the republic pursued a precarious policy of nonalignment and neutrality in relationship to the region's chief powers, the Ottoman and the Holy Roman empires, and the Mediterranean point man of this policy was the bailo. Indeed, despite Venice's weakened political position and its altered status in the Porte, the bailo remained the "*doyen du corps diplomatique*," and its mission the model on which other states patterned their own.[33] Because, as one seventeenth-century observer wrote, the Ottoman legation was "above all others full of inextricable difficulties, requiring a man of great resolution and prudence," Venice wanted its best men on the front lines.[34]

The responsibilities of the baili were extensive. In a report to the Senate in 1564, a former bailo, Daniele Barbarigo, provided some sense of these: "In my opinion, your Serenity does not give any charge . . . of greater importance, and of greater travail . . . than this one [bailo]; because if a bailo wants to do his duty he will never loaf about, as he has too much to do in preventing the merchants being mistreated, in holding audience with subjects, in meeting with those who can make known to him new information (for which purpose one would need never to leave the house), in addition to going to the Magnificent Paşa and negotiating important matters.[35]

Barbarigo's account suggests the range and burden of a bailo's duties: another bailo, Simone Contarini, simplified these into two principal areas: "The task of bailo in Constantinople . . . seems to me to be contained in two offices: one ambassador, the other consul."[36] First and foremost, then, the baili were present in the Ottoman capital to represent and protect Venetian political interests and to preserve the status quo. Once in Constantinople they devoted the lion's share of their time to nurturing Veneto-Ottoman relations. This was accomplished most often through a form of personal diplomacy wherein the baili maintained extensive networks of friendship and patronage through which they were able to establish relationships with influential Ottomans in positions to benefit and protect Venetian interests. These networks were created and maintained through liberal use of gifts, bribes, and hospitality (see chapter 6).

An important aspect of their diplomatic duties included gathering information on Ottoman afffairs.[37] The baili's information came from members of the household personnel; agents in the informal Venetian spy network, which included Venetian subjects in the Ottoman Empire, many of whom worked in the imperial arsenal in Galata; banished men and women; the merchants with their many connections; moles in the other foreign embassies in Constantinople; and numerous individuals within the Ottoman bureaucracy itself.[38] Venice's position as the sole regular courier between Europe and the Levant provided the baili with the opportunity to examine most of the mail from Constantinople to Europe, particularly that of other ambassadors and to control the flow of information in both directions.[39] The combination of diplomacy and espionage, then, was essential to the baili's accomplishing their diplomatic mandate. Overly zealous information gathering could, however, lead to a bailo's expulsion, as happened in 1491.[40]

The baili's second principal task was to serve as Venice's chief consular representative in the Ottoman Empire,[41] charged with both promoting Veneto-Ottoman trade and protecting it against potential interlopers such as the English, the Dutch, and the Florentines.[42] While scholars have often ignored this commercial role in favor of the diplomatic, it was an important part of every bailo's charge from the Signoria. In the commissions issued to them at their election, each bailo was directed by the Senate "to recommend the merchants, and our subjects" to the sultan and "not to fail in any of their necessities to give to these merchants and our subjects every help and favor possible, as this is one of the principal reasons for which you are sent there by us."[43] These onerous commercial tasks were little appreciated by the baili, and consequently often neglected. As Ottaviano Bon wrote in 1604, "This bailate is today a garden, in which the roses and flowers are the public affairs, and the thorns and twigs are the affairs of private subjects, because of their ships and the contracts they make and the *avanie* that are brought against them, on which it is necessary that I trouble myself every waking hour."[44]

Though often averse to the task, the baili nonetheless worked hard to defend Venice's Levantine trade. This was done chiefly by ensuring that the capitulations, which Venice renewed with every sultan, were observed. This required constant vigilance. Both Venetian and Ottoman records are rife with complaints of infractions of the capitulations on both sides that threatened both Venetian and Ottoman trade.[45] One particularly thorny issue that plagued the baili was the protection of the merchandise of Venetians and subjects who died in the Ottoman Empire.[46] The baili also arbitrated disagreements within the Venetian nation, and because of their reputation for fairness and the continuity of Venetian institutions in the Porte, the baili were often asked to arbitrate issues involving other European nations, their ambassadors, and even Ottoman subjects.[47]

As Venice's chief consular official in the Ottoman Empire, the baili's chancellery also notarized a wide variety of commercial and legal documents whose validity was accepted throughout the Mediterranean, including in Ottoman lands. Among these were bills of health given to ships and travelers leaving Constantinople, which certified that the city had been plague-free at their departure, and were necessary to avoid protracted quarantine time in Venice's *lazaretto*.[48]

Beyond political and commercial affairs, matters relating to Latin-rite Christians in the Ottoman Empire occupied a significant amount of the baili's time.[49]

For centuries Venice had been the de facto protector of Latin-rite Christianity in the *stato da mar*, in Ottoman territories, and in the Holy Land. The baili were also important figures in the confraternities of Galata and were protectors of the company of the Holy Sacrament. While holding the protectorate of Roman Catholicism in the region created many trials for the baili, it also returned certain liturgical and honorary benefits of precedence.[50] After 1600, however, Venice's position as the defender of Christianity in the Ottoman Empire was gradually usurped by the French, who were supported by the Jesuits.[51]

Another aspect of the baili's religious charge was the protection and eventual redemption of Venetians enslaved in the Ottoman Empire. While the capitulations dictated that all nobles, citizens, subjects, and persons in Venetian service be turned over immediately by Ottoman officials, the reality was that once captured, slaves were rarely released voluntarily either from private households or from official Ottoman institutions, such as the arsenal. Obtaining freedom for these slaves, who in 1588 were estimated to number at least 2,500, consumed much time and treasure.[52] Piero Bragadin in 1525 reported having already freed sixty-four slaves, though he hoped to free three hundred by the end of his service; forty years later Daniele Barbarigo freed ninety slaves during his bailate, and Paolo Contarini in 1581 obtained the release of forty-six slaves, including one Venetian patrician. Overzealousness in carrying out this duty, however, could create trouble. On at least two occasions, the sultans wrote directly to the doge complaining about the actions of the baili in freeing slaves held in Constantinople and requesting their recall.[53]

Freeing slaves, defending commerce, treating in the divan, the tasks of the baili required their full energy. For men of ambition and ability, the office represented a significant opportunity that outweighed the dangers and inconveniences it often presented. While some avoided the challenges of defending and representing Venice's commercial and diplomatic positions in Constantinople, more it would appear eagerly sought the posting as an important step on their *cursus honorum*. As the supreme representative, and indeed, the personification, of the Venetian state in the eastern Mediterranean, the patricians who were elected as baili represented the centerpiece around which the diverse Venetian nation was arrayed. Little wonder, then, that Venice's governing bodies carefully selected from their most accomplished and capable members those who would be able to meet the rigors of service in the Ottoman capital.

The men elected as baili were not expected to confront their responsibilities alone. In recognition of the unique challenges of being ambassador, consul, and head of the large Venetian community, the Senate authorized the baili to engage a number of officials and servants to assist them in their important missions.[54] The servants and officials attached to each bailo formed the rest of the official core of the nation, and were referred to as the *famiglia* (though not genealogically related in any way).

The size of the *famiglia* generally varied from twenty-five to thirty-five: when Simone Contarini traveled to Constantinople in 1608, he counted thirty-four members of his household, including a secretary, his assistant (*coadiutore*), an accountant (*ragionato*), chaplain, doctor, majordomo (*maestro di casa*), five drago-mans, six *giovani della lingua,* and seventeen men generically classified as ser-vants.[55] While the size of the *famiglia* fluctuated over time, there remained a clear difference between the quantity of servants permitted by the Senate, ten, and the number the baili actually retained.[56] Indeed, many baili complained that the Senate did not provide them with funds sufficient to maintain a household large enough to both carry out their duties and to make the necessary public impres-sion.[57] Image was especially crucial to the success of Venice's Ottoman diplomacy, because, as one bailo wrote, "one is unable to make oneself esteemed in that land except by dressing richly, maintaining an honorable *famiglia*, . . . with these means friendships are conserved and new ones acquired, and the Most Serene Republic's greatness is made known to the world."[58]

The *famiglia* of the baili was hierarchically organized. The secretary, *coadiutore, ragionato,* chaplain, doctor and barber, as well as the dragomans and the *gio-vani della lingua,* made up the *famiglia alta,* or upper family. The *famiglia bassa,* or lower family, comprised the remainder of the household—servants, pages, squires, couriers.[59]

Next to the bailo, the most important member of the Venetian diplomatic delegation was the secretary. As one Englishman in the Ottoman capital observed, Venice did not leave alone to the baili "the manadginge of theyre busines in that fickell state, but doe euer appoynte him a clarissimo to bee his secretory, without whom hee can doe noethinge."[60] Because of the sensitive nature of the mission in Constantinople, the secretaries selected to accompany the baili were certainly among the most prepared and capable members of the Venetian Ducal Chancel-lery. They were drawn exclusively from the estate of the *cittadini originari,* the citizen sub-elite immediately below the patriciate, which in 1569 effectively had been closed off to new families in a *serrata cittadinesca,* similar to the great patri-cian *serrata* of 1297.[61]

The secretaries' most important and time-consuming task was ensuring the regular transfer of information between the baili and their numerous correspon-dents: the Senate, the Council of Ten, and other magistracies in Venice, as well as consuls, rectors, and other officials in the *stato da mar*. Because of the importance of events in Constantinople, the Senate required regular, detailed communications from its representatives to the Porte. As Cristoforo Valier observed, the Senate desired "to be informed with frequent letters on what is happening at this court, even if there is no news of importance."[62] Late or missing correspondence often resulted in accusations of carelessness and negligence against the secretary, and could adversely affect a career.[63]

The volume of correspondence that passed through the Venetian chancellery was remarkable. Over a two-year period, Vettore Bragadin sent 141 letters to the Senate and Council of Ten, an average of five to six per month, almost all of which were written in a complex cipher for security. These letters varied in length from a single page to the more common five to ten pages.[64] In addition, during the same period he sent many other letters to the various Levantine consulates under the bailo's jurisdiction, as well as to the rectors, captains, and other ministers of the *stato da mar* and the Venetian armada. The most important letters had to be copied and sent to Venice via several different routes to avoid correspondence being lost or intercepted, and copies of all letters to and from Ottoman officials were archived in the chancellery.[65] It is not surprising then, that secretaries complained of the effects of this quantity of correspondence on their health: Antonio Milledonne reportedly lost the use of one hand as a result of the "burdens of writing" and so learned to write with the other.[66]

The secretary also served as the notary for the nation, and indeed for much of the international community in Constantinople, recording wills and last testaments and notarizing commercial and official transactions of all sorts. Secretaries played key roles in the information gathering efforts of the embassy by screening mail that went through the chancellery and gleaning items that could be of interest to the Council of Ten and Inquisitors of State.[67] Secretaries were also regularly called on to supplement the bailo in both his ambassadorial and consular roles. With the passing by the mid-sixteenth century of the era of direct patrician involvement in the Levantine trade, tasks that noble merchants had previously carried out were often entrusted to secretaries. For example, when Bailo Niccolò Barbarigo died unexpectedly in 1579, no other Venetian nobleman was present in Constantinople to fill the office temporarily, so his secretary Gabriel Cavazza acted for seven months as de facto bailo until the Senate could elect and send a patrician replacement.[68]

The secretaries also regularly substituted the baili in diplomatic capacities.[69] In 1613, Gabriel Cavazza (the nephew of the Gabriel Cavazza who replaced Barbarigo in 1579) was sent with the Grand Dragoman Marcantonio Borisi to Adrianople, where the sultan had retired for the hunt, to negotiate a border issue and obtain several commandments addressing difficulties with Ottoman provincial officials. The baili also sent their secretaries to treat for the release of slaves, to negotiate rivalries between the French and English ambassadors, to bear condolences to Ottoman ministers, and to investigate suspicious individuals who appeared in Constantinople.[70]

Recognizing the many duties of the secretary and the unique challenges of the Ottoman mission, the Senate in 1568 decreed "that the Baili in Constantinople, because of the multiplicity and importance of the correspondence that is required in that office, may take with them a *Coadiutore*," an assistant secretary. Only the ambassadors in Rome and Constantinople were allocated this assistant. The *coadiutore* performed many of the more menial, quotidian functions of the chancellery, such as maintaining the notarial protocols, writing and copying correspondence, and enciphering and deciphering letters.[71]

As with the secretaries, the *coadiutori* were drawn exclusively from the class of *cittadini originari*. The majority of those who went to Constantinople were quite young, usually aged between twenty and twenty-five. Most often they were extraordinary secretaries of the Ducal Chancellery, the first stage in a Venetian bureaucrat's career, and often Constantinople was their first posting. For an aspiring young man, service in the most important diplomatic post of the Republic could be a springboard for a fruitful and successful career.[72]

Another key official was the *rasonato*, or accountant, whose duties centered on the nation's commerce. On arrival in and departure from Constantinople, Venetian merchants and ships' scribes were required to declare before the *rasonato* the value of all goods and merchandise they received and shipped by both land and sea so that the duties owed to Venice, the *cottimi et bailaggi*, could be computed.[73] The *rasonato* also kept the embassy's financial records, including the customs books and an account book of the embassy's day-to-day expenditures from which a quarterly report was compiled and sent to Venice. At the end of the bailo's term the *rasonato* was required to present the embassy's account books for an audit in Venice by the *Proveditori del cottimo di londra*.[74] The *rasonato* also coordinated the embassy's mail service. Another important task of the *rasonato* was issuing letters of credit to facilitate the transfer of large sums of money safely over long distances.[75] Finally, as one of the chief Venetian officials in Constantinople, the *rasonato* might be sent to represent the bailo before Ottoman dignitaries.[76]

The secretary, his *coadiutore*, and the *rasonato* were the key administrative figures in the bailo's *famiglia*. They fulfilled crucial administrative tasks and were essential to the effective function of the embassy in both its diplomatic and its consular duties. They were joined by several other persons in supporting roles. The chaplain was charged with the spiritual well-being of the bailo's household, a task deemed of great import in the spiritually and morally dangerous Ottoman Empire. He celebrated mass daily for the bailo and the *famiglia* in the small chapel located within the embassy, which spared them the long trip to the main Latin-rite church of San Francesco in Galata, where the personnel of the diplomatic missions and Ottoman Latin-rite subjects usually heard mass on Sundays and feast days.[77] As was the case with the secretaries, favorite chaplains followed patricians as they moved from post to post and often served as personal spiritual adviser to a Venetian patrician throughout his career.

Another valued support figure was the *medico di casa,* or house physician.[78] Originally the bailo was accompanied by a barber who could only perform simple medical procedures. The barber was supplemented by Ottoman physicians, invariably Jews, who were renowned for both their medical skills and their political connections.[79] The most famous Jewish physician/diplomat, Solomon Ashkenazi, in 1573 played a key role in negotiating Venice's separate peace following Lepanto. Born in Udine, and thus technically a subject of Venice, Ashkenazi served as *medico di casa* to all Venetian baili and ambassadors until his death in 1583.[80] At his death, Ashkenazi was replaced, on the recommendation of many important Ottomans, by the Portuguese Marrano, David Valentino. Valentino's and Ashkenazi's political connections, more than their medical services, were what led the Senate to retain them, but these activities left little time for actual medical attention to the diplomatic mission. This, combined with the scandal of a Jew caring for Christians and the death from plague of Bailo Vicenzo Gradenigo and most of his *famiglia,* moved the Senate in 1600 to provide the embassy with its own Christian physician.[81]

The final members of the *famiglia alta* were in many ways perhaps the most important. The dragomans (derived from the Persian *terdjuman*)[82] and their protégés, the *giovani di lingua,* filled a role crucial to the functioning and success of the Venetian mission in the multilingual world of early modern Constantinople. Because of the regular rotations characteristic of Venice's diplomatic corps, and despite the recommendation of former bailo Marino Cavalli that diplomats posted to the Ottoman Empire "need to know the Slavic, Greek, and Turkish languages, otherwise [they] are like mutes,"[83] none of the baili in the period after Lepanto had any formal knowledge of the Ottoman language spoken in the Porte. In the early sixteenth century, Andrea Gritti appears to have had some command of the language, a result of his extended residence in Constantinople as a young merchant, but he was entirely exceptional.[84] Although the italianate *lingua franca* was widely used in the eastern Mediterranean, and indeed in much of Europe,[85] for formal negotiations and everyday activities, the baili were entirely dependent on their dragomans' mastery of the Ottoman idiom.

This dependence grew as the mission expanded over the course of the sixteenth and seventeenth centuries. In 1500 there was only one dragoman; by 1530 there were two; and from the war of 1537 to Lepanto there were consistently three dragomans serving Venice.[86] After Lepanto, the number increased in short order to six, and by the time of Alvise Contarini's mission in the mid-1630s, seven dragomans were in Venice's service.[87]

The different dragomans served in a variety of tasks. The grand dragoman was charged with treating the most important issues of state and spent his days in the divan and the palaces of the members of the Ottoman hierarchy. He was the face of Venice in the halls of Ottoman power as the baili spent most of their time in the bailate and only occasionally made the long trip across the horn to Constantinople. An eighteenth-century bailo described the ideal grand dragoman thus: "The tongue that speaks, the ear that hears, the eye that sees, the hand that gives, the spirit that acts, and on whom life and the success of every negotiation may depend."[88] The "little dragoman" spent his days in the port and merchant loggia of Galata and was charged with interpreting for the merchants and the *ragionato* and dealing with any commercial matters involving Ottoman officials and magistracies. The *dragomano di strada* was the traveling dragoman, who accompanied the baili on their trips to and from Constantinople and was sent on the road to treat matters related to borders and other local diplomatic issues.[89] Another dragoman was always expected to be in the bailate to assist in the myriad linguistic issues that arose daily. The remaining dragomans were usually younger apprentices who supplemented and assisted the four chief men.[90]

Though key members of any bailo's *famiglia*, the dragomans were in many ways unique. Most of them did not live in the bailate; rather they had homes in the Vigne di Pera in reasonable proximity to the embassy complex.[91] In contrast to most other members of the bailo's team, they were permanent residents of Constantinople, and indeed almost all of them were subjects not of Venice but of the Ottoman Empire. Indeed, Venice's dragomans, whether Ottoman or Venetian subjects, were invariably among the most important and influential members of the Latin-rite community.[92] This was a source of endless concern and constant complaints to the Senate by the baili, who feared that their most intimate discussions might be compromised, or that the dragomans might be intimidated because of their status and their exposed position as Ottoman subjects. Another common concern was linguistic ineptitude. It was endlessly frustrating for Venice's most effective diplomats to be effectively rendered mute in their dealings at the Ottoman Porte.[93] These concerns are laid out clearly in a 1594 assessment by Bailo Marco Venier: "The quality of the dragomans [who are] subjects of this Empire is such that having to depend in their jobs and in their everyday lives on those who have tyrannical authority [over them], they often adapt their interpretations more to the avarice and arrogance of the Turks than to the reputation and benefit of the affairs of [Venice], which creates indignity and burdens for the [ambassadors and baili] who cannot trust their translations."[94]

To free the baili from their dependence on non-Venetian dragomans, in 1551 the Senate conceived a program to train young men in eastern languages, so as to maintain a pool of loyal Venetian citizens and subjects who could fill this most important task and to free the baili from their dependence on foreign dragomans. This program established the Venetian embassy's famous and much copied school for *giovani di lingua*, or language apprentices.[95] The decree of the Senate that established the program also stated its raison d'être: "it being important to have in this office persons who are no less effective than faithful." A local teacher was retained to teach the young men, who lived in the bailate and ate at the bailo's table. Boys accepted into the program were to stay in the Ottoman capital for five years.[96] The initial number of *giovani di lingua* was set at two, but that number quickly expanded so that by 1625 there were regularly more than ten young men studying in the school at any given time who were dependent on Venetian support.

While the embassy language school proved successful in producing generations of dragomans, it failed in its goal to free Venice from dependency on non-Venetian dragomans. Into the early seventeenth century several citizen boys participated in the program, but as a result of several high profile cases in which boys converted to Islam, as well as concerns over health threats, Venetian citizen parents seem to have become more reluctant to send their sons to Constantinople.[97] Increasingly, then, the program served the sons of Ottoman Latin-rite subjects, especially those of the Ottoman dragomans in Venetian service who saw the *giovani della lingua* program as a way to insert their sons into Venetian service and thus effectively make their lucrative positions hereditary.

The secretary, *coadiutore, rasonato,* chaplain, and physician, along with the dragomans and *giovani della lingua,* made up the *famiglia alta.* Much more numerous, but also more anonymous in the records, was the *famiglia bassa.*

The most important figure in the *famiglia bassa* was the *maestro di casa,* the majordomo. As one ambassador wrote, "He is the overseer of all and . . . like the counterweight of a clock makes all the gears move, so the diligence of this man, the prudence, his modesty and severity ensures that everyone carries out their offices."[98] The majordomo oversaw the provisioning, staffing, and maintenance of the physical structures of the bailo's household. He traveled with the new bailo from Venice, always preceding the main party to arrange for accommodations and to prepare the bailate for the ceremonial procession and feast that was held at the arrival of every bailo in Constantinople.[99] Evidence of the majordomo's importance was the location of his bedroom, which directly adjoined the bailo's.[100] The majordomo was directly responsible for the nonprofessional staff of the embassy—the cooks, footmen, valets, and grooms, and was to "preserv[e] the *famiglia* from disagreements and fights, . . . and not give them time to gamble or go whoring."[101]

Second in importance in the *famiglia bassa* was the *cavaliere*, or marshal, who assisted the bailo in his consular and juridical duties. He was responsible for delivering summonses and other legal communications; conducting investigations and interviewing witnesses in civil and criminal matters brought before the bailo; ensuring the presence of witnesses subpoenaed to appear before the bailo's court; and discharging penalties, as far as this was possible and desirable within the limitations imposed by Ottoman law. The *cavaliere* sequestered merchandise, warehouses, homes, and other spaces that had been declared off-limits pending judgment by the bailo, and sold at public auction unclaimed items left in the chancellery. Finally, he was the keeper of the official iron seal of St. Mark, used to authenticate documents and weights and measurements.[102]

The rest of the household staff consisted of generic servants. While the *famiglia alta* was always made up of Venetian citizens, there were no requirements that these servants be Venetian, or even Venetian subjects. Of the seventeen servants Simone Contarini listed in his household in 1612, eleven were Venetian subjects, while the remainder hailed from towns in Italy, France, Armenia, and Anatolia. The baili also retained many local people—Ottoman Greeks, and even Muslims—to serve as cooks, footmen, valets, and grooms.[103] In addition, baili retained gardeners and bakers for the embassy.[104] Some baili brought painters with them to record their missions in Constantinople, and these artists were invariably in great demand among the Ottoman elite.[105]

While men constituted the bulk of the *famiglia*, there were occasionally a few women who served in the bailate. A 1590 letter mentions a man from Chioggia who had been a slave for nine years, whose wife worked in the bailate, perhaps to earn funds for his release; another document refers to a former woman slave, freed by the bailo, who promised to serve him until she could pay off the forty ducats she had borrowed to buy her freedom.[106] Perhaps there were other women in similar situations, who never appear in the records, which rarely mention lesser servants, male or female. On the whole, however, the *famiglia* was a man's world, and women existed only occasionally on its margins.

While most of the *famiglia* came from European lands, there were a number of Ottomans who were part of the larger embassy household. The most important of these were the dragomans and *giovani della lingua*, and their Ottoman-Muslim *coza*, or instructor of Turkish. Next in importance were the janissaries of the *casa*, or the *yasakçıs*. Every embassy in Constantinople had a contingent of janissaries assigned to protect and oversee their members. Foreign ambassadors in Constantinople engaged from two to eight janissaries; the Venetian baili had at least four.[107] These janissaries were known among their fellow Muslims as "swineherds" for their work among infidels, but it appears that generally good relations existed between them and their charges.[108] Of the bailate's janissaries, one was needed to assist the merchants; one to escort the dragomans, baili, and other officials when they left the house; and at least one to be present at all times to protect the bailate.[109] The janissaries of the *casa* had a variety of roles. They served the bailo "for his gard, conservation or surety of his person, his house and family, so as to them or none of theirs be done any wrong or injury, which if any should attempte to doe, these janissaries have full authority for to punishe siche by beating them with a staffe upon their belly, buttocks, yea and sometimes under the soles of their feet, without that any dare withstande or resist them, such is their greate authority."[110] If there were a bread or grain shortage, the baili might also send his janissaries "to gather bread with violence and authority," as Lorenzo Bernardo did 1586.[111] In an interesting blurring of jurisdiction, the janissaries were also charged with guarding Venetian prisoners, who were held in chains in the janissaries' room, though this arrangement proved relatively unreliable as prisoners regularly escaped.[112] Janissaries also occasionally served as intermediaries between the bailo and his Ottoman-Muslim neighbors and others in the Porte whom the bailo might desire to encounter outside the somewhat restrictive confines of the divan. In addition, they were charged with protecting Venetian merchant ships as they arrived in Galata and were unloaded at the customs house, for which service they received a small percentage of the goods they were assigned to protect.[113]

The final, and largest contingent of the *famiglia* was the *portalettere*, the couriers of the Venetian mail service. All Venice's couriers were Ottoman subjects, usually from the region of Montenegro, and as one informant observed, "Though they are poor and of very low condition and live rustically, they are all, however, robust and strong youths, well-disposed to carry out their charge and resolute in defending themselves in their journeys."[114] Besides carrying the mail, the couriers also worked in the bailate as cooks' helpers or in other minor support positions. They also provided numbers to fill out the honor guard that accompanied the bailo to church and on other ceremonial occasions, dressed in livery for the greater honor of the household.[115]

Except for the occasional married dragoman, all these men physically resided with the bailo in the complex in the Vigne di Pera. Given the size of his household (fifty to a hundred people), it is no surprise that the bailo often described supervising them as one of his greatest burdens.[116] The documents are replete with instances of gambling, scuffles, and thefts among household members, as well a number of cases of moral turpitude and even several murders. These sorts of disturbances were quite dangerous because they opened the door to potential Ottoman interference in the household's internal affairs, which presented a threat to the sovereignty and authority of the bailo over his nation.

This examination of the *famiglia* of the Venetian baili in Constantinople gives some suggestion of the size and diversity of the mission to the sultans. No other European embassy in Constantinople was so large, and provided the number and level of services as the Venetian. The baili's diplomatic and commercial mission required a large supporting cast of secretaries, servants, couriers, and guards. The services the baili and their *famiglia* provided to the larger nation were critical to its effective functioning. In addition to services, the bailo, the *famiglia,* and the embassy itself provided an institutional presence and focus for the larger community of Venetians in Constantinople. Whether merchants or diplomats, slaves or renegades, Greeks or exiles, all who considered themselves Venetians interacted in some fashion with the officials and institutions of Venice in Constantinople.

The bailo and his *famiglia,* along with the merchants (who will be examined in chapter 2), represented the core of the *official* Venetian nation, which is to say they were sanctioned by the state and their presence in Ottoman lands was legally recognized and sustained. Although they composed the core official element of the nation, behind the seemingly homogeneous facade of the Venetian nation existed diverse groups of individuals who identified in varying degrees with Venice. While the patrician baili and their *cittadini* secretaries had the closest and clearest tie to the state, they were greatly outnumbered both in the bailate and in the larger nation by newly minted citizens, subjects from throughout the empire, and many non-Venetians, including Christian and Muslim Ottoman subjects. These men, and the occasional woman, living and working together in Ottoman capital suggest the variety and disparity of groups who identified with and functioned under the aegis of the Venetian nation.

CHAPTER TWO

The Merchants of Venice

On the first day of the Venetian new year, March 1, 1594, Bailo Marco Venier convened the governing body of the merchant nation in Constantinople, the Council of Twelve, in the great room of the embassy. In attendance were the principal merchants of the nation, gathered to discuss a ship which had foundered carrying valuable merchandise and goods belonging to many of their number. As he did at every such meeting, the bailo's secretary Gabriel Cavazza registered a careful list of all the participants, seventeen in total: Andrea Soranzo, Piero Bragadin, Girolamo Pianella, Edoardo da Gagliano, Pasqualino Leoni, Zuanantonio Perla, Giacomo Balbi, Francesco di Niccolò, Benetto Bozza, Agostino Agazzi, Bernardin Agazzi, Marcantonio Vidali, Zuanmaria di Ventura, Demosthene Carrerio, Zuanbattista Mocello, Zorzi di Gianna, Piero di Grassi, Antonio di Cavalli.[1]

This list of names, one of literally hundreds recorded in the notarial protocols of the Venetian nation, seems at first glance of little potential historical value. Yet these names open a window onto an aspect of merchant nations which has often been overlooked. While there is an extensive literature on the commercial activities of medieval and early modern merchant nations, we have an incomplete picture of the actual merchants who made up trading nations.[2] The regularity with which lists such as Cavazza's appear in the records of the bailate permit a unique prosopographical reconstruction of the merchants who made up the Venetian commercial nation in Constantinople.

It has generally been assumed, though not necessarily substantiated, that trading nations were culturally homogenous, "closed ethnic and social enclaves."[3]

Niels Steensgaard describes the merchant nation as "a society of merchants of common origin," while Frédéric Mauro writes of "an ethnology" of merchant nations bound together by a common geographical provenance and a shared culture and language.[4] A cursory examination of the merchants comprising the Council of Twelve, however, gives a clear sense of the social, political, and cultural diversity concealed by the label "Venetian nation." The only patricians in the group were Soranzo and Bragadin, and Soranzo was merely passing through Constantinople at the time. Bragadin was the sole Venetian patrician trading in the Ottoman capital in this period, and one of the few trading anywhere in the Levant.[5] Of the sixteen remaining men, none were noble, but each was rather variously described as a "Venetian merchant," a "Venetian citizen," or a "Venetian Gentleman." A careful study of their backgrounds, however, clearly reveals that this categorization too is overly simplistic. While several—Pasqualino Leoni, Zuanmaria di Ventura, Benetto Bozza—may have been born Venetian citizens, most of their colleagues clearly came from much more diverse backgrounds. Agostino and Bernardin Agazzi, two brothers originally from Bergamo, had just recently been granted Venetian citizenship, which permitted them to trade in the Levant. Demosthene Carrerio was also a Venetian subject, from the area of Capo d'Istria, and was brother-in-law to Cristoforo Brutti, the recently deceased grand dragoman of Venice in Constantinople.[6] Perhaps most surprising were Girolamo Pianella and Edoardo da Gagliano, both of whom were Ottoman-Christian subjects trading as Venetian merchants. Behind the list of merchants who convened in 1594 there existed a community of traders infinitely more variegated and heterogeneous than initially meets the eye, which suggests the need to recast our views of the composition and character of early modern merchant nations and of merchant identity.

NOBLE MERCHANTS

Commerce in Venice, particularly international commerce, historically was the perquisite of the patrician class, a right they jealously guarded because of its fantastic worth. This system also guaranteed the patriciate's continued economic and political monopolization of the expanding city-state. Indeed, the state itself organized and carefully regulated patrician trade in a protomercantilist system, the objective being to encourage Venetian commerce and the involvement of as many nobles as desired to participate. The emblematic merchant of Venice during the city's medieval golden age was like Marco Polo or Andrea Barbarigo: an intrepid patrician working with family members, who made his fortune trading exotic Asian goods in ports throughout the Mediterranean.[7] In Venice there was never much debate over the legitimacy of noble commerce.[8]

While patrician commercial investment remained significant into the early modern era, as our list of the merchants in the Council of XII in 1594 makes clear, direct participation in trade progressively became the exception rather than the rule. In effect, by the late sixteenth century the romanticized patrician merchant world traveler of medieval Venice no longer existed. After Lepanto, Venetian commerce in the Mediterranean came to be practiced not by adventuresome patricians but almost entirely by non-noble factors and agents. The cultural rationale for this is evident in Girolamo Muzio's 1571 work, *Il gentilhuomo*, in which he wrote descriptively, rather than prescriptively, that trade "is honorable if it is large scale . . . the gentleman must not dirty his hands with it, but administer everything through factors."[9] This development was in reality already under way well before Muzio wrote. In 1523 Sanudo reported that only four noble merchants traded in Galata, while the rest of the nation was made up of "popular factors." By 1555 there were only two nobles active in Constantinople, and after Lepanto this number shrank even further.[10]

The patriciate's abandonment of its commercial roots has been depicted "with monotonous insistence" as one of the central causes for the decline of Venice.[11] Observers since Girolamo Priuli in the early sixteenth century (who regarded the *terraferma* as "a malignant tumor sucking the maritime vitality that had made Venice great") have pointed to the patriciate's renunciation of commerce as evidence of a cultural and therefore commercial reorientation that led, in part at least, to Venice's economic decay. Birthed by the sea, and symbolically wedded to it each year, Venetian greatness was portrayed as intimately intertwined with the Mediterranean.[12] Niccolò Donà's famous nostalgic speech to the Senate in 1610 lamented that "the nobility wants no part in trade, everything is spent on lands, dwellings, and the pleasures of the city. He who has money to spare lends it at interest, instead of investing in eastbound voyages."[13] Although recent years have seen more nuanced discussions of early modern Venetian transformation rather than decline, the image of Venice as primarily a "Maritime Republic" persists.[14]

Linking Venetian decline to the end of patrician trade has obscured a more involuted and elusive reality. While patricians more rarely traveled abroad themselves to trade, and invested proportionally less capital in international commerce, this was a transition which happened gradually throughout the sixteenth and seventeenth centuries.[15] Noble entrepreneurs continued to invest their funds in international trade and other commercial endeavors, but instead of traveling abroad, they contracted their business from the comfort of the Rialto in Venice. The bailate's records include many incidents of patrician merchants trading through factors in Constantinople, as does the archival collection, *Giudici di petizion, rendimenti di conto*.[16] An early-seventeenth-century report prepared for the Venetian Senate, the *Notta de tutti li Nobelli hanno negotio in Levante*, listed eighty-three families—including some of the most important—who still regularly invested in international trade. Patrician investment in the Mediterranean trade may also have been partly cloaked by the use of intermediaries, as the Marquis of Bedmar suggested: "the greater part of the business on the Rialto market is transacted on account of noblemen, whether they are openly involved or engaging in commerce under other people's names."[17]

Ample evidence of patrician participation in commerce abounds: around 1600 the Venetian merchant fleet included fifty ships owned by nobles and another fifty belonging to *cittadini*.[18] Another new area of patrician investment was the expanding market in maritime insurance, made indispensable by the threat of the Uskoks and corsairs to Mediterranean shipping. Insurance's high returns in this troubled time may have made it seem a more secure investment than commerce.[19] Another potential source of patrician income was government service, which was a form of government welfare for patricians and other citizens. Ugo Tucci has argued that expanding opportunities for government service helped extinguish the spirit of commercial initiative. While perhaps true for some of the impoverished majority of the patriciate, this angle should not be exaggerated; as James Davis's study of the Donà family shows, political office was a poor way to obtain or retain great wealth. In his long political career, Leonardo Donà made some small profit on his offices, but the same money invested in commerce would have provided a greater return. Indeed, Donà was probably exceptional, as most Venetian nobles lost money through holding high public office, leading to the widespread efforts to avoid appointments which Donald Queller has identified.[20]

While these other financial options attracted some patrician ducats, the most attractive way to diversify was investment in real estate. A lucrative and secure investment, land was often viewed by patrician families as a form of insurance, a safe haven for capital preservation, and a significant source of income. Capital investment in land holdings was nothing new: the great twelfth-century merchant doge Sebastiano Ziani made his fortune in commerce and then invested in land, and fifteenth-century observers complained that the *terraferma* expansion was leading to the abandonment of traditional patrician practices. In what one historian has aptly described as the "land/sea dichotomy," early modern Venetian patrician investments increasingly came to be diverted in two directions: east and west, sea and land.[21]

The decline paradigm was for many years widely embraced, but more recent research based on statistical as opposed to anecdotal evidence, which examines the entire economy rather than single sectors, has pointed to an economic transformation rather than regression.[22] In this view, patrician economic diversification represents not a decline from some essentialized Venetian commercial character, but rather a canny assessment of a continually changing economic landscape. Given Venice's lost hegemony in the Levantine market, the insecurity of the seas, the declining returns from traditional investments, and the regular failures of international merchants, as one merchant stated in 1555, "it is less bad to keep capital at home than to put it in circulation with so many risks and without profit." If overall international commerce experienced a reduction, advances in other sectors of the economy, particularly industry, and a shift of the port of Venice from international to regional trade made up for it. Venice's decline in absolute economic terms, then, does not coincide with the gradual loss of its role as middleman between East and West over the course of the sixteenth and the first decades of the seventeenth centuries.[23]

Although many, probably most, early modern Venetian patricians diversified their investments and increasingly worked through agents, some did continue to go to sea. Often they came from among the second tier of less wealthy and powerful Venetian families, such as Alessandro Magno in Egypt in 1561, or Andrea Dandolo, who accompanied his brother-in-law, the bailo Girolamo Ferro, to Constantinople. Niccolò Donà, father of the future doge Leonardo, profited on several short trips to the Greek islands for wines, cheeses, and cotton, and he lost money on longer voyages to Syria for spices and oil in the years following Lepanto.[24] Still, in the sixteenth century these men were exceptions to the emerging rule.

This transformation is evident in the merchant nation in Constantinople after Lepanto, when only one Venetian noble merchant was in residence for any significant time. Pietro (or Piero) Bragadin was the eldest of the four sons of Zuanne di Alvise and Beatrice di Ottaviano Grimani. Born in 1565, he died in 1614, apparently without marrying. The family, from the Campo Russolo branch, had a long history of involvement in the Levant: Bragadin's great grandfather, Piero di Girolamo, had been elected bailo to Constantinople in 1506, and his family still had significant investments in international commerce in the late sixteenth century.[25]

Piero Bragadin was in many ways an anachronism, however, a holdover from an earlier period in which Venetian patrician families sent their teenaged sons abroad to gain commercial and life experience, the first step in the *cursus honorum* they followed in preparation for a life of commercial and political leadership. Gasparo Contarini in his *De Magistratibus et Republica Venetorum* perpetuated this ideal patrician upbringing, even though by its publication in 1541 such an ideal was already exceptional. Following a formal school education, he writes, the young patricians "shoulde apply themselves to navigation, being thereunto (as it were) even drawen by their owne inclination and nature."[26] In the case of Piero Bragadin, it seems clear from a letter written by his father, Zuane, that he envisioned his son's sojourn in Constantinople in the same terms, as a chance to "train" him for his future role in the Venetian state.[27]

Piero Bragadin first appeared in Constantinople in July 1584, at age nineteen, and he remained there until March 1594.[28] He was active in the nation both as a merchant and a leader; as the only noble merchant, he served by default as the nation's vice-bailo. He was well known and moved comfortably among the highest echelons of the Ottoman court. The sultan's mother, for instance, passed communications via a servant to Bragadin, who served as her intermediary with the baili.[29] Some sense of Bragadin's character is conveyed by the laudatory dispatch composed by the bailo Marco Venier recommending him to the Senate when the young man finally departed Constantinople. Venier described Bragadin as a "person of great valor, prudence and experience in affairs, especially regarding this government, in no way inferior to any of the older or more experienced men: he had free access to the seraglio of the King, and to that of the Queen, and he was intimate with many Grandees of the Porte who had become friends because of the sweetness of his nature, his liberality, and because he speaks the Turkish language with confidence, as well as reading and writing it."[30]

Piero was the field representative in Constantinople of a much larger family trading network, involving both his immediate and extended families, along the lines of the historic Venetian *fraterna*, or family partnership.[31] The Bragadin clan was engaged in commerce throughout the Adriatic, the Balkans, the Levant and the Venetian *terraferma*. They were also significantly invested in shipping: Piero bought and sold at least four ships during his time in Constantinople.[32] The family traded in cereals, too: Piero sent a number of ships with Ottoman grain throughout the *stato da mar*, and his father traveled the breadth of the *terraferma* buying up grain. Other evidence suggests that Zuane Bragadin and his family were "at the center of a vast traffic in golden cloth which from Venice ended up in Constantinople, by way of Ragusa and Adrianople." Like many other patricians, the Bragadin also invested in insurance.[33] In sum, it appears that the family of Zuane Bragadin was in line with the diversified investment strategies pursued by their patrician contemporaries, even if Piero's residence in Constantinople and direct involvement in commerce was no longer representative of his estate.

In their varied business activities, the Bragadin also had extensive dealings with Ottoman Greek, Muslim, Jewish, and Christian merchants. When a Bragadin factor, Ludovico Ludovici failed, the Bragadin were held partially responsible, despite their own losses, by important Ottoman Jewish and Muslim creditors, including an influential çavuş. The reason was in part because Piero, known by all as an honorable man "and especially in the imperial seraglio where his noble conduct has always been accepted by the Queen," had recommended Ludovici to the çavuş, who had "trusted Ludovici on the word of Clarissimo Signor Piero Bragadin."[34]

Piero experienced firsthand the difficulties and rewards of the life of a merchant. He lost two members of his merchant household to the plague. In 1586, Piero, a "most virtuous youth," was caught up in a controversy when he was implicated by a Muslim servant of the household's janissaries in the murder of two women, whose bodies were found dumped in a nearby well. The charges were a pretext to extort money from Bragadin, and the bailo was able to get Ottoman officials to drop the case.[35]

Although Piero Bragadin was the only patrician present in Constantinople over an extended period of time, other nobles would appear temporarily in the city for commercial dealings. Bragadin was occasionally joined by extended family members, such as his cousin Giacomo and his younger brother, Polo.[36] In 1594, Andrea Soranzo accompanied the new bailo Marco Venier to Constantinople to treat some commercial issues, and three years later Zuane Foscarini passed through Galata with two servants on his way to Poland "for his trade." In 1603, Giacomo Trevisan, "who is here for trade," purchased a ship, the Bonaventura, "for a good price." He was in Constantinople sporadically from 1602 to 1605 but was much less active commercially than Bragadin.[37]

After Piero Bragadin departed Constantinople in 1594 and Giacomo Trevisan in 1605, no Venetian noble merchant was again to trade or reside in the city for any extended period. Bragadin's departure represents the end of an era. While patrician money would continue to be invested in Levantine commerce, nobles no longer sent their sons to learn the trade of their forefathers. Many came temporarily to observe the Ottoman state, but no more did they come for commerce.[38] Thus, a trend that had been developing throughout the sixteenth century culminated in 1594, and from this date onward, all trade in Constantinople was carried out by common, or *cittadino*, factors.[39]

CITTADINI

The void left by patricians in the Levantine trade was filled by three groups— *cittadini*, subjects, and nonsubjects—though of these three, the majority of merchants in Constantinople were *cittadini*. Already by 1550 the conflation of merchant and *cittadino* was becoming apparent. As one observer describing the order of Venetian society noted, "The nobleman employs his talents in letters or public office, sometimes in the affairs of Mars . . . the *cittadino* of lower standing either takes up the career of government secretary or is employed in trade; the plebeian is entirely occupied with crafts."[40]

By law, participation in the Levantine trade was limited to Venetian patricians and to the elusive group situated between the nobility and *popolani*, the *cittadini*, or citizens. Though for much of their history, the *cittadini* were not a clearly defined estate in Venetian society, by the end of the sixteenth century, they had come to be divided into two main groups: the so-called *cittadini originari* (citizens by nature or birth), and citizens made (citizens by privilege or culture).[41] Between 1563 and 1642, the number of citizens of both varieties fluctuated between 7,000 and 13,500, or approximately 5 to 10 percent of the population, compared with 3.5 to 5 percent patricians.[42] All citizens were not created equal, however. Contemporaries considered *cittadini originari* to be the true Venetian citizens because of their historically close ties to the patriciate, and indeed in the sixteenth century they were becoming an increasingly closed caste like the nobility.[43]

The number of citizens by privilege, by contrast, was constantly being replenished; indeed, this regular in-migration was an important source of activity and innovation in the evolving Venetian economy. A deliberation of the Maggior consiglio in midcentury lays out quite clearly Venice's motivations in granting citizenship to non-Venetians: "Our ancestors have always striven to take those measures which have seemed in the circumstances to be most necessary and vital to the well-being of this city, . . . especially by giving the benefit of Venetian citizenship to various foreigners." This policy was inspired by "the wars, because of the shortage of inhabitants, so as to fill the city for the good of trade, customs, industry and other benefits."[44]

Venetian officials were correct in their assessment: many non-Venetians granted citizenship made important contributions to the prestige and wealth of the city. Examples include the explorer John Cabot, made a citizen in 1476; Pasquale Spinola, a Genoese noble and merchant of oil and grain in Venice from 1560 to 1583; and Vicenzo Valgrisi, a typographer of French origins. The silk weavers guild by the fifteenth century was dominated by men from Bergamo, a situation that continued into the next century. After the sack of Antwerp in 1576 and the Spanish blockade of Scheldt in 1585, wealthy Dutch merchants also settled in the lagoon.[45]

During the period under examination, it would appear that few *cittadini originari* were active as merchants in the nation in Constantinople. It is difficult to say this with surety, however, because Venetian chancellery records in Constantinople identify individuals as *cittadini veneziani,* but do not clearly distinguish whether these were citizens by privilege or by birth. A second problem is that the laws that would lead to the "crystallization" of Venice's social order into "precise categories—nobles, *cittadini originari,* citizens by privilege, subjects, foreigners," were only gradually being worked out between 1569 and 1583. While we cannot say with certainty whether any *cittadini originari* traded in Constantinople in the years immediately preceding and following Lepanto, after 1590 it seems clear that they, just as the patricians, were almost entirely uninvolved in direct commercial dealings in the Ottoman capital. Increasingly, they were engaged more as bureaucrats in the state administration and as rentiers than as merchants.[46]

The majority of the trading nation's merchants fell under the second rubric, citizens made. The requirements for Venetian citizenship were relatively simple, if time-consuming: there was a residency and a taxation element. Two levels of citizenship were possible, *de intus* and *de intus et extra.* In the former case, an individual was required to live in Venice and pay taxes for fifteen years; *de intus et extra* citizens had to be resident and pay taxes for twenty-five years. Another way to acquire *de intus* status was to marry a Venetian woman and pay taxes for eight years.[47] *De intus* status opened up certain avenues not available to noncitizens and ensured the new citizen a lower tax rate than foreigners paid. To participate in the Levantine trade, however, a merchant needed to have *de intus et extra* status, which allowed him to enjoy the protection and financial assistance reserved for members of the Venetian nation.[48]

Obtaining citizenship was an important step on the path to economic advancement and social acceptance in Venice, as well as assimilation into the elite fabric of the city. Despite changing patrician and *cittadini originari* attitudes toward commerce, large-scale merchants still generally enjoyed respect and a privileged status in early modern Venetian society. This is evident in the temporary opening of the patriciate to citizens who were able to buy nobility during the economic and political problems of the mid-seventeenth century. Of the 121 families who bought nobility between 1646 and 1718, seventy-two were engaged in commerce. A revealing statistic is that of these seventy-two families, twenty-three originated in the region of Bergamo, almost 50 percent more than the number of merchant families from Venice proper who were admitted into the patriciate.[49]

The reason for this conspicuous Bergamasque contingent is that the largest number of applications for Venetian citizenship came from the *terraferma*, especially the rugged areas around Brescia and Bergamo. Because of the challenges of eking out an existence in this region, its subjects were declared a *"nation privilegiata"* and granted a fast-track to citizenship in 1525, and many men from the region became important merchants and industrialists in Venice. Among these were the jewel merchant Salomon Rigola; the Zois brothers, who were merchants and cloth manufacturers; and Cesare Federici, a jewel merchant who traveled to Malacca and Burma early in his career and used the capital gained in this enterprise to fund many Levantine commercial activities.[50] Matteo Bandello wrote, with only a degree of hyperbole, "there exists no place in the world, however distant or remote, where there is not a Bergamasque doing business."[51]

Men from the region of Bergamo were also disproportionately represented in the Venetian nation in Constantinople as new citizens and citizens in the making; indeed some of the most active traders came from this region. Among these were the Agazzi brothers, Agostino and Bernardin *quondam* Lorenzo, who first appeared in Constantinople in early 1594. They settled in a house in Galata, just a few months after having been granted *de intus et extra* citizenship by the Senate upon the recommendation of the V Savii (the board of trade charged with protecting and encouraging Venetian commerce), who described them as "merchants with much trade and of good fame."[52] While the granting of full citizenship should have been the necessary prerequisite to the Agazzi becoming involved in the Levantine trade, both brothers had been active in the Levant since at least 1588, several years before they obtained official sanction—a practice that was technically illegal but quite common. The brothers left the Levant in 1600 because of difficulties with an Ottoman official they represented commercially, but both remained active in international trade as late as 1637.[53]

After acquiring citizenship, the Agazzi quickly came to play an important role in the nation: in 1595 Bernardin was elected one of two merchants charged with defending Venetian commerce and representing the merchants before Ottoman magistracies in cases where they were "mistreated" or "tyrannized" by the sultan's officials. In 1598 Agostino was elected to the highest position among the merchants, *capo dei mercanti*. The brothers also achieved important posts in the Latin-rite religious community of Galata; in 1597, for example, Bernardin was elected a guardian of the church of San Francesco.[54]

The Agazzi dealt in a wide range of goods, including relics, such as the "an-

cient effigy of Our Lady in the Greek style finished in silver," which they purchased in 1597 for 5600 *akçe*. Their main trade, however, was in jewels, precious
stones, and metals. At the time of their abrupt departure from Constantinople,
the goods in their possession were valued at almost 200,000 ducats. They represented and traded with many merchants in Venice but seem to have worked
especially with a group of immigrant Dutch.[55] Their commercial endeavors were
successful enough that in 1593 they purchased a large ship to use in their Levantine trade, and another several years later, which, though Ottoman in construction, was granted Venetian status because of the shortage of native ships.[56]

One of the reasons for the Agazzi's success was their extensive trade with
Ottoman-Muslims. Abdi Çelebi, for example, traded with Agostino Agazzi in
Silivri, on the Sea of Marmora, where he entrusted Agazzi as his representative in
a shipping dispute with several merchants. The Agazzi also traded with and for
some important figures in the Ottoman court, including several *çavuşes*—Hamza
Ağa and Ahmed Ağa—and Mustafa Bey, an intimate of the grand vizier.[57] This
involvement with Ottoman merchants and officials was probably due to one or
both of the brothers being able to speak some Turkish.[58] While these dealings
were quite lucrative for the Agazzi and their partners, they also proved to be a
source of difficulty and even danger, which ultimately forced the brothers to leave
the Ottoman capital permanently.

Soon after their arrival in Constantinople, the Agazzi entered into an agreement with an influential Ottoman official, Ali who was ağa of the Janissaries, and
a protégé of Gazanfer Ağa, a Venetian renegade. Ali Ağa provided the Agazzi with
an initial investment of 23,872 ducats to manage on his behalf. As part of his
investment they purchased a ship, the *Santa Maria et San Francesco*. The investments did not turn out well, and the Agazzi returned only 8,000 ducats on the
investment. Not surprisingly, Ali Ağa was infuriated and insisted that his initial
investment be returned, threatening both the Agazzi and the bailo if he was not
reimbursed.[59] It was this dispute that impelled the Agazzi to flee Constantinople
because of fears that Ali Ağa would assault their house. They left behind, as
Bernardin described it, "great amounts of goods . . . [and] the trade of this house
progressing so well with all my efforts in the course of my youth the past eleven
years . . . from which I had been able to hope for much honor and profit."[60]

The flight of the Agazzi created a serious political incident that threatened
Veneto-Ottoman relations for a time. Bailo Agostino Nani eventually resolved the
affair, but not without great effort and expense, and somewhat begrudgingly. He
observed: "I will not fail to help in this difficult negotiation especially because of
the interest that many nobles and others have in it, even though the Agazzi would

deserve punishment rather than protection as against the laws that expressly prohibit them entirely [from making] commercial companies, or even trading with the principal Ministers of the Porte, they have placed in danger all the capital of their principals."[61] While the Ali Ağa controversy forced both brothers to flee Constantinople, and created serious problems for them with Venetian officials, this proved only a temporary interlude. Both remained active in the Levantine trade in subsequent decades, administering their fortune from their home in the parish of San Cassan, neighbors to many other important Levantine merchants.[62] The Agazzi, then, are a classic example of the new Venetian merchant, the citizen made, who came to control the bulk of the trade with Constantinople. And they were by no means unique: we could examine Iseppo and Antonio Albrici, the Zois brothers of Bergamo and many others who followed similar paths in becoming the most important Venetian citizen merchants in Constantinople.

VENETIAN SUBJECTS, OTTOMAN SUBJECTS, AND OTHERS

If patricians and *cittadini originari* made up a small minority and citizens constituted the majority, it still remains to establish the identity of the remaining traders of the merchant nation in Constantinople. In an influential essay on early modern Venetian commerce, a respected historian of Venice categorically states that "all foreigners were rigorously excluded" from the Levantine trade. This is only true in the sense that Venetian magistracies created numerous laws that attempted to defend the monopoly citizens and patricians enjoyed in this trade.[63] In practice, many men who had not been approved as Venetian citizens participated; indeed, in Constantinople at times their numbers rivaled those of the legally recognized citizen merchants. These men came from a variety of backgrounds: most were Venetian subjects, either from the *terraferma* or the *stato da mar,* but some non-Venetians and even Ottoman subjects also traded under the aegis of the nation. While forbidden by law, they traded in Constantinople with the tacit recognition and the open acceptance of the official nation.

The majority of these noncitizen traders came from the Venetian Greek islands, especially Candia, and Venice and its officials in Constantinople regularly ignored the activities of this group. Candia at the end of the sixteenth century underwent a significant economic upsurge, and one of its major outlets was the Ottoman Empire. Giovanni Moro wrote in 1600 that Candia, which was "in the jaws" of the Ottomans, had much more trade with Constantinople than with Venice; this evidence would support one scholar's recent contention that Cretan international trade diminished in this period and was supplanted by a regional trade nexus between Constantinople, Candia, Egypt, and Venice.[64] Phane Mauroeide has compiled a series of tables showing the shipping activity of Greek-Venetian subjects in Galata from 1580 to 1599. In this twenty year period, she finds that on average 14.8 ships with connections to the Greek-Venetian islands docked in the port of Galata every year.[65] Given the amounts of contraband that circulated between Venetian and Ottoman Greek territories, the actual number of ships and value of goods involved in this trade was likely much higher.[66]

The most lucrative Candiot commercial product was wine. Cretan wines—malvasia, muscatels, sweet wines—were renowned and traded as far afield as England, Flanders, Spain, and Portugal. Niccolò Barbarigo in 1578 wrote "It is normal for 1000, 1200 and even 1500 barrels of Candiot wine to come here to Constantinople every year, and the major part of this, perhaps two-thirds, is chartered for the port of Şile in the Black Sea, whence it is put on carts and goes to Poland."[67] The troubled times at the end of the sixteenth century made the Black Sea passage often dangerous, and in 1592 several Candiot merchants petitioned the Senate to establish a more secure route through the Friuli.[68] Describing this commerce as regional perhaps is inaccurate: while Cretans may have been supplanted in the trade with western Europe and especially England, they continued to be active throughout the eastern Mediterranean, into the Black Sea, and even further north. To encourage and defend this Cretan eastern trade, in 1592 a Genoese physician was elected consul in Tana and Kaffa, where many Candiot and Venetian merchants were actively trading for morone, caviar and other goods.[69]

Besides these large scale wine merchants, many Cretans came to Constantinople in small boats loaded down with lemons, olives, and oil which were all highly sought after on the Ottoman market because of their quality. Other lucrative Cretan exports to Ottoman territories were cheeses, oil, cotton, honey, wax, raisins, fruit and citrus juices: it was reported that the Ottoman capital annually consumed 3–4,000 barrels of orange and lemon juices imported from Candia. This trade was important not only to the Ottomans but also to the baili, who collected a variety of duties on the merchandise of Candiot traders. Given the reduced flow of Venetian commerce through Constantinople, these duties were an important source of income.[70]

The majority of these Greek subject traders remained on the periphery of the official nation. They generally did not participate in the governance and other formal activities of the nation, but they did enjoy the protection of the baili. In some instances, however, Greek subjects did participate as members of the official nation. Leonin Servo, for example, was a Venetian subject from Candia who was active in Constantinople in the decades prior to and after Lepanto. In his role as a factor for many Cretans in the Ottoman capital, Servo became very wealthy. Indeed, his wealth and commercial activities led him to acquire a reputation among Venetian officials for arrogance and as a troublemaker. Yet he was permitted to participate in the workings of the nation, voted in meetings of the Council of Twelve and traded as a Venetian.[71]

Besides the Greeks, subjects of Venice's *terraferma* were also present in Constantinople, and some of them traded as Venetian merchants without official status. The policy seems to have been one of "don't ask, don't tell": when sanctioned merchants in Venice requested permission to allow non-Venetians to represent them in Constantinople, the V Savii and Senate opposed it, though increasingly not without vigorous debate as Venice's commercial situation deteriorated. The fear among these magistracies was that by relaxing the legal requirements for trading in the Levant, commerce would pass from the hands of legitimate patrician and citizen merchants to foreign interlopers, who would take over the entire trade and block out Venetians, to the detriment of the city and its citizens. This issue arose regularly: it was addressed in 1524, 1536, and 1603, with always the same negative response. The issue arose again in 1610 when Paolo Santorini proposed to allow foreigners to trade as Venetians without the residency and tax requirements of citizenship. Because of the greatly reduced commercial position of Venice, this proposal was entertained more seriously as a legitimate innovation to rescue Venice's failing fortunes; in the end, however, it too was rejected.[72]

This official hesitance did not prevent unsanctioned merchants in Constantinople from trading openly as Venetians. In 1597 several merchants in Venice proposed to send Ludovico di Damiani, a subject born in Salò, near Brescia, who had married a Venetian and lived in Venice for twenty-one years, to open a "house of trade in Pera." They did not even request that he be exempted from paying the higher duties of non-Venetians, and they openly acknowledged that he was "a foreigner." The V Savii opposed this proposal because "it is not permitted that any except *cittadini originari*, or those made [citizens] by privilege . . . , may navigate or trade in the Levant." Thus, though Damiani was a subject, he did not yet meet the requirements for citizenship, and the V Savii opposed the idea as a "terrible innovation." Despite this ruling, five months later Damiani was in Constantinople, and remained there until 1600, trading with the nation, participating in the Council of Twelve, and in short functioning as a regular Venetian merchant, even though he had been denied official sanction. Finally, in 1604 Damiani, citing his long residency, his marriage to a Venetian and his contributions to the city's trade and customs, requested and received *de intus et extra* citizenship.[73]

Damiani's experience was quite common: a subject from the mainland would settle in Venice and commence trading in the Levant before having fulfilled the residency and financial requirements necessary for citizenship. Instead of being punished, he would subsequently receive citizenship, ironically based in part on the success of his technically illegal commercial enterprises. In 1564, Marcantonio Stanga, as part of his request for full citizenship, emphasized that he had lived in Venice and traded in Constantinople and Syria as a factor for many years and had paid many taxes that benefited Venice's coffers, "and in Constantinople he had also readily served in [times of] public need, as is demonstrated by diverse statements from baili and consuls."[74] Even though he did not meet the residency requirements, and had by his own admission traded illegally in the Levant for years, the V Savii nonetheless recommended him for citizenship. The Agazzi brothers were in a similar situation; they reported that they had traded for some time in the Levant prior to fulfilling the residency requirement, which was widely known throughout Venice. Notwithstanding, the V Savii recommended them unequivocally as taxpaying "merchants with much trade, and good reputation." Lorenzo Girardi used the same logic, and because he had lived in the city forty years, he too was recommended.[75] These are but a few of the many examples of what seems clearly to have been a common practice that Venetian officials did little to stop. Indeed, despite the repetitive legislation to the contrary, Venetian magistracies tacitly accepted, and even rewarded, merchants who, though technically acting illegally, brought commerce and income to the city.

To further complicate the notions of nation and what it meant to be a Venetian merchant, in the years after Lepanto, unsanctioned Venetian subjects trading in the Levant were joined by a number of nonsubjects who also enjoyed the protection of the nation, and benefited it and the sponsoring city's coffers in a time of commercial transition. One example is Girolamo Pianella, a merchant active in the Levantine jewel and cloth trade with several of Venice's most prominent noble merchants, including members of the patrician Sanudo clan and important Ragusan officials.[76] From 1590 until at least 1607, Pianella was in Constantinople openly and actively trading in the nation as a Venetian merchant.[77] He participated often in the Council of Twelve, and indeed was elected on several occasions to important positions of responsibility. In 1596 he and Edoardo Gagliano were elected *procuratori* to deal with issues related to the failure of Ludovico Ludovici (interestingly, all three men—Pianella, Gagliano and Ludovici—were acknowledged non-Venetians openly trading as part of the nation). The next year, based no doubt on his service in the Ludovici case, when the merchants reorganized the nation and created new positions of leadership, Pianella was elected nearly unanimously by the council as the first assistant to the *capo dei mercanti*.[78]

What is striking about Pianella is that despite his long activity and leadership in the Venetian nation, and his representation of important patrician families, he was not a Venetian citizen or even subject. Rather, he was, as Bailo Girolamo Lippomano described him somewhat paradoxically, "Girolamo Pianella, Venetian merchant, and *haracgüzar* of the Grand Lord" (that is, a tax-paying, non-Muslim Ottoman subject). Such a statement clearly indicates that the baili were aware of Pianella's schizophrenic situation, and that what would at first glance appear as seemingly contradictory elements of Pianella's public and private identity, were not viewed as such by the nation or its head.[79] Indeed, despite Venice's attempts to conceal the fact that non-Venetians traded under its auspices, the Ottomans may have been aware of this fact. In a command of 1530, the sultan ordered the *kadı* of Gallipoli to protect Venetian merchants and "other wayfarers who are under the name of the Venetians."[80]

While on one level accepted as an influential, contributing member of the nation, a merchant in Pianella's situation represented a distinct risk as well, as evidenced by Lippomano's report of an incident involving the Ottoman. Accompanying a caravan of more than thirty horses carrying jewels and other goods, Pianella was detained by a local official in the Ottoman lands neighboring Ragusa, who was intent on taking his merchandise and perhaps his life. Through the bailo's intervention, Pianella was freed unharmed. But, as the bailo warned, "If it had been discovered that he is a *haracgüzar*, everything would have been finished and lost."[81] The dangers of this type of situation were clear: as an Ottoman subject, Pianella was not legally subject to the jurisdiction of the bailo, even though he traded as a Venetian and represented other Venetian merchants. Were he to die or encounter legal or commercial problems, according to Ottoman practice his goods, even if they belonged to Venetian patricians, were subject to confiscation. While clear laws, applying to both Muslim and non-Muslim, governed questions of inheritance, and confiscation rarely occurred arbitrarily, the danger did exist. This could make even more problematic the already sticky situation of disposing of the estate of a Venetian merchant deceased in Ottoman lands.

Despite these very real dangers presented by Ottomans trading as Venetians, Pianella was by no means unique. A similar case involved Niccolò Soruro, who traded as part of the nation in Constantinople from April 1601 to his death in March 1624.[82] Soruro was an active merchant: in 1603 he and several partners acquired a ship, the *Santa Caterina*, in Constantinople. In later years, he partnered with the Venetian merchant Gianmaria Parente, and they maintained a thriving trade with the French ambassador and many Ottoman-Muslim officials, including the chief *Defterdar*, who invested some 100,000 *akçe* with them.[83] Soruro traded mostly in large quantities of cloth: in 1613 he received two shipments via caravan in the span of three months, valued at 667,600 and 563,000 akçe respectively.[84] Soruro also established close ties with Venetian officials; he traded for Simone Tosi, *ragionato* under Simone Contarini, and stood as godfather (by proxy) at the baptism of Tosi's child.[85]

Soruro is an example of the protean character of identity in the Mediterranean world. He was born in Famagosta, Cyprus, and although his parents were Venetian subjects, they came under Ottoman rule with the fall of the island in 1572. We do not know his birth date, so there is a chance Niccolò was born a Venetian subject, but certainly by a young age he was an Ottoman subject. The status of former Venetian subjects from Cyprus after the Ottoman conquest is somewhat byzantine: following the loss of the island, many Cypriots who had escaped were permitted to settle in Venice, and some were granted early citizenship before they had met their residency requirements. Indeed, two of the most important brokers in Venice in this period, Michel Siro and Cesare Nixia, were both Cypriots who were enslaved at the fall of the island and escaped to good fortune in Venice.[86] While Cypriots received some preferential treatment, Venice openly acknowledged that the *Nation cipriotta* was "subject to the Signor Turk."[87] In Soruro's case, while he was publicly labeled and treated as a Venetian merchant, the documents make explicit that he was a *haracgüzar* of the sultan. Giorgio Giustinian acknowledged this when he wrote "though he was Cypriot he traded as a Venetian."[88] Like Pianella, Soruro functioned entirely as if he were a Venetian citizen merchant, though he was in reality a subject of the sultan.

There was some danger to Venice in granting citizenship to Cypriots who sought it; the Ottomans clearly considered them their own subjects and thus as liable to Ottoman taxes, laws, and courts, regardless of Venice's policies.[89] In Soruro's case, his subject status led the Ottoman woman he had married to claim his estate for the son she had born him months before his death. She took her case to Ottoman officials, including the Müfti, and Soruro's business partner was even imprisoned for a time. Eventually the bailo was able to free the man and recover Soruro's goods, but not without substantial trouble and expense.[90]

Ottomans were not the only nonsubjects who traded as Venetians. In 1596 Marco Venier reported the failure and flight of a merchant in Galata, "a Ludovico, who had himself called dei Ludovici . . . who had in his hands the business of several of our men from Venice, and though he was held to be an Anconitan, he passed as a Venetian and was treated as a Venetian, as I saw happen when I came to the Bailate, and as has continued since."[91] During this time Ludovici was prominently involved in the nation in Constantinople: he represented some of the most important Venetian Levantine merchants, patrician and citizen, and purchased a ship in Constantinople in association with several other merchants; this may have precipitated his collapse. In addition, Ludovici was extensively invested with Ottoman merchants—Jews and Muslims—and also a number of Ottoman officials.[92] What ultimately ruined him was excessive debt; as Marco Venier said, "his having wanted to spend much and at the same time to borrow much." Venier estimated his indebtedness at thirty thousand *scudi* and blamed Ludovici's failure on his Jewish creditors, though this was an exaggeration, as other sources show that Ludovici had debts "from many parts," including members of the Venetian community.[93]

Ludovici's case created numerous problems for the nation, and in response the Council of Twelve elected two merchants to oversee the case. In addition, because so many Ottomans were affected, the *kadı* of Galata elected a Jewish and Christian subject of the sultan, "according to the Turkish practice," to do the same, whom he submitted for the approval of the council, which was given.[94] This initial cooperation broke down over the division of Ludovici's remaining assets, and the matter escalated to the grand vizier, who ordered all Venetian ships held in port until Ludovici's influential Ottoman creditors were reimbursed.[95] Bailo Venier tried mightily to have the matter returned to his jurisdiction, but Ludovici's Ottoman creditors argued that as Ludovici was not a Venetian, he was subject to the French ambassador, under whose protection all persons from states not officially recognized by the sultan had to trade. Venier's counter is revealing; he argued that Ludovici "did not deal with French, but with Venetians . . . since he was a Venetian factor who traded the capital of those in Venice, who had constituted him their factor here, he was under the jurisdiction of the Venetian Bailate, he entered into our Councils of Twelve, and in all things was treated as a Venetian, and if it had been otherwise, the Ambassador of France would not have allowed me to insert myself in the persons and matters of his subjects."[96]

The Venetian representative acknowledged that Ludovici was not legally recognized as Venetian, but since he had identified himself as part of the nation, had associated and traded with other Venetian merchants, juridical recognition was unnecessary. Because Ludovici had been accepted and traded with the Venetian nation, he was, de facto, a part of it and thus subject to its head, the bailo. For Venier, and indeed for Venice generally, merchants' identities were flexible; one could become a merchant of Venice simply by acting as if one were Venetian. Legal recognition, while desirable, was not essential.[97]

The cases of the Ottomans Pianella and Soruro and the Anconitan Ludovici clearly demonstrate both the presence of and the trials associated with non-

Venetians trading in the nation. Although their trade was coveted and their service needed, their presence opened a Pandora's box of potential problems. As
Venier observed, failures such as Ludovici's led Ottoman creditors to attempt to
bring political pressure to bear on deliberations regarding the resolution of the
bankruptcy and the division of assets. This situation, already fraught with difficulty, would become impossible "if some chief Turk and Hebrew merchants,
greatly favored by the principals of the Porte, . . . heard that a Foreigner under the
name of a Venetian merchant and factor had sent elsewhere ships and merchandise without them having received any payment from them . . . This would cause a
disturbance to public affairs [i.e., diplomatic relations]."[98] The disturbances included Ottoman expectations that all damages involving Venetians be covered by
public funds, and that Ottoman claims be satisfied before Venetian ones, which
meant that someone like Piero Bragadin's father, Zuane, who had lost much
capital as a result of Ludovici's failure, probably would never recover his money.

Given the difficulties faced with some regularity in recognizing Ottoman and
other non-subjects as de facto members of the nation, one might wonder why
Venetian authorities would ever accept, let alone facilitate, this practice. Clearly,
the most compelling reason for doing so can be found in the commercial challenges Venice faced in the post-Lepanto era. The expanding role of French, then
English and Dutch, traders, as well as the ongoing competition of Ottoman and
Jewish merchants all coalesced to make the Levantine trade an extremely com-
petitive and dynamic commercial milieu, and one in which Venice no longer held
a dominant position. This increased competition, combined with the flight of
the patriciate and the general disinterest of the *cittadini originari* in commercial
matters, forced Venetians to innovate. One such innovation was the creation of
the V Savii, or board of trade, early in the sixteenth century; another was the
reduction of customs duties on eastern goods. A final transformation was in the
city's commercial personnel; Venice increasingly came to rely on new groups and
individuals to keep the still significant Levantine traffic alive. Preferably these
merchants would be naturalized citizens, but in order to encourage eastern trade,
authorities were willing to turn a blind eye to the participation of subjects and
foreigners who had not met the requirements for citizenship. Driven by the same
imperative, the Signoria embraced, somewhat hesitantly to be sure, the participation of Jewish merchants in this trade and granted them unique privileges not
available even to most Christian subjects.[99] For the same reasons, Venice increasingly encouraged and facilitated Ottoman-Muslim merchants trading in Venice
with favorable customs rates and the construction of the *fondaco dei turchi*.[100] The
same motivation, then, explains why the baili and other Venetian officials were

willing to permit men like Soruro, Ludovici, Pianella, and many others, to trade under the aegis of the nation in Constantinople and why they continued to accept the challenges that often arose as a result of this practice.[101]

Whatever the motivation, it seems clear that the monochromatic image of the typical Venetian merchant, and of the complexion of the Venetian trading nation, for the early modern period at least, must be dramatically revised. In the Venetian trading nation in Constantinople, by the middle of the sixteenth century noble merchants were effectively absent. Venetians made easily outnumbered Venetians born and were supplemented by a sizable cross-section of merchants drawn from throughout the Mediterranean littoral. In this fluid world, categories of identity such as Venetian, Ottoman, Greek—perhaps even Muslim, Jew, and Christian —were not set in stone; rather they were adaptable and situational. The merchants of Venice, in many ways then, represent the multiplicity and multilayered character of identities possible in the frontier world of the Mediterranean.

CHAPTER THREE

The Unofficial Nation

Banditi, Schiavi, Greci

The Venetian nation in Constantinople in the early modern era was, in narrow legal terms, limited to the bailo, his *famiglia,* and the merchants possessing legal status as full Venetian citizens. These groups arrayed themselves around the institutions and physical space of the bailate, and represented the official nation, sanctioned and recognized by the sponsoring state, the Republic of Venice. Surrounding this small core of the official nation, however, there existed a much broader community comprising men and women who identified themselves, and were identified to varying degrees, with Venice, its rulers, and its institutions.

In strictly institutional and juridical terms, these individuals were not members of the official nation. Their presence was without official sanction; they had no legal or constituent status or right to participate in the official community; and they maintained only minimal claim on the services and protection of the nation. But if we break free of this structuralist view with its rigid boundaries and instead consider community in a broader sense, as a number of important recent studies have, then these marginal individuals and groups constitute an integral part of the larger whole.[1] Despite their murky legal status, these peripheral members of the Venetian community were acknowledged by the institutions of the nation, participated in their activities and life, and benefited from these associations. These individuals existed on the fringes of the nation yet were in many ways a central part of it, and their existence forces us to reconsider both nation and community in the context of the early modern Mediterranean.

At any given time in the period after Lepanto, Venice's diplomats, their *famiglie,* and the sanctioned merchants numbered probably no more than a hundred individuals total. They were significantly outnumbered by the several thousand men and women who moved in and out of the orbit of the official nation and who resided in Constantinople without official approval. Some came from Venice proper or the *terraferma*; the majority, however, were Greek-Venetian subjects. Their motivations for coming to the Ottoman capital varied: some were slaves, others *banditi*—men and women banished from Venetian territories for criminal activities, unpaid debts, or other infractions. Some were small-scale traders who came to sell lemons, oils, or wines independent of the official nation; others sought work as artisans in Ottoman industries, especially shipbuilding and textiles. Some were travelers drawn by the allure of the Mediterranean's largest city.[2]

The status of this unofficial contingent was ambiguous. Some individuals, while not officially incorporated into the nation, nonetheless worked closely with its members and provided useful services, carrying out many of its more onerous tasks, such as bagging and transporting cloth, loading ships, and baking bread. In addition, they often functioned as an unofficial intelligence network for the baili. At the same time, Constantinople was the front line in the always sensitive relations between Venice and the Ottoman Empire, and the maintenance of this balance was often precarious. Thus the presence of unauthorized persons in the Ottoman capital posed a potential political risk to the republic. Often such individuals possessed knowledge of artisanal techniques in shipbuilding, glassmaking, and other industrial activities which the Signoria did not want passed on to Venice's powerful neighbor. Many soldiers and sailors with detailed knowledge of the extensive defenses of Venice's *stato da mar* also ended up in the city. And the fear of spontaneous conversion to Islam always loomed large as well. Thus, Venice's rulers attempted to control the presence and activities of all its citizens and subjects in Constantinople, wavering between tolerating these groups and encouraging them to return home with promises of pardons and employment.

This chapter examines the various parts of this diverse but unofficial community, their reasons for being in Constantinople, and some of the problems they encountered and created while in the city. The focus is primarily on three groups—banished people, slaves, and Greek subjects. To understand their roles provides a more nuanced understanding of the constituent elements of the Venetian nation in Constantinople, and the need to problematize and progress beyond strictly juridical and political definitions of community and of early modern trading nations.

I BANDITI

While popular views of Venetian justice often conjure images of secret hang-
ings and poisonings carried out by the malevolent Council of Ten, the reality is
that many individuals were condemned but few were actually executed. Much
more common were monetary fines or banishment.[3] During the "hot years" of
crime in the late sixteenth century, increasing population combined with agricultural shortfalls, rising prices, and expensive military and political ventures by the
Venetian Signoria created an environment in which levels of criminality, and thus
of banishment, increased precipitously. At any given time a significant group of
banditi—banished men, women, and even families—existed on the periphery of
the Venetian state. Many of these remained as close as legally permissible to their
own homes and often contributed to an increasing lawlessness and banditry on
the borderlands of early modern states.[4]

While exile in the Venetian *terraferma* has been extensively studied, the *stato da
mar* has attracted less attention. The records of the baili, however, provide a
window onto crime and banishment in the most distant corners of the empire
and suggest the place within the broader Venetian community of the many banished men and women who worked their way to Constantinople. *Banditi* were
drawn to the Ottoman capital for two chief reasons: first were the economic and
social possibilities the city presented; second, many more *banditi* came seeking an
audience with the baili, who were legally empowered with broad authority to
review and rescind sentences issued by courts from throughout the Venetian
Empire. At their discretion, the baili could grant "liberation, safe-conduct, permu-
tation, moderation of sentence, or other criminal pardon," which permitted *banditi* to return to their homes, or at least to Venetian lands under the protection of a
salvacondotto, or safe-conduct, recognized throughout the empire.[5] These safe-
conducts were highly sought after because they permitted the banished person to
return to clearly specified areas within the Venetian state, often for a limited
period of time. With this permission of passage, exiles were able to visit family
and friends they may have not seen for years and to attempt to clear their names,
often by paying off debts, which were the most common cause of banishment.

It is not entirely clear when the baili obtained these broad powers, which very
few Venetian officials enjoyed.[6] Certainly they resulted from a recognition of the
unique nature and location of their mission. The chief councils of Venice awarded
this right, and encouraged its liberal application, because of political more than
legal expediencies. The *banditi* had potential to cause greater disturbances to the

sensitive diplomatic dealings in Constantinople than to the public order in Venetian lands. The challenge, however, was to grant *salvacondotti* in such a way as to
avoid giving the impression that the law could be broken with impunity. This
balance proved elusive and led to regular questioning of the baili and their use of
their ample powers, particularly as the Council of Ten became the dominant
political and judicial institution in the Venetian state over the course of the sixteenth century.[7]

In 1586, for example, the Council of Ten decided that the baili could remand
sentences imposed by most magistracies inside the city and throughout its empire, except for those issued by either the Council of Ten itself or the judicial body,
the Quarantia, which could not be altered without these bodies' permission. But
confusion and overuse by the baili continued, and the council issued numerous
reaffirmations and clarifications of its rulings in an attempt to reign in the abusive
use of *salvacondotti* throughout the Venetian state.[8] Indeed, despite the evolving
laws, many *banditi* still trekked to Constantinople hoping for a sympathetic hearing of their cases.[9] The baili had the power to commute a wide range of offenses,
so as to maintain order within the Venetian community in the sensitive environment of Venice's powerful Ottoman neighbor. Yet, paradoxically, by trying to
remove *banditi* and other unofficial elements from the city, they probably attracted
many others who came in hopes of having their sentences modified.

While there are no statistics on the *banditi* in early modern Constantinople,
figures do exist for the Venetian state as a whole, which indicate how commonplace banishment was. For the period 1600–1607, for example, one scholar has
counted 17,294 sentences of banishment issued throughout the Venetian state.
The actual total is certainly much higher, as this figure does not include sentences
issued in Corfu and Candia, areas where banishment was widely used. Another
source reports that in 1601, six hundred banished men and women lived in Zante,
a striking figure given that the island's total population was less than twenty
thousand.[10]

The number of exiles resident in Constantinople almost certainly exceeded
that in Zante. Very often, a sentence of banishment required the guilty party to
stay out of all Venetian territories, as in the case of Alvise Morosini, who killed two
men in a rival's gondola and was banished "in perpetuity from the city and the
Dogate, and from all the other cities, lands, and places of the landed and maritime
Dominion, and ships both armed and disarmed." A law of 1443 prohibited *banditi*
from coming within fifteen miles of any Venetian territory.[11] In situations of total
exile, the only option was to find refuge in some non-Venetian territory, and for
Venetians, and especially subjects of the *stato da mar*, the immediateness of the

Ottoman Empire made it an attractive option for two reasons. First, for economically uprooted exiles the Ottoman capital represented a much more promising destination than a small island like Zante or some minor regional town; second, the presence in Constantinople of a high Venetian official with authority to review sentences issued by almost all Venetian magistracies made the city even more inviting.

The many *salvacondotti* recorded in the voluminous chancellery protocols give some sense of the *banditi*'s numbers in Constantinople. Without exception, safe-conducts are the most common actions registered in the protocols after Lepanto. For example, the rubrics of Giovanni Cappello from February 1630 to February 1633 contain 188 *salvacondotti* granted to supplicants guilty of offenses ranging from unpaid debts to murder. Several years later, Bailo Alvise Contarini issued more than double this number, 399 from early 1636 to October of 1640.[12] These numbers are particularly striking when viewed in the context of the small size of the Venetian community in the Ottoman capital.

The majority of the *banditi* who appeared in Constantinople were Greek-Venetian subjects; many others came from the Venetian *terraferma* and Dalmatian coast. There were also occasional cases of Jewish exiles whose causes were often taken up by important Porte figures.[13] While most *banditi* came from the lower classes, there were instances of noble banishment, such as Giulio Marini, described as "one of the falsest men born in this world," and Zuanne Boldù, banished for unpaid debts by the Council of Ten in 1591 and only granted permission to reenter Venice's *stato da mar* in 1611. In general, however, noble *banditi* from Venice proper were the exception. More common were local nobles banished from the island possessions of the *stato da mar*.[14]

The crimes that led to banishment varied: some were for moral offenses, such as the man excommunicated and banished after being caught *in flagrante* during a nocturnal visit to a cloistered nun, or Margarita of Tínos, banished in 1615 for "carnal commerce," or the Jew Afrizele banished for gambling.[15] Much more common were banishments resulting from poverty or inability to pay debts, as in the case of Boldù, who was expelled because of "his poor and lamentable state" due to a debt he owed another patrician.[16] While most banishments seem to have been for lesser misdeeds, there were cases of serious crimes as well, such as the man from Canea banished for fratricide, or Antonio Senessene and his wife, both banished from Candia for murder.[17]

It was not unusual for exiles who appeared in Constantinople to have spent five, ten, even twenty years in exile. Boldù lived under a sentence of banishment for twenty years, and a man from Rettimo described spending twenty-one years of his life "wandering."[18] Neither of these men probably passed his entire exile in Constantinople, but evidence suggests that in many cases *banditi* came to Constantinople for its economic opportunities and often stayed on for years and even decades working in Ottoman industries and on Ottoman galleys. However long they spent in Constantinople, it is clear that at any given time the city was inhabited by a significant contingent of *banditi* from Venetian territories.

A *parte* issued by the Senate in 1620 indicates the several alternatives the baili possessed for dealing with the unending parade of *banditi* who appeared in their chambers. One option was to commute a sentence entirely, effectively allowing the exile to repatriate. Alternatively, the bailo could grant a safe-conduct and permission to travel and settle in certain restricted areas within the Venetian state, though in "atrocious cases" the exile was generally not allowed to return to the scene of the original offense.[19] A third possibility was to free the supplicant conditionally, dependent on a certain period of service, usually on the war galleys, in return for a recision of the banishment.[20] Finally, of course, the baili could refuse to grant any alteration to the sentence.[21]

Despite the many *banditi* who passed through Constantinople, and the seriousness of some crimes, this latter option was rarely utilized. The potential danger to the affairs of state and to the soul of the supplicant made it generally in the best interests of both parties to move the exiles out of the city expeditiously and quietly. Exiles seem to have understood that due to the sensitivity of the situation in Constantinople *salvacondotti* could be obtained more easily there, which attracted many men and women to the city. Even when he could not legally modify a sentence, a letter of support from a bailo could often sway the Council of Ten or Quarantia; thus many people banished by these magistracies came to Constantinople to present their case in hopes of obtaining a favorable recommendation.[22]

The relative ease of obtaining alterations to sentences in Constantinople resulted from Venice's desire to control its subjects and citizens in the city. The Ottoman capital was considered a physically and morally dangerous space, and the presence of any unauthorized persons, particularly criminals, represented a significant risk both to themselves and to the state. As one bailo wrote, "the liberty of Turkish living, the lasciviousness of the Turkish women and the corrupt customs of the renegades would have the power to make a saint a devil."[23] Individuals or groups who might potentially upset the sensitive Veneto-Ottoman relationship, or might agitate or impede the diplomatic and commercial missions of the nation, were classed *persone non grate*. Marco Venier's statement suggests the baili's challenge: "It pains me extremely that many men banished . . . end up coming here with much greater danger and with much greater travail for me."[24]

To avoid this peril, Venetian policy was first to try and prevent *banditi* from coming to Constantinople at all, and failing this, to encourage them to leave quickly by issuing safe-passages, commutations of sentences, and even financial incentives.[25] The motivations behind the policy are made clear in the experience of Giandomenico Moro from Venice, who "had lived here [Constantinople] evilly for some time." Despite this, Simone Contarini granted him a safe-conduct, contingent on his serving three years at half pay as a *uomo da spada* on a Venetian galley. Contarini did this because Moro "has truthfully given me very great travail because of his bad behavior, . . . I came to the resolution to remove this Giandomenico from here as a person of great scandal, so that in serving on a galley . . . he may not have occasion to commit a greater evil here to the public detriment, and in particular to his soul. Your Excellency is very prudent and knows very well how much better it is to eschew a lesser evil, so as not to incur a greater one."[26]

As the case of Giandomenico Moro suggests, *banditi* and other unauthorized persons presented a number of dangers to Venice and its subjects by their presence in the sultan's capital. These were at least threefold—political, commercial, and spiritual—and all were closely interconnected. Although Venice ideally wanted no subjects or citizens in Ottoman territory without official sanction, there were certain categories of people earmarked for a quick return to Venetian lands. Primary among them were men who possessed specialized knowledge or technical skills that could be of use to the Ottomans either militarily or commercially. As Marco Venier indicated, the objective was "to prevent the Turks taking advantage of our people in the production of the most important things to use against us . . . because by our own men in this Arsenal have been made, and has been taught the making of among other things, large galleys no different than our own."[27] Not surprisingly, then, many of the *salvacondotti* issued in Constantinople, particularly to men from Venice and the *terraferma*, went to artisans with specialized and sensitive skills.

The most common examples involved workers from the famed arsenals in Venice and Candia—carpenters, caulkers, and other master craftsmen.[28] One bailo reported, with some exaggeration, that there were so many *banditi* in Constantinople that "they make up a great part of the workers in the Turks' arsenal." A report of 1591 placed the number of skilled *banditi* in Ottoman arsenals at three hundred, a significant portion, if accurate, of the 838 permanent craftsmen who worked in the Galata arsenal in 1604.[29]

The fear among Venetian officials was that once banished, these men would come to work in the sultan's arsenals and reveal closely-guarded trade secrets, out of either desperation or revenge. Experience proved such fears to be well-

founded. One carpenter banished from Venice for a "minimal affair" was discovered working in the arsenal in Galata and given a safe-conduct to encourage
him to leave. Another, a master carpenter convicted of murder, came to Constantinople and was offered by no less a figure than the *kapudanpaşa* a position in
the arsenal that would allow him to live "very comfortably." Despite the seriousness of his crime, the bailo immediately began working to remove the man from
temptation's way. It was important to catch potential problems before they mush-
roomed: a carpenter from Candia and five other men banished from Venice were
"continually solicited to enter and work in this Arsenal," and so the bailo had
them retained "because once [they] would have begun [work], dragging them
away would have been perhaps more difficult."[30]

Another targeted industry was cloth manufacturing. One cloth-worker, banished from Venice by the *Signori di notte*, received "very vigorous incitements to
exercise his art from several of these Turkish merchants, who gave him great
hopes of earnings and profit because of the desire they have of introducing the
silk industry into Constantinople." The bailo wanted to get the man out of Constantinople as quickly as possible, particularly because the Ottomans were at the
same time trying to start up a wool industry through the efforts of a number of
Marranos.[31] In another case, a silk-worker was given a safe-conduct, though his
papers' reference to a number of Venetians who were still "making . . . canvasses
and other cloths," confirms that there were many expert craftsmen willing to shop
their services whom the baili could not deflect from the city.[32]

Sailors and other men with maritime experience also found ready opportunities in Constantinople. In the years before Lepanto, Bailo Antonio Tiepolo
estimated there were enough *banditi* from Candia alone to man at least thirty of
the sultan's galleys; a decade later Giovanni Moro put the number at twenty
galleys. These Greek-Venetian sailors and ship workers were commonly known
as *marioli*, "Candiots," as Tiepolo described them, "who, banished from Candia,
entertained themselves in the taverns of Pera." By 1600, their numbers seem to
have been reduced somewhat due in part to Venetian policies to discourage immi-
gration by creating opportunities on the Greek islands, though this flow was
never entirely stanched.[33]

Besides these strategic and industrial dangers, there was also a spiritual danger in allowing *banditi* to remain in Constantinople. Considerable concern existed
that men would renounce their faith and become Muslim, or even Protestant, as
in the case of a friar from Chios who scaled the wall of his convent, went to the
English embassy, and entered "the errors of Luther."[34] If Constantinople was
dangerous for men, it was even more perilous for women and children, who were

believed to be spiritually weaker and morally more susceptible. While the baili complained that conversions made it more difficult to spirit subjects out of Constantinople, they also seem genuinely to have felt a paternalistic burden of providing spiritual protection to their charges. One example, not at all isolated, involved a thirteen-year-old boy from Rettimo who appeared in Constantinople, having fled for fear of being accused of a murder he did not commit. Of this case, Almoro Nani wrote, "I decided not to allow him to wander in any part of the city because of the danger that children of a tender age run here, so I kept him in my palace . . . having decided it good to remove him from here."[35]

While motivations were often sincere, the issuance of safe-conducts and commutations was a complicated question, and a source of debate among Venice's *stato da mar* officials. While all agreed that excessive banishments and commutations produced significant problems, the solution did not generate any such unanimity. At work were conflicting exigencies of public order. The baili and the Signoria wanted to limit the presence of Venetians and subjects in Constantinople to a small, controllable, official contingent. To do this it was necessary to facilitate the departure of undesirables who possessed specialized knowledge or might create disturbances among, or bring unwanted attention to, the Venetian community. In contrast, the rectors and other officials in the Venetian *terraferma* and *stato da mar* wanted to be able to use banishment liberally in order to rid their lands of disruptive criminal elements.

Alvise Giustinian, *proveditor generale* in Candia in 1591 described the tension between these two objectives. He recounted an incident when several criminals implicated in murders, burglaries and other illegal acts fled Candia before appearing in court. He was certain "that they were about to have recourse to the Illustrious Bailo in Constantinople to obtain a safe-conduct . . . I know that ejecting these types from the Kingdom is *ragione di stato* because of the consolation and respite that the people feel from it, and so returning them would have a contrary effect." Granting such criminals *salvacondotti*, he believed, "produces bad fruits, because it serves as an invitation to all Candiots to commit crimes and to free themselves from their caprices, as they can be certain, because of the experience they see every day, to receive absolution quickly through a safe-conduct. With this opportunity to travel to Constantinople, . . . that which Your Lordships had hoped to avoid occurs, because it is certain that many for mediocre sins without the hope of a safe-conduct would accept their banishment, or would attempt other means, which are not lacking in that Kingdom, to absolve themselves. They would not go to Constantinople, where they are easily able to interact with and befriend Turks, and where many of them remain."[36]

Another official in Candia, Tommaso Priuli, further observed that many *ban-diti* returned from Constantinople with safe-conducts that required them to serve on the galleys in the event of a mobilization, "and in the meantime they go freely wherever they please." During Priuli's tour of duty, a man who was indebted to the state was banished and told that "if he did not pay the debt that he had to the Prince he could not be absolved." He went directly to Constantinople and obtained a safe-conduct with a few minor stipulations; this was not in Venice's best interests in the long run, as "many debtors by hiding all that they have, obtain everything."[37]

Bailo Simone Contarini, in defending his handling of the *banditi*, presented the other side of the equation. He reported, "I regulated myself in the wisest manner that I believed conformed to the commissions of Your Lordship," even though the rectors at times did not think so. In his time, he "with great affliction of soul, saw two or three times" that when men banished from Candia came for commutations, and he was not forthcoming with them, they "turned Turks before my very eyes" and joined with the *kapudanpaşa*. For Contarini, the great danger of this was that through these men the Ottomans not only obtained their services as carpenters, pilots, and sailors, but also important information about the situation in the few remaining, vulnerable Greek islands in the *stato da mar*.[38] Gianfrancesco Morosini complained of the same problem, that desperate *banditi* often "became Turks" to remedy their situation; he suggested "it would be good to command in Candia and in the other islands . . . that they abstain as much as possible [from banishment] because the people of this sort who end up here are the cause of many *inconvenienti*."[39]

In spite of these inconveniences and the repeated calls for reform, the Signoria did not temper the use of banishment or the baili's authority to grant safe-conducts. Exile was a key means of punishment in the Venetian legal system, and the Senate and other legislative bodies were unable to conceive of a workable alternative. There were suggestions: one official proposed that Venetian officials in Candia be allowed to issue safe-conducts to those banished from their island because "reason dictates that it would also be good if the *proveditor generale* could give [*salvacondotti*] in that Kingdom so that [the *banditi*] would not have need to go [to Constantinople]." Another official suggested creating a sanctuary, a sort of internal prison colony, so that *banditi* would not be compelled to go to Constantinople to receive commutations. These ideas were never implemented, perhaps because to do so would have reduced the already relatively ineffectual penalty of banishment.[40]

Despite the best efforts of the baili to remove the *banditi* from Constantinople, then, there was always a significant number present in the city, and while many came only temporarily to seek a safe-conduct, a certain number remained and even settled in the city. Although their legal situations compromised their status as subjects, most *banditi* still considered themselves, and were received as, a part of the larger Venetian community. Many participated in the life of the nation and submitted themselves to the jurisdictional authority of the bailì, and in general the official core of the nation, the diplomats and merchants considered the *banditi* as legitimate parts of the broader Venetian community.

Gregorio di Giana, for example, was banished for murder in 1586, came to Constantinople, and became a useful member of the nation. Because he had worked in the Venetian arsenal, the bailo sent him to Anatolia to observe the construction of some Ottoman ships there. Such a mission was not uncommon, as the bailì regularly used *banditi* for espionage activities; indeed, one scholar has argued that banished men working in the Ottoman arsenal were "subsidized as agents of the Signoria." Another banished subject, who still "conserve[d] devotion towards" Venice, reported on happenings in the household of the *kapudanpaşa*.[41] An exile from Treviso lived in the embassy for three years because the bailo found him to be a man of "lively intellect who works in stucco and painting." So accomplished was the man that the Persian ambassador in Constantinople invited him to Baghdad to work for the shah, who was a great lover of art. The bailo granted him a safe-conduct in return for a promise to inform on affairs in the court there.[42]

Men accused of serious crimes in Venice were not ostracized from the nation. Bernardo Argiti was banished by the Quarantia for homicide and eventually arrived in Constantinople. He worked closely with the nation's official merchants, several of whom specifically requested that Argiti be given a safe-conduct to accompany several other exiles to the Greek peninsula to purchase grain. This was no small responsibility, either, as these men were entrusted with large amounts of cash and sent to oversee Ottoman ship captains retained to carry the grain to Venice and its dominions during the difficult famine year of 1591.[43] Another banished man, Domenico Balsarino, went on a similar mission, with eight thousand ducats "from public funds"; he was chosen in part because he had been in Ottoman lands long enough to become acquainted with its "language and customs." He used this experience to his benefit and in 1610 was elected Venetian consul in Chios. Eventually his son became consul, and in 1637, his grandson Carlo was accepted as a *giovane della lingua*.[44] Finally, there is the case of Marcantonio Zuccarini, a *cittadino originario*, who in 1591 with several other men chased the son of a butcher into a church in Venice and killed him. Zuccarini was banished, but the Quarantia conceded him a safe-conduct that permitted him to travel to Constantinople, where his brother was the *rasonato* to Matteo Zane. Despite his crime, he too was used "in several expeditions . . . in the public service" and in 1593 was granted a safe-conduct to return to Venice.[45]

As these cases indicate, *banditi* were regularly included in the normal life of the larger Venetian community. While not officially sanctioned, they were known and trusted by the diplomatic and mercantile core of the nation; they offered services, provided espionage, and even lived in the bailate. Such service often translated into important evidence in support of their requests to repatriate. In other cases, they parlayed their experience into highly desirable positions and important responsibilities. They represent a constantly changing, sizable, and important segment of the unofficial nation.

SLAVES

Joining the many *banditi* on the margins of the unofficial Venetian community in Constantinople was another large group of individuals with ties to Venice, slaves. While more peripheral and often restricted in their engagement, they nonetheless were seen as constituents of the broadly defined Venetian nation, and their care and protection was considered a significant responsibility for all baili and other members of the community.

Because slavery was legally and morally acceptable in Islam (one bailo felt slaves were esteemed "on par with women and horses"), there were many slaves throughout the Ottoman Empire. The most recent study on Mediterranean slavery estimates that between 1 and 1.5 million European Christians were enslaved on the Barbary Coast alone between 1530 and 1780.[46] For Constantinople, İnalcık estimates that the total number of slaves, prisoners-of-war, and boys of the *devşirme* numbered sixty thousand in 1568, and one hundred thousand in 1609, or approximately one-fifth of the city's population. An apostolic visitor in 1581 estimated that there were eight to nine thousand slaves in Galata alone, though this probably refers only to Christian galley slaves, whose numbers İnalcık puts at ten thousand.[47] While many in the city owned slaves, Morosini's claim that every household had at least one Russian slave was probably an exaggeration. Rather, the great majority of the slaves belonged to the sultan, with the bulk of the rest in the hands of important Ottoman officials. Under Süleyman I, for example, the official Iskender Çelebi owned six to seven thousand slaves, many more than the grand vizier's approximately 1,700. Even midlevel officials had slaves: a 1557 inventory of one such man's possessions included 156 slaves; most were from the Caucasus, Bosnia, and Hungary and just ten from Western Europe.[48]

The number of slaves in the Ottoman capital was not static. Periods of open warfare produced large numbers of slaves: the decade following Lepanto, for instance, was marked by intense efforts to exchange prisoners,[49] including Cervantes, who lived five years in the *bagno* of Algiers.[50] Over the long run, though, the most consistent source of slaves was the undeclared warfare of the Mediterranean corsairs. Times of peace generally produced a gradual reduction in the number of slaves: Lorenzo Bernardo reported in 1592 that the number of slaves in Constantinople had dropped dramatically from eight or ten thousand to perhaps three thousand. This drop was due, he believed, "to death, to escape, to ransom, and to conversion."[51] Alvise Contarini in 1641 reported that where previously three thousand slaves arrived annually in the city, now only about seven hundred did, which made it more difficult to obtain their freedom. Another factor in the ebb and flow of slave numbers was the Muslim view that slavery was a temporary state; thus the manumission of slaves was encouraged as an act of charity.[52]

Actual length of captivity varied widely. In cases in which ransom funds were readily available, and the location of a Venetian slave was known, "several months were the minimum time necessary for obtaining liberation," though the process more often took several years. It seems, however, that much longer captivities were the rule: one slave, a carpenter in the arsenal, was held for eighteen years because of the demand for his skills. Another slave, taken at Famagosta, was held twenty-two years and still another for twenty-six years.[53] Giacomo Nores, descended from a Cypriot noble family, was enslaved "at a year and a half in the arms of . . . his wet-nurse." Fifteen years later Lorenzo Bernardo obtained his release, and he eventually became Venice's "chief interpreter" and married his daughter to a patrician.[54]

Though some lists have survived, it is difficult to establish with any accuracy the actual number of Venetians among Constantinople's slaves. In 1588, the Senate estimated the number of Venetian captives in all the Mediterranean at more than 2,500, a number perhaps still somewhat inflated by the large numbers enslaved in the previous war.[55] One difficulty in making estimates is that Ottomans who held Venetian slaves often attempted to hide them because according to the capitulations, all Venetian slaves were to be freed into the baili's custody as soon as their identity became known. In practice, of course, this happened only with great difficulty. Ottoman masters, particularly the largest holder of the sultan's slaves in Constantinople, the *kapudanpaşa*, regularly went to great lengths to keep the presence of enslaved Venetians hidden from officials. Alvise Contarini reported that Ottoman ship captains either kept their Venetian slaves outside the city or locked up in their ships "so that they do not have recourse to the Bailo."

The *beylerbeyi* of Tripoli "*per prudenza* immediately [sold] in Fez or in Algeria the Venetian slaves that [he] captured, so as to avoid their being ransomed."[56]

Conversely, the baili often resorted to subterfuge to free Venetian slaves as quickly and inexpensively as possible, as the experience of Gianantonio Barozzi suggests. Born a Venetian noble, at the age of sixteen in 1593 he was banished by the Council of Ten "for a serious crime." He ended up in Hungary fighting as a mercenary, was captured, enslaved, and taken to Constantinople by a janissary captain who secretly sequestered him. When word reached Marco Venier of Barozzi's plight, he was able to free him by hiding the boy's identity as a Venetian patrician (which would have led to a much higher ransom) and obtaining the private intercession of a Venetian merchant as a cover for the bailo's interest.[57]

Caring for and freeing slaves was, of course, one of the principal duties of the baili; indeed, Alvise Contarini listed this as one of his greatest burdens. After 1586 the baili had at their disposal funds to ransom Venetian slaves, raised primarily by the Provveditori sopra Ospedali e Luoghi Pii and the Scuola of the Santissima Trinità. These resources attracted many slaves to Constantinople, including even some who had renounced Christianity for Islam.[58] In order to qualify for the funds available to the baili, a slave had to be either a patrician, citizen, or subject of Venice or to have been taken captive while in the republic's service. To verify slaves' eligibility for diplomatic and financial assistance, the baili regularly held inquiries into the circumstances of their capture.[59] Once freed, these ex-slaves were often lodged and fed at the bailate, at least temporarily, which was a drain on its resources. In certain cases, slaves received financial assistance to obtain their release and in return promised a certain period of service to pay off their debt. Alessandro Pelegrini, slave of the "sultana of Piyale Paşa," received funds to purchase his liberty, as did a Donna Marietta. Both agreed to serve the bailo a stipulated number of years in payment, until the debt was satisfied.[60]

Even in legitimate cases that met the requirements for financial assistance, limited resources prevented the baili from freeing many Venetian slaves. In deciding where to concentrate funds, patricians and citizens were always favored, followed by Italian subjects; subjects from the Greek islands were often overlooked. Marco Venier reported that corsair activity in the archipelago produced large numbers of Cretan slaves, but his inability to pay for their freedom produced "the universal discontent of those peoples, who believe themselves almost gone from the memory of their Prince, . . . Even though I do not fail to assist them as I am able, . . . that which I should do I am not able."[61]

Besides providing financial assistance, the baili occasionally assisted slaves in escaping; indeed, there was a secret passage in the bailate which was used to hide slaves until they could be shipped to Candia or Zante. Alvise Contarini reported having helped many slaves, Venetian and non-Venetian, to escape "without ever any complaint, indeed not even a suspicion." In one instance when a slave was missing, his favorable reputation in the Porte led the grand vizier to state publicly "that the escapee might be hidden in any other place than in the house of the bailo," even though that, in fact, was where he was.[62] In general, however, the baili avoided this practice, as overzealousness could land them in trouble. In the late sixteenth century, in fact, the baili had the reputation, unwarranted they claimed, of hiding slaves and spiriting them out of Constantinople. On at least two occasions, the sultan wrote directly to the doge complaining about the actions of baili in freeing slaves and requesting the diplomats' immediate recall.[63]

In addition to the baili, many members of the Venetian nation engaged in what Braudel termed the "traffic in ransoms and the exchanges of men," liberating slaves for piety and profit.[64] A 1616 dispatch reported that ship patrons and scribes "drawn by greed for gain, without the knowledge of the Baili, hide slaves in great numbers and of great consideration . . . and since this trade is very perilous, one day some serious problem could happen." In another instance, several members of the embassy household were ordered to cease hiding slaves there without permission.[65] Jewish merchants also played an important, though not uncontroversial, role as middlemen in freeing Christian slaves. The terms of this trade, at least in Venice, were that merchants worked through intermediaries and earned a percentage on the ransom price, receiving the full sum only on delivery of the slave.[66]

However their freedom was obtained, as with the *banditi,* Venice was eager that its slaves be removed from Constantinople as soon as possible, and for very similar reasons: the fear that they might pass on crucial information or provide services to their Ottoman masters or that they might convert to Islam. An example of the former was Tommaso Venetiano, a carpenter in the arsenal, whom the Ottomans refused to release for eighteen years because of the demand for his skills. Lorenzo Bernardo eventually obtained his release by making a gift of several sand-glasses to the *kapudanpaşa.*[67] The demand for skilled workers led the *kapudanpaşa* to offer artisans, carpenters, rope and sail makers, locksmiths, and coopers their freedom in return for ten years of service, after which they would be free to settle and work in Constantinople or to return home. These sorts of agreements were very common in the Ottoman Empire: Islamic jurisprudence permitted these *mukataba* contracts, which allowed slaves to work independently and apply earnings toward their ransom. Another option was to work a certain period in return for freedom, in some ways a Mediterranean form of indentured servitude. Many urban craftsmen in the Ottoman Empire held slaves on these terms, as has been shown in the Bursan silk industry. The system guaranteed the owner good service for a certain period of time in return for manumission, which was important since lifetime slaves were less productive.[68]

Venice's second concern was the increased potential for apostasy that captives ran during long-term enslavement. This was particularly true in cases involving young slaves, such as Pietro Cavazza, a *cittadino originario* whose father worked for an important Venetian magistracy. Captured by corsairs at age fourteen and sold to the *kapudanpaşa,* the lad was forcibly converted and circumcised. He recounted this experience in a letter to his father: "Still being a child, and having tender flesh, and not being able to resist the great pain, I was forced to say that I believed them, and I made myself a subject with my mouth, but maintaining my heart consistent with my omnipresent God and our patron, whom I never abandoned, nor thinking of his divine majesty, will I ever abandon him." Despite his claims of coercion, his letter to his father also emphasizes the educational benefits he was enjoying as a result of his conversion, including learning to read and write Turkish. "Here . . . I am not a *scarf(i)aro* nor am I a tailor; I do nothing but read and write, praise be to God who gave me a little bit of a brain so that I know how to read and write a bit in Turkish, and I do nothing but attend to exercising that art which could be of use to me."[69] At his father's request, the bailo tried to free the boy, whose letter suggests that he may not have been entirely discontented with his new life. Perhaps young Pietro hoped to translate his linguistic experience into a lucrative position upon his release. Venice had something of a welfare system for former slaves who returned to Christianity. A number of those who learned Turkish, Arabic, Greek, and other more exotic languages were elected as *sansari,* or brokers, to assist Ottoman merchants trading in the lagoon.[70]

In most cases, slaves who obtained their freedom wanted to flee Ottoman lands and return home as quickly as possible. However, a certain number did settle in Constantinople following their releases, drawn by the possibilities that the great city offered. A papal visitor in the 1580s found five hundred freed slaves living in Galata and sixty more in Constantinople proper; a similar survey in 1630 found approximately the same numbers. These *libertini* often married and set up houses throughout greater Constantinople, a visitor reported. "They live as subjects of the Turk, and there are some of them who are very comfortable working in industry and commerce," as was the case with a group of *libertini* who began trading wine after their release.[71] İnalcık's findings support this: freed slaves "occupied an unusually important place in the economic life of Bursa as rich silk manufacturers and merchants engaged in distant caravan trade, in money exchange, in usury and in tax farming."[72]

Because of their familiarity with the Ottoman world, these former slaves often assumed roles as cultural intermediaries: Wenceslas Wratislaw mentions an Alfonso di Strada, a Spanish merchant and former slave settled in Galata, who helped free the imperial ambassador Frederic Kregwitz.[73] During the bailate of Marino Cavalli, one of Venice's dragomans was a former slave who had been freed by a previous bailo and who was in turn assigned the responsibility of negotiating other slaves' freedom. He also instructed the *giovani della lingua*, though he left Venetian service in 1559, citing poor pay.[74]

These *libertini* existed in the interstices of the Ottoman and Venetian communities, and their political and religious identity was not always immediately apparent, nor necessarily fixed. It was not uncommon for *libertini* who settled in Constantinople to have recourse to both the *kadı* and the bailo on commercial and other matters. It was also not uncommon for former slaves, after marrying a local woman and raising a family, to return to die in Christian lands. There are also cases of slaves escaping to Europe and then subsequently returning to their owners. In other instances, slaves who obtained their freedom remained in the service of their former Ottoman masters. After purchasing his freedom, Pietro Brea, became "scribe of the slaves to ʿUlūg ʿAlī." He learned Turkish and customs of the land, and when he eventually left Constantinople, he soon returned to the city in the pay of the king of Spain.[75]

Slaves and the *libertini*, then, constitute another element of the larger Venetian community in Constantinople that might at any given time have comprised hundreds, if not thousands, of patricians, citizens, and subjects. The nation felt a responsibility to obtain the freedom of these unfortunate men and women and often went to great expense and effort to do so. As with the *banditi*, slaves represented a burden for the baili, but they also provided certain critical services. Once freed, some former slaves remained in Constantinople and even settled down, some working directly with the nation, others becoming Ottoman subjects but never renouncing entirely their Venetian identity.

GREEKS

Of the several different groups existing on the margins of the official nation, the most numerous were the Greek subjects of Venice, that is the culturally and linguistically Greek inhabitants of the islands of the *stato da mar*. In the late sixteenth century Venice's Greek Orthodox subjects numbered 480,000, almost 20 percent of the empire's total population.[76] The label of Greek-Venetian is a shorthand, of course, which masks the great diversity that characterized Greek speakers in the early modern Mediterranean. While Venice's policy regarding the Greek-Venetians in the Ottoman Empire was not fundamentally different than that toward *banditi* and slaves, Venetian authorities seem to have recognized, and perhaps accepted, the deeper causes of the significant Greek exodus to Constantinople and in the end did little to prevent it. Indeed, the baili effectively facilitated the presence of these men and women in the Ottoman Empire by annually providing them with a certification of their status as Venetian subjects, which carried with it important economic and legal rights. The Venetian chancellery also supplied other important services to these subjects, adjudicated their disputes, and furnished some with employment in the embassy and the commercial wing of the nation.

Venice's ties with eastern Mediterranean Greek culture dated back to the city's early status as an outpost of the Byzantine Empire and its later role in the blossoming Levantine trade. With the Fourth Crusade in 1204, Venice extracted from the Byzantine emperors a series of island and mainland possessions, which provided the foundation of the city's near monopoly of Levantine commerce in the later Middle Ages. This eastern empire, the *stato da mar*, was expanded after 1204 through conquest, purchase, and dynastic succession.[77] The rise of the Ottomans, however, set in motion a gradual waning in Venice's presence and influence in the region. In the two centuries following the conquest of Constantinople, Venice progressively lost many of its Aegean and Ionian possessions: by the end of the War of the Holy League in 1573, a "turning point in the history of the *Stato da mar*," as one historian has described it, Venice's holdings in the Mediterranean were reduced to a few small islands—Zante, Kíthira, Cephalonia, Corfu, Tínos, and, most importantly, Crete.[78]

Crete, or Candia as it was called by contemporaries after the principal city of the island (modern-day Hērákleion), was considered the "the loveliest crown that adorns the head of the Most Serene Republic," and indeed it was the largest of the *stato da mar* possessions, with a population of around 160,000 in 1571, comprising about a third of *stato da mar*'s total population.[79] Candia was one of Venice's earliest possessions, acquired in 1204 and held until the Ottoman conquest in 1669. A strategic linchpin in Venetian defenses, the island was also important for its agricultural production, particularly its famous wines, and as a market for Venetian goods. Additionally, Candia in many ways functioned as the backbone of

Venice's commercial empire, serving as a crucial stop on Venice's Levantine shipping routes.[80]

The island of Candia was unique in that it was the only possession of the *stato da mar* that Venice attempted in any systematic way to colonize, a process that led to numerous popular revolts that earned the island the reputation of the most difficult area of the empire to govern.[81] Colonization efforts met with limited success, however, and the Venetian families that settled on the island over time became Hellenized and effectively assimilated into the much larger Greek Ortho- dox population, creating something akin to a composite Veneto-Cretan culture. By the sixteenth century, partly in response to Ottoman encroachments in the *stato da mar*, Venice adopted a more tolerant policy and treated Crete as an integral part of the larger Venetian state, rather than a colony.[82] This shift signaled a tacit acknowledgment by Venice of the necessity for local support in retaining its hold on the island, which was especially clear after the loss of Cyprus in 1571.

It has been argued that this liberalization of Venetian policy resulted in a Cretan renaissance. An urban class began to arise in the chief cities of the island, with a commensurate rise in commerce and shipping, which produced an in- crease in living standards and a cultural flowering.[83] This boom was relatively brief, however, and the shipping sector began to decline significantly by 1600. Additionally, Crete was a predominantly rural society, thus most Cretans did not benefit directly from this urban economic expansion; in the countryside peasants still lived in abject misery. They were exploited by feudal lords and often pressed into service by Venetian authorities on the republic's galleys and public works, especially the island's massive fortifications built in the latter sixteenth century. Other factors contributed to misery on Crete: significant tracts of land originally planted in grain were switched to grapes to supply the lucrative wine trade, producing chronic grain shortages. Piracy paralyzed shipping, and seven major outbreaks of plague between 1570 and 1645, exacerbated the situation. As one Venetian official reported in 1589, "anyone who has not seen the wretchedness of those people is unable to believe it."[84]

Because of the harshness of the *dominante*'s policies, rural peasants were often antagonistic towards their Venetian masters in a way that urban Cretans were not. One observer noted that the peasants "considering that it is not possible to sink into a worse state than that in which they live today, burst into cries of pain and despair . . . Some of them, contemplating their wretchedness and lamenting their fate, have uttered these words: 'In the end we shall prefer to go and find those dogs,' meaning that they will prefer to go and live in Turkish regions."[85]

This was not an idle threat: during the previous war when an Ottoman force briefly landed on the island, peasants revolted and even attempted to join with the invaders.

The desperate conditions of their islands drove many Greek-Venetians to migrate to Ottoman lands, as well as Venice and other European cities.[86] In Constantinople they found work in the cloth industries, in shipyards, and often with the Venetian nation. The number of immigrants was significant: Matteo Zane wrote, "so many Levantine subjects are in this city . . . that I remain truly amazed." While no precise record remains, contemporary estimates give some indication of their numbers: Leonardo Donà, in 1595, calculated that in Galata alone there were two thousand Greek-Venetian subjects; Simone Contarini in 1612 put the number at over three thousand subjects, mostly from Candia. These estimates are probably inaccurate as they include only those subjects who, in order to avoid paying the *harac*, annually registered in the bailate's chancellery. Behind these numbers there certainly existed many more Greek-Venetians who quietly assimilated into the capital's large Greek population.[87]

Many Greek-Venetians came to Constantinople intending to remain only briefly, and they retained ownership of houses and farms on Candia. If their original intention was to seek their fortune and then return home, many ended up staying in the city for extended periods. As Leonardo Donà reported, they came "to earn a living" with the intention of returning home but gradually settled down, married, and had children and made the Ottoman Empire "almost their *patria*." Paolo Contarini in 1581 wrote of "many Candiots with wives and children who have lived in these parts for fifteen years"; Ottaviano Bon described "subjects . . . from the island of Candia and Tínos . . . the more part aged with wives and children, so that they do not think any more of returning to their *patria*."[88]

The experience of Francesco Calogna from Rettimo was probably quite common. He was seventy years old and resided in Constantinople with his wife, "living in great comfort." He gave two houses in Rettimo to his sister's sons, indication of his intent to live out his remaining years in the Ottoman capital.[89] In another case, a man who had settled with his wife in Constantinople turned over two houses on Crete to his father-in-law. Transfers of property to relatives such as these were very common among the acts of the baili, to the point that the chancellery appears to have served as something of a real estate office for Greek-Venetian subjects in Constantinople.[90]

On their arrival in the Ottoman capital, the Greek subjects of Venice found work in a variety of sectors. Simone Contarini reported that the expatriates were "for the most part sailors, coopers, shoemakers, and grocers."[91] A Venetian document of 1627, listing "Tinots and Candiots living in Constantinople and their professions," supports this assertion: it lists eighty men divided according to profession and place of origin. Forty-nine came from the Venetian island of Tínos; most of the rest from Candia. Of those whose profession was specified, seventeen worked as coopers, three as sailors, one a shoemaker, and one was listed as a beggar. The majority of this group, however, worked in the woolen industry—forty-one of the sixty-one whose jobs were indicated.[92] The number of men listed as involved in shipping and shipbuilding is certainly low, and the census was not intended to be exhaustive, as a number of baili reported that men from Candia "make up a great part of the workers in the Turk's arsenal."[93] So numerous were the Greek-Venetian subjects in the arsenal that they organized themselves into at least one guild, the *Arte del Bottaro*. Other Greek-Venetians entered into contracts of apprenticeship with young men from the islands. A man from Candia living in Galata, for instance, accepted custody of a thirteen-year-old boy from Canea "with the obligation to maintain him, to clothe him, and to provide him with shoes for the space of two continuous years, and to teach him the barber's art." The documents record Greek-Venetian clockmakers, merchants, tradesmen, and storekeepers, such as Dimitri Carpoforo who was in business with an uncle and had a *bottega* in Galata and one in Candia.[94]

In addition to trades, Constantinople was the focus of a thriving commerce in Cretan agricultural products—lemons, oranges, olives, oil, wax, honey, cotton, raisins, fruit, and cheeses. The most sought after and lucrative product of the island, however, was its wines. Malvasia, muscatels, and sweet wines all were in great demand in Constantinople and were carried from there into the Black Sea and beyond into Poland, Russia, and even as far as Calicut where Vasco da Gama's men found barrels of malvasia for sale in 1498.[95] All of the trade that flowed into Constantinople was subject, at least in theory, to paying Venetian *cottimi*, and while there was much tax evasion, still the income from Greek commerce was not insignificant. Despite the good tax return on this trade, the Signoria and the baili pursued a policy, if inconsistently, intent on discouraging its Greek subjects from coming to Constantinople.

One reason for this policy was to control the flow of news into the Ottoman capital. Because of the sensitivity of their task, the baili wanted to monopolize information and to have the independence to put whatever spin on it would benefit their negotiations. The Cretans represented a dangerous, uncontrollable source of information on the islands. Some passed intelligence along innocently: Giovanni Correr complained that "because of the continual commerce that the

Candiots have in Constantinople, the ships that come and go are very frequent, and as soon as one arrives, the passengers and the merchants are interrogated by renegades, and by other people they know who buy their goods, concerning goings on in Candia, and if the harvest has been or it appears will be good, and other similar inquiries. These men respond, [and] immediately it is publicized and discussed that because of that shortage of foodstuffs, [the Ottomans] ought to conquer Candia."[96] Giovanni Mocenigo believed the miserable situation of the Cretan peasantry represented a serious security risk because loud complaints about their bad treatment might incite an Ottoman intervention, "as the experience . . . of Cyprus may have taught us."[97] Gianfrancesco Morosini expressed concerns that expatriates in Constantinople sought to weaken the Venetian hold on the island by passing along the plans of Candia's defenses and spreading rumors that its people were on the verge of rebellion "because they are not less tyrannized than were the Cypriots, affirming that a few great and rich men are those who keep the people suffocated."[98] Two hundred years of shared history with the Ottomans, combined with the recent loss of Cyprus, made Venice very aware of the fragility of its hold over its few remaining *stato da mar* possessions.[99]

Avoiding controversy and complications was another motivation for Venice to keep its subjects out of Constantinople. Alvise Contarini maintained that the Cretans caused more trouble to Venice's representatives than did the Ottomans: they were always fighting with Muslims, Greek-Ottoman subjects, the customs officers, or among themselves. None of these problems were unique to the Greeks; members of the nation, both official and unofficial, regularly created similar disturbances. Probably it was the sheer numbers of the Greek-Venetian subjects that contributed to this impression, though some among the Venetian patriciate did believe that because "the nature of the Greeks is extremely cruel and savage," they were more inclined to create problems.[100] In one case, in which a Cretan "broke a Jew's head open," the bailo fined the man, and the matter seemed closed. But the injured Jew carried the issue to the divan, and it was resolved only with some difficulty and expense of political and financial capital. In another instance, a Cretan suspected of piracy was turned in by Greek subjects of the sultan, and once again the bailo was drawn into the fray.[101]

Venice's fears that its discontented subjects would revolt were also projected onto those Greeks living in Constantinople. When a wealthy man banished from Candia for killing a farmer came to the city, the bailo quickly issued him a safe-conduct so he could plead his case in Venice, which he granted "judging it more than necessary to remove from these lands such a person who has the following of all the Candiots that are here, and trying to quiet the noise that was being made" regarding his case. The man apparently had won the sympathies of his fellow expatriates by lamenting the sufferings of his five children, "which things are not only heard willingly here, but are caressed and fomented greatly by the Turks."[102]

In addition to these security risks, the Greek presence created problems of a more economic nature, such as the thriving contraband trade between Constantinople and Candia. One Cretan ship was intercepted by Ottoman authorities carrying contraband fish. A 1592 dispatch to the Venetian Inquisitori di stato reported that certain Ottomans and Greeks were taking vegetables and other foodstuffs to Candia in small boats, which they traded secretly for sword blades and other prohibited goods. The modus operandi was "to let a man ashore, who then with a small boat carries the merchandise to their great profit . . . I believe that no ship from Christianity turns up here that does not carry arms of diverse sorts for merchandise."[103] As this intelligence report indicated, smuggling was not solely a Greek problem, but there was an impression, accurate or not, that the Greeks were widely involved in it. Because they were not allowed to participate actively in the life of the nation, Greek-Venetian traders may have been less opposed to working outside the vale of the nation's regulations. This certainly was the case with a Cretan ship patron who was caught trying to smuggle three slaves from Constantinople, something the nation's officials had warned him against "many times . . . as he was accustomed to doing similar things."[104]

Besides smuggling activities, Venetian authorities were vexed by the Greek-Venetian merchants' persistent evasion of consular duties and fees. This became such a problem that in 1615, Venice effectively acknowledged its inability to police its own subjects when it requested that the sultan issue an extraordinary command to the kadı of Gallipoli and the Castellans of the fortresses at the mouth of the Dardanelles, ordering them to ensure that Cretan ships leaving Constantinople for Venetian territories paid their ten ducat duty to the consul of Gallipoli. The order stated that to avoid paying their duties, "they depart from here and exit past the mouth of the Castles without saying a word or making anything known." Any ship that refused was to be detained by these Ottoman officials.[105]

To avoid these and other problems, Venice's policy was first to discourage the Greek-Venetians from settling in Ottoman lands and, failing this, to encourage them to leave as quickly as possible. Venetian officials experimented with a variety of solutions—some prescriptive, others proscriptive—to stanch the continual hemorrhage of subjects. One governor of Candia, to prevent Cretan banditi from leaving for the Ottoman Empire, set aside a space where they could remain on the island in a sort of internal exile. This did not prove particularly effective because "this place is at times restricted so greatly, that the *bandito,* perhaps being poor, unable to find a way to sustain himself and earn a living in that place, he must, so as not to die of hunger, leave the island."[106] In another attempt in 1606, the Senate directed Ottaviano Bon to encourage the men of Candia and Tínos working in the arsenal in Constantinople to return to Candia with the promise that there was much work to do in the island's arsenal arming twenty galleys and that afterward there would be work as sailors and workers on these ships. In this way "the opportunity to move themselves from home and to return to Turkish lands will be removed." To encourage their return, the bailo was permitted to make small donations to offset expenses and to give safe-conducts to any *banditi* among their number.[107]

These attempts suggest that Venice was aware of the economic causes that drove so many to Constantinople, though the appropriate response was much debated. The root of the problem seemed quite simple, as one bailo indicated to the Senate: "I found that in reality they came here because they did not have provisions on the islands." Another made clear why this was the case: they "do not have sustenance and are not able to live by their art."[108] Alvise Priuli, on his return from duty in Candia, concurred with this view. In his opinion men went to Constantinople seeking work because they had such irregular employment and low wages in Candia that they were unable to feed themselves. The way to stop this outflow was to construct more ships in the arsenal there, and to pay a fair wage. In Constantinople workers in the arsenal started at eight *akçe,* but specialized men could rise as high as one hundred *akçe* a day.[109] Another Cretan official reported that the number of skilled artisans in the arsenal there had plummeted to fifteen caulkers and seventeen carpenters, due in part to the plague, but more to the shortage of ships and shipbuilding on the island: "Not finding, therefore, either work or shipping, nor even work in the arsenals, all the men in these industries decide to hunt for a living in other parts, and especially Constantinople."[110] He too suggested the solution was to build more ships and maintain them in Candia's arsenal. The Senate's response was that this was impossible: Candia's depressed shipping industry was part of a much larger problem affecting the whole empire, due in part to overexploitation of its limited forest reserves.[111] The shortage of ships, combined with an oversupply of sailors, produced a diaspora of Cretan seamen, many of whom went to work on Ottoman ships.[112]

One byproduct of the shortage of work in the islands was piracy, which resulted in regular diplomatic difficulties for Venice and its baili in Constantinople. Alvise Giustinian, *proveditor generale* in Candia, reported in 1591 that due to the lack of legitimate shipping work, Greek men regularly went into the archipelago to prey on Ottoman subjects. When some of these men were captured and a trial ensued it was discovered that there were "many, many interested parties, and thus this represented a matter of great consideration, because the desire to castigate all the guilty would be to destroy all that people [the Candiots] whom Your Lordships esteem highly, and of whom you have great need. And castigating a part and leaving the other part unpunished would be an injustice."[113] The solution: build more ships so that men would have work and not resort to illegal activities.

It would be inaccurate, however, to imply that officials were interested solely in ridding Constantinople of its Greek-Venetian subjects. The Signoria and the baili turned a blind eye to the presence and activities of Greek subjects, and indeed even acted in ways that facilitated and thus encouraged their remaining in the city. One reason was that the coffers of the baili, which suffered from the reduction in the official nation's long-distance trade in the early seventeenth century, desperately needed the customs duties and other fees that these Greek subjects paid. The Venetian mission in Constantinople also relied on the foodstuffs, especially wine, that Cretan merchants provided. Greek-Venetians resident in Constantinople also provided many services crucial to the functioning of the diplomatic and commercial nation, particularly in treating and working cloth. And finally, though a point of contention, the Ottoman Empire served as something of a release valve toward which problem-makers among the poor and disaffected of Venice's island possessions could be directed.

It is something of an irony, given the energy and resources expended in trying to prevent Greek subjects from leaving the islands, that once they arrived in Constantinople the baili facilitated their residency there and that these migrants became extensively involved in the activities of the larger Venetian community. Despite the problems that their presence created, and the attempts by Venice to get them to leave, the unofficial subjects and the official Venetian nation were interconnected, as each furnished the other with necessary services and support. The Venetian chancellery provided for Greek-Venetians the same sorts of functions it did for the official community: registering wills and testaments, administering justice, registering sales of properties, providing deposit services, and so forth. In addition, because of their status as Venetian subjects, the Greeks were also able to use the Latin-rite hospital in Galata.[114]

The baili, as leaders of the Venetian community, served as arbitrators in resolving guild labor disputes, despite their opposition to Greek-Venetian involvement in Ottoman industries. In a particularly revealing instance, twelve members of the Coopers Guild, all from Rettimo, appeared before the bailo and stated, "as subjects of the most serene Signoria they desired to have as headmaster of their guild one of your subjects, not wanting any more that man who at present exercises that office named Constantin from Rhodes, a Turkish subject, because of the many tyrannies done to them."[115] In Constantin's place the Rettimites elected one of their own compatriots, a certain Giorgi from Rettimo. That men providing a skilled trade to the Ottomans, against the wishes of their Venetian lords, had no qualms about appearing before the bailo to resolve their dispute gives some indication of the unusual relationship between the official and unofficial elements of the community.

Most important of all the services the baili rendered, however, and the one that permitted the Greek-Venetian subjects to retain their legal status despite their extended sojourns in Constantinople, was the annual issuance of *fedi*. The *fede* was a legal document issued by the chancellery which attested to the status of the resident Greek men and women as Venetian subjects. Though these were Venetian certifications, Ottoman institutions accepted them as valid, legally binding documents and as proof that the bearer was indeed a Venetian subject and therefore not subject to the special taxes required of all non-Muslim, *dhimmi* subjects of the sultan. In addition, the *fede* ensured that the baili's court would be the ultimate authority in legal and other matters involving the bearer. These documents were issued in great numbers, often at the beginning of each year when lines of subjects would appear at the embassy to have their papers renewed. While occasionally a Venetian or Italian subject from the *terraferma* might appear, the vast majority of these documents were issued to people from the Greek islands.[116]

Venetian authorities jealously defended both the rights of Greek-Venetian subjects before Ottoman officials and their jurisdiction over them. Attempts to declare long-term inhabitants Ottoman subjects, especially if they married a local man or woman, so that officials might collect the *harac*, were repeatedly fended off by the baili's diplomatic efforts.[117] As Venetian subjects, the baili also held legal authority over the Greek-Venetians, a right they protected vigorously. One evening, while Simone Contarini was out walking, "a great number of Candiot subjects came to me complaining strongly that while they were making fun of a certain Greek from here in Galata, he complained to one of the Ministers of this place, who commanded that two of them be put down and beaten according to the local custom."[118] Contarini sent his dragoman to the divan to request that the minister that had done this be punished, to which the vizier immediately agreed, and he further reaffirmed that all Venetian subjects would be sent to the baili for such matters. Venice's jurisdiction over its subjects, as well as those subjects' Venetian identity, was recognized and often respected by individuals outside the nation, as in the case of a Ottoman-Jewish merchant who bought some Cretan wine for "important people," which was delivered watered down. He appeared before bailo as the Cretan merchant's "Prince . . . not desiring to seek any other Justice."[119]

The baili also protected the commercial activity of its Greek subjects in the Ottoman Empire. Lorenzo Bernardo described one case in which a Jewish Cretan customs official and an influential Ottoman Jew, David Passi, tried to block the many vessels from Candia that passed through Constantinople on their way to Poland-Lithuania with wine, in an attempt to monopolize this trade for themselves. Bernardo took this matter before the grand vizier, "for the benefit of these poor men [the Candiots] and much more for the dignity of Your Serenity." He pointed out "the ancient usage, that it has always been customary for their personal vessels to pass into the Black Sea" after paying duties of 7 ½ ducats per barrel of wine. The bailo was eventually able to obtain an imperial commandment ordering the Jewish customs officials to leave the Cretan merchants alone.[120]

In another case, a man from Canea died on a ship belonging to the *kapudan-paşa*, and the sixty-three barrels of wine he had loaded on an Ottoman caramousal were confiscated by several officials who claimed them. The bailo intervened and was able to save the Greek's goods, just as he would have for any deceased, official merchant of the nation. Another way the official nation both assisted and benefited from the unofficial was through the bestowal of official, but menial, positions within the nation. For example a Tiniot who had worked in the cloth industry for twenty years in Constantinople was elected as a *cernitore ordinario* by the Council of Twelve, as was a Cypriot who had been working in the same industry for thirty years.[121]

The relationship, then, between the official nation and the much more numerous Greek-Venetians of the unofficial nation was quite uneven. Ottaviano Bon summarized quite well this unusual situation: "I have observed that in Constantinople are found infinite artisans and many work-people who work as carpenters and as caulkers, subjects of Your Lordship from the island of Candia and Tínos who work indifferently both in the Arsenal and outside . . . These live as subjects of the Most Serene Republic so as not to pay the ordinary *harac*, and not to be subjected to other taxes. They preserve themselves [from this] with a *bolletino* that is made for them by the baili witnessing that they are subjects, which they renew every year for their greater security."[122]

Bon was careful about distributing these *bollettini* or *fedi* in an effort to encourage the Greek subjects to return home, and he argued that the Senate ought to provide "some recompense to make them stay in Candia." Venice's Greek subjects left the islands, he held, because "they do not have employment and they cannot live on their trade." The great benefit of this steady stream of people went to the "Turks who use them on their galleys as rowers and workers, making them obey by force," and in the arsenal and other industries. "The worst thing," in Bon's view, "is that they are so weakly edified in religion, that for every little unpleasant encounter in which there is danger to life or some other interest, they easily become Turks." Yet, Bon reported, despite these conditions, the Greek-Venetians still loved Venice and held "Saint Mark in their hearts."[123]

Perhaps there was an element of wishful thinking in Bon's final observation that the Greek-Venetian subjects in Constantinople still held Venice dear. In many ways, the Greeks illustrate the complexity and variability of nation and identity in early modern Constantinople. By going to the Ottoman capital, these men and women were voicing discontent with Venice and Venetian rule in their homelands. Yet in Constantinople many of them became even more dependent on their status as Venetian subjects. By identifying themselves as recognized, card-carrying members of the Venetian community they were able to avoid being subsumed into the much larger population of Greek-Ottoman subjects. Though religiously and linguistically Greek, the Cretans distinguished themselves from their cultural and linguistic "nation" and played an integral and reciprocal role in the life of the official nation in Constantinople. The multiple layers of their identity allowed them to move with reasonable ease between Greek, Ottoman, and Venetian poles.

RELIGIOUS, WOMEN, AND OTHERS ON THE MARGINS OF THE NATION

The Greek subjects, slaves, and *banditi* represented the bulk of the unofficial nation, but there were also present in Constantinople a number of Venetians—citizens and subjects—who fit into none of these categories. These include religious, small-scale merchants and tradesmen, women, and a variety of others who existed on the margins of the Venetian community.

By the post-Lepanto era, the Latin-rite community of Galata (which will be examined in detail in chapter 5) had shrunk to a mere shadow of its former self. Few religious remained to serve in the churches and monasteries of the city, and many of those who did hailed from lands subject to Venice. One church official wrote that the five or six monks in the church of San Pietro were "for the most part from the state of Venice" and barely survived on the income of the church supplemented by gifts from the baili.[124] The bailo in 1632 reported that in the convent of Santa Maria di Galata all the monks were Venetian subjects. Indeed, the patriarchal vicar, the most senior Roman Catholic official responsible for the church in the Ottoman capital, was for many years almost always a Venetian because of the city's traditional role as protector of the Latin churches in the Ottoman Empire.[125] This primacy was challenged in the seventeenth century by the French, but accepted practice remained that the religious were under the jurisdiction of their prince's legate.[126] This is clear from an incident in 1632 in which a Bergamasque monk was punished for disrupting his monastery; both the French ambassador and the patriarchal vicar readily admitted the bailo's authority to discipline the man because he was a Venetian subject.[127]

That these prelates were Venetian did not necessarily mean that they favored their sovereign's interests. One vicar, Giuseppe Bruni, was from Venice but "dependent entirely on the Jesuits." A "Brescian friar" attempted to spy on the Venetian embassy on behalf of the Holy Roman emperor. Almoro Nani rather sweepingly decried the activities of the religious community in Constantinople, "who for the most part are out-of-control carts who come down here either to live after their own fashion, licentiously, or also moved by a spirit of ambition they procure to advance themselves in Rome and other places by examining the dispatches of the Porte." Certain church officials shared this view as well.[128]

More numerous than the few remaining religious were men and women who came to Constantinople of their own will for motivations quite similar to those of the Greek-Venetians: the hope of improving their social and economic position. Many came to work in the Ottoman cloth and shipping industries; there were always numerous specialized artisans from Venice and the *terraferma* who worked in the sultans' shipyards. Pietro Zen, early in the sixteenth century, complained of the "caulkers, carpenters, and other such" who came from Christian lands and provided critical technological assistance to the Ottomans. İnalcık has found that by the mid-sixteenth century in the Kasımpaşa arsenal district of Galata, the majority of the skilled workmen were Christians, Greeks, or Venetians.[129] Many other Venetian tradesmen were attracted to the city to ply their crafts, too.

One commercial sector that continued to be lucrative for Venetian Levantine exports was precious stones. A number of Venetian jewelers lived and worked in Constantinople, including Sebastian Danese who lived there for years with his three children. At Danese's death he left land and houses in Venice to his daughter Moisa, who had married into an important Ottoman Latin-rite family.[130] There was an ongoing demand for jewelers and goldsmiths in Constantinople: Mordecai Cressi, described as a "Venetian-Jew," arranged to bring a goldsmith from Venice "with the promise that he would have the opportunity to work and make great profits." Another man agreed to teach a Portuguese Jew *l'arte del diamanter* and to provide him with raw materials in return for his assistance.[131]

Other specialized artisans also worked in Constantinople, such as the furrier Giacomo Frieste from Venice. A man from Bergamo maintained a *hosteria* in Galata, and though he was not an official member of the nation, he submitted himself to the baili's authority in return for their defense and protection of his interests. In the first decades of the century, Sanudo mentions the presence in Constantinople of a number of "lower-class Venetian subjects . . . artisans, shoe-makers, tailors, and tavern keepers," as well as doctors, surgeons, apothecaries, and watchmakers.[132]

There were also merchants who traded in Constantinople, as we have seen, but not under the auspices of the official trading nation. The testament of Iseppo Sanzonio from near Bergamo, who died in Galata in 1627 leaving a pregnant wife and three daughters in the city, gives us a picture of the networks of a merchant outside the official nation. In partnership with a Venetian dragoman, he carried on a significant trade, principally in jewels, from Venice to the Black Sea and Moldavia. His commercial circles included a recently naturalized Venetian citizen from Salò, as well as another *paesano* from Bergamo, who traded in the Black Sea for fish and who was also not a member of the official nation.[133]

As in the case of the Greek-Venetians, these unofficial men (and some women) were often supported and subsidized by the official community, in effect facilitat-ing their continued presence. In 1596, for example, Marco Venier conceded to one such man "that you may make good bread, enough for this our household, and for all our merchants, and others of our subjects, but being in no way able to sell it to Turks, nor to Perots, nor to any *haracgüzar*."[134] This man had accom-panied Marco Venier to Constantinople and married a Chioggian woman living in Galata who served as the embassy's washerwoman. Eventually both left Con-stantinople in 1603, but by 1606 another Venetian subject, "Francesco Padoan, baker in Galata," was filling this role.[135]

The reciprocally beneficial relationship between official and unofficial nation is particularly evident in the experience of Venice's *cernitori,* or appraisers. *Cerni-tori* were officially sanctioned functionaries of the nation, charged with appraising the quality of merchandise and finalizing sales of cloth, leather, and other goods traded by the official merchants. They were especially important in transactions involving raw wool: they ensured the quality of the wool, and that it was not damp, as this ruined the material and could damage other merchandise loaded with it. *Cernitori* were assisted in their activities by several *argati,* or porters, who carried the heavy merchandise and might assist in its appraisal. Though they were not officially members of the nation, the *cernitori* played an important regulatory role in its trade. Venice's merchants were obligated to trade only through the nation's official *cernitori*, who were required to keep wool and other goods under lock and key until they had verified the weight and quality of the merchandise. Following this, the *cernitori* sealed the bundles of merchandise with an official seal and registered the transaction in the Venetian chancellery. As a further level of oversight, merchants were required to ship their goods only on Venetian ships, and captains were forbidden to receive any goods that did not have the official seal. In return for their services, *cernitori* typically received a 1–2 percent commission on the value of the goods.[136] *Cernitori* were almost always subjects, not citizens, and their presence in Constantinople was almost never legally endorsed. Yet their services were vital to the commercial activities of the nation, as well as the collection of duties that were the lifeblood of the Venetian bailate.[137]

Indeed, the *cernitori*'s unusual status vis-à-vis the nation is evident in the process by which one was elected a *cernitore pubblico*. To be considered, an aspirant required an acceptable guarantor and approval of the Council of Twelve. The nation's merchants often maneuvered to place someone they favored, such as one of their *giovani*, or even the bailo's *cavaliere*, in one of these highly sought after positions. In most cases, *cernitori* had to be Venetian subjects, though in some areas where this was impossible, non-Venetians were elected.[138] A recurring problem was that the nation's merchants would use unauthorized *cernitori*, especially Armenians, Jews, and even Muslims, an infraction punishable by a fine of one hundred ducats. Finding qualified individuals in Constantinople was not an issue, however, and indeed the positions were in such great demand that with Venice's diminishing Levantine trade after 1600, a glut of *cernitori* resulted and a number of initiatives were proposed to limit their numbers. These met with limited success, however, as the positions were seen as a form of social assistance for needy, unsanctioned members of the community.[139]

While not heritable, families tried to maintain a hold on the positions, which were often passed from father to son. Bernardin Corniani, a Venetian citizen from an established family, first appeared in Constantinople in 1590 and was soon elected as a *cernitore*. Corniani owned a house in Venice which he rented out, and he left behind his wife and at least one daughter, to whom he eventually provided a dowry of twenty ducats. He was accompanied to Constantinople by sons Bartolo and Lorenzo, both of whom also were elected as appraisers through their father's intervention. Lorenzo was sent home to Venice in irons after committing several unspecified "errors," probably fraud or theft, though he eventually returned and regained his position in Constantinople, where he died in 1615.[140]

Despite their status as official appraisers for the Venetian nation, the Corniani also aggressively sought work with Jewish and Muslim merchants, something quite common among all Venice's *cernitori*.[141]

Many of the *cernitori* had worked in the cloth industry, in Venice or Constantinople, for long periods—eighteen, twenty, even thirty years.[142] In applying for a position, Giuseppe Sanzonio emphasized that he had "worked in wools and hides all the time in my youth at [my] home, . . . and likewise in these lands."[143] Other supplicants emphasized their neediness: a Venetian *cittadino*, Marco Albriga, who worked in the wool industry came to Constantinople "because of several misfortunes" but could not find work. Cristoforo Mazzon from Brescia was in debt and was elected when he threatened that, if not approved, he would "alienate myself from the service of the nation and merchants of Venice."[144]

A similar situation was that of Niccolò Gonale, a subject from Venice, who may originally have come from Candia. Initially he appeared in Constantinople trading with a Muslim merchant in 1592, and in 1594 he requested election as a *miserator ordinario* of the nation and described his story. He had a wife and three children, and "hoping more easily to find a solution to my poverty, and to the needs of these children, I decided to come to these lands with the little substance that I had, and to set up a *bottega* of cloth, in which I worked for some time the best I could, and because of the cruel famines that reigned, having left my wife and children in Venice, I decided to have them come here [to Constantinople]."[145]

Gonale's gambit in moving to Constantinople did not pan out. His affairs "got progressively worse"; he fell into serious debt and was imprisoned for a time. He requested election so as "to maintain my poor family as long as it pleases the Lord God that I am able to remain free, so as to return to my *patria* with my family." Additionally, Gonale argued for special consideration as a Venetian subject, as "many who are not subjects of Your Serenity" served the nation in these positions. Moved by his sorrowful tale, the council elected Gonale to the position of *cernitore* by a unanimous vote.[146] The family never left Constantinople: Gonale died in 1611, and his daughter married a Venetian subject from Brescia who served in the household of several Venetian merchants in Galata.[147]

Gonale's case raises the question of women and the Venetian nation. The focus of this study has been predominantly male, mostly because men made up the majority of the Venetian expatriate community, but also because of the relative archival silence regarding early modern women's experiences, particularly on the margins of the Mediterranean.[148] There are records regarding enough cases for a picture of the women of the Venetian community, however anecdotal and incomplete, to emerge. In some instances women came to Constantinople for reasons

very similar to men—opportunity, slavery, absolution. For example, Fatima Ca-
dun, née Beatrice Michiel, came to Constantinople in late 1591 to join her brother,
the renegade eunuch Gazanfer Ağa, a trusted adviser within the sultan's harem.
Her motives for fleeing and renouncing her religion seem to have included "the
hope of deriving great gain, and maybe also from being little contented with her
husband," who was intent on controlling assets from her first marriage and
economic privileges the Signoria had granted her.[149] Another woman, Anzola
from Chioggia, came to Constantinople alone but then entered into a relationship
before the local *kadı* with Valerio Palmi, who worked as the embassy's baker while
she nursed ill members of the nation and served as its washerwoman.[150] These
women, however, are exceptional. Although an occasional woman came alone to
Constantinople, the majority came in the company of men—fathers, husbands,
lovers—and their experiences, from what little we know, were strongly influenced
by the decisions and experiences of the men they accompanied.

While the great majority of *banditi* were men, there were some *bandite,* women
expelled from the Venetian state for a variety of crimes. Some were banished
alone for their indiscretions, such as the woman who injured a male notary;
Margarita of Tínos, exiled in 1615 for "carnal commerce"; or the Cretan sisters
Elena and Regina, banished for an unspecified crime. In the case of Margarita,
after three years of banishment, the bailo granted her a safe-conduct in recognition of "the fragility of the female sex" and her "great poverty."[151]

Venice's paternalistic policy toward its men was even more pronounced toward its female subjects. The Aristotelian and Christian view of women as ir-
rational and morally weaker than men still obtained, and thus the fear that a
woman would "lose her soul for being far from her *patria*" was strongly held.[152]
The baili went to great lengths to remove women from Constantinople as quickly
as possible in order to distance them from the dangers of the city. This policy was
not uniquely Venetian; religious redeemers of slaves were instructed to ransom
first women and children, who were "judged to be more exposed to the pressures
of the Muslims." The French went so far as to forbid women from embarking for
the Levant, and a 1679 list grouped women with vagabonds and criminals as
equally undesirable elements in the Levant.[153] Although lacking an explicit policy,
the Signoria shared these attitudes: while the English and French ambassadors
often were accompanied by wives and children, the baili always left their families
in Venice.[154]

The case of Donna Jacoma shows the ends to which Venetian political and
religious officials would go to remove women from the corrupting influence of
Constantinople. How she ended up in Constantinople is unclear, but her extreme

poverty and her desperate situation led a Venetian priest to fear she might be on the verge of apostasy. To avoid this, he arranged a marriage with a young man of twenty from Urbino, Simone de Bartolo, who had run into unspecified difficulties while doing business in Constantinople and made a solemn vow to marry whomever his spiritual advisor proposed if his affairs turned out in his favor. When this occurred he agreed to wed Jacoma; she, however, "protested somewhat." Threatened by the priest "that if she did not accept this match . . . God would chastize her, and that having fallen into such a miserable state she would be abhorred and ostracized by everyone," she finally was bullied into accepting the match.[155]

As was the case with exiles, so too most Venetians enslaved in Constantinople that we know about were men. Women do appear, however, and their numbers may have been greater, but simply less likely to appear in official records because their slavery often played out in Ottoman homes and other private realms. In one case, funds from *Proveditori sopra gli Hospitali* and a special allocation of 150 ducats from the Senate provided a large ransom to free Laura Gritti and her two young daughters, almost certainly from the noble Gritti family. A woman of less exalted status, Donna Marietta Venetiana, who had a Jewish master, Abram Calipin, was also manumitted with official funds, though in her case she was constrained to work in the embassy to repay the money the bailo had spent to free her.[156]

Although some women were banished or enslaved alone, most often they came in the company of a man. Some were banished as a couple, such as the husband and wife expelled from Canea for their involvement in a murder there, or Ludovico and Paolina Cagnola, banished from Padua. Most came by choice, having elected to accompany husbands into exile. In some cases, *banditi* would bring their entire families to Constantinople: Horatio di Marchi, banished from Vicenza, came to Galata with his young wife and "four little children of tender age." To facilitate his return home, the bailo gave the young father a pardon because he was a good "carpenter of artillery carriages, and also a cooper" but especially because of his family, "all of whom in this land run the manifest risk to be lost in an instant."[157]

In another case, an arsenal worker banished from Venice went initially to Naples, where his banishment was rescinded on the onerous condition that he not work in the shipping industry. Upset at this ruling and unable to provide for his family, he brought his pregnant wife and two young children to Constantinople intent on conversion and to find work in the sultan's shipyards. It seems likely that this threat, backed up by the presence of wife and children, was intended to elicit sympathy and the reversal of his banishment, which is exactly what occurred. More commonly, however, banished men used tales of the impoverishment of the families they left behind as a bargaining chip in obtaining a safe-conduct.[158]

Some women were brought from Venice by merchants to serve as maids or cooks and not infrequently, as mistresses. In one instance, Francesco Spiera brought a Madonna Betta Biscontina from Venice to work for him. When she became pregnant, Spiera was ordered to pay the wages he had promised her, to arrange for her return to Venice, to support her during her pregnancy at five ducats per month, and to have his parents receive the child whom the bailo ordered Betta to consign upon its birth.[159]

Madonna Betta's case is quite unique, however, as most merchants' partners were not imported from Venice but rather were found among Constantinople's women. European merchant nations in general were made up mostly of bachelors, and while there were occasional exceptions, married merchants were almost never accompanied by wives or children.[160] Occasionally a merchant might wed a local woman, such as Giulio Croce, who married the noblewoman Cecilia Pisani in the church of San Francesco. Pisani had been enslaved following Lepanto and taken to Constantinople, where Croce paid 150,482 akçe to free her.[161] It was also not uncommon for merchants to have female slaves—usually Greeks, Circassians, Russians, Hungarians, Bulgarians, but also an occasional Ethiopian—whose duties included sexual services. The Venetian merchant Marcantonio Stanga, for example, owned a slave and produced several children with her.[162]

Much more common than Christian marriage, however, were temporary, relationships with Ottoman-Christian women which were formalized before local Ottoman magistrates. George Sandys wrote of merchants in Constantinople "They live freely, and plentifully: and many of them wil not lye alone where women are so easily come by. For besides the aforesaid markets [of slaves], it is a use, not prohibited but onely by our religion, to purchase for their concubines the beautifull daughters of the Grecians, . . . recording the contract in the Cadies booke."[163]

It was licit for foreigners to take a local spouse temporarily by presenting a contract, or *kâbin,* before a *kadı.* These temporary marriages did not extend to Muslim women, however, who were reserved solely to Ottoman men, at least in theory.[164] Maffio Venier described these legal ceremonies: the *kadı* asked the prospective husband what financial settlement or allowance (*kâbin*) he proposed and, if acceptable to the woman, he took "the thumbs of both and touche[d] them together from the inside out as a sign of the faith that they give."[165] Legally recognized "contractual concubinage" relationships of this sort were commonplace among merchants: the patriarchal vicar reported that "this is a thing in which are involved the greater part of the merchants, both Venetians and French, and also [those] from Pera."[166] Andrea Gritti fathered three sons with a Greek woman during his long years in Constantinople, including the controversial Alvise Gritti. Indeed, one of the charges of opponents to Gritti's election was that "one who has three bastard sons in Turkey should not be made doge."[167] While we have no record of the baili keeping mistresses or entering into temporary marriages, some of their *famiglia* did, and other European ambassadors openly lived in such *kâbin* relationships: the French ambassador Brèves had three children with a Greek women, whom he legitimized upon his subsequent marriage to a French noblewoman.[168]

As one man accused of adultery for maintaining a wife in Venice and a mistress in Galata (a not uncommon phenomenon)[169] explained, merchants entered into and justified these relationships "in the land of infidels so as to not run the risk of greater danger, as people are fragile, and inclined to sin."[170] These legal relationships with Christians helped prevent merchants from engaging in more perilous intimacies with Muslim women. While in theory contact across gender and religious lines was forbidden, in reality it was not unheard of.[171] In 1604, a Venetian merchant in Cyprus was caught in the house of a Muslim woman and only narrowly escaped being burned.[172] In 1596, Marcantonio Borisi, one of Venice's most important dragomans, carried on an extended intimate relationship with a Muslim neighbor whom he would sneak into his room in the embassy, at great danger to himself and to Venice.[173] When a band of four hundred French soldiers, who had abandoned their post in Hungary and gone over to the sultan's service, arrived in Galata, they sequestered a number of Muslim women in their private rooms.[174] This behavior was not limited to soldiers and merchants: in 1609 an ecclesiastical authority inspecting the religious institutions of Galata reported that "several of the monks of San Pietro had been immoderate with some Turk women who neighbored their garden."[175]

Punishment for such relationships was often swift and harsh. One Venetian merchant was hung for "having dared to cast his profane glance upon the beauties of the harem," with a spyglass pointed toward the seraglio. In another case, a Christian boy was quartered, and his Muslim lover dragged nude behind a horse.[176] Most relationships, however, seem not to have ended so badly. As the always observant Fynes Moryson reported, the reality of Christian-Muslim intimacies was less straightforward than the laws and occasional expiatory execution suggested: "If a Christian man committt fornication with a Turke woman both are putt to death, and this Common danger to both, makes them more wary of others, and more confident to trust one an other, but the sinne is Common, and at Constantinople the houses of the Ambassadors being free from the search of magistrates very Turkes, yea the Janizaries guarding the persons and howses of these Ambassadors, will not stick to play the bawdes for a small reward."[177]

As Moryson makes clear, Ottoman officials were not always energetic in enforcing the letter of the law; they even might collude in circumventing it. This is supported by another case, involving the Venetian merchant Zuanantonio Nordio, who was caught with a Muslim woman in his house. As the bailo reported, "This is the greatest crime, which is punished with impalement of both parties without trial, and with the loss of all merchandise. Nonetheless, everything was quickly resolved and assuaged with 300 ducats paid by him before the incident reached the ear of the *paşa* or some other important minister, who the bigger they are take bigger bribes."[178]

The baili roundly condemned these sorts of dangerous liaisons, less on moral grounds than on the intractable economic and political problems that arose if a merchant died in Ottoman lands and left behind children from these *kâbin* marriages. While considered bastards in Christianity, children from such relationships were recognized by Islamic law, which did not recognize illegitimacy, and extensive negotiations frequently ensued over the financial obligations owed the children and their mothers.[179] Giorgio Giustinian clearly delineated the risks of such immorality among merchants: "The lack of control and the extreme sensuality of some of our merchants can cause their principals grave damage, and the baili of Your Lordship many travails, because these women . . . arrive unexpectedly to declare themselves *haracgüzar* of the Grand Lord and to place the merchandise in manifest peril."[180] Despite oft-repeated injunctions, however, merchants and others continued to enter into these relationships.

As the numerous cases above suggest, there was a close relationship between the official nation and the broader community that existed on its periphery. Clearly these unofficial individuals saw themselves as, and were considered, part of the larger Venetian community. One way the nation affirmed and strengthened this bond was by supplying opportunities for Venetians and subjects to work in association with the nation, if not to trade officially under its auspices. A paternalistic impulse among the baili and merchants helped provide for the needs of the impoverished in the community and to protect them from the perceived dangers of life in Constantinople. This was particularly true in the case of women and children. While officially the presence of unsanctioned individuals was discouraged, in practice the nation's merchants and diplomats needed many of the services that such men and women could provide, and thus they effectively facilitated their continuing presence by providing them jobs and support.

SAILORS, TRAVELERS, AND OTHER TRANSITORY PEOPLE

The Venetian community in Constantinople included both stable and more transitory elements: among these latter were the many travelers from Venice and its territories who made the pilgrimage to the Porte, and the crews of the ships that regularly anchored in the port of Galata. It is difficult to establish accurately the number of such travelers passing through at any given time. One visitor in 1581 estimated that there were five to six hundred transient residents in Galata alone; a seventeenth-century churchman estimated some one hundred travelers in Constantinople.[181] Published reports on the splendors of the city created among Christians what one Englishman called "an itching desire to see . . . Constantinople . . . the seate of the Turkish Ottoman." Similarly, Sir Henry Blount declared in 1635, "He who would better behold these Times in their greatest glory could not find a better scene than Turkey."[182]

Because of Venice's historic link with the Ottoman Empire, Venetians were regular and enthusiastic travelers to Constantinople. One such traveler wrote that the city was "set in the most beautiful and charming site that man can imagine." Another enthused upon his departure, "I still cannot calm my soul nor my eyes, . . . having fixed [in them] the graciousness of Constantinople, nor can I wait to have the occasion to return and enjoy it; I feel I have died and gone to heaven."[183] Venetians were among the most prolific writers of travel accounts on the region: of 449 travel reports written in this period, fully 20 percent were composed by Venetians. As one scholar has written, "among the voyages most noted and dear to the Venetians, . . . Constantinople undoubtedly held first place, . . . There was not a man of politics or of business that had not removed himself at least once to the shores of the Bosporus, and very few had withstood the desire— when there was not a political duty—to note down, often for publication, the experiences of this voyage."[184]

When Venetian diplomats traveled to Constantinople to take up office, they were invariably accompanied by fellow patricians. Pietro Foscarini was joined by several Venetians, including his two sons, who were inspired to travel to the Ottoman Empire by a *virtuosa curiosità*.[185] Jacopo Soranzo reported that when word of his 1582 embassy became public, "an infinite number of gentlemen scrambled with warm requests . . . to be admitted to the number of those that would accompany and serve your most Illustrious Serenity on this voyage, considering the noble and rare occasion to see the Porte, the security and comfort of the trip, the information that one could acquire about many things, and that which is most important, to insinuate themselves in the grace of that Lord."[186]

A visit to the Porte was requisite preparation for a patrician's future career in state service. After completing his studies, Agostino Gussoni resided in Constantinople for over a year, studying Ottoman government so that "by seeing the world [he might] make himself more expert in these matters."[187] Tommaso Priuli came to Constantinople after having been to all the major European courts, saving the most important for last, after which, "according to custom . . . he would begin to dedicate himself to the most important offices."[188] Patricians also traveled to the Ottoman capital temporarily to resolve personal and familial matters. Andrea Soranzo and Marchio Zane, for example, accompanied Marco Venier on his voyage to Constantinople. Soranzo was involved in a number of commercial dealings there, and Zane came "with the desire to see the greatness of this grand Porte, and also to assist in some skillful way the pretensions of the brother-in-law of his brother, Signor Zuanne, in his request for the principality of Wallachia."[189]

Galata was also regularly filled with crew members from the many merchant ships docked in its port. Although by 1600 Venetian maritime commerce had certainly declined in absolute terms (in many cases replaced by overland caravans passing through Split), ships of Venetian registry still came to Constantinople every year. Some were large merchant craft that sailed the waters between Venice and Constantinople, stopping at many of the islands of the *stato da mar*. More numerous were the many smaller boats of Greek-Venetian subjects that plied the route between Candia, Tínos, Zante, and other islands.[190] By the sixteenth century the medieval galley had been replaced by larger round ships of 600–700 tons, such as the carrack. These ships employed between fifty and eighty crew members—oarsmen, masters, seamen, deck hands, and a noble "bowman of the quarterdeck." Though Venetians occasionally served on these ships, the majority of the crews were drawn from the *stato da mar*, the *terraferma*, and increasingly from outside Venetian dominions.[191]

When a ship dropped anchor in the port of Galata then, there was a significant, if temporary, influx of men into the Venetian community, with an attendant transformation of its makeup. While in port, these men, whether Venetian subjects or not, were the responsibility and under the jurisdiction of the baili, and numerous court cases in the chancellery's records attest to the frequent problems the mariners caused. In one case, a ship's cook was charged with insubordination and blasphemy after a dustup with a shipmate over a woman. Another time, two

Greek-Venetian sailors fought a duel over a debt. The first man to fire killed his opponent with a direct shot to the heart, and the surviving duelist was condemned to five years on a prison galley.[192] One of the reasons for these recurring problems, was that Venetian ships generally remained in port for up to four months, much longer than the typical one month stay of English and Dutch ships. In part, Venetian ships remained longer because crews were permitted to carry a certain amount of merchandise to trade on their own—this had long been Venetian practice, and change was slow in coming.[193]

In the case of ships' crews, the men's necessarily extended stays in the city made Venice's paternal policy of trying to keep its charges out of Constantinople's libertine atmosphere clearly untenable. The baili did try to limit the number of young men who came to the capital. In 1580 Giovanni Cappello reported that numerous young men serving as *mocci*, or ship's boys, upon arriving in Constantinople regularly abandoned their ships, their families, and their faith, "led astray by those already involved" in licentious practices. He proposed that the Senate forbid youths under age eighteen to serve in any capacity on ships that would bring them to Constantinople.[194] Venetian patricians were particularly concerned about the danger that youth of their caste encountered while serving as ship's nobles. The practice of sending young nobles on Venetian ships as *balestrieri di popa* or *nobeli di galia* had a long history as a sort of apprenticeship for aspiring young merchants. As merchants retreated from international commerce, these positions became a popular form of state welfare to subsidize the impoverished majority of the patriciate. A young noble received free passage, food, a salary of approximately sixty ducats, and the right to carry merchandise that could be traded at a good profit.[195] While potentially a significant subsidy for a poor patrician family, there were still concerns about this policy in the dangerous Mediterranean world. As Gianfrancesco Morosini reported in 1583, sending nobles to learn the "art of navigation" was a good idea,

> But doing it as it is now done is surely damning, and of manifest peril, because youths of fourteen or fifteen years are sent to learn every other thing than the art of navigation and once they arrive here we run the manifest peril that they be stolen by Turks with the loss of their souls . . . Your Serenity would be more secure if you commanded that in these parts nobles under the age of twenty years did not come on your ships, so that at least we could be more at peace from the danger that they might be stolen, as I have already experienced with one boy who is here in my house with me . . . [Fathers who] think they are providing for their children [will have] to give account to the Lord God for the education that they will have given them.[196]

"Stolen," of course, could mean being captured and enslaved involuntarily, as in the case of Francesco Pisani, *nobile* of the Colomba. It could also refer to voluntary conversions, such as the ship's noble from "Ca' Lombardo" who under "his own pure and spontaneous impulse, turned Turk."[197] Conversion was not the only danger facing these young nobles: in 1601 a ship's noble, Niccolo Zane, "a minor child," gambled with the older men on his ship (which was against the law) and lost his money and merchandise.[198]

If youths provoked the baili's paternal concern, mature crew members in the end created many more problems through their contraband, violence, and conflicts with local authorities. In 1612 there was a row between sailors and janissaries, in which some of the latter were badly wounded, which cost a bribe of a crimson vest and ninety ducats to resolve.[199] These sorts of incidents created unwanted expenses for the baili, and also potentially serious political complications. In 1638, for example, several sailors from the *Nave Nuova* fought among themselves and two were gravely wounded, as was an Ottoman customs official. "At the uproar the *Bostancıbaşı* came in person, and he took the Barber and another sailor to the Seraglio's prison, not so much as promoters of the trouble as the wounders of a Turk in the hand." Alvise Contarini tried to secure the men's release, arguing that the Capitulations gave the bailo the right to punish Venetians. The Ottoman official, who wanted to cut off the men's hands, responded that this was true only "when they came to blows among themselves as sailors on Venetian ships, but when these same sailors railed against Turks, this was clearly not covered by the Capitulations." Contarini finally obtained their release through his good offices, but similar incidents were all too common.[200]

Another problem was sailors jumping ship. Because of the demand for qualified seamen in Venice and Constantinople, there was competition for their services. Some ships' officers paid to release debtors from prison in return for their services. Thus, Venetian crewmen regularly abandoned their posts while in port, leaving their ships shorthanded. Such an act might result from mistreatment by the ship's officers, or because better wages or a pay advance could be obtained from another captain, either Christian or Muslim. Some men also jumped ship and converted to Islam.[201] Such experiences reaffirmed for the Signoria the wisdom of its policy to keep unsanctioned people out of Constantinople and out of harm's way as much as possible.

The definition of Venetian and the composition of the Venetian community in Constantinople was much more diverse than its merchant and diplomatic core might indicate. Venetian law and tradition had a very narrow definition of what constituted the Venetian nation. In practice, however, the Venetian community was much broader and more fluid than just its two official elements, merchants and diplomats. Individuals from a wide range of cultural, social, economic, and linguistic backgrounds considered, perhaps imagined, themselves to be part of the larger community. Men and women from the Greek islands of the *stato da mar*, individuals and families banished from Venetian lands, sailors, soldiers, slaves, and travelers all came to Constantinople. While there they became de facto part of the nation, at least peripherally. Not only did these individuals imagine themselves as part of the nation, but the official nation also considered them to be part of the larger Venetian community, if on a different footing than the diplomats and merchants. The official policy of the baili and the Venetian government was to discourage the presence of these groups in Constantinople for a variety of political, economic, and moral reasons, but in practice they went to significant lengths that facilitated the long-term residency of these people and asserted and protected their rights as Venetian subjects.

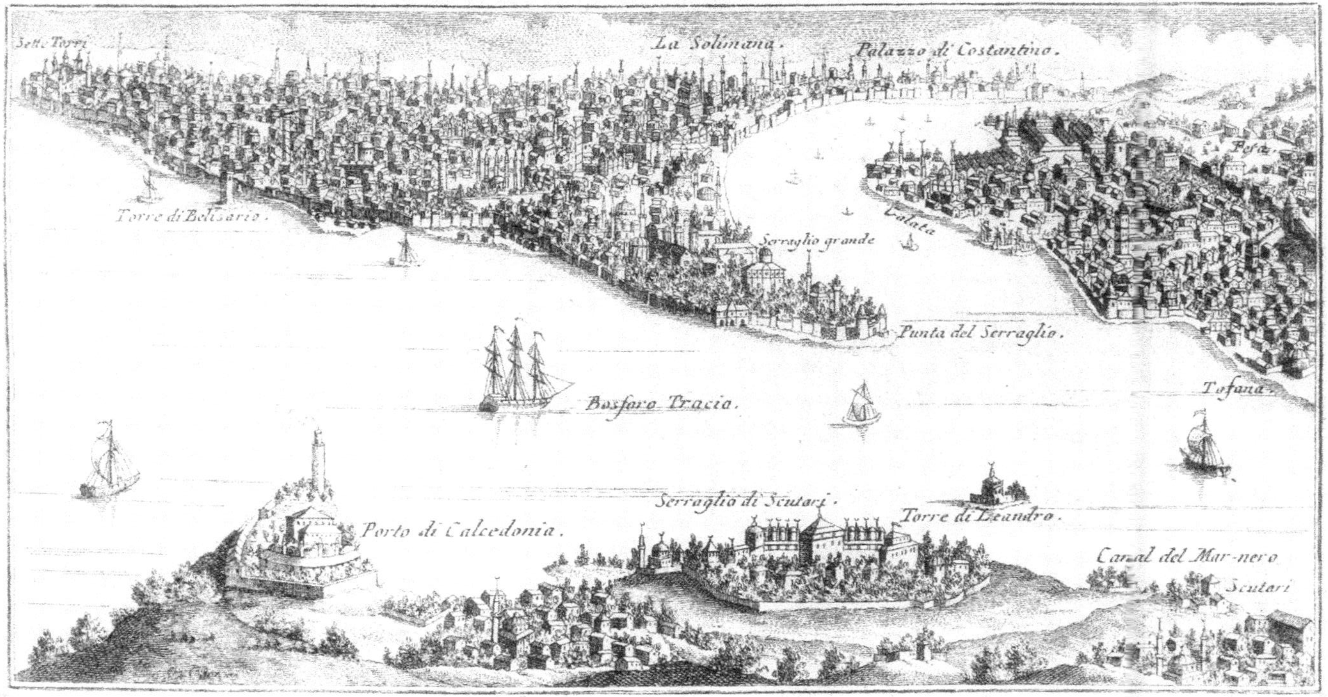
Sette Torri
La Solimana.
Palazzo di Costantino.
Pera
Galata
Torre di Belisario.
Serraglio grande
Punta del Serraglio.
Tofana.
Bosforo Tracia.
Serraglio di Scutari.
Torre di Leandro.
Porto di Calcedonia.
Canal del Mar-nero
Scutari

Late sixteenth-century view of Constantinople. Correr, Cod. Sagredo, PD 5702

Inside the Venetian bailo's residence in Constantinople. *Alt-Stambuler Hof-und Volksleben, ein türkisches Miniaturenalbum aus dem 17. Jahrhundert*, no. 48

Simone Contarini, Venetian bailo in Constantinople, 1608–12. Correr, Ritratti, Cicogna 423

Bailo's audience with the grand vizier. *Alt-Stambuler Hof-und Volksleben, ein türkisches Miniaturenalbum aus dem 17. Jahrhundert,* no. 51

Dragoman interpreting for Venetian bailo and Ottoman officials. *Memorie turche,* Cod. Cicogna 1971, c. 35r

Marketplace scene in Constantinople. *Memorie turche,* Cod. Cicogna 1971, c. 19r

Merchant shops in Constantinople. *Memorie turche,* Cod. Cicogna 1971, c. 31r

Hasan Paşa, Ottoman *kapudanpaşa* and Venetian renegade. Bodleian Library, Ms. Bodl. Or. 430:1588, c. 48r. Also *Life in Istanbul, 1588*

CHAPTER FOUR

Jews, Renegades, and
Early Modern Identity

With the burgeoning travel literature of the sixteenth and seventeenth centuries, accounts such as Pietro della Valle's description of his voyage to Constantinople in 1614 became increasingly common.[1] Julien Bordier, squire of the French ambassador to Constantinople Jean Gontaut, baron of Salignac, produced a similar narrative of his travels into the "Orient" in the first years of the seventeenth century. Housed in the Bibliothèque Nationale is a manuscript of this intrepid traveler's "Relation d'un voyage en Orient," the fifth book of which contains an account of Bordier's travels to the Black Sea entrepôt of Trebizond (modern day Trabzon) in 1609. As was typical of travel accounts of this era, Bordier devotes considerable space to a careful description of the historical and religious attractions of the city. In addition, he records his encounters with the region's populations: these include "all sorts of diverse nations, both from Persia, Armenia, Georgia, Mangrelia, Cherhasia, Tartaria, Syria and from many other nations." He also described meeting "not only Georgians, Greeks and other Christian nations of the Levant, but also Muhammadans."[2] Bordier's account conveys the multicultural complexity of the early modern Mediterranean and provides a window onto the way he described and ordered the diverse world he encountered during his travels. As was the case with della Valle, Bordier's taxonomy comprised two chief categories, religion and nation.

While nation and religion were among the primary categories early modern people employed both to order their world and to define themselves, they also recognized the variable and composite character of identity. In the mid-sixteenth century, the imperial ambassador Busbecq wrote of encountering a man who was

"an Italian Greek, i.e., both in birth and manners half Greek and half Italian."
Sandys referred to "the Greeke Genoeses in Pera," whom he distinguished from
the "normal" Greeks, as well as "European Turks," and a Jesuit described a dragoman as a "Greek-Turk." Fynes Moryson described sailors as Greek "though subject to the State of Venice."³ Similarly, the English organ builder Thomas Dallam
reported meeting two men: one "was a Turke, but a Cornishe man borne," the
other, "an Inglishe man, borne in Chorlaye in Lancashier; his name Finche. He
was in religion a perfit Turk, but he was our trustie frende." A man described as a
"Florentine Turk" gave two lamps to decorate the church of San Francesco in
1622, and a French consul reported meeting a Süleyman Ağa, whom he described
as "of the French nation [*français de nation*], and a Turk of some consideration."⁴
The pilgrim Arnold von Harff wrote of finding in Cairo "two German Mame-
lukes, one born in Basel, . . . The other was born in Denmark." Busbecq reported
a friendship he struck up with an Ali Paşa, "by birth a Dalmatian, he is a thorough
gentleman, and has (what you will be surprised to hear of in a Turk) a kind and
feeling heart." Finally, an English traveler recorded his encounter in Ragusa with
"Mr. Wyllyam Robynsoun, ane Inglyshe man, a man of many words but slo in
performing, for tyme hathe so allterred the man that he ys becom a Slavonyan
in natur."⁵

    In the Ottoman context, Stéphane Yérasimos has shown that in Ottoman
documents there was significant "inter-penetration" and interchangeability in
use of ethnic and religious categories.⁶ By combining "national" and religious
categories, these early modern observers suggest both the composite, "horizon-
tal" character of identity, as well as its malleable nature, in the same way that we in
the modern age evoke the multiple layers of self through hyphenated identities—
African-American, Italian-American, Jewish-American.⁷

    The temptation in confronting the multiple elements of identity evident in
these descriptions is to try to order them, to categorize them, to create a hierarchy
or taxonomy of identity that ranks its various elements according to importance.
In the infinite variety of the past, historians are trained to try to make order where
disorder exists. In the case of identity, we must be very careful in doing this. When
attempts are made to reduce identity to its essence or even to its various constituent parts, we run the risk of making fixed and concrete what was really a fluid
and protean process rather than an apprehendable object; identity in the early
modern era was "a bundle of shifting interactions" and a step along "a continuum."⁸ Early modern identities were not defined by some essence or "primordial quality." They did not necessarily depend on political boundaries, linguistic, religious, or cultural factors though all of these could and often did come

into play. Rather, early modern identity was a process of definition and redefinition, of imagining communities, of perceiving or creating boundaries, as well as
challenging these boundaries. It was, as it is today, "contingent and relational."[9]

The simplicity and clarity of objectifying identity, of reducing it to some foundational characteristics that define the essence of being French or Venetian, Muslim or Christian, male or female, Ottoman or European, or any combination of
the above can be very seductive, however. Cemal Kafadar has described this as the
"lid model," which assumes the "more or less sealed cultural identities of peoples
(Turks, Greeks, Spaniards, Arabs) who have come into contact within the framework of a larger bipolar division of equally sealed civilizational identities (East/
West, Muslim/Christian, etc.)."[10] Studying individual and group identities as
process rather than object, as fluid rather than fixed, reveals a picture that, while
often contradictory and ambiguous, nonetheless gives us a much more historically sensitive and accurate image of the premodern, prenational world. Building
on the previous chapters' deconstruction of the Venetian nation, the next two
chapters address the question of early modern identity more directly, in the context of individuals and groups who existed within or on the periphery of the
Venetian nation in Constantinople and who both navigated and embodied the
composite and dynamic nature of identities in the early modern Mediterranean.

JEWS

When considering groups who moved between the various cultural and political poles of the Mediterranean, perhaps the most familiar case is that of the Jews.
The label Jew, of course, masks a much more complex religious and cultural
identity. Recent research has emphasized the diversity, and even antagonism, that
existed within the broad community of Jews. For example, the Ottoman city
Thessaloníki was known as the "the Jerusalem of the Balkans" because of its high
concentration of Jews, yet it was not a homogenous or a united community.
Rather, the Jews of Thessaloníki represented "a conglomeration of diverse, independent groups, often at odds with one another." Each congregation bore the
name of its provenance, spoke its own language, had its own rabbi, and generally
lived in a common section of the city. Indeed, each congregation "was like a city
unto itself, . . . Each congregation zealously guarded its identity."[11] In Venice, a
similar situation existed within the *università degli Ebrei*, a collective term used by
Christians and Jews that masked a very diverse, even divided, community of Jews,
who separated themselves into three nations—German (which included Italian-
born Jews), Levantine, and Ponentine.[12] The homogeneity of these "national,"

regional, and cultural subgroups of Jews should not be exaggerated, however. There is ample evidence of the porosity of their communal boundaries and of migration between them, and of the constantly evolving, negotiated process of communal definition and redefinition.[13]

In the early modern era, one of the most compelling Jewish communities, and also the most elusive in terms of identity, was that of the conversos, Iberian-Jewish converts to Christianity, more commonly known as Marranos.[14] Christians had a great deal of difficulty categorizing Marranos: one observer complained, "these Marranos are worse than the Jews since they are not Christians nor are they Jews." In 1550 when the Senate forbade trade with Marranos, Christian merchants on the Rialto were upset because of the difficulty in deciding "who is a Marrano and who not." The problem was "we know neither the background nor the way of life of these men, nor what they believe or what they do not."[15] To further complicate matters, in Venice "Marrano" came to indicate almost any Spaniard or Portuguese regardless of religion, and in the Ottoman Empire "Spanish" generally signified Jewish until the twentieth century.[16]

This difficulty in precisely categorizing the Marranos was not uncommon, even for other Jews, as the case of Righetto, alias Anriquez Nuñez, alias Abraham Benvenisti, reveals. An Italian, a Portuguese, and a Jewish name "concealed three different social identities, which Righetto manipulated as . . . the occasion called for." Though at one point he insisted that his essential self was Jewish, his self-constructions and reconstructions indicate a much more fluid identity.[17] One leader of the Jewish community in Venice charged Righetto, a Marrano, as being " 'a ship with two rudders,' a man willing to trim his sails to the prevailing religious and political winds . . . because he is neither Jew nor Christian." This indeterminancy seems to have been a family trait: it was said of Righetto's father, "he is neither Christian nor Jew nor Turk, and could not himself tell you what law he follows, save that of making money."[18]

This chameleon-like ambiguity—religious, to be sure, but also political and social—was not unique; the records contain many references to Jewish merchants as members of a class "which knows no frontiers."[19] One of the most famous examples is that of the man described in the chapter title of a popular history of the Venetian ghetto as "João Miches, Giovanni Miguez, Joseph Nasi, Duke of Naxos: Four Names and Many Diverse Identities for One Man."[20] A study of rabbinical responsa literature for this period reveals that religious leaders perceived the number of Jews who converted to Christianity and Islam as a significant problem. These documents also suggest motives for Jewish conversion, including as a means "to escape from a difficult situation, to spite an enemy or to attain a selfish ambition." Conversion was also a quick way to resolve marital problems: "In one instance, it was a man's desire to marry another man's wife, for by embracing the Moslem faith, he obtained the aid of its religious authorities. In another case, it was the man's eagerness to rid himself of his wife." Women who converted to free themselves of undesirable husbands were also not uncommon.[21] In Venice there are also numerous instances of Jews who were baptized as Christians; the Senate even provided housing and religious instruction to these Christian neophytes at the Casa dei Catecumeni. At times, Venice also provided male converts with positions as commercial brokers "so that [they] may have the means to sustain [themselves] and continue in the most holy Catholic faith."[22] Even the great Jewish Messianic mystic Shabbatai Sevi (1626–76), when captured and given the choice between death or conversion, chose the latter and assumed the name Aziz Mehmed Efendi and received a royal pension and an honorary position in the sultan's household. During the remainder of his life he attracted "some two hundred Jewish families" to Islam, though he and they continued to observe some Jewish traditions.[23]

As these cases suggest, both Jews and Christians looked upon the Marranos with suspicion because of their functional identity and the seeming ease with which they transgressed traditional social and cultural boundaries. As one scholar has observed, "Jews in Italy were inclined to see Portuguese Marranos as prevaricators, and were hostile to them on the grounds that in religion they were half-breeds or hermaphrodites, neither Christian fish nor Jewish fowl." One convert to Christianity similarly commented, "The way of these Portuguese is that they go to Ferrara and have themselves circumcised, and then they come to Venice and depart for the Levant where they stay for three or four years, and then they return to Venice with Levantine turbans upon their heads . . . Portuguese of this type are neither Christians nor Jews nor Turks nor Moors . . . They are hated by the other Jews because they bear nothing but the headgear of Jews."[24] Altering identity was often as simple as changing clothes: when Righetto saw important Venetian officials on the street, he put on the yellow hat all Jews were required to wear, "and when he passed them he took it off and put it under his arm and placed on his head another hat or cap which was black." Indeed, it was not uncommon for residents of Venice's ghetto to obtain exemptions permitting them to remove the yellow caps that marked them as Jews.[25]

Righetto was finally tried before the Inquisition for his overly and overtly malleable identity. In his own defense, he argued that it was legitimate to assume "a Christian identity from motives of self-preservation, as and where appropriate . . . [and that] Christianity had never been to him more than a protective skin."[26] He was convicted and imprisoned, but he soon escaped to Constantinople, where he lived openly as a Jew and was active in the Duke of Naxos's circle. Righetto's permutations were not done, however, as he eventually returned to his native Spain and reconciled with Catholicism because he "had felt himself distanced from the 'Lei de Moises'" during his Constantinople sojourn. He acknowledged having observed Jewish law and practices "but only because he did not have the grace of God, and, since being in prison in Portugal, he had practised none of the Jewish rites, which he had even begun to detest."[27] Righetto's is a fascinating case of a man whose public and private religious, social, and political selves were constantly in flux; who he really was is in many ways immaterial.

The malleability of the Marranos, and other Jews, was both beneficial and troubling to Venice and other European powers. The benefit they provided was clear, whatever religious misgivings they may have raised, as beginning in the sixteenth century the Jews became an important, perhaps even dominant, part of Venice's commercial fabric. Jews had been forbidden to participate in the Levantine trade in the Middle Ages, but by the sixteenth century the evolving commercial situation led the rulers of Venice and other Italian cities to compete for important Jewish merchants, granting them special charters and commercial privileges usually reserved for patricians and citizens. Indeed, English, Dutch, and Flemish merchants in Venice sought similar special privileges but were never granted them.[28] The combination of religious pogroms in parts of Europe and the relative religious tolerance of Islam made Ottoman lands another magnet for displaced Jews from across Europe, and very quickly they came to occupy an important position in the Levantine trade.[29]

Some scholars have argued that by 1600 the Jews were the largest player in Venice's Levantine trade, occupying perhaps even a hegemonic position, though this has been more often asserted than demonstrated.[30] Passing observations of travelers and the ferocious complaints of Venetian officials suggest that the Jews were making important inroads, but as some scholars have argued, this picture is based on anecdotal sources often inclined to exaggeration. A truly statistical picture, based on hard data, of the relative and absolute strength of the Jewish position is still lacking.[31] Still, we do have some numbers: in 1625 the V Savii estimated that Jewish business interests drew 100,000 ducats annually to Venetian coffers, and in Ragusa Jews represented 60 percent of the brokers and brought in large quantities of goods.[32] There is no question that in the early modern era Jews became an important and influential trading bloc within the Venetian and Mediterranean economies. Merchants traded through them in Constantinople to avoid certain customs and other duties, and it was widely believed that patricians profited in Venice by allowing Jews to trade under their names. During times of war, Venetian merchants regularly traded through Jewish merchants who were able to remain active.[33]

Relations between Venice and its Jewish communities were characterized by commercial and political expediency, cooperation, and indulgence, but there also could be hostility, anger, and fear. Jews feared the arbitrariness of Venice's control over them, a concern founded in several sixteenth-century expulsions. Venice was anxious about both the takeover of commerce by the Jews and their polluting influence within the Christian social fabric of the city.[34] Jews were perceived as wanting all the benefits with none of the costs of being Venetians; the baili complained repeatedly that the Jews "want all the comforts that the subjects of Your Serenity enjoy, and also to withdraw all the trade of our city to themselves, and then they do not want to pay even a minimal thing."[35] Perception of the Jews as having very malleable identities made them, and especially the Marranos, appear a greater threat than other groups. Venice was relatively tolerant of religious heterogeneity, even among Protestants, as long as it could be classified and therefore controlled.[36] Marranos, and to an extent Jews in general, could not be pinned down easily, either by their own or by Christian officials, and the assumption that they had "neither *Patria* nor Prince" contributed to their liminal status.[37]

Part of the problem for Christians in this uneasy marriage was the ambiguous and often transitory relationship of Jews to the polities in which they resided. During the Middle Ages, some Jews, the so-called white-Venetians, had traded alongside patrician merchants in Constantinople, and some had received a form of citizenship. In the early modern period, however, while many Christian immigrants obtained Venetian citizenship by residing in the city a certain amount of time and paying taxes, Jews could not become citizens no matter how long they stayed in the city or how much income they brought into its coffers.[38] In the Ottoman capital, there were many Jewish merchants who either were born or had resided in Venice for some period of time and many who had family members in Venice's ghetto. Despite their privileged commercial status in Venice, these Jews were never considered part of the official Venetian nation in Constantinople. Indeed, it was never quite clear what their relationship to the nation was, and many traded as often as Ottoman subjects as they did as Venetian. Jews never appear listed among the merchants' governing councils, and the records of the embassy are rife with complaints about the unwillingness of Jewish merchants with Venetian ties to pay their required duties. This situation became so bad in the early seventeenth century that Bailo Simone Contarini turned to the sultan to order his own customs officials to collect duties from Jews because Venetian officials were unable to do so.[39]

This does not mean that Jews were not considered in some limited ways as members of the broader Venetian nation. Occasionally, an individual was distinguished as a "Venetian Jew" in the bailo's notarial protocols.[40] Jews also periodically occupied official positions, such as consuls or dragomans in remote locales, while others possessed plum jobs among the nation's brokers.[41] Jews interacted regularly with the official and unofficial elements of the nation; they often registered transactions and other legal affairs before the nation's notaries; and in some instances they submitted to the legal judgments of the baili.[42] This should not be overstated, however, as in the end Jews generally were considered part of their own nation rather than subjects of Venice or the Ottoman Empire. This Jewish nation was perceived primarily in religious terms, though Venetians had a clear sense of the cultural and regional diversity masked by the label Jew.[43]

Venice generally maintained a comparatively favorable policy toward Jews, despite the ambiguity of their position.[44] Beginning in the sixteenth century, Jews in Venice were collectively granted charters allowing them to reside in the city, which gave them certain special privileges, though their juridical relationship to the Venetian state remained decidedly murky. There was some sense of the Jews in Constantinople existing on the periphery of the Venetian community as subjects of Venice, at least in the opinion of the nation, and perhaps also of the Jews themselves. One bailo intervened in the Porte on behalf of Gallata Valenzin, a "Jewish-Venetian subject [ebreo suddito Veneto]," who had died in Galata and whose goods had subsequently been confiscated and whose nephew and heir, "Jesurun Venetiano," had been imprisoned. In this case, both the sultan and the bailo concurred that Valenzin and his nephew while Jewish were nonetheless also Venetian subjects, and as a result the merchandise and the boy were ordered turned over to the bailo as the capitulations prescribed for all Venetian subjects who died in the Ottoman Empire.[45] Salomon Ashkenazi, who played a key role during the War of the Holy League, was described as a "subject of Your Serenity [suddito di Vostra Serenità]." Ashkenazi was exceptional, though, as he had been born in Udine and studied in Padua before going to Constantinople, and his role in the crisis of the early 1570s earned him special recognition and privileges from the Senate.[46] In contrast to the seemingly exceptional loyalty of Ashkenazi, Gianfrancesco Morosini reported that the Levantine Jews in Venice were disloyal and communicated sensitive information to Jews in Constantinople; this attitude was shared by many other patricians.[47] Most Jews, and especially Marranos, were immigrants and of little individual importance to Venice. Rather, their significance was collective in nature. And collectively, Jews were guests in the city, granted certain favorable rights but maintained at a distance and only on the good will of the patrician rulers of Venice, who could and did revoke these rights.

The ambiguity of the Jewish position is evident in the case of David Passi, a Marrano. Passi was a commercial agent in Ragusa; his wife lived in Ferrara, his father in Thessaloníki; his uncle was a doctor in Constantinople. Situated in the interstices of the major Mediterranean powers of the day, where did his loyalties lie? He was a double agent for Spain and Venice in the 1570s and provided information to the sultans from his network of agents in all major European courts. Despite this political ambiguity, in 1584 he wrote the Senate from Constantinople, where he was an intimate in the divan, asking for its intervention in a matter involving another Marrano. Passi invoked his Venetian identity, pointing to his eighteen years residence in the ghetto, his service to Venice, and his wife and children, "who are also subjects of that most excellent Republic and were born under its wings."[48]

Passi was not exceptional; it was not uncommon for Jews to move between Venice and Constantinople and other regions, claiming subject status in one or the other and using it to obtain immunity from local prosecution and persecution.[49] In 1600 in reaction to the economic and political troubles plaguing Constantinople, and the targeting of their community for reprisals, many Jews considered migrating, or re-migrating, to Venice. There was a constant fear of retaliation for the role of Joseph Nasi in the previous war, but these Jews also recognized their importance to both Venice and the Ottoman Empire. One family, the Abudenti, already had representatives in the lagoon and negotiated the terms of their transfer. They would consider migrating only if granted several guarantees: a house in the ghetto with the rent paid, freedom from the Inquisition, a safe-conduct for ten years, and three years time to get out of Venice should the Jews be expelled. The Senate acceded to these demands, justifying its policies toward families such as the Abudenti not in religious terms but as political expedients to prevent the strengthening of an enemy.[50] In another instance, a Marrano merchant who had left Portugal for Venice moved to Constantinople where he became a *haracgüzar*. Several years later, he and his family decided to return to Venice, and despite what might have been perceived as their betrayal, the bailo recommended to the Senate that they be allowed to return.[51]

Other examples also suggest the ambiguity of the Jews' status: when Jewish merchants in Pesaro, subject to the Papacy, encountered problems with Maltese corsairs, they wrote to the Duke of Naxos in Constantinople, asking for the assistance of the Ottoman fleet. When Esperanza, the famed Jewish intimate (or *kira*)

of the queen mother Safiye, heard about problems the Jews in Venice were encountering, she chastised them for not allowing her to intervene: "Inform me and
I will not fail to help you with all my spirit and diligence, as I must and as I am
able."[52] Even after the main branch of the Abudenti family relocated to Venice,
Ottoman officials dealt closely with a remaining brother in Constantinople and
regularly intervened with Venetian authorities on the family's behalf.[53] The question remained, however, whether Jews were Venetians, Ottomans, or some privileged, interstitial group. The various "nations" that composed the Jewish università epitomized in many ways the multivalence of identity in the Mediterranean
world: they moved easily between religious, political, and economic poles and
were often a confusing anomaly within the body politic wherever they resided.

RENEGADES

Jews were not the only group alleged to know no frontiers. In recent years
much has been written about the chrétiens d'Allah, the many men and women who
migrated from Christianity to Islam, and in so doing violated what was perhaps
the most elemental boundary of early modern societies.[54] In Christendom these
individuals were termed renegades; in Islamic lands they were welcomed as
converts.[55] The period from 1500 to 1650 represents the golden age of the renegade; their numbers were so great that the flow from Christianity to Islam has
been characterized as a "hemorrhage of men" and a "religious nomadism."[56]

It is impossible to establish the renegades' actual numbers, but travelers and
other observers offer at least an impressionistic sense. Arnold von Harff in 1496
reported fifteen thousand renegades in the service of the Egyptian sultans.[57]
Writing a century later, Diego de Häedo estimated that renegades constituted
almost half the population of Algiers, approximately six thousand households, or
sixty thousand people. These figures are clearly exaggerated, however, as the city's
total population was probably no more than seventy-five thousand.[58] Fifty years
later the French Trinitarian Father Dan counted eight thousand men and twelve
hundred women renegades in Algiers, and three to four thousand men and six to
seven hundred women in Tunis.[59] Whatever their numbers in individual cities,
scholars generally agree that in the sixteenth-century Mediterranean, renegades
numbered into the hundreds of thousands.[60]

Though renegades fled from all over Europe, the majority came from areas
bordering the Mediterranean. In southern Italy, especially Calabria, the "consistent flight of men toward the Ottoman Empire," had the "character of a social
revolt." Observers were struck by the number of renegades, and the ease with

which seemingly impassable religious frontiers were regularly breached. Della Valle noted chidingly that "you could not believe . . . the ease that there is in many people in renouncing the faith."[61] If religion was one of the most important constituent parts of identity in the premodern world, then the presence of so many who traversed boundaries of belief suggests the malleability of even this aspect of identity.

The motivations behind conversion were myriad, but the most important are suggested in Blount's observation: "Many who professe themselves Christians scarce know what they mean by being so; finally, perceiving themselves poore, wretched, taxed, disgraced, deprived of their children and subject to the intolerance of every Rascall, they begin to consider and prefer the present World, before the other which they so little understand."[62] Poverty, ignorance, oppression, and the hope of better socioeconomic conditions all were powerful motivations for religious nomadism. Many renegades resulted from the constant Mediterranean corsair activity: slaves, in an attempt to better their desperate condition, often felt compelled to convert. Still others converted to escape complications in the Christian world, to start a new life, or simply in search of adventure. Cynical Christians believed that men converted because Islamic laws permitted multiple wives, and in French literature the most frequent cause of apostasy was erotic, a prisoner caught in flagrante delicto in the arms of a Muslim wife, widow, or daughter. The famous renegade *kapudanpaşa* Çigalazade Sinan Paşa (also Cicala, Cağalazade) was motivated to renounce Christianity in return for the release of his father, who along with his son had been captured by corsairs.[63] A Mediterranean saying of the time suggests still another motivation: "out of spite, I will become a Turk."[64] Antonio Fabris summarizes well the varied motivations of conversion: "We are dealing with artisans driven by a yearning for income, with Europeans, slaves of Muslims, desirous of a better life, with men greedy for adventure or in search of a power precluded them in the West."[65] It is not surprising that periods of increased conversion usually coincided with crises in European society, economic depression, and religious and/or political persecution.[66]

As these passages suggest, many renegades were inspired by reports, which circulated widely, that Islamic society knew no "social discrimination or privileges" and that opportunity existed for all, regardless of background.[67] Contemporaries noted the attractiveness of this world without perceived social barriers: an ecclesiastic noted that men "have themselves circumcised hoping to achieve a more excellent rank." Blount echoed this sentiment: "Generally I found them Atheists, who left our cause for the Turkish as [being] . . . fuller of preferment."[68] Luther believed that one explanation for Ottoman military success was the "social injustice" of the time, evidenced during the peasant revolts by the flight to Islam of common folk, who looked on the Ottomans "as possible deliverers from oppression."[69] This popular perception was not unfounded: in early modern Muslim societies, birth meant less than "merit, audacity, *savoir-faire* . . . Many men, condemned by the status of their birth in Christianity to a subordinate condition, saw themselves offered marvelous opportunities for social promotion."[70] Examples of men of low station in Christendom rising to the summits of the Ottoman state were well known throughout Europe. Indeed, the baili in Constantinople had to grapple regularly with men, women, and sometimes families who came to the city seeking entry into the divan, hoping to be awarded some office in return for their conversion and the information they claimed to possess.

Just as rumors of a more open society intrigued Europe, so too did the belief that renegades could make their fortunes. For example, a Jew in Venice told a friend of the "astounding news of the prosperity swiftly attained by the convert in the lands of the Ottoman Empire."[71] Renegades were often seen as the benefactors of their native lands, the local man (or woman) made good who might share his (or her) newfound wealth at least in part with family and *paesani*. Not infrequently renegades maintained close economic ties with their families, and Scaraffia speaks of "Euro-Barbaresque family businesses that saw members of the same family, in part renegades in part Christians, involved in the same business." One such figure was the Genoese renegade Giaffer, *kadı* in Tunis, who was at the center of a trade and slave-exchange network between a cousin in Marseilles and a brother in Genoa.[72]

A brief survey of the cases of several renegades suggests the variety of potential motivations to convert. Niccolò Algarotti, a Venetian merchant in Cairo, accrued a large debt spending lavishly and gambling with Muslims, and became a "Turk" to achieve a change of venue for his case to an Ottoman court, hoping to receive a favorable judgment from the *kadı*. Another merchant converted to avoid paying debts and returning goods that he owed to several important merchants in Venice. These conversions for commercial motivations were common enough to be dramatized in Robert Wilson's play *Three Ladies of London* (1581–84).[73] The regularity of such conversions led the baili to obtain a firman stating that if Venetian agents turned to Islam, their goods were to be returned to their principals.[74] Ladislaw Mörten, the majordomo of the Holy Roman ambassador in Constantinople, committed "a capital crime" and was confined to the embassy. He shouted out the window that he wanted to become a "Turk" and was taken to the divan, where he was rewarded with a lucrative office. Another man in the imperial entourage converted in response to the offer of a horse and an office worth twenty *akçe* a day. Giovanni Moro reported meeting two men being sought by the pope, who "not knowing how to save themselves . . . fled to Turkey, and to avoid being made slaves there, became Turks."[75]

Renegades were not limited to the lower classes: Girolamo Fasaneo was a Dalmatian lawyer banished with a price on his head as a result of a controversy with a local Venetian official. In requesting rescission of the banishment, he warned that he would "be constrained to become a Turk," which he ultimately did, and he immediately turned to the Ottoman courts "to obtain the justice that he felt had been denied him by Christians."[76] It was not uncommon for educated Christians, or those possessing specialized knowledge, to convert in hopes of using their skills to advance and prosper, such as the German military engineer trained in artillery and fortress design who came to Constantinople to convert at the invitation of several Jews. Geoffrey Parker has found many instances of European renegades who served Muslim masters in Kongo, Calicut, and Malabar. Indeed, he argues that in the Ottoman Empire the founding and management of artillery "became the exclusive preserve of small cadres of foreign specialists, most of them renegades and adventurers."[77]

Individual conversions were the norm, but occasionally larger groups converted en masse. One example is the French mercenary contingent defending the Habsburg frontier garrison at Papa in Hungary, which defected collectively in 1600, in part because their pay was months in arrears. Military defections were common: Bennassar has found records of many soldiers who abandoned their posts in Spain's Algerian citadels of Oran and Mers el-Kébir for Islam. The reasons are clear: "the impossibility of honoring their debts, bad luck gambling, a quarrel with a comrade, the threat of a sanction, the ragging of a superior," as well as hunger and pay sometimes several years in arrears. A Seville court found that in a twelve-year span, some five hundred soldiers had abandoned the forts due to their "extreme penuriousness." Many of them became Ottoman mercenaries, and some of their leaders even were awarded important positions with the sultan's forces. Others fled their posts believing that they had a better chance to return home through being freed by the priests in the region who redeemed slaves, or that they could earn enough as Ottoman soldiers to return to Spain and confess before the Inquisition, rather than serving their sentences in Spain's frontier fortresses.[78] In 1579–80 five Maronite villages in Syria converted en masse, and as did two groups of a thousand and four hundred inhabitants of Cosenza in Calabria, "who were not able to tolerate the government of the Spanish in those parts." And in perhaps the most curious mass conversion, at Chios some three hundred Christians publicly converted to Islam, with the approval of their Jesuit pastors, though in secret they continued to live as Christians.[79]

While the river of renegades generally flowed from Christianity to Islam, movement in the other direction was not unheard of.[80] Simone Contarini, for example, reported meeting a man in Corfu "who though he once was a Turk, he became however a Christian, and lives here with his wife and children."[81] Economically motivated conversions were not limited to Christians: there were frequent instances of Muslim merchants in Venice becoming Christians and decamping with the goods of their principals, often important Ottoman officials, prompting requests from Constantinople for official Venetian intervention.[82] A Muslim in the household of the grand vizier stole goods valued at almost a million *akçe*, sold them in Venice at a public auction, and renounced his faith, which provoked a request for direct intervention by the doge; in another instance, an Ottoman official in Venice loaned funds to a fellow Muslim there who was down on his luck; the man absconded and went to the Duke of Florence "to become a Christian." Early in the sixteenth century, Piero Bragadin reported on seventy janissaries "with wives and children" who fled to Candia and whom Venetian authorities agreed to assist as they had done previously in similar cases.[83] Political circumstances motivated some Muslim apostasies: the Ottoman historian Naima wrote of a governor of Syria who after protracted hostilities with a grand vizier, "to save his own life became a French proselyte, . . . promising he would assist a French army in acquiring a conquest in the environs of Jerusalem."[84] Muslim women also occasionally converted, such as the young bride of an Ottoman *kadı* who fled with her mother and two sisters to Venetian lands and converted to Christianity, and the three Muslim converts who hid in a Greek nunnery.[85]

Violations of religious boundaries in the early modern era were not limited to Islam and Christianity. The most notable example after 1517, of course, is the many millions of converts to the various Protestant sects. Donia and Fine have shown that after the Ottoman conquest of the Balkans, there were many Roman Catholic conversions to Islam but also to Orthodoxy because of its favored status in the empire. Religious change was multidirectional; Islam acquired most converts, but Orthodoxy, too, won many.[86] Venetian observers reported several instances of Persian, Shiite Muslims becoming "Turks": Gianfrancesco Morosini recounted the case of a Persian ambassador who "renouncing the faith of the Persians, declared himself a Turk," and Paolo Contarini described a similar occurrence. These "conversions" were really political defections, and the fact that Christian observers interpreted these occurrences in a religious light suggests a fundamental misunderstanding regarding the universal nature of Islam, even among its various sects.[87] Of course, there are many cases of Jews converting to Islam and Christianity. Christians also occasionally converted to Judaism: Pullan cites the case of a Venetian patrician who argued with a Jewish man that Jews converted to Christianity but never the reverse. The man countered by pointing out that a Leandro Tisanio, son of a local shoemaker, was living in Thessaloniki as a Jew. He preferred Judaism's religious unity to the myriad divisions among Christians, as well as for certain theological reasons. Also striking is the case of Ni'matallah, the Syrian Jacobite patriarch, who was so troubled by the problems of his church that he converted first to Islam but finding "no peace as a Muslim," fled to Rome and was admitted into the papal fold.[88]

Although practical economic, social and political catalysts for conversion were common, it would be wrong to overlook the element of sincere belief and of a more transcendent religious conversion.[89] Religion and belief in the sixteenth century had meaning and the power to mobilize significant passion and commitment. Islam was attractive to some because of its promise of "eternal health to all believers." As Blount observed from his many encounters with them, renegades often "left our cause for the Turkish as the more thriving in the Word."[90] A certain Pere Bedellia, for example, was initially captured as a boy and became a "Moor to the core." He was a janissary for thirteen years, then a corsair; when he was captured by Christians, instead of revealing his identity, for three and a half years "he passed himself off as a 'Turk by birth'" chained in a Christian galley, hoping to be ransomed and to return to Algiers.[91] Leonardo Donà described a renegade Venetian noble of the Querini family who had studied Muslim law, went on the hajj to Mecca, and in general appeared greatly impressed by Islam's doctrines: "He says that the life of Venetian gentlemen is more secure than his, but that here at least he will save his soul." He tried to persuade his mother "to embrace that light of salvation that he said God had given to him, by abandoning that Religion to which she had attempted to persuade him to return."[92]

While some people converted out of sincere religious conviction, this was probably not the predominant motivation. Indeed, acceptance of Islam, rather than conversion, is probably a more accurate description of the nature of religious refashioning. As Donia and Fine have shown in the case of Bosnia, "Few Bosnians in accepting Islam underwent any deep changes in patterns of thought and life . . . retaining most of their domestic customs and many Christian practices."[93] In the eighteenth century a merchant from Marseilles observed much the same of two renegades, one of whom continued to drink wine and eat pork after his conversion and the other who when sick asked a monk to say masses for him.[94]

That these conversions in many cases were in name only is evidenced by the many renegades who returned to Christianity in their twilight years, in some instances to flee problems encountered in their Muslim lives, in others simply to die in the bosom of the holy mother church.

In case after case that appeared before the Inquisition, renegades would claim that their conversion had been solely external, more functional than spiritual, and that in their hearts they had always remained Christian. The assumption of this internal-Christian / external-Muslim dichotomy is at the core of an Inquisition manual of 1625, which suggested a leading dialogue for use in interrogating renegades: "At the persuasion of the Turks, and for fear of being mistreated by them, you had externally renounced the Holy Christian Faith, and said expressly that you wanted to be a Turk, lifting the finger . . . and freely allowing yourself to be circumcised, but retaining from thence onward the Holy Christian Faith in your heart."[95] Instances of renegades who qualified their conversions as "incomplete" in this fashion abound: for example, one slave encouraged another to convert "because God [knows] the secret of our hearts." In another case, a Greek woman who was forced to convert by her Muslim husband reassured friends, "although I am supposed to be a Mahometan, yet I remain a Christian in heart, as I was before, and perform my customary devotions."[96] A man whose whole family had converted explained to the Pisan Inquisition in 1627 that "in our house we lived as good Christians and I did my orations as I used to do here, but outside it was necessary to live as Turks."[97]

In a great majority of the cases that appeared before tribunals of the Inquisition throughout Mediterranean Europe, the men and women were welcomed back into the fold with little or no punishment, their trials being little more than a "bureaucratic practice," their freedom "a sort of prize for the renegades who had fled from the hands of the Turks, or those captured at a young age."[98] In line with this general attitude toward penitent renegades, Venice maintained a liberal policy toward its subjects who returned to Christianity: it did not seek vengeance against those who wanted to return, and even sought to incite them with gifts and promises of lucrative jobs as interpreters and brokers.[99]

Although the Inquisition did not censor renegades too severely, both Muslims and Christians often looked upon them with disdain and suspicion. Sherley described them thus: "The renegadoes are for the most parte roagues, & the skumme of people, whyche beinge villanes and atheists, vnable to liue in Christendomme, are fledde to the Turke for succoure & releyffe." An ecclesiastical observer considered them "more villainous, pillagers, insolent, cruel, arrogant, proud, boasters and ignorant" than the average "Turk."[100] Venetian observers often distinguished between "Turks" born and converted and divided the latter category between forced and voluntary converts. Of these voluntary renegades, Simone Contarini said, "there are no worse people found, not even among Turks, let alone the world, or even in hell."[101] From the Muslim side, Mustafa Ali referred to converted Slavs as half-Turks and "Islamicized rogues," and the Bey of Tunis remarked of renegades, "a pig still remains a pig, even if they do cut off its tail."[102] Converts from Islam to Christianity were also viewed with suspicion: Teodolo Dandolo, a Persian converted by the patrician Venetian consul in Aleppo, immigrated to Venice and held several lucrative offices. Concerns remained, however, regarding the sincerity of his conversion and his loyalty: "since he was born a Turk, even though he has become a Christian, he could always have some greater inclination toward his nation, not being a [Venetian] subject."[103] Just as with the Jews, renegades were interstitial individuals whose loyalties were never entirely clear or beyond reproach.

While some renegades eventually returned to Christianity, the vast majority probably did not. The growing historiography of the renegades has almost entirely ignored this group, in part, no doubt, because these individuals do not often appear in the Inquisition records that have been the base of all studies of renegades. Fortunately, the Venetian documentary sources help illuminate this elusive group. One particularly revealing example is Gazanfer Ağa.[104] For many years, Gazanfer Ağa's origins were something of a mystery: while Hammer and many other historians described him as being of Hungarian origins, it is clear from Venetian records that he was born in the Venetian lagoon, perhaps in Chioggia, sometime around 1550.[105] He claimed descent from noble parents, though there was some doubt of this among the patriciate, who believed he might have come from a natural branch of the Michiel clan, the Ca' Zorzi, or perhaps even common stock. He was captured as a boy—with his mother, a brother, and two sisters—in 1559 while traveling from Budua, a Venetian possession in the eastern Adriatic where his father held a governmental office.[106] His mother and sisters eventually obtained their freedom, but Gazanfer and his brother, Ca'fer, were enslaved. Both were sent initially to Hungary and became favorites of the future sultan Selim II (probably this is the source of Hammer's mistaken identification), who convinced both boys to undergo the knife and become eunuchs so that they might serve in the imperial harem. Ca'fer died in the operation, but Gazanfer survived and on Selim's ascension to the throne in 1566, he accompanied the new ruler to Constantinople.[107]

Gazanfer Ağa, who had "a lively and penetrating spirit, [which] he developed through study," advanced rapidly in this setting and by 1580 had risen to the heights of the Ottoman state. He held simultaneously the two most important offices within the inner service of the Harem—*kapıağası* (chief of the gate and of the white eunuch gatekeepers) and *odabaşi* (chief of the Privy Chamber)—and for a span of more than thirty years he was "one of the most influential persons in the government, . . . a tenure longer than that of any grand vizier."[108] The *kapıağası*'s office was located at the Gate of Felicity, which led from the outer to the inner palace. The holder of this office was "the sole mediator between the Sultan and the world outside the Palace." Any person or communication into or out of the palace was transmitted through the *kapıağası*.[109] As one bailo observed, "There is ordinarily no one who can give or have given memorials or *Arz* to the King that it does not pass through his hands, and he is the one who has the ear of the King for his every pleasure and who governs the family within the Seraglio."[110] Gazanfer demonstrated remarkable staying power in a period of great challenge for the Ottoman Empire and its rulers: he served and advised three sultans over more than thirty years before his execution in 1603. At his death, Francesco Contarini reported that the renegade had tried numerous times to leave the seraglio, but Mehmed III had insisted he stay "because of the singular affection that he bore for him, keeping him always near by." Whenever important matters appeared before the sultan, Contarini continued, he always asked his *kapıağası* "what he wanted him to write, and whatever he recommended, without any modification, was written."[111]

At the height of his influence, Gazanfer was part of "an important network of influence in the bosom of the leadership elite" in the Porte.[112] This included a number of fellow Venetians, as well as the Italian renegade, Çigalazade Sinan Paşa. Gazanfer was one of the champions of Çigalazade's attempts, temporarily successful, to obtain the grand vizierate and was influential in the successful careers of numerous other important Ottoman officials of the later sixteenth century.[113] He was a patron of literature, and many appreciable works were dedicated to him; among those who benefited from his largesse was the historian Mustafa Ali.[114] So far-reaching was his influence that he was considered among the handful of men and women widely believed to dominate the sultans during the period of the so-called sultanate of the women.[115]

Gazanfer's demise came much more quickly than had his ascension. In the troubles that plagued the empire at the turn of the century, the military came to exercise increasing influence over their sovereigns and, according to the historian Naima, "the *sipahi* legion requested his majesty, the emperor, to call a divan for the purpose of taking into consideration the state of the empire, everywhere torn and afflicted with rebellion and insubordination." Naima attributed Gazanfer's fall to his reputation as the power behind the throne, which made him an easy target as one of the chief figures responsible for the empire's problems.[116] Gazanfer was also reported to be highly favored of the sultans but "much envied of this people." The sultan tried to protect his favorite: as an English diplomat reported, the ruler turned over to his soldiers "all, except one, the Capiaga, his cheffe chamberlen, who he desyred might be spared and presented him; for which he wold not only give them a liberalitye but encrease of their pay. Towards whom they [the rebellious troops] seing his fervent love, refused, sayeng they wold have his headd only, and all the rest their lives should be spared." In the end, to save himself the sultan was forced to sacrifice the Venetian renegade, though he wept fiercely "for having seen murdered before his very eyes the dearest person that he had in the world without being able to find some remedy."[117]

The story of Gazanfer Ağa is fascinating on a human level, but it also reveals the complex nature of identity in the early modern era. While he had converted to Islam at a young age, had lived in Constantinople for much of his adult life, was a patron of Ottoman letters, and was intimately involved in the government of the empire, still Gazanfer Ağa continued to consider and describe himself as Venetian: he told Girolamo Cappello "I am still Venetian because I have an interest in that blood." A close Ottoman ally of Gazanfer's reported him saying "he remembers very well his *patria*, and as a true patriot [*patriota*] he would not fail to favor it." Marco Venier reported similarly that the *kapıağası* "protested that he was a good Venetian, lover and partisan of the *patria*."[118] Despite his important offices and his great influence in the Porte, members of the Ottoman ruling class also considered Gazanfer a Venetian and chastised him for not using this status in his favor: the sultana was reported to have told him "these Venetians, your relatives, hold you in no account, and you are always ready to favor them." The bailo Gianfrancesco Morosini acknowledged the complexity of the *kapıağası*'s identity: he described Gazanfer as a Venetian, but also "a true Turk."[119]

In his early years in the capital, Gazanfer avoided openly treating with and favoring the Venetians because he did not want to compromise his potentially unstable position as a renegade in the Ottoman court, a concern very common among new converts. As Lorenzo Bernardo reported, "This man has the ear of the Grand Signor when he wants it, but, either from timidity or for prudence he does not want to involve himself in negotiations, and especially those of Christians, and principally of Your Signoria, so as not to enter into suspicion with the Grand Signor." In another report Bernardo explained further that early on Gazanfer avoided helping Venice "to escape the perils that overshadow whoever intervenes in such matters . . . so as not to give suspicion to anyone as a Venetian."[120] Matteo Zane believed that something of an anti-Christian atmosphere reigned in Constantinople during this period, in which "everyone wants to act the good Muslim, opposing the Christians, and showing themselves their enemies without any reason."[121] To avoid suspicion, Gazanfer required the baili to visit him clandestinely. Agostino Nani described one such visit: "I went to visit him privately as usual with just one dragoman, and a few servants, knowing that he did not like it to be known publicly in the Seraglio and in the Porte that the bailo of Venice had entered to treat with him, who is a Venetian, therefore he industriously had Ömer Ağa waiting for me to let me in as soon as I had arrived, so that I would not tarry in the view of the people."[122]

If in earlier times Gazanfer was very reticent in treating with and assisting his *patria*, in his later years when he had solidified his power, he became much less concerned with appearances. Clearly inserted and accepted in his adopted milieu as Muslim, Ottoman, and high official, he also willingly accentuated his Venetian identity to gain favors and benefits for family members still in Venice, even to the point of personally visiting the baili in their embassy.[123] In 1584 the Venetian Senate granted a petition from Gazanfer Ağa, who invoked his many "relatives and relations by blood" still in Venice and requested that his mother, Franceschina Michiel, be given the proceeds of a governmental office, worth ten ducats monthly. In 1590 the Senate forgave a 350 ducat debt that Gazanfer's sister owed as a sign of goodwill to him. In the same year, he tried to obtain a lucrative office for his brother-in-law in Venice and received the support of the bailo, Girolamo Lippomano.[124] Gazanfer also arranged favorable marriages with Ottoman officials and lucrative offices for other relations whom he convinced to join him in Constantinople.[125] His assistance was not limited to family: in a 1594 document he requested that a Jew, Jacob Parenzo, and his heirs be allowed to make bread and sell it in the Ghetto, with no tax.[126]

In return for Venice's assistance in his official and personal activities, Gazanfer increasingly favored his native city's policies in the Porte. As Francesco Contarini wrote, "He promised me as a Venetian to protect the negotiations of Your Serenity, and to provide every favor possible to me."[127] When the bailo was having difficulty concluding a prisoner exchange with the *kapudanpaşa*, Gazanfer "showed himself very ready" in facilitating the negotiation, resulting in the release of twenty-five individuals. Through the efforts of the *kapıağası*, his fellow renegade Çigalazade, who had historically been quite opposed to Venice, softened his position somewhat, aided by bribes of "sweet muscat, which he drinks with great reserve and very secretly."[128] In another incident, Gianfrancesco Morosini tried to get Gazanfer's assistance in having the *Sancak* of Lecca removed, even going so far as to enlist the assistance of the Ottoman's mother who was visiting her son. She remonstrated with him and counseled him "to do in the future that which one who was born a Venetian gentleman ought to do in the service of his *patria,* in addition to that which he must do as an obligation which every child is held to do to please his mother." Gazanfer's response is revealing: he reported he had many enemies "watching his every action, and who said he was a *Giaur,* . . . and said that for the love of [his mother] he favored Christians more than he should have, which when it would reach the ears of the Grand Signor could cause his ruin, and as a result it was necessary to proceed with reservation." Still, he agreed to intervene as he was safely able in the matter.[129]

The story of Gazanfer Ağa vividly exemplifies the multiple, seemingly contradictory poles of identity that might exist within an individual: while it presented certain potential political complications, Gazanfer's sense of self permitted Ottoman and Venetian to coexist. Clearly he was an Ottoman by choice and adoption, and he was intimately inserted into the highest echelons of the Ottoman leadership; nonetheless, he also retained a clear sense of himself as a Venetian, and felt an enduring loyalty to and connection with his extended family. The composite nature of Gazanfer's sense of his own identity permitted him to benefit his Ottoman master, Venice, himself, and his family. It was not necessary, indeed perhaps not even possible, for him to choose one or the other; as contradictory as it may seem to us, to himself and his contemporaries he was an Ottoman-Venetian.

Gazanfer Ağa's case while striking, is not exceptional. Another Venetian renegade who rose to the summits of the Ottoman hierarchy was Hasan Ağa (eventually Hasan Paşa). Despite some disagreement among the various accounts, we have a fairly detailed picture of Hasan's life.[130] Hasan, whose Christian name was Andretta, was born into a poor Venetian citizen family, the Celesti. At age sixteen, he was sent to sea "to earn his living." In 1563 the famed corsair Draghut snatched him from a galley on which he served as scribe and gave him to another corsair, 'Ulūg 'Alī (called Occhiali in Italy). Andretta converted to Islam and came to be highly favored by his owner, who was said to have stated of the lad "that he did not know any[one] more able in the service of the Grand Signor than Hasan Paşa." Under the patronage of 'Ulūg 'Alī Paşa, Hasan became a highly effective corsair and rose in reputation and official rank in North Africa, eventually becoming *paşa* of Algiers in 1577, and again in 1582.[131]

In this influential position Hasan achieved great power and wealth. He was known for his ambition and his ruthless effectiveness as a tax collector. He successfully claimed one-fifth of the booty of the corsairs under his command, rather than the traditional one-seventh. He also compelled merchants to sell food to his agents at a discount and generally collected more and higher taxes from all levels of Algerian society. Hasan augmented his revenues through active involvement in the gold and silver trade. So fabled did his wealth become, in fact, that he had to endure at least one, and perhaps two, confiscations of it by the sultan. He was also known as a harsh master, especially to his Christian slaves, one of whom, for a time, was the young Cervantes, who wrote of "a Venetian runagate, who being a ship-boy in a certain vessel, was taken by Uchiali, who loved him so tenderly as he was one of the dearest youths he had, and he became after the most cruel runagate that ever lived. He was called Azanaga [Hasan Ağa], and came to be very rich, and King of Algiers."[132] Hasan eventually became *kapudanpaşa* in 1588, in part through a large gift of slaves and cash to the sultan, a position he held for three years before dying, perhaps poisoned, as rumor held. He was the last of the corsair captains in the tradition of Barbarossa to hold this important office.[133]

As was the case with Gazanfer, Hasan also retained close ties to the Venetian community in Constantinople and with his *patria* itself. Whereas Gazanfer seems to have forgotten much of his native tongue, Hasan had a good remembrance of it: when Lorenzo Bernardo went to visit him in 1591, he "spoke for a piece in Turkish for reputation, in which language it seems he is not very prepared, and then spoke in Frank very comfortably, interspersing many Spanish words."[134] He also often registered legal transactions in the Venetian chancellery, and from 1575 retained the services of Cristoforo Bertolotti, a Venetian merchant in Constantinople.[135] Like Gazanfer, Hasan emphasized his native roots in describing himself, saying "in the end he was born Venetian, [and] he could not forget his *patria*."[136] As evidence of his goodwill, on several occasions he did not harm Venetian ships even though he would routinely sack those belonging to other European states. He reported, for instance, encountering a Venetian ship transporting grain to Zante from which he did not claim his customary gift; it was reported that he even offered refreshments to the crew and passengers. Hasan also utilized the bailo to intervene in his business affairs, asking him to have certain goods sequestered in Venice and turned over from one agent to another.[137]

Hasan left a sister, Camilla, in Venice, and in 1590, after becoming *kapudanpaşa*, he sent at least two letters to the doge, written in his own hand, seeking favorable treatment for her and her husband, "Marcantonio Vedova, Christian, relative of our love."[138] In this correspondence he acknowledged the favor Venice had shown his family and requested that Vedova be made one of the Senate's secretaries, one of the most prestigious offices in the Venetian bureaucracy. He admitted that this request was unusual and might even be against Venetian laws, but he also emphasized that he had worked ceaselessly on Venice's behalf and would continue to do so. While it appears that Vedova (who traveled to Constantinople to try and obtain a gift of a thousand ducats from his brother-in-law) never was awarded his office, Hasan did arrange for Camilla to receive the proceeds of a rich office, four hundred ducats annually, and he intervened in another instance involving the confiscation of a bakery that was part of his sister's dowry.[139] In return for these services, Hasan favored Venetian policies as he was able, especially in matters relating to the troublesome Uskoks.[140]

Like Gazanfer Ağa, Hasan was a man of two worlds. On the one hand, he was a feared and famed corsair and commander of Ottoman naval forces. To a certain extent he seems to have genuinely embraced his adopted religion, suggesting that his transformation went beyond the superficial level one often encounters in forced conversions. When a famine struck Algiers in 1579 and tensions in the city mounted, Hasan assembled the population and publicly burned three Christian images. In this way "the city restated its profoundly Islamic identity in this symbolic recreation of Muhammed's destruction of the idols in Mecca."[141] On the other hand, he acknowledged his Venetian roots and considered and described himself as a Venetian, despite his years away from the city, his renunciation of Christianity, and his very real awareness of the social limitations of his position in Venice.[142] His protean sense of identity seems to have fused Venetian, Ottoman, Muslim, and familial elements, which he apparently inhabited reasonably comfortably, and between which he moved as was necessary and appropriate.

The cases of Gazanfer Ağa and Hasan Paşa provide clear evidence that ties and identities associated with the places and cultures of their births remained important among Ottoman elites. As influential Venetian-Ottomans, both were at the center of a ring of men of shared regional, religious, political, and cultural filiation.[143] Around Gazanfer especially there existed a coterie of men (and several women) who had renounced their religion, but not, it appears, their cultural and political identities as Venetians and Venetian subjects. These included Ömer Ağa, a eunuch in the seraglio from Zara who was a close ally and protégé of Gazanfer, and a Venetian patrician of the Querini clan, Mehmed, captured as a youth, "who with his virtue and ability and with the favor of the *kapıağası* advances each day in rank, and he aspires soon to be *defterdar*."[144] Gazanfer's patronage even extended to Venetians who had not renounced their faith. Pasqualino Leoni and Antonio di Cavalli, two important merchants whom Gazanfer "loved greatly," had access to his private seraglio and were involved in trade with him; their status with the Venetian renegade directly benefited their commerce and position in Constantinople.[145] Other Ottoman officials often privileged Venetians to curry Gazanfer's favor. In one instance an Ottoman gave a Venetian renegade a high position in his household to demonstrate his "favor [for] that nation." He did this to win over Gazanfer, whom he had alienated by opposing Hasan Paşa for the admiralty, which had exposed him politically because Hasan "has always conserved with solicitude and with much courtesy the friendship of the *kapıağası* . . . [Who] has been able to favor him greatly, and he has always done it because [he is] of the same *patria* as the Captain."[146]

In the past the associations and affinity based on shared backgrounds, such as Gazanfer and Hasan exhibited, were believed not to have existed. The very idea of the *devşirme* was "to provide the sultan and the central government with an efficient, well-trained and loyal professional army . . . without root and without ties." This practice, according to one scholar, successfully "mold[ed] aliens of widely divergent race and creed to the Turkish type, [in a] process of assimilation," which resulted in a corps of soldiers and bureaucrats highly loyal to the sultans.[147] This view in which the *devşirme* effaced all memory of the past was also common among contemporaries: Nicolay, for example, wrote that the boys of the *devşirme* never acknowledged their friends or families and allowed their poor relatives to be reduced to begging.[148] Metin I. Kunt, however, has shown that ethnic-regional affinities endured and formed an important network and buttress for those making careers within the Ottoman bureaucracy. Indeed, he argues that one "factor which seems to have played a significant part in shaping the career of an individual slave was his ethnic and/or regional origin and his relations with others of the same background in the Ottoman world," or *cins* solidarity as Kunt calls it. In the case of the *devşirme*, "theoretically, a slave was brought into the system at an early age so that his identity as a Muslim Ottoman could be established irreversibly." In practice, however, the children of the *devşirme* were recruited between fourteen to eighteen years of age. Thus, "they remembered their birthplace and exhibited a special tie to it."[149]

Suraiya Faroqhi likewise has discussed the importance of patronage relationships in the factional life of the early modern divan in which *devşirme* officials often associated on basis of common ethnicity. Ultimately this undermined the system's efficacy. She writes, "Today we know that to be a *kul* was not the same as to be a slave to a private person, and that a *kul* retained family, regional and factional loyalties which they needed to 'fit in' with their loyalty to the Sultan as best they might."[150] In a more recent work, Kunt has demonstrated that people in the palace service often tried to obtain positions for acquaintances and family members through the *devşirme*, indeed pages in the palace often provided recom-

JEWS, RENEGADES, AND EARLY MODERN IDENTITY   127

mendations for friends from their villages. This trend was common enough to attract the disdain of Ottoman commentators: the bureaucrat and historian Geli-bolulu Ali complained about individuals given positions because they were the "compatriot of this vezir and brother of that aga."[151] Scaraffia similarly points out that while there were cases of renegades "ill with 'forgetfulness', who to cancel every trace of their previous identity" became the worst torturers of Christians, they were rarely the ones who reached the apex of their new world. Rather the ones who succeeded were those who knew "how to act as mediators between the two cultures." Renegades tried "not to cut off the past, but to make the two different worlds to which they belong[ed] coexist."[152] This is certainly evident in the cases of Gazanfer and Hasan.

Evidence of the importance of regional and ethnic identities within the Porte abound. The Grand Vizier Mehmed Sokullu, for example, was born to minor noble, Orthodox parents in Visegrad in Bosnia. Early on he was earmarked for an ecclesiastical career and studied with a monk uncle at the important monastery in Mileseva. When he was taken to Constantinople as part of the devşirme, he was eighteen years old and had already achieved the deaconate. After reaching the summit of Ottoman officialdom, he became patron of the Patriarchate of Peć—the first three patriarchs were his brother and two nephews; other family members received bishoprics in Hercegovina. Sokullu also was protector of his former monastery school and was responsible for the erection of the bridge on the Drina made famous by Ivo Andrić's novel.[153] Though he scaled the heights of the Otto-man hierarchy, "this Muslim convert from Bosnia still remembered his child-hood community (and especially his own family)."[154] Indeed, Mustafa Ali com-plained quite bitterly about Sokullu who "advanced his relatives and relations whenever he saw a chance to do so, thus promoting many parvenus and appoin-ting them to lofty positions. Consequently, the ordered system of the affairs of mankind was changed in a way, and many of the great men as well as the common people gulped down bowl after bowl of poison at the banquet of his effrontery."[155]

Another grand vizier who maintained close ties with his birthplace and culture was İbrahim Paşa, originally born in 1493 or 1494 on the Venetian island of Parga, off Dalmatia, to commoner parents. Kidnapped by corsairs as a youth, İbrahim became a trusted friend of the future sultan Süleyman, and he parlayed this friendship into an appointment as grand vizier in 1523, at the expense of a more experienced rival. İbrahim held this office until his death in 1536 and, by all accounts, effectively ruled the day-to-day affairs of the empire. During his time he was one of the most influential figures in the Porte, though he was not without enemies. He led the successful invasion of Hungary in 1526, which saw the Hungarians routed at the Battle of Mohács and their young king, Louis II, killed on the battlefield,[156] and in 1534 he assumed command of the war with the pesky shah of Persia and captured Baghdad and Mesopotamia.[157]

The Venetian vizier did not hide his connections to his past; indeed, he was a frequent visitor to Galata where he patronized European artists and watched ballets on classical themes. Under his influence, both his mother and father converted to Islam, though rather half-heartedly: they described themselves as "affectionate to our most illustrious Signoria, . . . we know well that we were born subjects." İbrahim, like Sokullu, used his position to benefit his family and the state of his birth. He procured positions for two brothers in the palace, as well as an important office for his father, and "was largely responsible for the good standing of [the] son of the doge," the bastard Alvise Gritti, one of the sultan's most important advisers. İbrahim was generally favorably inclined to Venice's political and diplomatic position and avowed that he "greatly loved the Signoria since he was born under its dominion," and he described himself as a subject of the republic. The Venetians saw his favor as a key to their successful balancing act between the Habsurgs and Ottomans in the 1520s and 1530s. Indeed, one bailo went so far as to recommend Christian prayers for İbrahim's safe return from the front.[158] Ultimately, this interstitial position, in combination with political machinations in the palace, led to İbrahim's downfall, and he was strangled, during a lunch with Süleyman.[159] His meteoric rise to power and subsequent fall provided great fodder for European novelists and playwrights. Rouillard records three seventeenth-century dramas which portray the story of İbrahim, and a vast four-volume work by Mlle de Scudéry, *Ibrahim ou l'illustre Bassa*, 1641, further assured the romantic perpetuation of the vizier's tragic story.[160]

Çigalazade, as we have already seen, was another renegade who maintained close ties with his family, whom he tried to convert, or at least to benefit through his influence, as when he obtained the duchy of Naxos for his brother Carlo.[161] In another case, an Albanian-born grand vizier was described as "very inclined" to men of his region and language, regardless of their religion.[162] Such shared identities often benefited Venetian dragomans of the same region but from the Venetian side of the border, who emphasized regional over political and even religious identities in order to facilitate their access to and negotiations with officials at the highest levels of the Ottoman government. Salignac reported in 1606 that Venice was giving Ragusa the island of Auguste, which he thought would make the *kapudanpaşa* "more softened . . . on their position, as he is Slav by birth (*de nation*) and affectionate to the Ragusans."[163] A renegade Venetian subject from Arbe, "a Turk here for many years . . . a person of much honor, of good repute, who was previously Chief Horse Trainer of the late Grand Signor," requested that the Senate award his brothers a small villa or some properties in their homeland, a request supported by the *kapudanpaşa* and the bailo. There were so many Serbs in the Porte that Serbian became a "private patois" in the Ottoman court; Süleyman may have spoken it as well.[164]

Even among women of the harem memories and identities remained vivid: the Sultana Nūr Bānū who was captured by Barbarossa and became mother of Murad III (whom she allegedly had baptized as a baby), retained her identity as Venetian throughout her life. Though she was almost certainly of Corfiot common stock, after her rise to prominence in the imperial harem, she began to depict herself as a Venetian noble. Venetian officials were privately skeptical of this claim, but publicly they embraced the fiction. This benefited them as Nūr Bānū regularly intervened to prevent policies unfavorable to Venice's interests and territories. The Sultana's case is also suggestive of the power of regional, cultural roots, as "even after rising to the vertex of the Ottoman state, this Greek girl . . . of elevated social status, native of a Venetian colony, probably imbued from childhood by Venetian social values, apparently preferred to be considered as a scion of a Venetian patrician family."[165]

The numerous cases studied in this chapter suggest the need to revise the way in which we understand identity in the early modern Mediterranean world. Identity in this era, both individual and group, was much more complicated than simple adherence to modern notions of religious or political belonging. The experiences of Jews such as Righetto or David Passi and of Gazanfer Ağa, Hasan Paşa, and the many other renegades who populated the Ottoman Empire clearly illustrate the degree to which even the most elemental boundary—religion—was crossed and re-crossed in the early modern Mediterranean. Their cases also suggest the degree to which cultural and geographical provenance, as expressed in the elusive idea of nation, constituted a central element in the mosaic of identity. Though this boundary was often breached, changing one's religion did not mean replacing or abandoning some former, essentialized self. Indeed, conversion signified simply a complication of identity, an addition to the important regional, ethnic, religious, and familial elements that were at the core of self and community in this period.

CHAPTER FIVE

Merchants, Patricians, Citizens, and Early Modern Identity

The cases of Gazanfer Ağa and Righetto are fascinating and suggest the malleable and composite nature of early modern identities. It would not be unreasonable to argue, however, that because Jews and renegades existed on the margins, their experiences cannot be seen as normative. To a degree it is true that these groups inhabited the interstices of society, but we should not ignore the fact that they also circulated in and participated at all levels of Ottoman society. This is particularly true of the renegades, who penetrated Ottoman society so completely precisely because they were not anomalous; their experience of "migration and conversion" was not uncommon in the sixteenth and seventeenth centuries. In fact, between 1453 and 1623, thirty-three of the forty-eight grand viziers were of Christian extraction.[1] The chameleonlike qualities renegades displayed seem to be emblematic of a much broader ambiguity in issues of identity in the early modern Mediterranean, particularly among the admixture of cultural, linguistic, ethnic, and religious groups that composed what one scholar has described as the "Levantine subculture."[2] The pliancy and porosity of identic boundaries is also evident among members of the commercial and diplomatic core of the official Venetian community in Constantinople, as well as on a broader, communal level by the Perots, the small group of Latin-rite Ottoman subjects who inhabited Galata and Vigne di Pera.

MERCHANTS

As chapter 2 shows, the label "merchant of Venice" in early modern times was a facade that masked a heterogeneous and ambiguous physiognomy. Venetian

Levantine commerce from 1540 on was carried out almost exclusively by non-noble agents. Legally, these merchants had to be Venetian citizens, born or natu-ralized; in practice most were the latter. Many came from Venice's empire; others were not even culturally Venetian or Italian. There were also numerous instances of merchants trading in the Venetian nation who never obtained citizenship, and some were even Ottoman subjects. The archetypal Venetian merchant, then, was Venetian not by birth but by adoption, which suggests the degree to which mer-chant identity shared the malleability and adaptability demonstrated by renegades and Jews.

The experience of one of these naturalized merchants and a longtime member of the Venetian nation in Constantinople, Marcantonio Stanga, illuminates the variability of early modern merchant identity. Stanga was born in Cremona but spent most of his adult life trading in Syria and Constantinople. He came to Constantinople sometime around 1550 and resided in the city until his death in 1593. Stanga owned a house and vineyard in Galata, and though he appears not to have married, he did produce a son with a slave he owned. He was not a particularly wealthy merchant, but he was well known and respected by impor-tant Ottoman and Venetian officials. There is no evidence that Stanga lived for any length of time in Venice, yet in 1564 the V Savii recommended him for full *de intus et extra* citizenship, emphasizing his many years as a merchant and the income he had brought the city, despite the fact that he did not meet the residency requirement.[3]

During the War of the Holy League, Stanga led an interesting double life. At the outbreak of the war, Venetian merchants in Constantinople were imprisoned and their goods confiscated (as happened to Ottoman merchants in Venice). In anticipation, "for the security of his person and merchandise," Stanga refash-ioned himself as the official treasurer, and therefore a member, of the French nation in Constantinople. Some charged that Stanga became an Ottoman subject during the war to protect his commercial activities, though he vehemently denied the accusation. Despite this transmutation, throughout the war Stanga remained closely affiliated with the Venetian nation as a key link in the communication network between the imprisoned bailo, Marcantonio Barbaro, and Venice. He received and sent crucial communications in his own mail and passed these on surreptitiously in the church of San Francesco. The Council of Ten declared that "if it had not been for Mr. Antonio Stanga," communication would have been impossible "because of the great guard that was around this bailo."[4]

After the peace of 1573, Stanga returned to the Venetian nation, to the dismay of the French ambassadors. Because of Stanga's serial self-refashioning, his death in

1593 precipitated a struggle over his estate among French, Venetian, and Ottoman authorities, who all claimed him as their own. Venice maintained that Stanga had been a citizen of the city since 1564; the French claimed him because "at the time of the last war he had made himself a French subject"; and the Ottomans alleged that because of his long residency, the property he owned in Galata, and a bastard son he had fathered there, he was a *haracgüzar* of the sultan.[5] Stanga's identity was furthered complicated by the revelation that since at least 1582 he had served the Spanish crown as one of its "most esteemed spies in Constantinople," reporting regularly on the activities of the Venetian baili and activities in the Porte. Indeed, Marcantonio Stanga was not even his real name; he was born Bartolomeo Pusterla.[6] While clearly an opportunist, Bartolomeo Pusterla alias Marcantonio Stanga seems a good example of the malleability of political identity in this period and the importance of his vocational identity as a merchant in this calculus. Stanga migrated from non-Venetian to citizen, citizen to French subject, perhaps Ottoman subject as well, back to Venetian citizen, all the while serving as a Spanish informer.

The shifting sense of political affiliation demonstrated by Stanga/Pusterla is also evident in another Venetian merchant, Poloantonio Bon. Bon first appears listed as a Venetian merchant in Constantinople in 1604, and he reappears sporadically to 1611. Cristoforo Valier described him as a Venetian, "though married in this land," suggesting his may have been a more permanent union than the concubinage normally practiced by expatriate merchants.[7] In Constantinople, Bon moved among the highest circles of both Ottoman and European society: he was a silk and wool merchant who traded with the most important Venetians and other merchants, including the English ambassador. His most significant commercial and political connection was with the influential Ottoman official, Halil Paşa, whom he served as a dragoman for some time.[8]

Halil Paşa was key in bringing Dutch merchants into the Levant; as part of his efforts, he offered Bon, an "essential functionary from his own entourage," as dragoman to the new Dutch ambassador, Cornelius Haga. The existing trading nations in Constantinople, led by Venice, had worked mightily to block the introduction of a new and potent competitor into their markets. Unable to convince the Ottomans to keep out the Dutch, the baili tried to use their influence as head of Bon's nation to dissuade the merchant from entering the service of a competitor, though with no success. Bon's relationship with his new patron proved short-lived, however, as within a year he and Haga had a falling out. Having alienated both the Venetians and the Dutch, Bon attempted to obtain satisfaction by taking the matter to the divan, probably with the hope of leveraging his relationship with

Halil Paşa in his favor. This too failed, and the Ottoman grandee withdrew his support. Unwilling to abandon his grievance, Bon next wrote the States General about Haga's dissolute lifestyle and large debts, trying in this way to achieve his objectives. The last record of Bon was from Cyprus, where he passed in 1614 on his way to Holland.[9]

Stanga and Bon were not exceptional among Venice's merchants in Constantinople. The Gagliano brothers provide another example of the fuzzy and elastic nature of identity in the Venetian merchant nation. Edoardo and Domenico Gagliano were among the most active and successful merchants in the late sixteenth century, trading between Venice, Ragusa, Constantinople, and as far afield as Poland-Lithuania.[10] The brothers' trade network included Venetian patricians and *cittadini*, merchants and ambassadors of other European states, numerous Ottoman traders—Christian, Jewish, and Muslim—and even the highest officials in the Porte.[11] They also operated several ships, at least two of which were foreign-built but declared Venetian by the Senate at the Gaglianos' request.[12] Domenico was a well-known merchant in Venice, and he used his reputation to benefit colleagues and acquaintances in legal matters before various Venetian magistracies. The Gagliano brothers, then, would appear exemplary merchants of Venice. Except that they were not Venetian at all, but rather Latin-rite subjects of the Ottoman sultans.[13]

The details of the Gaglianos' early life are sketchy: they appear to have originally come from Ragusa where they were part of an important local banking family. Domenico first went to Venice in 1575 to live and work with his uncle Domenico, who appears to have become by then a Venetian citizen. The younger Domenico resided in the city almost continuously to the end of his life. He married a Venetian woman who bore several children. At his uncle's death, Domenico took over the family business, and resided in the parish of Santa Maria Mater Domini, where he maintained a large household, until at least 1624. He also owned a number of houses and shops throughout the city as well as properties on the *terraferma*. In 1603, after more than twenty-eight years of residency, Domenico requested and received *de intus et extra* citizenship status. In its recommendation, the V Savii noted that Domenico was "a merchant with a good name, and with his commerce and navigation of several ships he and his uncle have brought much benefit to [Venice]'s customs and trade."[14] Citizenship technically opened the door to Domenico's participation in the Levantine trade, which he had already been actively engaged in for many years, as he traveled to and from Constantinople and traded as a member of the Venetian nation there.[15]

While Domenico lived out his life in Venice and became a citizen, his brother

Edoardo settled and did business in Constantinople. Edoardo first appears in the rosters of the Council of Twelve in 1582, and remained one of the most active merchants of the Venetian nation until 1606.[16] His fellow merchants regularly elected him to positions of importance in the nation: in 1595 he was selected to supervise the recovery of a ship that had gone down with the goods of many of the nation's merchants aboard; the next year he was chosen to oversee the sticky issues surrounding the failure of a Venetian merchant; in 1598 he was elected to one of the most important offices in the merchant nation, *sindico* (assistant) to the *capo dei mercanti*. Further evidence of Edoardo's influence is the 1602 commandment from the sultan to the *kadıs* of Constantinople and Galata describing him as the "representative of the merchants of Venice" and enjoining their cooperation in the fulfillment of his responsibilities.[17]

Despite his prominence in the nation, Edoardo never was a Venetian citizen; rather he remained a subject of the sultan his entire life.[18] He maintained a house in the Vigne di Pera near the seraglio there, married the daughter of a local Ottoman-Christian merchant, and raised two daughters to adulthood, having lost another daughter and a son in their youth.[19] Like his brother Domenico in Venice, Edoardo was an important landholder with numerous properties in both Galata and Vigne di Pera, including houses, shops, vineyards, and garden plots, which he rented to other Venetian merchants and locals.[20] He regularly served in the community of the sultan's Latin-rite subjects in positions of importance: in 1584 he was *procuratore* of San Francesco; in 1603 he was *procuratore* of the Holy Land. He was also elected to one of the highest civic offices in the Latin-rite community, prior of the Magnifica Comunità.[21] Edoardo was respected among Ottoman-Muslims as well. He was designated by an influential *çavuş* as an arbitrator in a commercial dispute with a Venetian merchant, and he often stood as guarantor in matters between Venetian and Ottoman-Muslim merchants. He was an intimate of high-level Ottoman officials, including Çigalazade Sinan Paşa; he conveyed letters from the renegade to family members in Christendom, all the while reporting on their contents to the baili.[22] In 1599, when Constantinople was suffering a severe food shortage, certain Ottoman ministers approached Edoardo with a proposal that he bring food into the city on his ships, which would not be charged any duties. In another instance, in an extended dispute with an Ottoman-Muslim merchant, the *kadı* of Galata kept Edoardo apprised of his adversary's strategy and worked to resolve the matter in Gagliano's favor.[23]

Legally, Edoardo should not have been permitted to trade as a Venetian, yet for years he did just that. This was no case of mistaken identity: for over two decades he was publicly recognized as a "citizen of Pera" and "Perot," and thus an Ottoman subject, and yet again and again the chancellery records referred to him as a Venetian citizen and a "Venetian gentlem[a]n and merchant." When Gagliano was involved in a commercial dispute, Agostino Nani wrote the Senate that he would "not fail to assist him," even though, as Nani added in code, Gagliano "is a *haracgüzar*, . . . [and thus] one may encounter some greater difficulty."[24] Clearly Venice and its officials were aware of Edoardo's split identity.

In many ways the Gagliano brothers' trading company, with its various family members located in different Mediterranean ports, resembles the familial partnerships of Jewish merchant families in this period. Maintaining or obtaining citizenship or subject status from the two dominant eastern Mediterranean powers was clearly a strategy for developing and protecting family capital. In the case of the Gagliano brothers, this had been going on for at least two generations: Edoardo's and Domenico's father, Benetto, was trading with the Venetian nation in Constantinople already in 1545, just about the time that their uncle, Domenico, established himself in Venice.[25] Edoardo's marital alliances provide additional evidence of these family strategies. One daughter, Isabeta, wed Thomaso Navon (Naon), a Latin-rite, Ottoman subject of Genoese ancestry who was a dragoman of the Venetian nation; Libania, his other daughter, married an Orthodox Greek "gentleman" who was also an Ottoman subject.[26] When Venetian fortunes in Constantinople started to wane, Edoardo began to broaden his associations to include increasingly close ties with the French merchant nation, much as Stanga had done in 1570–73. He eventually became a consul for the French in the early seventeenth century, and after 1606 he seems to have ceased entirely his involvement with Venetian merchants.[27] While it is not clear what precipitated this break, it was perhaps related to suspicions that Edoardo was part of the Spanish spy network in Constantinople.[28]

The multivalence of Edoardo's identity is also evident in his use of the Venetian and Ottoman justice systems. At the death of his uncle in Venice, there arose a disagreement over the division of the inheritance that pitted him and Domenico against their sister, Caterina, who was married to a Venetian dragoman in Galata. In order to settle the matter "amicably," the litigants agreed initially to submit to the bailo's judgment and, as was a standard requirement in accepting Venetian jurisdiction, to avoid taking the matter before the local Ottoman *kadı*. Indeed, the agreement explicitly stated that both parties would accept the decision of the arbitrators selected to consider the matter, and that neither would have recourse to Ottoman justice.[29] This agreement broke down when the opposing camps refused to abide by the bailo's settlement, and over the next several years Edoardo and the other litigants turned to Galata's *kadı* court in an effort to maximize their portions of a Venetian inheritance matter. At the same time they continued to pursue the matter before a series of Venetian magistracies. The strategy of non-Muslim use of Ottoman courts when communal institutions failed, and playing the magistracies of various polities off each other, was exceedingly common in the early modern period.[30] Eventually the Gagliano matter was resolved by Bailo Girolamo Cappello, as the estate, valued at 680,000 *akçe*, was divided with twenty percent going to Caterina, and the remainder split evenly between her two brothers.[31]

The Gagliano case, like that of Stanga and Bon, clearly suggests the diversity masked by the label of Venetian merchant; it also reveals the mechanisms and motivations that permitted a certain ambiguity in merchant identity. The variety of Venetian merchants' backgrounds and their objectives made their Venetian-ness a part, but clearly not the all-encompassing or exclusive sum, of their identities. Familial and commercial, much more than religious or political, considerations seem to have been at the core of the Gaglianos' identity. Although in all three of these cases, the merchants had close ties to Venice and the nation and were highly respected and influential members of it at different points in their lives, this association did not prevent them from reconfiguring themselves as members of other nations or from pursuing justice or advancement in a variety of forums, regardless of their political status. Their sense of identity clearly comprised a multiplicity of focuses and was adaptable and flexible as situations permitted or dictated.

PATRICIANS AND CITIZENS

As the merchants' stories suggest, identity in the early modern Mediterranean was anything but fixed or simple. Due to the transitory and composite nature of the many regional polities, identity and political status were not often tightly intertwined. Within the Venetian state, however, there existed groups whose privileged status might imply a willingness to identify themselves more readily and closely with their native or adoptive polity. The merchants were one such group; even more closely tied to the state, however, were the patricians and *cittadini originari*. Both groups enjoyed a close association with the ruling institutions of the Venetian state, and benefited politically, economically and socially from their favored status. Indeed, for the patriciate, the state was the expression and embodiment of their estate's political and economic aspirations. Of all the disparate peoples who constituted the Venetian empire, the patricians and *cittadini* would logically be those who most closely identified with and derived their sense of identity from their historical relationship to the institutions of the state. Yet even among these privileged castes, the documentary evidence suggests a certain mal-leability of identity.

In most instances, renegades came disproportionately from the lower eche-lons of society, those who stood to gain the most socially through conversion and who may have felt a more tenuous attachment to distant, often mutable sov-ereigns. Venetian nobles and *cittadini originari* had the most to lose by abandon-ing their faith and their state. Patrician conversions, if more rare, did nonetheless occur. In 1621, for instance, a Venetian "gentleman" of the Lombardo family, serving as ship's noble on the Pellegria di Rossi "became a Turk solely on his own, spontaneous motivation," after his ship docked in Alexandria.[32]

We know more about another Venetian patrician convert, Mehmed Ağa Frenk-beyoğlu, who was born Marcantonio Querini. Captured as a teen during the War of the Holy League while serving on the galley of his uncle, Vincenzo Priuli, he was taken to Constantinople where he embraced Islam. Although there has often been suspicion about the depth and sincerity of renegades' conversions among both contemporaries and modern scholars, Querini seems to have embraced Islam wholeheartedly. When Leonardo Donà met the renegade noble more than two decades later, he reported that Mehmed had studied Islamic law and theology and was convinced that Islam would "save his soul." He corresponded with family members in Venice and claimed to have convinced his mother "to embrace the light of salvation that God had given him," though she seems never to have left Venice to join him.[33] That in 1597–98 he made the hajj to Mecca also indicates the depth of his conversion. Aided by his fellow Venetian Gazanfer Ağa, Mehmed Querini progressed rapidly in the Porte, holding several high-profile positions with the janissary corps and warranting mention in the chronicles of the day. Eventually he became the commander of all the *sipahi;* he was killed in the tumults of 1602 by his own soldiers.[34]

We also have examples of Venetian *cittadini* who transgressed the boundaries of religion, such as Pietro Venier. Venier came to Constantinople in 1626 as a *giovane della lingua,* recommended by the Senate for this plum spot because he had shown great promise in his Turkish language studies in Venice. He not only remained in Constantinople for his allotted seven years, in 1632 he requested an extension of his stay, alleging that both of his parents had died in the plague of 1630–31, "whence resulted the collapse of all of [his] family affairs." Less than three months after this request, Venier secretly packed his belongings and fled the embassy under cover of darkness, leaving behind him in his room a sort of missionary tract instructing "whoever desires to become a Muslim, what he must believe, say and do." The bailo, Girolamo Cappello, suggested that Venier was driven to abandon his prestigious position and became a "Turk" by a combination of economic trials and a forbidden passion for a woman: Venier, he wrote, had "fooled himself . . . with the belief (which had been suggested to him) . . . that he could receive pay at the level of a *Sipahi* and be free to join with the woman with whom he had secret dealings."[35]

Following his flight, Venier was able to boast to his nephew, another *giovane della lingua*, that he had won the sultan's favor by being the first to show him how "the glass of Galileo" worked, as they used the telescope to spy on the French ambassador's house. To further his standing with the sultan, Venier also sought to pry information about Venetian affairs from his nephew. In response to this threat, the bailo discredited the renegade *cittadino* by spreading misinformation and slanderous rumors, including the suggestion that Venier had been born "of a father [who] passed from Hebrewism to our faith," though the truth of this assertion is unknown.[36]

Venier was not the first citizen *giovane della lingua* to abandon his post. Indeed, one of the first young men sent to Constantinople to learn Turkish, a certain Colombina, converted to Islam in the 1550s and enjoyed a successful career in the seraglio, no doubt benefiting from the linguistic instruction he received in the bailate. He appears to have played an important role breaking Bailo Vettore Bragadin's code in 1566, and in 1578 he was nominated to go as *çavuş* to Venice to announce the circumcision of the sultan's son. His saga became a cautionary tale for subsequent baili against the dangers of sending young men to Constantinople.[37]

Among the best documented cases of a citizen abandoning his privileged position in Venetian society and refashioning himself as an Ottoman in an attempt to rise higher than his social station in Venice permitted is that of Zuanbattista Locadello. Locadello initially appeared in Constantinople in 1614, and again in 1616–17, as a merchant trading with the nation; he returned three years later with the plum position of secretary to Bailo Giorgio Giustinian. This position was restricted to the narrow class of Venetian *cittadini originari* and was highly sought after. During the next two years Locadello continued to carry on an active trade while serving as secretary, despite the fact that this violated Venetian law and he had been chastised by Giustinian for doing so. Locadello ran up substantial debts, including one of 400,000 *akçe* to a Venetian dragoman for cloth purchased on his behalf.[38] His largest debts, however, resulted from his dealings with influential figures in the Porte, including the sultana. With his access to the women of the seraglio, he dared to dream of obtaining no less a prize than the Principality of Moldavia, in quest of which he advanced the sultana increasing sums of money. Locadello also tried to gain the support of the ambassador of Poland-Lithuania in

Constantinople, promising him a portion of the almost 500,000 thalers in taxes that the principality allegedly produced. The Venetian also befriended the sons of the grand vizier, "by eating and drinking together," and secured their intervention with their father on his behalf. They helped him obtain accommodations with the secretary of the vizier, which opened a whole new circle of supporters of his claim. When it became apparent that because of the strident opposition of the bailo, Locadello would not receive the post in Moldavia, he turned his attention to the Duchy of Naxos, less lucrative but still important, but was rebuffed in this as well.[39]

Eventually, by exposing Locadello's impending bankruptcy, the bailo was able to have him imprisoned by order of the grand vizier. Because Locadello continued to confess and take communion, Giustinian was confident that he would not "turn Turk" to free himself. But, through the intervention of several Muslim and Jewish friends, Locadello did in fact convert, and was awarded a position in the seraglio. In explaining his actions to his father, Locadello claimed he had converted because he feared that the "bailo had conspired with certain janissaries to come into the Tower and to strangle me." The bailo's motivation, according to the renegade, was to get his hands on some pearls valued at 25,000 ducats: "Thus to save my life and to have time to be able to restore our afflicted household, it was very necessary for me to do this."[40]

Locadello's position, however, was not what he had anticipated, as he was effectively sequestered in a "miserable and most difficult" situation. He tired very quickly of the new situation and tried to obtain his freedom, "declaring that in a few days he would die of desperation."[41] Locadello was soon reduced to sending letters to everyone he knew, including the French and English ambassadors, imploring assistance and claiming to know the Venetian cipher to try to win support. But, Giustinian wrote, "he was derided, and as I appeared not to care about him or his renouncement at all, as he was a person worth nothing, . . . his scorn and humiliation grew even greater." In the end, Locadello's gambit failed, and he died in the same tower room in which Venier and another renegade Venetian had been previously held, and where both had apparently died at unknown hands.[42]

One final example of the self-refashioning of a Venetian citizen official is Paolo Mariani. Mariani cut a wide swath throughout the Mediterranean in the late sixteenth century, appearing in the documentary records of most of the states active in the region. The Englishman John Sanderson served as Mariani's viceconsul in Cairo and left a scathing description, which nonetheless suggests the range of his involvements and influence: "Now for Signor Paulo Mariani, as very atheist as Tipton, a chefe counselour to the ambassiatour. He, after many broyles and Machievile turmoyles, went consull of Fraunce to Alexandria and Cairo in Egipt. Ther beinge settled in his chefest desiered pompe . . . Paulo his witt was a maker of patriarks and princes, a setter up and pullar downe of them and ambassiators, a poysoner and filthy liver, a warrs and peace maker, a graboyler."[43] Mariani associated intimately with and often served the English (Sanderson describes him as Ambassador Barton's secretary), the French, and Ottomans of many ranks. Yet Mariani was a Venetian merchant and citizen, probably by birth rather than privilege, and his brother was a priest in the city.[44]

In Cairo where he was married and had a child, Paolo and his brother Pietro dominated the consulates of France, England, and perhaps Venice for the two decades following Lepanto.[45] In 1579 he had rented the office of French consul in Cairo from its holder, Cristoforo Vento, in Marseilles, for three and then six years. When the consulate began making a good income, Vento wanted to regain the office and accused Mariani of being a spy and of having drowned a Genoese merchant in his household. Mariani was able to fend off these charges with the support of several important Ottoman officials. Inquiries by both Ottoman and Venetian magistrates asserted that the Genoese had died of natural causes. After the resolution of this affair, in 1585, Mariani was appointed consul of the English nation in Cairo, apparently holding both consulates simultaneously. At some point he also became a *haracgüzar* of the sultan, though there are no surviving details of the motivations and necessities that drove him to make this move.[46]

A Venetian serving as an official for a commercial rival was not in and of itself unique: Nadalin Testa, for example, was the *emin* (sultan's agent) of Alessio (modern Lezhë), for six years, but this did not prevent him proposing a way to protect Venetian shipping from corsairs out of Vlora, and describing himself as a Venetian "most faithful to Your Serenity."[47] Earlier in the century, Marin Sanudo recorded the departure of two Venetian patricians, Zuanfrancesco Contarini and Zuan Contarini, who went to Constantinople seeking adventure and positions in the sultan's naval forces. A Venetian subject, Niccolò Orlandi, was elected consul in Cyprus by the V Savii in 1624, and also served as French and Dutch consul concurrently until his death in 1638.[48] This practice was "a dangerous thing and always of some degree of prejudice," as Alvise Contarini observed, suggesting that it be forbidden the new consul, but again such a practice was not uncommon in the dynamic world of eastern Mediterranean ports.[49] In the case of Mariani, it is perhaps more the ease with which he fashioned and refashioned himself repeatedly that set him apart.

While serving as consuls of both France and England, Mariani was a close associate and trading partner of the English ambassador or, as Marco Venier wrote, "a companion with him [Barton] in his intrigues, a most shrewd person." Indeed, Venier believed that in the relationship with Barton, Mariani was "the one who guides this boat."[50] Despite his close and long-standing association with Venice's commercial competitors, Mariani still considered himself (and apparently was accepted) as part of the Venetian nation, and he regularly participated in meetings of the Council of Twelve in Constantinople when he was there. In 1590 he even was selected from the council's numbers to carry out an inheritance inquiry for creditors of a deceased goldsmith.[51] As a citizen of Venice, though also an Ottoman subject and an official of the English and French nations, he still acknowledged the jurisdiction of the bailo in a matter involving a disputed debt he and Barton owed to a deceased Venetian merchant.[52]

Mariani's identity balancing act ultimately resulted in his death. In 1596, the French ambassador discovered that yet another Venetian was sending information on matters in the Ottoman Empire to Spanish ministers in Italy.[53] The ambassador inculpated Mariani with the grand vizier, and an Ottoman and French official were sent to Cairo where Mariani was consul, "and they had him hung by the neck with [a] letter attached to his feet." Sanderson expands on the event: "He hanged by the necke in his redd velvett goune under the chiefeste gate of Cairo; beinge privatly by force fetched out of his house in the eveninge, for otherwise his death had bine prevented, he had so besotted and was so beloved of most in the citie." According to Sanderson, the Moors especially favored "Mallem Paulo (Master Paul), as they commonly called him."[54]

The cases of Mariani, Mehmed Querini, Venier, and Locadello demonstrate the elites' ability to redefine and refashion themselves, even though they dominated Venice politically, socially, and economically and their individual and group identities were therefore most tightly intertwined with the state. While their motivations for transgressing political and religious boundaries varied, in all of these cases Venetian birthrights did not prevent association with English, French, and even Ottoman competitors as circumstances permitted and dictated. These men did not abandon their Venetian selves; rather, their identities were complicated and supplemented by their individual metamorphoses.

THE MAGNIFICA COMUNITÀ

The community of the Latin-rite Christian subjects of the sultan—called Perots after Pera, the name often used by Europeans for Galata—was technically outside of the Venetian domain, yet it was closely affiliated with it. Because of its location in the interstices between the Muslim, Jewish, and Orthodox populations of Constantinople, the Perot community sheds further light on the nature of communal identity in the diverse world of the Mediterranean.

During the conquest of Constantinople in 1453, Mehmed II was eager to spare Galata in order to protect the city's commercial life, which he regarded as "vitally important for the reconstruction of his new capital and the economy of his empire." So supportive of the merchants of Galata was Mehmed that he ordered his fleet to intervene in Chios on behalf of one of their most influential representatives, Francesco Draperio, who owned alum mines there and was owed a significant sum by the Christian Chiots.[55] While many Genoese fled Galata both before and after its fall, a core group remained and was organized into what was known as the Magnifica Comunità. This community was led by a council of twelve officials who replaced the preconquest office of the Genoese podestà and met regularly in the church of San Francesco. The Magnifica Comunità was granted certain legal and ceremonial rights, the most important of which was authority over the affairs of the remaining Latin churches in greater Constantinople. Unlike the other much larger minority *taife* or millets officially recognized by the Ottomans, such as the Greeks, Jews, or Armenians, the Magnifica Comunità was directly under the political jurisdiction of the *kadı* and *voyvoda* of Galata and did not enjoy administrative, legal or political autonomy. Its members were *dhimmi* subjects of the sultan, and not *harbi,* or non-Muslim foreigners, like the Frankish merchants with whom they lived and dealt.[56]

Early modern Constantinople's Latin-rite Christians were not numerous: in 1580 a papal legate reported there were five hundred Roman Catholic subjects of the sultans in Galata. They were joined by two thousand slaves, five hundred freed slaves, and seven hundred merchants and embassy staff temporarily in the city. A 1600 report estimated there were only between seventeen and twenty-eight Perot families, and a slightly later report added 150 Protestants to the city's Christian population.[57] Other contemporary reports generally support these figures.[58] These few families represented the last vestiges of the Genoese community that had thrived in the area for centuries, joined by refugees from Kaffa forced to move to the Ottoman capital after the capture of the Black Sea port in 1475. For the most part the Perots lived in the center of Galata, near the great tower that had been the heart of the city in Genoese times, though in the sixteenth century some of the most successful and important members of the community joined the exodus to the Vigne di Pera suburb outside Galata, neighboring the several European embassies that were located there.[59]

Because of its small numbers, the Latin-rite community had to struggle continuously to retain its separate identity and avoid being assimilated into the larger Greek Orthodox or Muslim populations. Della Valle reported, for example, that the Perots observed the Latin rite, but in their "customs they are greekified [*grecheggiano*]." Visitors to Pera acknowledged the hyphenated character of Perot identity, describing them as "Greeke Genoeses," "Greeks, of Genoese origins," and "Greek Franks."[60] This process of assimilation is found also in the language of the community: while the Perots originally had spoken a Genoese variant of Italian, by the seventeenth century Greek had replaced it as the everyday language of the community, though Italian continued as its administrative idiom and the lingua franca of the Levant, and many, most notably the dragomans, were multilingual.[61]

One way the Perots attempted to defend their identity was by avoiding marriages with Orthodox Greeks. Indeed, in 1627 the Roman Catholic patriarchal vicar of Constantinople tried to prohibit all intermarriage between Orthodox and Catholic.[62] The records of the Venetian chancellery, however, provide ample evidence that these marriages did occur often. Edoardo Gagliano married a daughter to a Greek noble, as did the dragoman Ambrosio Grillo.[63] Another external expression and defense of identity was the Perots' dress. Travelers to Constantinople often commented on the distinctive costume of the Perots, who wore "high collars, capped with calpaks [a characteristic black wool or felt cap worn in Turkey], with Ragusan bonnets and Mantuan hats," which made them readily identifiable within the cosmopolitan milieu of Galata.[64] Another means of defending their community's identity was through education; the Perots aggressively sought Jesuit and other teachers for their children, "so that no rapacious wolf enters in among us, or rather our children, who with bites of false doctrine might come and poison these poor souls."[65] Their objective was simple: to defend their children's sense of cultural and religious identity as a small minority in the larger Muslim and Orthodox cultures of Constantinople. Despite these efforts, many Perots gradually assimilated into broader Ottoman society. Maffio Venier estimated in 1582 that the Magnifica Comunità had lost four hundred Latin-rite households to the Orthodox alone, and the community's numbers continued to decrease.[66]

Religion was a central element of the Perots' identity; they maintained their religious distinctiveness chiefly through the control and perpetuation of their community's sacred edifices and rituals. As the last vestiges of the Latin-rite community in the Ottoman capital, the Perots ardently defended their right to govern the city's Roman Catholic confraternities, hospitals, and monasteries, as well as its ritual life of processions and holy feasts. Most important, however, was the control of the community's churches. In 1600 there were twelve Latin-rite churches in greater Constantinople, though most had only a few religious left inhabiting them, and several were abandoned except for the occasional, exceptional mass. Situated in the heart of Galata, in the old Genoese quarter, the church of San Francesco, with its monastery and nine friars, represented the geographical and spiritual focal point of the Latin-rite community in Constantinople. Also important was San Benedetto, built in 1420 by the Genoese, which had a library of 10,593 works.[67] The Magnifica Comunità took very seriously its protectorate role; as one church official reported, the Perots had "an incredible zeal for the Latin-rite."[68]

The Perots' zeal to superintend their churches often resulted in controversy with religious representatives sent from Rome, as well as with the resident Roman Catholic ambassadors who patronized and protected the churches. The fundamental issue centered on the question of who had legal authority over the churches. Despite its strong identification with the Roman church, the Magnifica Comunità traced its sovereignty over the Ottoman capital's Latin-rite churches to Mehmed II. As Cristoforo Valier reported, the Perots claimed "absolute dominion over all the churches of Pera, donated, as was seen in their statutes, by Emperor Sultan Mehmet . . . to whom the Perots made voluntary submission of themselves in return for the privileges and other immunities that they still enjoy today."[69] This claim was contested both by Venice and Rome who heavily subsidized the churches and the community. As a Roman official wrote to the bailo in 1590, "You will do well not to give any authority here to the Perots over these places, nor over the monks, because unfortunately they usurp the authority of the Religious, and of the monasteries, to their damage."[70]

Disputes over the jurisdiction of the churches were common and often bitter, and the patriarchal vicar assigned by Rome to oversee the churches had regularly to threaten the priors of the Magnifica Comunità with excommunication because of their refusal "to give account of their administration"; indeed, in 1643 the community was cut off, though only temporarily.[71] In an effort to take control of the situation, in 1622 Rome decided to replace the patriarchal vicar with a bishop, a move the Perots opposed greatly, fearing that a bishop would make a stronger adversary in the struggle to control their churches.[72] These machinations should not mask the fact that in the end both the Perots and Rome depended greatly on each other and strived to work together. The Perots claimed sovereignty over the churches of Constantinople, but in practice they were not financially or politically capable of maintaining them and thus were dependent on subventions from European powers and popes. For example, in 1603 the Venetian Senate voted to grant the Perots thousands of ducats to cover the costs of maintenance and restoration of the community's churches, which were in a terrible state. Conversely, Venice relied on the community for a variety of religious, commercial, and linguistic services. The papacy was dependent on the Magnifica Comunità to maintain a Roman Catholic presence in the Ottoman capital so as to protect the rights of believers throughout the sultan's lands, as no papal representative was sanctioned to reside or treat in the Porte.[73]

This interdependence meant that the Venetian nation and the Magnifica Comunità generally tried to maintain good relations. Perots regularly functioned as Venice's dragomans and in other official capacities within the embassy; from at least 1550 on, the majority of the dragomans and *giovani della lingua* were Latin-rite Ottoman subjects, and these lucrative posts were highly coveted within the community. Part of their allure was that dragomans and other dependents of foreign embassies were exempted from paying the two Ottoman taxes required of *dhimmi:* the *harac* and the *cizye.* Dependents also had recourse to the Venetian embassy's legal and notarial institutions and thus were able to avoid tangling with Ottoman courts and officials if they desired.[74]

While they were almost always constrained to depend on Ottoman dragomans, the baili clearly considered the Perots to be Ottomans and thus outside the Venetian nation, despite their shared religion. When possible, the baili always preferred Venetian citizens as dragomans and officials over "Perots and other nations distant from the Chancellery."[75] The obligation to rely on Perots in sensitive positions was a continuous, bitter lament of the baili. Lorenzo Bernardo warned in his *relazione* of the danger in having to rely on "Turkish subjects" like the Perots in treating delicate matters of state. Indeed, the problems with one Perot dragoman, Matheca Salvago, became so serious that the Council of Ten seriously considered having him poisoned. The *giovani della lingua* language-training program arose in response to this undesirable reliance.[76] The motivations for this lack of confidence seem clear: Perots lived in the interstices of Ottoman and European society or, as one scholar has described, "astride [the world] of the 'Franks' and that of the Ottoman 'minorities.'"[77] Like the Marranos, the Perots were difficult to pin down; they were neither fish nor fowl, but rather men and women with unique, seemingly contradictory identities that permitted them to move comfortably between the various political and religious spheres of the early modern Mediterranean world.

This evasiveness was evident in the community's dealings with Venice on matters of religion. During the sixteenth century, Venice had been the protector and patron of the Magnifica Comunità and its churches; after 1608 the Perots transferred this role increasingly to the French ambassadors, whom the Perots eventually declared their *protecteur générale*.[78] They switched their allegiances to France partly because of a sense of Venice's creeping commercial and political decline in the Porte and partly for religious motivations. The French were the patrons of the Jesuits in Constantinople, and after a first attempt to initiate a mission failed when all the fathers died of the plague in 1583, the Jesuits were able to establish a presence in Constantinople in 1609. The Magnifica Comunità, supported by the French ambassador Salignac, had been very vocal in petitioning the papacy to send the Jesuits, in part because they wanted them to establish a school in Galata but also to wean the community from dependence on the other orders, which were supported by Venice.[79] Because the baili vigorously opposed the Jesuit presence, a rift arose with the Perots, causing the baili to lament their "ancient devotion to this house that they are [now] alienating." So influential did the Jesuits become that they were the only order that attracted any Perot youth, which forced the other religious orders to import religious to staff their facilities.[80]

Commercial concerns also affected the Perots' relations with European powers. In 1608, for example, Ottaviano Bon obtained permission for Venetian merchants to open *botteghe* in the Bedestan of Galata. This move was vigorously opposed by Constantinople's Jewish merchants, who enlisted the opposition of the Perots as well. Both were keen to defend their advantage as Ottoman subjects in this crucial commercial venue, which served as a procurement center for clothing for the Ottoman military. To protect their stake in this lucrative market against Venetian merchants, the Jews and Perots did not hesitate to utilize connections with Ottoman officials and institutions, and to emphasize their status as Ottoman subjects, to achieve their aims.[81]

The Magnifica Comunità clearly represents a little-studied community situated in the interstices between the various polities and cultures of the eastern Mediterranean. Culturally and religiously they imagined themselves as linked to the broader community of European Christians in Constantinople, but this close relationship did not mean that the Perots did not consider themselves Ottoman subjects or benefit from that status. They regularly migrated between the legal institutions of Venice, the Ottomans, and the other European powers in Constantinople as circumstances dictated. Many Perots' sense of identity was clearly a composite of their status as Ottoman subjects, their historical and cultural identity as Genoese Italians, their vocations as Venetian functionaries and dependents, and their religious identity as a Roman Catholic minority. It is impossible and unnecessary to rank these elements; the Perots emphasized them instrumentally in the diverse ways they adapted and refashioned themselves within their unique situation.

The case of the Piron (Perone) family of Pera illuminates the protean nature of Perot identity. The four families of the Casa Piron were the largest of the twenty or so clans that made up the core of the Perot community. The Piron may have had some claim to nobility, though how well founded a claim is unclear.[82] We know little of the history of the family, where its members originated, or when they settled in Galata. They were certainly among the wealthiest members of the community: in 1590 the fourteen chief Perot families donated 400,000 *akçe* to prevent the church of San Francesco from being made into a mosque, and almost 20 percent of this sum, 75,000 *akçe*, was paid by Niccolò and Stefano Piron alone. The Piron were involved commercially in cloth, hides, and slaves, and in the early part of the seventeenth century they owned a ship that traveled between Constantinople and Venice. They had extensive commercial relationships with the French, English, and imperial ambassadors, important merchants from the various European trading nations, and many influential Ottoman-Muslim merchants and officials.[83] The Piron also served in responsible and influential positions in the Magnifica Comunità as "elders of Pera" and owned valuable land in Galata and the Vigne di Pera.[84]

Despite, or perhaps as a result of, their importance in the Ottoman Latin-rite community, the Piron were also actively involved with the Venetian nation. Although never recognized as members of the nation, several different family members appear repeatedly in the rosters of the Council of Twelve, and one, Matteo Piron, appears regularly from 1607 to 1635.[85] Clearly the Piron were respected and influential members of the nation: in 1616, Matteo and Stefano Piron called a meeting of the council to recommend one of their *giovani* as an official *cernitor* of the nation, and their motion was approved. The Piron also loaned the baili large amounts of cash when the duties collected were insufficient to cover consular costs. Though widely and openly recognized as Perot subjects of the sultan, Matteo and Stefano Piron appear at the head of a 1619 list of "Venetian merchants" ordered to pay their *cottimi;* Stefano and two other Piron merchants also appear on a list of Venetian "merchants" and "subjects" in 1616. Antonio Piron also played, at the request of the bailo, a role in an official investigation into serious allegations against the Venetian *cittadino originario,* dragoman and *coadiutore* to Marco Venier, Girolamo Alberti.[86]

As was the case with Edoardo Gagliano, the Piron also pursued marriage alliances to align themselves closely with the Venetian nation. Piron women often married Venetian dragomans: the influential Venetian grand dragoman, Marcantonio Borisi, married Caterina Piron, and had to obtain a dispensation to do so through the offices of the bailo, after the death of his first wife, Caterina's cousin.

The bailo intervened in this matter to ensure that his most important dragoman would not "be linked to other households."[87] In the 1630s a Piron became a Venetian dragoman, and several others acquired lucrative positions as *giovani della lingua*. One Piron boy benefited from the patronage of "several most excellent senators," including a number of former baili, among them Matteo Zane, who became patriarch of Venice and patronized the lad's study in the seminary of the Somascans in the lagoon.[88] Clearly ties of patronage and marriage with Venice were an important part of the Casa Piron's strategy, yet they also jealously guarded their Ottoman identity. When an inheritance matter that had been entrusted to the bailo's adjudication was not resolved to their satisfaction, family members did not hesitate to take the matter before the *kadı* of Galata.[89]

The Piron moved with ease between the various religious, cultural and political poles of Galata, using instrumentally their relationships with Venice, the Ottoman Empire, and other entities to advance their family's fortunes and position. Their eight hundred *botte* ship, for example, though of foreign construction, was recognized by the V Savii as one of the twenty-six Venetian ships trading legitimately in the Mediterranean, which allowed Venetian merchants to ship goods on it. The Piron also used it and other ships to ferry Venetian soldiers and slaves in the Levant. In one instance, the bailo removed the accreditation of a Jewish broker who had cheated Antonio Piron of some cattle hides that Piron had purchased from a Muslim merchant.[90] In another case, when some six thousand ducats of their goods were held as suspected contraband in Zante by a Venetian official, Niccolò and Antonio Piron asked Marco Venier to assist them in freeing it, which he did willingly, even though an inquiry produced evidence that the goods were indeed illegal. Venier's reasons are revealing: though Ottoman subjects, the Piron had assisted the imprisoned bailo Marcantonio Barbaro in the past war at great risk to their lives and fortunes, "employing themselves as if they were vassals of the Most Serene Republic." They were still "most loyal," Venier reports, and informed Venice's representatives on the Ottoman fleet's movements and other sensitive affairs in the Porte. Another motivation Venier cites for nurturing this relationship was the extensive network of the Piron family. They were in great favor with important officials in the divan, including the vizier, the sultan, and his mother (the Piron had been responsible for bringing Mehmed III to the capital when his father died). Antonio was an intimate of Ferrat Paşa and many other "principal Turks [were] his friends." The Piron wives, too, "practiced familiarly" in the households of influential Ottomans, rounding out the network of Piron connections within the Ottoman hierarchy.[91]

Because of the breadth of their relations and their reputation, the Piron often bridged the Ottoman and Venetian worlds. Antonio Piron was elected by the *kadı* of Galata to resolve the matter of a failed Venetian merchant, and his selection was accepted by the Venetian nation. Zorzi Piron was chosen by an Ottoman-Muslim merchant to resolve a dispute he had with two prominent Venetian merchants; all parties agreed Piron was a dependable and honest broker and that they would abide by his ruling. In another instance, an influential Ottoman official employed Antonio Piron, "his friend," to act in a fiduciary role in resolving an issue between him and a Venetian merchant.[92] The Piron existed comfortably in the liminal space in which the Ottoman, Venetian, Genoese, Muslim, Ortho-dox, and Christian ambits intersected. They seem to have been perfectly at ease navigating these seemingly incompatible realms and to have perceived no contra-diction in their composite identity of Ottoman subjects, Latin-rite Christians, and Venetian allies.[93]

While it is difficult to make broad generalizations about early modern identity, the adaptability and multivalency of identity exhibited by the Jews and renegades of the previous chapter was not limited to the margins of society. Patricians and *cittadini originari*, despite their privileged status, still transgressed political and religious boundaries, albeit less frequently than subjects with their more ephemeral and less direct relationship to the ruling class and its institutions. In doing so they added layers to their sense of self rather than substituting an old identity for a new. As new Muslims they embraced a new Ottoman political and religious identity; at the same time they preserved their memory and identity as members of the ruling classes of Venice and their sense of belonging to a specific family.

The unique community of Latin-rite Christians in Constantinople, the Perots, further demonstrate how seemingly incongruous and even conflictual pieces can combine into an intricate mosaic of individual identity. In many ways this small group felt threatened with assimilation into the much larger Greek and Muslim society with which it coexisted. Its members achieved self-definition and preserva-tion of communal boundaries through dress, marriage strategies, and education. The role of the Magnifica Comunità as sole representative and defender of the Roman church in the Ottoman capital was central to this identity, yet the Perots' sense of purpose derived as much from their status as subjects of the sultan as it did from their Christianity. In the conflicts that arose with the French, Venetians, and even the papacy over the administration and control of the churches, the Perots made much more of their status as Ottomans and the legal right to control their churches granted them by Mehmed II than they did of their religious identity. By the same token, when Ottoman officials threatened their churches with closure, the Perots did not hesitate to refashion, or better, reorder their collective identity as they sought the intervention and protection of these same Christian adversaries. For the Perots, Roman Catholic and Ottoman identities were complementary, rather than mutually exclusive categories.

CHAPTER SIX

An Urban Middle Ground

Venetians and Ottomans in Constantinople

Cultural confrontation, what Samuel Huntington has called the "clash of civilizations,"[1] has fascinated historians from the earliest days of Herodotus's *History of the Persian Wars*. Tales of human conflicts have seemed more compelling, and perhaps more representative of the human condition, than have tales of cooperation. This has certainly been true in the historiography of the engagement of Islam and Christianity and, more narrowly, that of the Venetian and Ottoman empires, which has privileged discussions of war almost always over peace. Conflict and misunderstanding have certainly informed this relationship; however, an overemphasis on these factors obscures the striking, unanticipated fact that for the majority of their shared history, coexistence as much as conflict characterized Veneto-Ottoman relations. Volumes have been devoted to the history of conflict, but the moments and mechanisms of coexistence have been largely overlooked.

In recent years historians have begun to reconsider the nature of the intersection of cultures in more nuanced and sophisticated ways that avoid reducing cultural interaction to an encounter between oppositional metacategories such as East and West, Christian and Muslim, and instead recognize its inherently messy, contradictory, and variable nature. In the context of the early modern Mediterranean, a few scholars have tried to move beyond broad, geopolitical generalizations, focusing on local and regional contexts that suggest the complexity and ambiguity of relations between people of diverse religious, political, social, and cultural backgrounds.[2] The binary certainties of the past, in which the early modern Mediterranean "was composed of isolated blocks, secure and content in their foreignness,"[3] have been convincingly undercut, and a more variegated and equivocal understanding of Mediterranean culture in this time has emerged. This sophisticated analysis of identity and cultural exchanges has produced a more subtle and nuanced portrait of the real rather than the rhetorical nature of every-day existence and of the ways that potentially discordant individuals and groups were able to live in close proximity and in relative harmony.

One of the keys to this accommodation was the often fluid and functional nature of identity among early modern peoples, their ability to accept inconsis-tency and discontinuity in ways that may seem confusing or impossible in a world such as ours in which rigid religious, racial, sexual, and political boundaries are often conjured. However, it seems clear that instead of imagining the early mod-ern Mediterranean in our modern image, inspired by the primacy of the nation-state paradigm, we would do better to view this age as a shared world of soft boundaries,[4] of porous frontiers inhabited by culturally, politically and religiously diverse groups who struggled to be sure, but often succeeded in living together as neighbors in relative tranquility.

Three general areas serve to illustrate the character of the peaceful relations between Venetians and Ottomans in early modern Constantinople—geography, economy, and sociability. A detailed study of each reveals that Venetians and Ottomans did not exist in isolation from each other but in fact had regular and meaningful interactions across a wide spectrum. These relations were similar to those of most complex societies: at times they were characterized by cooperation, support, and even amity, at times by controversy and disagreement. While we cannot ignore the ample evidence of antagonism and discord that have informed past discussions of the early modern Mediterranean, a more complete under-standing of relations between religious and cultural groups in this age must also make room for the very compelling evidence of regular, recurring "cordial interaction."[5]

GEOGRAPHY

Greater Constantinople—comprising the capital, Galata, Eyup, and Üsküdar (formerly Scutari)[6]—was an immense, diverse metropolis that drew people from all over the Mediterranean, Near East, and Europe. The beauty and allure of the seat of the sultans were part of the draw, but most attractive were the many opportunities that it promised. The city itself was huge: Thomas Sherley thought it "the greatest citye that euer I sawe."[7] He was certainly right: contempora-ries hazarded wild guesses at Constantinople's size, ranging from 600,000 to

1,231,207.[8] Modern historians estimate the city's population was from 300,000 to 500,000.[9] Whatever its actual size, Constantinople was without peer: it was the largest city in the Mediterranean, Europe, or the Near East.

Behind these population figures lay an extremely diverse community. A 1535 survey found the city divided into 46,635 Muslim, 25,292 Christian, and 8,070 Jewish households. Similarly, a 1550 census found that the total population was approximately 400,000, composed of 40,000 Christian houses, 4,000 Jewish, and 60,000 Muslim. In both of these surveys the population was approximately 58 percent Muslim and 42 percent non-Muslim.[10]

Constantinople's mixed character would seem to suggest that the city functioned as something of a cultural middle ground in which communal and individual boundaries were softer and more porous. In fact, scholars have argued quite the opposite, positing an image of geographical isolationism in which individuals and groups rarely mixed, or even crossed paths, living instead in separation, both self-imposed and mandated by their rulers. Seen in this fashion, Constantinople conformed to the model "Oriental city," composed of "an array of closed and compact societies, each leading lives separate from the other."[11] For Braude and Lewis, the Ottoman Empire represents a classical plural society in which "the medley of peoples" inhabits the same geographical space but never combines, living "side by side, but separately." In this segregated setting, "each group holds its own religion, its own culture and language, its own ideas and ways."[12] Robert Mantran similarly describes Constantinople's population as concurrently mixed and separated: minorities grouped around a church or synagogue in "isolated cores amidst the Turkish masses."[13]

In Constantinople, this proximate isolation was expressed spatially in the separation between Constantinople and Galata, the suburb facing the capital from across the Golden Horn. Despite its propinquity, Galata historically had been quite distinct from its much larger neighbor. No bridges connected the two cities until the nineteenth century, so crossings were made in one of the fifteen to sixteen thousand small boats (*perme*) that plied the waters of the Golden Horn. This expanse of sea symbolized and accentuated the fissure between the two cities.[14] Prior to 1453, Galata was home to the sizable and largely independent Genoese merchant community. After his conquest of the Byzantine capital, Mehmed II left the suburb relatively untouched so as not to interrupt its commerce, but he did incorporate it entirely into the larger metropolitan institutional structures of his new capital. The area became something of a ghetto for most of the capital's non-Ottomans, who gradually relocated there. The Venetian community in Byzantine times had been located within Constantinople proper, but following the Ottoman conquest, despite Venetian attempts to regain their old quarter, the community and the bailo's house were removed to Galata.[15]

In the sixteenth and seventeenth centuries, many travelers commented on what they perceived as the European, or "Frankish," character of Galata, or Pera. George Sandys reported "Pera hath three Christians for one Mahometan: for no Jew dwells in Pera, though they have their flops there." Pigafetta challenged this last assertion, but generally agreed with Sandys: "Most of the inhabitants are Greeks, then Venetians, French, a few Turks and very many Jews . . . Here, in sum, one appears to be in a city of Italy." Nicolay acknowledged that there were Muslims in Galata but described the city as being divided by three walls, which separated the Greeks from the Muslims and from the "Peratins."[16] Ottomans too considered Galata as "part of *Frengistan* or Europe"; indeed, for Ottoman-Muslims, Galata represented the morally dangerous other to Istanbul. For writers from the sultan Mehmed II to the famed seventeenth-century traveler Evliya Çelebi, Galata was the city of the Franks and as such symbolized "vice and depravity."[17]

This geographical separation, according to an earlier generation of scholars, had broader social implications. Mantran argues that as a result of the demographic engineering of the sultans, Galata became the "City of the Infidels" facing the "City of the Ottomans." By 1650, it had effectively become a "European residential city," with an insignificant Muslim minority of several hundred. Not only did a meager number of Muslims inhabit Galata, but those who did rarely mixed with the Franks, who in turn "were not . . . in contact with the Turks." In the Vigne di Pera suburb of Galata where their embassies were located, Europeans were even more completely insulated from contact with "Turks." For Mantran, this situation resulted in a minimum of xenophobia and interreligious strife in Constantinople, as there were so few actual encounters between Franks and Turks.[18]

There is increasing evidence that this clean division between Muslim Constantinople and infidel Galata, and the simplistic vision of cultural encounters and interaction it suggests, has been seriously overstated. The view that Muslims were forbidden to settle in Galata is based on the misinterpretation of the *ahidname* granted by Mehmed II to the Genoese in Galata in 1453. As İnalcık has shown, the passage "no *doghandjı* or *kul* shall come and stay as guests in their households" was a common stipulation in Ottoman grants that guaranteed no military men would be quartered in private houses.[19] It did not imply that Muslims were forbidden to settle in the city, and there is ample proof that many did.[20] As Galata grew after the Ottoman conquest, it came to be peopled by as wide a spectrum of people as Constantinople. One traveler's observation suggests the cosmopolitan face of the city: "The natural inhabitants of this city are Greeks, Turks and Jews; infinite then the other men of other various and distant nations who are living here." These included Spanish, Italians, Germans, Russians, English, French, Dutch, and even men from far away Peru.[21]

Beyond travelers' anecdotes, the multicultural, and increasingly Muslim, face of Galata appears clearly in Ottoman documents. Indeed, settling Muslims in Galata was a deliberate part of the sultans' demographic policies: Süleyman established a community of Egyptians in Galata, and waves of Moor and Morisco refugees from Granada settled in the city in the sixteenth and seventeenth centuries.[22] A survey of 1455 shows that within two years of the conquest of Constantinople, a Muslim quarter had been established near the Tower of Galata. A document of 1477–78 reports that Galata was inhabited by 535 Muslim, 592 Greek, 332 Frank, and 62 Armenian households.[23] Kasımpaşa, the main arsenal of the empire; the cannon foundry at Tophane; and the Acemioğlan school of Galata Seraglio were all products of Mehmed II's resettlement efforts, and they attracted increasing numbers of Muslims. There were also numerous Ottoman officials and their subalterns in the city, as well as a group of five to six hundred soldiers responsible for maintaining the peace. By 1500, despite its physical separation, Galata ceased to be a distinct entity but was fully assimilated into the broader, Ottoman, Muslim capital complex of cities and suburbs. By 1600, Ottoman Galata had a Muslim majority, and by 1700, there were only six non-Muslim churches, as opposed to twelve mosques, in the city.[24]

Contemporary observers noted the evolving Muslim character of Galata. Giovanni Moro in 1590 reported that while Galata was previously inhabited only by Christians, "at present, because the city of Constantinople is not sufficient for the great concourse of Turks, the long tract of marina [Kasımpaşa] . . . is occupied for the most part by" Ottoman-Muslims. A few years later, della Valle indicated that Galata had grown "particularly with a great number of Turks," and an ecclesiastical report of 1625 indicated that its inhabitants were "for the most part foreigners of diverse nations, though the Turks, who hold the government of it, inhabit the greater part."[25] Far from being an infidel ghetto, then, Galata was a place of encounter and engagement at the heart of the diverse population of Constantinople.

Exact demographic figures for Galata are difficult to establish with precision. Certainly Evliya Çelebi's estimate of 200,000 infidels and 64,000 Muslims is highly inflated. More reflective of the city's makeup perhaps, is his report that by the mid-seventeenth century, Galata had ninety-three neighborhoods—seventy Greek, seventeen Muslim, three European, two Armenian, and one Jewish. According to Stoianovich, a typical neighborhood (*mahalle*) contained an average of forty houses, with approximately seven people per house, which translates to a population of perhaps 26,000. Mantran's estimate is higher: he estimates Galata's population as approximately one-tenth of Constantinople's, for a total of perhaps 40,000 to 50,000 people.[26]

There was no agreement on the number of non-Ottomans and Ottoman-Catholics in Galata: in 1581 Pietro Cedulini counted 500 free Ottoman-Catholic subjects, 500 freed slaves (*libertini*), 5–600 foreigners passing through, and 100 persons attached to embassies. In addition, he estimated that there were 6–7,000 slaves in the arsenal and port. A 1616 Ottoman census of all Europeans revealed approximately 1,000 resident in Galata, and a report from 1626 indicated that the remaining families of Genoese extraction totaled 43 *casate* comprising 55 families, or 550 people, as well as perhaps 500 *libertini*, and an unknown number of slaves.[27] Galata's Jewish population too increased steadily in the period after Lepanto: a tax register of 1690 listed 1,033 Jews in Galata who paid the poll tax, second in number only to the Jews in Constantinople proper, as well as a small group in the Vigne di Pera.[28]

While people of all religious and cultural backgrounds lived throughout the city, they did tend to congregate around geographical poles. The most important Perot concentration was near the Galata Tower, which had been formerly the aristocratic center of the Genoese community. The old center of the city was also the focus of the growing Jewish population. Lagiro was inhabited predominantly by Greeks, in the area where four Greek churches still exist. Azapkapı, to the west, was mostly Muslim, with a Dominican church converted into a mosque there. The Muslim inhabitants of Galata generally grouped together to the west of the Galata Tower, particularly in the area of Kasımpaşa, as many Muslims worked in the naval yards. There was also a Christian population in this area, grouped around the church of St. Demetrios.[29]

The city's divisions into religious and ethnic neighborhoods might suggest that the urban fabric of Constantinople included diverse groups living in proximity but ultimately separated from each other. However, the city had a more multifarious complexion in which boundaries were dynamic and often overlapped. Hints of this more varied urban, cultural geography emerge from scattered documents found in the notarial records of the Venetian chancellery, which register land transactions involving members of the nation but also the larger community of Galata. These records are not sufficient for mapping the ethnoreligious geography of Galata, or for constructing any concrete statistical picture; however, they contain data indicating that while neighborhoods might have had a predominant religious or ethnic makeup, such did not preclude people of diverse religious and cultural backgrounds living in close proximity.

The widowed Perot, Isabetta di Battista Salvaressa, for example, owned a house near the Porta del Cula that bordered on properties belonging to two Ottoman-Muslims. The Venetian dragoman Tommaso Navon inherited a house near Galata Seraglio, which was also near the house of Edoardo Gagliano. Another dragoman, Marcantonio Borisi, received as dowry a portion of a large house near San Francesco, on the main city street next to the house of a Muslim. He also had a summer house in the area of the seraglio to the east of a Muslim cemetery.[30] A Venetian merchant who died in Galata held a long-term lease on a house that belonged to a mosque, and a compatriot sold a house with two shops on the main floor, a courtyard and a well, located next to several Muslim neighbors.[31]

Religious property was not isolated either, as Borisi's property near the Muslim graveyard of Galata demonstrates. Some Muslims purchased Latin-rite ecclesiastical property: a document in the Vatican dated 1653 mentions the sale of a garden and a house on the edge of the church and convent of San Francesco, which "were sold to a Turk friend of ours to pay a tax of 30,000 reals to the grand vizier." The church of San Pietro also had neighboring Muslims, including a number of women.[32]

Economic and social considerations, as much as religion, played a role in residence location. This is particularly evident in the Vigne di Pera, even though this area has often been described as a predominantly Greek and Frank suburb. Most foreign embassies were moved there from Galata in the sixteenth century, and many merchants built luxurious stone houses in this desirable neighborhood as well. But as in other villages along the Bosporus, wealthy Jews, Christians, and Muslims lived next to each other.[33] The main road of Galata, now İstiklal Caddesi, was the axis of this tony suburb. Pigafetta reported that in Galata "at the top of the hill beyond the walls and the prison tower there are many houses with large gardens, both of Turks and of Greeks." The French embassy, and by 1620 the Dutch embassy, was also located close by.[34] In this same area were located a mosque (the former church of St. Catherine), across from the public baths, and the Galata Seraglio, where the pages of the sultans were trained. The earliest convent of the Mevlevi dervishes, founded in 1492, was also located in this area.[35]

Along this same main street, directly next to the French embassy, was the bailate of Venice.[36] Venetian documents record numerous Muslim neighbors of the baili. A renegade Muslim ship captain from Sebenico had a house immediately adjacent, and a "Hagi Jusuf Abdulla, head of a team of Caulkers in the arsenal," purchased a plot of land between the Venetian and the French embassies.[37] Many other Muslims also inhabited the immediate area. The baili were often on familiar terms with these neighbors and sometimes served as their patrons. One Muslim neighbor who was hoping to be awarded an important Ottoman office petitioned Marco Venier to intercede with the vizier on his behalf. Venier did so and reported that "the *paşa* indulged me very willingly."[38]

Living in close proximity also produced occasional problems. The bailate had a ceremonial portal that at some point in the sixteenth century had been bricked up at the instigation of the house's owner, the Venetian dragoman Matheca Salvago, and some Muslim neighbors. When Marco Venier tried to have it reopened, a group of "more than 2,000 Turks gathered from the streets and shops" and went to the divan shouting "come Muslims to defend the cause of the religion against a *Giaur*, who wants to overwhelm our houses," calling "Allah, Allah" and throwing their turbans to the ground. Venier collected testimonies from twenty neighbors who were "affectionate to this house" and also the testimony of a former *kadı* of Galata who was in favor of his initiative. With these he was able to obtain an imperial promise to punish anyone who blocked the action, and the door was reopened.[39]

COMMERCE

One of the chief areas of cultural intercourse in Galata was commerce; however, as one historian recently observed, we know comparatively little about the day-to-day nature of interactions between Ottoman and European merchants.[40] Rather than specific evidence, scholars have often relied on generalizations and assumptions: one such foundational assumption has been that although significant trade occurred between European states and the Ottoman Empire, it did not translate into tangible contacts between individual Muslims and Christians. Rather, commerce was carried out by resident European merchants with Ottoman minority populations—Greeks, Armenians, and especially Jews. A corollary to this is the widespread belief that Muslim Ottomans did not travel outside *dar al-Islām* to trade with infidels.

The historical roots of the binary view of early modern Mediterranean commerce are deep. Among contemporary European travelers it was a common assumption that "Turks" did not engage in trade directly, depending instead on non-Muslim intermediaries. The English traveler Fynes Moryson, for example, reported "all the precious traffick of Turkey, by reason of the inhabitants slothfulnesse, is in the hands of Jewes and of Christians, and was long in the sole hands of the Venetians." He continues: Turks "traded in Natolia, and other parts of their owne Empire . . . but they take no voyage by sea into forraigne parts, excepting some few that come to Venice . . . So as the Jewes, the Greeks subject to the Turks, and other confederate Christians, exporting their commodities, they themselves have very few ships." The Scottish traveler William Lithgow observed in 1632, "The whole commerce of all commodities in Turkey is in the hands of Jewes and Christians, . . . who so warily manage their businecs that they enjoyed the most profits of any trading there, disappointing the Turks owne subjects of their due and ordinary traficke." A Venetian source states it more bluntly: "Turks are not merchants."[41]

This picture of Mediterranean commerce permeates influential nineteenth and early twentieth century works on the Ottoman Empire and Mediterranean trade—Hammer, Iorga, Heyd—in part because of their reliance on travel narratives. Heyd maintains, for example, that "Turks . . . had no taste for trade . . . but rather [an] insatiable passion for conquest."[42] Gibb and Bowen's *Islamic Society and the West* similarly states, "The European trade was entirely in the hands of Christians (European and Levantine) and Jews."[43] Mantran, too, subscribes to this vision of Mediterranean commerce: he argues that Muslims found commerce with non-Muslims "repugnant," and thus avoided travel to trade outside the *dar al-Islām*. Foreign, non-Muslim merchants did travel to Constantinople and other Islamic ports, but they traded through intermediaries because doing business with fellow Christians created a climate of comprehension that could never be duplicated with Asiatic Muslims who had a different language, religion, and culture.[44] This same view is evident in Bernard Lewis's work: he argues, in language clearly inspired by Mary Douglas's *Purity and Danger,* that Ottoman-Muslims attempted systematically to avoid what he calls the "dirty trades"—banking, diplomacy, commerce, in short anything that involved "dealing with foreigners, [who were] seen by strict Muslims as tainted and dangerous to the[ir] souls." They "were preserved from contact and, as they saw it, contamination by a large class of intermediaries" composed of non-Muslim subjects, manumitted slaves, refugees, and renegades who "served as a cushion, or perhaps more precisely as an insulation protecting the host Muslim society from the culture shock of European impact."[45]

Whether Ottoman-Muslim merchants ought to trade among infidels was, of course, also widely debated among medieval and early modern Muslim scholars. Some forbade any commerce with the infidel, who might use profits to pursue war against Islam. Others maintained that trade and travel to the West were permissible only to get food in time of shortage. One school of thought held that Muslims could travel outside *dar al-Islām* only to ransom Muslim captives. Other

Qur'anic scholars believed that it was acceptable to travel abroad for trade, as well as to accept infidels into Muslim lands for the same purpose.[46] Clearly there existed no single attitude in the Islamic world toward trade with outsiders. One reason Muslims were discouraged from venturing abroad was the intolerance, amply demonstrated over one thousand years of shared history, of Christians for Muslims. Another danger was that exposure to the tainting influence of the West would induce conversions among peripatetic Muslims, something that did occur often enough to warrant concern.[47] Interestingly, this same argument was used to discourage young Christians from traveling to Muslim lands.

If the theological explanation for Muslim indifference to commerce with Christian Europe is not entirely convincing, some scholars have advanced an even more problematic ethnocultural reading that depicts the "Turks" as warrior steppe peoples who had no inclination to sea-travel or to trade. Thus, the powerful Ottoman navy and merchant fleet was manned not by Ottoman-Muslims, but by Greek subjects more inclined to seafaring. The "Turks" wanted to make Constantinople the economic center of the Mediterranean, but as steppe warriors with little commercial acumen, they relied on minority subjects—Jews, Armenians—with a strong background in trade.[48] A variant on this view acknowledges that some European Muslims did trade in the *dar al-Harb* but implies that these newer adherents to Islam were somehow less Muslim than their Asiatic co-religionists, and thus more inclined to travel abroad.[49]

In recent years, however, this paradigm has been challenged by Ottomanists who have expressed a "growing discomfort" with this "older school of thought."[50] Chief among these is Çemal Kafadar, who has argued that there is no evidence of any action or law by Ottoman political or religious authorities aimed at preventing Ottoman-Muslim merchants from trading with foreigners in or out of the empire. On the contrary, he has found traces of significant, long-term mercantile operations involving Ottoman-Muslims trading outside *dar al-Islām*, which enjoyed governmental and legal protection under Islamic law.[51] Other scholars have echoed this position, showing the occasional presence of Muslim merchants in Venice, for example, already in the fourteenth century, as well as extensive direct commerce between Ottoman-Muslims and Genoese in the fourteenth and fifteenth centuries.[52] Persian Muslim merchants too have been shown to have traded widely with non-Muslims both domestically and abroad.[53] Indeed, Maxime Rodinson sees this regular commercial contact as an engine for expanding cultural interaction and even comprehension. He has suggested that the increased factual knowledge of Islam in the late medieval and early modern periods was driven in good measure by the growth in commercial contacts and "the quest for commercial profit."⁵⁴

That early modern Ottoman-Muslims were extensively and directly involved in face-to-face commerce with Venetian merchants throughout the Mediterranean is amply, indeed exhaustively, borne out by Venetian sources.⁵⁵ These demonstrate that Ottoman trade was one of the few sectors of Venice's economy that remained relatively immune to the commercial troubles that became apparent in the late sixteenth century.⁵⁶ Appearances of Ottoman-Muslim merchants in the chancellery protocols of the Venetian nation in Constantinople are so common as to preclude a systematic consideration. While it is difficult to paint a comprehensive picture of individual merchants and their trade networks, in part due to the notational inconsistencies of Venetian secretaries and notaries, the experiences of several merchants emerge quite clearly from the documentary record that show the nature and extent of Veneto-Ottoman commercial contacts.⁵⁷

One such merchant was Çelebi Mehmed Reis of Ankara. Mehmed maintained a wide-ranging commercial network between Ankara, Constantinople, Venice, and Candia: he dealt primarily in woolen and silk cloths, leather, foodstuffs, and cash transfers.⁵⁸ He began shipping goods to Venice immediately following the end of the War of the Holy League in 1573, and he may well have been involved in trade prior to, and perhaps even during, the war when commerce was only partially and temporarily interrupted.⁵⁹ His chief contact in Venice was Lorenzo Girardi, one of the city's most important merchants, whom he addressed in letters as his "amico carissimo Signor Lorenzo."⁶⁰ Perhaps they had met in Venice or Constantinople, though both generally traded through agents, often family members. Mehmed usually sent his goods to Venice with several men, including his brother-in-law, Yusuf Çelebi. He also retained a number of agents in Galata, including Ottoman Jewish and Christian subjects.

Mehmed considered Girardi "a good and loyal man," and he authorized him to appear on his behalf before Venetian councils, and to trade in his name without other intermediaries or official brokers. By circumventing the normal channels of trade, Mehmed was obviously trying to avoid incurring additional operating costs. To further protect his interests, he had an agent in Galata register an official declaration in the Venetian chancellery and obtain a hüccet from the kadı of Constantinople stating that Girardi owed him no money and was authorized to buy and sell in his name. These documents were then sent to Venice to legitimate Girardi's status as Mehmed's representative.⁶¹ By utilizing both Venetian and Ottoman channels, which was very common, Mehmed effectively nurtured and protected his lucrative trade in the lagoon. By his own estimate, his commerce annually brought more than two thousand ducats into Venice's tax coffers.[62]

At one point, Çelebi Mehmed Reis had to defend himself against Michel Membrè, the dragoman of the Venetian chancellery, whom he claimed was overcharging on the fees paid to him by all Ottoman merchants in Venice. Grievances against Membrè were quite common: in 1587 a group of Muslim merchants and brokers complained that Membrè's monopoly of the dragoman's office was detrimental to Veneto-Ottoman commerce because of "the great quantity of merchandise belonging to these Turks that is conducted, purchased and sold, and which each day grows larger." They argued that more dragomans were needed to better deal with this expanding market. Indeed, after Membrè's death two men were granted his office in response to the increased trade of Ottomans in Venice.[63]

Another Ottoman-Muslim merchant trading in Venice was Resul Ağa, commercially active from at least 1600 to 1620.[64] Resul Ağa traded on a larger scale than Mehmed: by his own account, he sent annually between Venice and Constantinople 550 bolts of camlets, 40 bales of silk, 200 bales of wax, as well as other goods, in addition to 20,000 ducats in cash. These brought in more than 700 ducats to Venice at the special 2 percent customs rate that Ottoman merchants enjoyed. In 1620 it was rumored that he had in Venice 8,000 ducats worth of goods—including wool and silk cloths and paper—and specie.[65] He shipped these goods by caravan from Constantinople to Spalato and then by ship to Venice, where at various times he engaged Jewish, Venetian, and Muslim factors. Besides this overland trade, he also regularly sent ships to Candia.[66] In 1620, Resul Ağa and several other Ottoman merchants lost a ship to corsairs in the Adriatic; the resultant controversy threatened the Veneto-Ottoman peace and ended in the execution of Marcantonio Borisi, the Venetian grand dragoman. The situation was resolved through diplomatic channels, and a "gift" of 3,700 ducats to Resul Ağa, who quickly became deeply invested in Venetian commerce again, to the point of lending 3,000 ducats to the bailo to cover the embassy's expenses when funds could not be raised from within the Venetian nation.[67]

Ottoman officials appear to have been among the most active participants in the Veneto-Ottoman trade. Though they rarely traveled outside the empire, they nonetheless invested significant capital in this lucrative enterprise. The importance of commercial dealings by the Ottoman elite has often been overlooked; some scholars have argued that the "administrative bourgeoisie" of upper- and mid-level functionaries were first-class consumers but uninvolved in commerce. Suraiya Faroqhi has allowed that occasionally important administrators used their privileges to profit from trade, but she argues that most Ottoman officials in the early modern period subscribed to Ibn Khaldûn's view that "commercial activity on the part of the ruler is harmful to his subjects and ruinous to the tax revenue" and that such involvement would lead to political decline.[68]

Venetian records, however, present compelling evidence that many Ottoman grandees did actively participate in trade, suggesting that views like Khaldûn's may have been more prescriptive than descriptive. Naima, the great Ottoman historian, acknowledged as much when he included political authority, *emâret*, as one of three main ways to gain wealth, the other two being agriculture and commerce. More recently, Metin Kunt has shown how an important Ottoman official of the seventeenth century, Derviş Paşa, was actively engaged in agriculture and commerce, and annually imported forty million *akçe* of luxury goods alone, all non-taxable. Derviş appears not to have been alone: Peçevi, a seventeenth-century Ottoman historian reported that in the previous century the income of frontier *paşas* and beys far exceeded that of the viziers, and de Groot has argued that if early modern Ottoman grandees "did not enter the marketplace in person . . . [they did understand] how to profit from foreign trade," often retaining merchants who traded for them, even in contraband if profitable.[69]

Officials' involvement in commercial activities can be traced back at least to the conquest of Constantinople, when Çandarlı Halil Paşa traded with prominent Venetian merchants immediately following the cessation of hostilities. Indeed, some gazis believed he had favored peace to advance his own business affairs. Early evidence of "*Askeri* entrepreneurialism" became more common in the sixteenth century. Both İbrahim and Rüstem Paşas, grand viziers under Süleyman Kanuni, had important commercial considerations, and Kafadar has found that, despite efforts to discourage it, even the famed janissary corps often engaged in commerce, including in contraband goods.[70] Because Italian cities were willing to pay higher prices for grain than the capital's command economy would, a widespread illegal trade arose involving timar holders, governors, janissaries, and even the ulema, who could earn up to 20 percent above official grain prices by selling to Venetians.[71] As one historian has suggested, by the late sixteenth century "contraband carried the day," and Ottoman officials were not opposed to benefiting from this economic situation, despite its real dangers: one vizier was executed, due in part to charges that he had stolen goods from the people and traded them in Christendom.[72]

There was significant commercial activity by Ottoman officials and soldiers with the Venetian nation in Constantinople. For example, a janissary, Mahmud, who had "a fruit shop in the Tophane," is mentioned, as are several other janissaries who sent seventeen sacks of cotton to Venice and were granted a customs' exemption because they needed to leave for the Persian front.[73] Another group which naturally tended toward commerce was the *çavuşes*, members of the Birun-u hümayun, or the palace's external service, who, because of their frequent official travels outside the empire, were in a position both to carry their own goods and to make contacts with agents who could represent them. As Pedani-Fabris has shown, some fifty-four of these representatives traveled to Venice between 1570 and 1645. In some instances the *çavuş* came specifically for official, commercial purposes on behalf of the sultan or some other important figure in the Porte, functioning as something akin to a "marchand de la Cour." More often, they engaged in trade on the side for their personal benefit.[74]

One such emissary actively involved in Levantine commerce was Hamza Çavuş. He owned at least two ships (the *Santa Maria di Loreto* and the *San Giovanni Battista*) that plied the Mediterranean from Chios to Venice and on which Venetian merchants regularly bought space, despite laws which forbade their use of foreign vessels: Hamza also transported his goods on Venetian ships.[75] He utilized the bailo's court to resolve commercial conflicts, and in one instance he agreed to accept a Christian, appointed by the bailo, as an arbitrator in a commercial disagreement involving Piero de Grassi, a Venetian merchant. The arbitrator's resolution, accepted by both merchants, favored Hamza and ordered Grassi to pay him 6,000 *akçe*.[76] From the available records it seems that Hamza never traveled to Venice in an official capacity, but he did retain the services of a merchant who had been active in Constantinople for some years, Pasqualino Leoni, whom he knew personally, to ship silk from Venice. These goods were sent in the name of Hamza's son, Mehmed, perhaps as a ruse to avoid duties or legal entanglements.[77]

Commercial involvement was not limited to the *çavuşes*. Other, more influential Ottoman officials also participated, as the case of Ca'fer Paşa suggests. Ca'fer (written variously by Venetian scribes as Giaffer, Cafer, Ga'fer), a Calabrian renegade who was probably initially captured by corsairs (Selaniki says he came to the Porte from Tunis), was described in Venetian records as a *"homo savio, amico de cristiani."*[78] While he held a variety of important positions, Ca'fer made something of a career as *beylerbeyi* of the newly conquered *eyālet* of Cyprus, serving there on three separate occasions. In 1587 he turned down a more prestigious office in favor of remaining on the island, and in 1603 he paid bribes of 6,000 ducats, and gave an advance of 25,000 ducats to the sultan on the monies he anticipated collecting, in order to be reappointed *beylerbeyi* of Cyprus.[79] From both Ottoman and Venetian sources we can follow Ca'fer's later career: Naima reports that "Ja'fer Pasha, the European, who had been three times the *beylerbeyi* of Cyprus" became *kapudanpaşa,* though he was almost immediately replaced. According to Selaniki, "Frenk Ca'fer Pasha" then became *beylerbeyi* of Tripoli, though he "was dismissed upon it being said, 'He has not sent the Treasury shipment on time.'" A Venetian document indicates that Ca'fer then became *beylerbeyi* of Cairo.[80]

One reason Ca'fer coveted the governorship of Cyprus was his extensive involvement in Levantine trade, stretching from at least 1587 to the last years of his life. The fact that his house was located in the *bedestan* of Galata, amid all the European merchants, is some indication of his commercial involvements.[81] Ca'fer was especially active in the cotton trade, which had been an important Cypriot export since at least the fourteenth century: in one transaction he sent cotton valued at 4,536 ducats to Venice via a Candiot merchant; in another, eighty-one sacks of cotton were shipped to the lagoon.[82] Ca'fer utilized his high positions as a means to increase his own personal wealth; technically his cotton exports were considered contraband, as cotton cloth and thread were classed as strategic material needed for ship sails. It is possible he used his status to procure an export license, though these were in theory difficult to obtain.[83] He sent his goods to Venice marked with his official seal so that they would be recognized and given preferential treatment, had Venetian secretaries come to his residence to create legal documents that were presented before the V Savii, and in several instances corresponded directly with the doge regarding his financial dealings.[84] He also informed the baili on matters in the divan and worked to free Venetian slaves and to protect Venice's interests in the Ottoman Empire, no doubt to curry favor for his own interests, both political and economic.

While Ca'fer personally managed his commerce and intervened with Venetian authorities on his own behalf, he employed a variety of Greek, Muslim, and Jewish agents to carry out the actual trading. This is not surprising given the importance of his government offices and the weighty responsibilities associated with them. He also worked with Venetian merchants, such as Giacomo Biasii, who carried a shipment of Ca'fer's cotton to Venice, where he was to turn over the profit to either the *beylerbeyi*'s Cypriot or Muslim agent in the city. Biasii eventually died en route to Venice, and Ca'fer commissioned the Ottoman-Jewish merchant David Abudenti's agent in Venice, Rabbi Mosè Mazaod, to recover the goods from Biasii's heirs. In addition, Ca'fer engaged Pasqualino Leoni, who also traded with Resul Ağa, to recover money owed him by a Cypriot merchant and the former Venetian consul of Cyprus, and he did business with a Venetian patrician from the Ruzini clan.[85] Ca'fer also owned and operated a ship on the route between Constantinople and Candia in partnership with a Greek, perhaps Candiot, merchant.[86]

After becoming *kapudanpaşa* in 1607, he continued in his commercial dealings. In that year, he had the Venetian secretary come to his ship and, "speaking in Frankish," declared he had received 5,000 ounces of gold from Abudenti, whose agent had collected them from the office of the V Savii in Venice. By 1609, Ca'fer had lost his position as head of the Ottoman fleet but still sent ten sacks of cotton to Venice, again through Abudenti's agent in the city. He died in 1620 and left a fortune of 200,000 ducats.[87]

Ca'fer Paşa is not the only Ottoman official involved in commercial activities to appear in Venetian records.[88] It was quite common for the "upper administrative class" to invest their fortunes with merchants involved in international commerce.[89] Indeed, Muslim agents trading on behalf of the sultans at times came to Venice; the shahs of Persia likewise often sent goods with factors to Venice, and even as far as London.[90] Grand viziers were quite active in the Venetian trade, as in the case of Süleyman's viziers. In 1598 Bernardin and Agostino Agazzi, two successful Venetian merchants in Constantinople, received 190,680 *akçe* from Mustafa Bey, agent of the Grand Vizier İbrahim, as payment to their partner Pasqualino Leoni for silk cloths. Several years later, a Mehmed Ağa sent 130 bolts of camlet belonging to the Grand Vizier Nassuf to two Venetian agents.[91] In 1613, a grand vizier sent to Venice with Derviş Çavuş "fifty quantities of camlet that are his own goods, and another sixty quantities of silk which belong to the *casna* of the Grand Signor, so that they may be sold, with the profit being reinvested in an equal amount of silk cloths to be conducted to Constantinople." In Venice, Derviş requested a customs exemption for the goods, which the V Savii opposed because of the bad precedent it would set for other Ottoman officials trading in Venice. The reasoning is illuminating: "under this cover of exempting the merchandise of the principal Turkish ministers, all the merchandise from here on out would be made out as belonging to these subjects," suggesting that commerce by Ottoman officials was significant enough that such a precedent could threaten Venetian customs' income.[92]

Despite the V Savii's negative response, Ottoman grandees regularly requested special treatment for their goods and agents. In 1590, another grand vizier preparing to send twenty thousand ducats' worth of raw silk to Venice requested that Girolamo Lippomano provide a letter recommending his factor as a form of insurance. The bailo reported to the Senate: "I considered all the perils of the voyages, of the negotiation, and even though I was very pleased for him to send his capital to that city [Venice], and that he might become increasingly involved by having his goods there . . . [nonetheless] I did not want to put either my pen or my word on this enterprise."[93] Instead, the bailo convinced the vizier to send his goods with the Venetian-Ottoman merchant Edoardo Gagliano, thus avoiding taking official responsibility for the safe arrival of the merchandise.

As this dispatch suggests, involvement in trade with Ottoman officials could be a double-edged sword. While their commerce was greatly sought after, direct involvement in facilitating this trade had the potential to open the door to requests for special treatment, tax exemptions, priority in loading goods on ships with limited space, trade in contraband goods, avoidance of customs duties, and especially Venetian liability for damages incurred in transit.[94] Despite all these negative ramifications, Venetian officials tried to accommodate these influential merchants because of the value of their official trade. They helped them penetrate the Venetian bureaucracy, introduced them to agents, intervened in disputes, and even occasionally reduced duties on their goods. When one grand vizier requested a customs exemption, the V Savii, in recognition of the "temper of this negotiation," recommended that he be given an expensive gift of clothing and that his goods be assessed only a half duty. They reasoned that it was important to retain his friendship because he was in a position to "bring great benefit to the port of Spalato," which was one of Venice's most successful commercial initiatives at the turn of the century. In a similar incident, a commercial dispute prevented the departure of a caramousal owned by a high Ottoman official. The V Savii recommended that the matter be expedited since the patron was "of the Turkish nation . . . [and] has conducted diverse goods in this city; it is not convenient that he be impeded in his negotiations with length and difficulties and litigations."[95]

It was also not uncommon for merchants representing high Ottoman officials to be caught with contraband, or goods on which the appropriate duties had not been paid. Venice had to proceed with caution in these instances, as strict enforcement of commercial laws had potential political ramifications. In 1615, for example, contraband merchandise belonging to three officials was confiscated. In an attempt to avoid controversy, the Senate directed the bailo to explain that while Venice favored Ottoman merchants, this case was too serious to be overlooked, and had to be pursued in order to ensure that other merchants respected Venetian laws. In another instance, several Ottoman-Muslim agents carrying merchandise belonging to "a very important Turkish minister of the Grand Signor in the city of

Bursa" asked for the return of some silk that had been concealed among other goods without a bill of lading. The V Savii granted this request, though they required that the appropriate duties be paid on the cloth.[96]

Despite such incidents, Venice's policy was to facilitate all Ottoman trade, regardless of who brought it to the city. With Ottoman officials this was accomplished by sending secretaries and dragomans to register their commercial transactions, by providing safe-conducts and letters of introduction, and by obtaining a range of special privileges for them. This policy was maintained in recognition of the reciprocal nature of the relationship between the Ottoman and Venetian officials. Each provided important services to the other and facilitated his (or occasionally her, as in the case of several influential Ottoman women in the harem) political and commercial objectives—personal or public. Again, the case of Ca'fer Paşa is illustrative: he assisted Venice by carrying important correspondence to Cyprus at the request of the bailo and wrote personally (in Italian) to various baili informing them on internal machinations, private meetings and important developments in the Porte. Ca'fer also attempted to influence Ottoman policies in Venice's favor. In a 1594 letter to Marco Venier, written to reassure him "that I have not forgotten our friendship and promises," Ca'fer reported on his efforts to free a number of slaves and his intervention with the kapudanpaşa to protect Venetian territories, concluding "God knows that which I have done . . . for every one of your territories, both on sea and on land."[97]

The relationship was not one-sided, of course. Ca'fer was neither a turncoat nor a Venetian mole, but rather engaged in a personal diplomacy that furthered both his personal political and economic fortunes, as well as those of the sultan, and benefited Venice at the same time. Because of the complex layers of his identity—former Christian, Ottoman-Muslim official, international merchant, personal friend—it was not a stretch for him to serve his Ottoman master and benefit from contacts with his former co-religionists. In implicit exchange for his assistance, the baili provided Ca'fer with information and interventions that favored him economically and politically. In 1601, when a dispute before the V Savii between Ca'fer and his agent was proceeding "with some lukewarmness," Agostino Nani encouraged the Senate to expedite the matter because, he wrote, the Ottoman was in a position to help or hurt the city. Two years later, the bailo Francesco Contarini discussed with the grand vizier some problems that had occurred in Cyprus "because Ca'fer Paşa had not been found there, whose governance of the island was very pleasing to our merchants because of his good qualities." Contarini intervened at the Porte "at the request of Ca'fer," and this combined with the six thousand ducats in gifts Ca'fer expended, certainly played a role in his reappointment as *beylerbeyi* of Cyprus two months later.[98] While merchants such as Ca'fer Paşa, Resul Ağa, and Hamza Çavuş were certainly among the more important Ottoman merchants trading with Venice, the template of their experiences was not unique or exceptional. Evidences of numerous other Muslim merchants also appear in lesser detail in Venetian notarial records.[99]

Just as Ottomans engaged directly in commerce with Venice, so too Venetian records reinforce that Ottoman-Muslim merchants did travel extensively outside Islamic lands, either carrying their own goods, or those of other merchants and officials. Compelling evidence from throughout Europe and the Near East supports this assertion: in the late sixteenth century there was an Ottoman-Muslim merchant community in Calicut, a similar enclave of 400 traders in Diu in western India, and numerous "Turkish and Arab merchants" in the Javanese town of Bantam. Ottoman-Muslim (and Persian) merchants were present at fairs in central Italy already in 1524, and a Florentine document of 1521 refers to "Turks and Greeks [in Florence] to buy good loads of cloth."[100] An English account of the late sixteenth century mentions the visit of a Mustafa to London "come but slenderly attended with some dozen of Turkes," and Nabil Matar's recent work suggests that this was not an isolated incident.[101] And recently Gilles Veinstein has shown the importance of Ottoman merchants, both official and independent, in Poland-Lithuania and Moscow in the first half of the sixteenth century, who traded in furs, falcons, tin and hides.[102]

One of the most frequent destinations of Ottoman merchants was Venice: when Henry Blount sailed from the city for Constantinople in 1634, he reported that he was the only Christian on the ship and was surrounded by "Turks and Jewes" returning from trading to the Ottoman capital.[103] A small, intermittent Muslim presence in Venice can be traced back to the early fifteenth century.[104] Ottomans had received reciprocal rights to trade in Venice already in 1419, and reports of Muslims in the city appear throughout the fifteenth century. Indeed, Ottoman merchants were favored with lower customs rates and other special treatment that put them on the same level in many ways as the official patrician merchants of Venice.[105] This Muslim presence in Venice is underlined visually by the turbaned figures dressed in eastern garb who begin cropping up in late fifteenth century Venetian paintings, such as Bellini's *Procession of the Relic of the True Cross*, Mansueti's *Miracle of the Relic at San Lio*, and Carpaccio's *Healing of a Possessed Man*.[106]

By 1546 Ottoman merchants' extended visits to the lagoon seem to have become quite regular, as suggested by the rising number of complaints about damages and petitions for retribution both to Venetian and Ottoman authorities, and the increase in *çavuşes* sent to the lagoon to treat these types of issues. These visits became so frequent that the Grand Vizier Rüstem Paşa reportedly felt "embarrassed" by their regularity. By 1567, the number of Muslim merchants was notable enough that the papal nuncio to Venice judged that the "multitude of Turks" might prove a fertile ground for Jesuit missionaries. Statistics from the War of the Holy League give concrete numbers to this anecdotal evidence: seventy-five Muslims and ninety-seven Jews trading in Venice in 1570 were arrested and held at the outbreak of the war, and immediately following the peace of 1573 their numbers began to grow significantly.[107] While it is impossible to establish the exact value of this commerce, we get some indication from Bailo Matteo Zane who in 1594 indicated that if the "Turks" and Jews could be compelled to pay all their duties the *cottimo* in Constantinople would increase by four thousand ducats annually, almost double the five thousand ducats he was presently collecting. The *cottimo* on incoming goods at the end of the century was 0.75 percent, and on outgoing goods was 1.25 percent, thus the value of this Ottoman trade would appear to have been in the range of 400,000 ducats annually.[108]

Yet another indication of the growing presence of Ottoman-Muslim merchants in Venice is the growing number of brokers (*sensale* or *sansar* in Italian, from the Arabic *simsâr*) who were sanctioned by the V Savii. In 1587 their number was estimated at between fifteen and twenty, which was a significant increase in response to the great growth in the number of "Turkish" merchants trading in Venice. These brokers were described as "men of little good, some of them having turned Christian from Turk or Jew." In 1582, two Muslims, "Hasan and Risuan, heads of the Bosnian nation," requested that the V Savii appoint a Slavic-speaking broker, as they felt they were being taken advantage of due to language difficulties. The regular brokers opposed this, stating that of the twenty brokers in Venice who knew Turkish, four knew Slavic as well.[109] By 1621, when the much larger *Fondaco dei turchi* in its present location on the Canal Grande opened (yet another indication of the increasing presence of Muslim merchants),[110] there were thirty-three "Turkish" brokers out of a total of 190.[111]

Of course the presence of such a large number of persons regarded as infidels could create difficulties within the city, and not only commercially. In 1605 a "secret person" denounced a man who "publicly sells young men of bad life, conducting them in all places, even to Turks in their own hostels." Similarly, in 1603 several Ottoman-Muslims in Venice ran into difficulties with officials, including one man "accused of homicide," who had to pay a three hundred ducat fine, and a "Hungarian Turk" who paid a fifty ducat fine for drawing a weapon in piazza San Marco against Venetian officials.[112]

Veneto-Ottoman commerce was not limited to Muslims in Venice: though smaller than in previous centuries, as we have seen, the early modern Venetian merchant community in Constantinople was still involved in a wide range of commercial activities in which they traded and interacted directly with the Ottoman merchants of all stripes. One such example is long-distance shipping. Although the Senate, in an effort to stimulate Venetian shipping, forbade Venetian merchants from loading their goods on foreign ships, in the case of Ottoman ships this legislation was often ignored.[113] Venetian merchants regularly contracted with Muslim ship captains to carry merchandise, especially grain, to Venice and the *stato da mar*. In particular in 1592, when the Levantine wheat markets were temporarily reopened to foreign traders in response to the extreme shortage affecting Italy, numerous Ottoman captains and their ships were engaged to supply Venice's voracious appetite for grain.[114] Initially, Venetian merchants tried to send a Christian overseer with each ship, but this practice was quickly abandoned and Ottoman-Muslim captains were entrusted with large sums of cash to purchase grain, and the liberty to decide where and at what price to buy it, with no supervision.[115] Sales of ships between European and Muslim entrepreneurs were also quite common, as the cases of Ca'fer Paşa and Hamza Çavuş suggest, and even the renegade *kapudanpaşa* Çigalazade Sinan sold a ship to the French ambassador.[116]

Though in theory Venetian partnerships with Muslims, and indeed with all foreigners, were illegal, they did occur.[117] More common was intercommunal commerce: there is ample evidence that Venetian and Muslim merchants in Constantinople traded directly with each other, without intermediaries. In 1591, for example, Gianantonio and Francesco Perla, factors for the patrician Bertucci Ciuran, sold Ali, a merchant in Galata, sixty multicolored cloths. When a Venetian merchant, Pietro Pencini, failed and fled Constantinople "many Turkish merchants" came to the bailate trying to find him to resolve outstanding commercial matters. In another case, Tommaso Bonastori made a trade with Hasan Çelebi, "and they touched their hands two times saying that the bazaar was done, and that as a Muslim he would never back out on his promise." The Venetian had a *sensale* who interpreted the transaction, but he was directly involved in closing the deal. Bonastori also sold some Venetian paper directly to Süleyman Ağa, head of the Guild of Papermakers, who came to deal with him in person.[118]

One area in which Muslims were actively involved with Venetian merchants was money-lending. Though traditionally this activity has been associated with Jews, many Muslims, including members of the sultan's household, lent funds to European merchants and diplomats, often at rates significantly above those of their Jewish competitors.[119] Muslim religious endowments were also an important institutional player in the money-markets of Constantinople, and many Christian slaves received funds from them to purchase their freedom.[120] While Venetians, including members of the baili's household, preferred to borrow funds from within the trading nation, on occasion they turned to Muslim lenders, as when a Venetian dragoman obtained a loan of two hundred ducats at 15 percent interest from an Ottoman *çavuş*. The baili also borrowed, especially in the seventeenth century as *cottimo* funds became insufficient to cover the regular expenses of the chancellery, as evidenced in Resul Ağa's loan to Giorgio Giustinian. Related to this service, Ottoman-Muslims also served as pawn brokers for the international community.[121]

While scholars have often overstated the importance of minority intermediaries in Constantinople's commerce, there is no question that such figures were involved in commercial transactions, however, not to the exclusion of Muslim or Venetian merchants.[122] To a certain extent, intermediaries existed in both Venice and Constantinople to provide linguistic assistance and to ensure that neither party was defrauded, particularly in cases involving expensive goods. As the case of Bonastori indicates, this did not mean that Venetian or Muslim merchants did not treat directly with each other. In some instances, members of the Venetian nation even served as intermediaries for Ottoman-Muslim merchants, as when a Murad Paşa paid a Venetian *cernitor* two ducats to sell his wool for him. In other instances we find Jewish merchants sending goods to Venice under Ottoman names, as when David Abudenti sent some alum under the name of Kabil Ağa and his son Halil to Venice.[123]

While it is generally maintained that Jews were the primary intermediaries in Levantine commerce, in the Venetian sources they appear to have been more involved in their own trade. When an intermediary appeared on behalf of a merchant—Christian, Muslim, or Jew—that relationship was explicitly stated by the chancellery secretary. It is possible that Venetian merchants did utilize Jews (or other minorities) as intermediaries and simply did not indicate this fact in registering transactions. Given the sheer number of exchanges that occurred, however, one would expect a representative sampling to appear: instead they are quite rare.[124] This evidence would seem to support the contention that Venetian merchants, because of their long-standing experience and position in Constantinople, their familiarity with the modalities of commerce, their knowledge of local languages, and their relations with Ottoman authorities, generally did not rely on intermediaries. The exception to this was periods of war, when Venetian

merchants did resort to brokers, usually Jews, to continue their commercial dealings uninterrupted. In times of peace, however, because Venetian, Jewish, and
Ottoman-Muslim merchants all paid the same *cottimi*, any tax or customs benefit
available from trading through intermediaries was effectively removed.[125]

Recent research is showing more and more the inaccuracy of "old ideas received in the West [which] have generally exaggerated the reservations of Muslims
in the Ottoman Empire towards economic and commercial activities."[126] It is
clear that Ottoman-Muslim merchants, including important officials of the Porte,
were actively engaged in a lively, direct trade with Venetian merchants both in
Constantinople and Venice. The documentary evidence amply demonstrates that
Ottoman-Muslim merchants and their agents regularly traveled to and traded in
Venice. Minority intermediaries did not dominate the trade as has often been
held, though they certainly did play a role. Simple ethnocultural generalizations
about Muslims and commerce mask the more diverse and varied reality of trade
at all levels of society, both in Venice and in Constantinople, and they mask the
degree to which these commercial exchanges resulted in friendship and enduring
relationships between seemingly antithetical groups.

SOCIAL AND PERSONAL RELATIONSHIPS

In the decades after 1570 Ottoman society is generally depicted as becoming
increasingly xenophobic and closed, embracing traditional Islamic values and
refusing any real constructive relations with non-Muslims. In this era, it is said,
interaction between Ottomans and Europeans was confined "to an 'anomalous'
stratum of renegades." This view, however, overlooks the very real evidence of
interaction between the many groups present in the Ottoman capital, especially in
Galata. Renegades were able to penetrate Ottoman society with such ease precisely because they were not anomalies: "They already had much in common with
numerous others in this society, in which migration and conversion were common. There was a shared discourse even beyond the migrants and converts,
because there were shared interests."[127] The Venetian nation in Constantinople
provides extensive evidence of the existence of this shared intercultural discourse,
in which the malleable boundaries between Muslim and Christian, Ottoman, and
European permitted interaction across a wide spectrum of activities.

Given their long residences in Constantinople, and their regular interaction
with Ottomans of varying estates, it is no surprise that Venetians developed a
range of personal relationships with their hosts.[128] The dispatches contain many
references by baili and others to Ottoman-Muslims whom they describe as

friends. Gianfrancesco Morosini referred to a "Turk, an old friend of the household, a person of great consideration, who is *Müteferrika* of the scribes" of the sultan, who kept him regularly informed on the affairs of the palace. Similarly, Lorenzo Bernardo was accompanied on the first leg of his return trip home to Venice by "several Turkish friends of his household," and Ottaviano Bon refers several times to "Turks" who were his friends, including "Halil Paşa *amico mio*."[129]

Certainly this use of the term *amico* must be qualified and understood in its historical context. In Venetian diplomatic sources, *amico* was used to signify someone to whom a person was attached by affection, and someone who favored Venice and its representatives; a Venetian advice manual dating from the 1570s enjoins the ambassador "to gain for himself as friends the domestics and favorites of those that have authority."[130] Clearly a functional side to friendship existed; however, we cannot dismiss such relationships as entirely political. Certainly the pragmatic need not necessarily preclude the personal. Both aspects may, and often did, coexist. As one scholar has accurately observed, there existed in late medieval and early modern society a "tension . . . between the 'instrumental' and the idealistic sides of friendship."[131] The evidence suggests that the term *amico* was commonly used by Venetian and Ottoman representatives to describe relationships that went beyond official duties and pure, political interests. Regular diplomatic encounters, philosophical discussions, social engagements, and private correspondence all point to personal relationships that may more closely approximate modern, affective friendship.

Both the pragmatic and the personal elements of *amicizia* are clearly present in the experiences of numerous baili and Ottoman grandees. When Paolo Contarini arrived in Constantinople, he reported that Venice had no friends there due to changes in the Ottoman court, and so "I set myself with every means to procure several friendships, it appearing to me that they were necessary to terminate successfully negotiations, and to have the information which is so important and necessary to the government of [Venice]."[132] These means included personal visits with important officials, liberal use of gifts or bribes, providing a range of personal services, and the maintenance of an open table in the bailate to which many important Ottomans came regularly, and at which the wine flowed freely.[133] Another bailo, Ottaviano Bon, in referring to a vizier who was killed by order of the sultan, indicated "I cannot help but be pained by this mishap, because I had made him my close friend, and up to now I had obtained everything that I had asked."[134]

Ottoman officials similarly refer to Venetians as their *amici*, despite the belief of some observers that "Turks" were "not capable of real friendship toward a

Christian."[135] A *bostancıbaşı* who several times assisted Alvise Contarini, and indeed was reprimanded for being too favorable to the bailo, told the Venetian diplomat "you are my *buon amico*." When Giovanni Cappello visited the *kapudanpaşa*, "Seeing me before I had sat down, he took me by the hand and with words of affection called me his dear and beloved friend," and upon hearing that Cappello was leaving soon for Venice "he showed sorrow . . . trying to persuade me to have my family come here, with the promise that he would write to Your Lordship for my continued residence in these parts, adding that in any case he would never forget me."[136]

As this encounter suggests, because of the regular contact that their official duties imposed, it was not uncommon for the baili, secretaries, and other official members of the nation and important figures in the Porte to become friendly, even intimates. During a visit, an Ottoman official, sensing Cristoforo Valier was depressed, inquired, "What is wrong Bailo? Why are you in bad spirits? Why do you not laugh as you are wont to do?" When Agostino Nani went to congratulate a new vizier, "finding the *paşa* entirely unoccupied I remained for more than an hour reasoning with him about various pleasing things."[137] Official functions also provided opportunity for interaction. At the festivities celebrating Almoro Nani's presentation in the divan, an official commented that he looked like his brother, Agostino, who had been bailo a decade previous and said he hoped he would "be similar to him in other ways too." Because of the reputation of his brother, Nani also received several gifts usually reserved for extraordinary ambassadors, including two horses from the *beylerbeyi* of Greece, given as a "compliment for the friendship he already had with the brother of the new bailo."[138] Gifts could also be small, simple expressions of sentiment, such as the flowers that Halil Paşa, "having placed a hand on my shoulder," gave to Simone Contarini while both were waiting at the divan.[139] Friendships between Ottomans and Venetians were not limited to Constantinople: Sanudo reports that in 1522 the nobleman Gianfrancesco Mocenigo traveled from Mestre where he was *podestà* and *capitano* to Venice to visit with an Ottoman *çavuş*, with whom he had established a "close friendship" two years previous.[140] While gift-giving can be read in purely functional terms as intended to buy favor, gifts had a great deal of ritualistic importance in many early modern societies. This was especially true of the Ottoman Empire, where gifts, or *piskes*, were "a mark of respect and dependence."[141]

The dragomans of Venice, who spent most of their days at the divan negotiating and observing, because they spoke the language and were not regularly replaced as were the baili, not surprisingly established close relations with Ottoman officials. The grand dragoman Marcantonio Borisi in the first years of the seventeenth century was well known in the Porte for his regal dress and bearing; at Almoro Nani's reception, the *kaimmakan* playfully made sport of Borisi "who for his dress, which was very pompous, and for the way he carried himself, made him appear a Prince of Bogdania; thus the *paşa* responded with a smile on his face, that if it pleased him, it seemed good to name him that Prince whom he already appeared like," and then went on to praise warmly the Venetian dragoman.[142]

One of the most vivid records we have of the sociability between Ottomans and Venetians is that of Doge Andrea Gritti. As a young man Gritti lived for over twenty years in Constantinople as a grain merchant and fathered three illegiti-mate sons there by an Ottoman-Greek woman. During this time he became friendly with Sultan Bayezid II and Grand Vizier Ahmed Paşa. These friendships probably saved him from execution in the war of 1499–1503, when he was caught forwarding information to Venice. On his return to Constantinople as ambas-sador to treat for peace in 1503, he was joined by his friend the *çavuş* Ali Bey, and "a great many people" flocked to the shore to greet him, "he being loved and revered by all for his optimal customs known from the time that he was a mer-chant here in Pera." The sultan and vizier sent an honor guard of officials and mounted men, as well as gifts of delicacies and a horse for Gritti "which [was] not customary." So warm were Gritti's relations with the Ottoman Empire that at his election to the dogeship, his detractors argued that "one who has three bastard sons in Turkey should not be made Doge."[143]

Other baili, too, thrived socially in the Porte. Simone Contarini, for example, became so close with Grand Vizier Murad that, because "his perfect will toward me had passed to such a point," Murad's own servants would ask the bailo to intercede with their master on their behalf, which he often did, "and [he] always obtained" what they requested. Murad maintained this friendship, even though it apparently cost him politically: Contarini quoted him as saying "Bailo, every day it costs me more because you are my friend and my enemies have wanted to take advantage of your name to wound me."[144]

Contarini struck up a lasting friendship with another important Ottoman official, Halil Paşa.[145] Originally from Albania, Halil Paşa (1565–1629) was an influential figure in the Porte in the early seventeenth century, serving as *ka-pudanpaşa* and grand vizier, and was called by Sagredo "the best head in Tur-key."[146] Early in his career, as an official in Bosnia, he was assisted by Venice in a matter of importance, which "he conserve[d] in memory"; this became the foun-dation of a lasting, mutually beneficial, relationship.[147] Contarini and Halil Paşa maintained an active correspondence after the former left Constantinople in 1612. In 1614 the Ottoman grandee wrote the Venetian patrician thanking him for his friendship, expressing "the love and good will that we bear you," as well as his hopes that their paths would cross again in Constantinople.[148] In a 1616 letter, Halil wrote of his "sincere friendship" for "his most affectionate friend . . . God knows that if distance and separation of our persons has been necessary, the love and affection of our heart toward you has never ever wavered or moved apart, but always we remember your optimal condition and good friendship . . . we desire that the grace of contentment may be conceded to you and all our friends in this and the next world by the wise Creator."[149] The Ottoman also regularly sent his regards to Contarini bundled with official correspondence to the doge, and he carefully followed the patrician's political career from Constantinople.

Halil Paşa's relationship with Contarini benefited both Constantinople and Venice in practical ways. Immediately upon being made grand vizier, Halil moved to rescind an order forcing all Venetians resident in Ottoman lands for more than a year to pay the *harac*, even before receiving a request from the Senate to do so. When he was at the Persian front, he corresponded with *"amico nostro, il Bailo"* informing him of the progress of the war. His anti-Spanish position was also to Venice's advantage and encouraged the city to maintain this influential friend. In return, Halil drew on his relationship with Venice to obtain a safe-conduct for his "dependent" Mordecai Cressi, banished by the *Esecutori contra bestemmia*. He wrote the doge to recommend that the brother of one of his close advisers, Marin Pier who was bishop in Antivari, be considered for a higher position. Halil also used his connections to obtain food delicacies—Piacentine cheeses and Venetian sugars—for the sultan.[150]

A similar relationship existed between Grand Vizier Mehmed Sokullu and Bailo Marcantonio Barbaro. When Barbaro was imprisoned during the War of the Holy League, Sokullu permitted him to visit the baths twice weekly for his health and sent regularly "to inquire about my status, to comfort me that I might be in good spirits." Barbaro wrote, "I could not nor would I know how to desire a better disposition from the Magnificent Paşa, who on many occasions, with me and with others shows himself to be very humane and affable." Another striking evidence of the friendship between these two men is an inscription dictated by Barbaro to his portraitist, "hidden in a corner of the canvas," conserved in the Schloss Ambras near Innsbruck: *"IMO. Domino Mahomet Pacha Musulmanorum Visario amico optimo. M.A.B.F."*[151]

Halil Paşa was also quite involved with the international community in Constantinople. A Dutch gentleman, Ernst Brink, in the capital as secretary to Cornelius Haga, kept an *album amicorum* with dedications by members of the foreign community, as well as many Ottomans, including high court officials, among them Halil Paşa, who knew the young Dutchman personally.[152] The Ottoman official was also a regular participant in the French ambassador Salignac's hunting expeditions, often accompanied by other Muslims and court dignitaries. Salignac's secretary described one of these outings: they "provided us contentment and new friendships with Turks, who favored us, and accompanied us to where the game was. There were çavuş and ağas who entertained the Ambassador in their homes, where we were very well treated according to their custom." In the Ottoman homes, fêtes were organized and attended by women and children: "Thus we passed the winter gaily."[153] Robert Bargrave, who accompanied the English ambassador to Constantinople in 1647, similarly described in pleasant detail his time spent on the estate of an important Ottoman official: "We spent much of our time in a faire Country Pallace, about :6: miles from the City, where we had many pleasing divertissements, & sundry Priveledges graunted us by our noble Patron Mamout Effendee, Cadiliskièr (chief Judge) first of Anatoli (Asia) then of Romeli (Europe) . . . oftentimes came theyr great Families of Concubines (came) to recreat themselves, attended only by theyr Eunuchs, not contented unless they saw the Franks Chambers (by which name they call all western Christians) & there enterteining themselves & us, with Dauncing, Leaping, & roaring like wild persons let out of a Prison."[154]

Social encounters were not limited to hunting; erudite Europeans often met with their Ottoman counterparts for philosophical colloquies or discussions of current affairs, politics, religion, and books, not unlike what one might find among the political and diplomatic elites in any important European city. Francesco Contarini recorded a visit to the home of an Ottoman official who had formerly been quite influential, "with whom I have remained in close friendship . . . He introduced me with great domesticity into his most intimate rooms, where he admits no one, and he showed me his books, discussing Astrology and Medicine which he professes." Contarini also turned to Muslim physicians when his *medico* could not cure his lack of appetite, and was given a stone "cooked and scalded," which was applied to the bottoms of his feet.[155] There is no record if this treatment worked. Similarly, Girolamo Lippomano met a former vizier, Mehmed, "in his garden toward the Black Sea, who received me with great humanity," and together they ruminated for over an hour on the problems plaguing the Ottoman Empire.[156]

Pietro Contarini wrote of two religious officials who "had wanted to visit me and to stay with me in recreation and to taste my wine, knowing that I was a friend of the Turks." They talked at length about Islam, and, to Contarini's surprise, his guests were quite candid in their assessment of the sultan, whom they described as "not very intelligent" and unable to act without the influence of women in the seraglio. In another instance, the *beylerbeyi* of Greece invited Lorenzo Bernardo to his home, where they passed a "good space of time in several pleasant and courteous discussions."[157] Halil Paşa invited Cristoforo Valier to meet him outside the city because he wanted to "have me with him for a bit of recreation." Halil passed an hour "playing at *Zagaglia*" with his men, while Valier looked on, and then he took the bailo in his boat to one of his private gardens where they spent the rest of the day together "in most pleasing discussions."[158] Similarly, Ambassador Salignac met regularly in his garden for discussions on and practice using arms and archery, with "several Turks, his friends and men of quality."[159]

Ottomans, Venetians, and other Europeans often came together at the many banquets and other social events held at the embassies. It was the practice that a new diplomatic representative would offer a large banquet on his arrival, to which he invited both European and Ottoman guests. At Leonardo Donà's banquet, eighty *çavuş*es and their chief, as well as thirty to forty janissaries, came to the bailate, which was specially decorated for the occasion, and enjoyed a sumptuous meal. Most of the guests ate in the courtyard, but the chief *çavuş* and "several Turks of honor" joined the ambassador, his *famiglia,* the nation, and the French ambassador inside. At another such banquet in 1636, several hundred people were entertained, though after the "Turks" left, "another, more civil" banquet was held for the Greeks, Perots, and other European nations.[160] Other events in Galata also drew Ottomans of all varieties: Sanudo, for example, describes in detail the grand parties held in Galata, and in the next century the French ambassador sponsored performances of Corneille and Moliére.[161]

In addition to these formal, official events, individual Ottomans often came to visit the bailate. Piero Bragadin left an interesting account of a *sancak-beyi* and twelve *çavuş*es who came to his house to celebrate the wedding of a nephew of the sultan: "My house could be called a tavern, but without payment, I do it willingly, because when I go to the Porte to the houses of the *paşas*, they give me such honors both coming and going that it is not good to mention it."[162] Paolo Contarini echoed this sentiment and suggested another motivation for maintaining an open-door policy: he reported that to preserve an honorable reputation in the Porte, it was necessary "to feed whomever desires it; and I can say with truth to have had a continual tavern in my house, and I very often needed to set three or four tables a day, because in this way friends are conserved and new ones acquired, and the greatness of this Most Serene Republic is made known to the world."[163]

It was common for the baili to entertain diverse guests, especially influential Ottoman officials, at their private table. Orembei, the renegade grand dragoman of the Porte, was a regular dinner guest, often reporting on the affairs relating to other European diplomats for whom he interpreted in the divan.[164] The baili used such encounters to build networks, obtain information, and treat informally a wide range of problems. Girolamo Lippomano had a disgruntled Ottoman-Muslim merchant and minor customs official over, "in the company of other Turkish friends of the household," and together they were able to convince the man to resolve his complaint in a favorable manner. Ottaviano Bon entertained the *paşa* of Tunisia as he was preparing to leave for his post, no doubt using the occasion to ensure that the man would favor Venetian interests in North Africa. The baili too were often dinner guests of Ottoman grandees: Almoro Nani dined with the *kapudanpaşa* and had to explain that as it was Lent he was not eating meat, to which the Ottoman good-naturedly responded that he was the "Captain of the Sea" and he had no shortage of fish to serve.[165]

Relationships forged in these informal settings often endured well beyond the end of the baili's service and their return to Venice, as we have seen in the case of Simone Contarini. Giovanni Moro, in 1589, went to visit a newly appointed Ottoman official who "entertained me in diverse discussions more than an hour, telling me that he had served . . . as *hoca* of this house, and had taught the language to *quondam* Lodovico Marucini; nor has he forgotten the favors received from [Venice], and he offered himself to me in any way that he could assist."[166] Francesco Contarini, who returned to Venice in 1619 as extraordinary ambassador, reported meeting a Hasan Paşa Nacas, who "was very well-known by me . . . because in the time of my bailate he came in secrecy to this house . . . to drink merrily, which he remembers and which he discussed in our discourse; he is of a very liberal nature."[167]

WORSHIP, EMPLOYMENT, AND OTHER ENCOUNTERS

Interaction and even friendship were not limited to diplomats and high officials. The multicultural nature of Galata attracted a wide range of people, including many curious Ottoman-Muslims. It served as cultural middle ground in which "intra-urban interaction was often more intensive than ha[s] been assumed."[168]

One of the chief attractions that drew Muslim residents and visitors to Galata was the few remaining Roman Catholic churches in greater Constantinople, all but one of which were in Galata. As one observer noted:

Many of them [Muslims] come inside our churches, particularly San Francesco, out of curiosity to see the manner of our devotions, and they come here many times when masses are celebrated, and are amazed at the ceremonies. Also during the time of the sermon they come to hear, or better, to see the preacher, because few understand the language except the Christian renegades, and they depart without any problem. At Easter time, as they know it is our most solemn feast, at my sermon I saw more than 200 of them between the ambassador's janissaries, who are there for protection, and others on Friday, which among them is like Sunday. Most women and youths come from Constantinople on a stroll, out of curiosity sparked by those who other times have been there, and they ask to hear the organ, and then when they leave they give alms or a tip.[169]

In the fifteenth century, Mehmed the Conqueror was reported to have attended services in San Francesco.[170] Popular religious feasts also drew large numbers of Muslims. The feast of the Holy Sacrament especially drew a "crowd not only of diverse Christian nations, but also the Turks themselves," who came in such great numbers that no empty seats could be found. And during Christmas festivities, "Turks . . . [had] the habit of bringing many flowers in hand to give to Christians."[171]

The activities of the few Christian religious still active in Galata were also of particular interest. When four Capuchin monks arrived in Galata in 1626 to establish a school and a mission at the Church of Saint George, their unique attire attracted typical curiosity.[172] Initially the fathers experienced occasional mistreatment: one was attacked in the street by a boy who threw a stone at him; others claimed that Muslims who lived nearby regularly sent toddlers who could barely walk with knifes to harass the fathers, who would return the children to their mothers. Over time, however, relations between the Capuchins and their Muslim neighbors became cordial. The father accosted in the street, for example, was cared for by a "Turk of quality" who had the youth arrested. A contemporary dispatch reports that Ottoman-Muslims "embrace us, come to eat with us, and want especially to observe our rites, such as keeping silence, reading while eating . . . They listen to our vespers in the choir where we sing, and they say that they love us so much that if any movement against Christians were to arise, we would not experience a shadow of evil."[173] When the Church of Santa Maria in Constantinople was in danger of being closed by Ottoman officials, "all the Turkish women neighbors of the church" took to the streets shouting "we do not want anything bad done, or that any trouble be given this church."[174]

Of particular acclaim throughout Constantinople was the tiny, ancient church of San Antonio Abbate, which attracted "a universal and indistinct crowd of people, who flock there for its favors, . . . Latins, Greeks, Armenians, and the Turks themselves." The crowds made offerings in the range of six to seven hundred ducats annually. People were drawn because of the miraculous healings associated with the church, which at times became crowded with people "making vows for the sick, as in Christendom is done at Our Lady of Loreto, or Liège." Christians and Muslims would sleep in the church and listen to mass in the hopes of being healed. One papal visitor reported in 1622 that twenty-six men and women were sleeping in the church during his visit, and he claimed that one of the sultan's daughters had once slept in the miraculous church, though this seems highly improbable. The city's insane were brought, "their relatives allowing them to be tied and placed in irons, and if necessary beaten," in the hope they would be cured of their condition.[175]

Because of the importance of ritual ablutions in Islam, Muslims were especially attracted to the waters of San Antonio's well, which they viewed as holy and which they drank and even washed in during the winter. They would also "come bearing offerings of lamps, candles, money, and other things to the Cordelier monk who is there, throwing themselves on their knees at his feet, praying him to recount to them the Gospel of Saint John or about the feast of Saint Anthony on the roof, with the star, as do the women in Christendom. And what is wonderful about the bounty of God, is that without regard to their infidelity, he cures them miraculously."[176] Also enjoying a miraculous reputation among both Christian and Muslim was the small chapel in the *kapudanpaşa*'s slave quarters. It was widely believed that whoever slept there three nights in a row would be healed of all infirmities.[177]

One Muslim woman, whose hands were rheumatic, had been to a number of dervishes and Islamic "holy men" to no avail. She visited San Antonio, where a priest read a gospel over her head, and when he said *Verbum caro factum est*, her hands were healed, and she publicized throughout the city that she had been cured "by the Christians' law."[178] A Papal emissary in Constantinople attempted to explain the healing of the infidel woman thus: "Though they too receive on their heads these orations, they do not feel by this that they are doing anything against their belief because, beyond the fact that they believe in the Gospel, they told me additionally . . . that this Saint fulfilled them because he had been a Muslim, that is a Turk, and had believed in Muhammed, and . . . these opinions are of the vulgar masses and not of their wise men, who in encountering them pretend not to know of these miracles, or search for opportunities to find in them insidiousness."[179] The distinct divisions that scholars and theologians, both

Christian and Muslim, drew between their respective faiths, in practice were much more flexible and overlapped in the minds of the masses. Saints could be venerated as Christian or their religious identity adapted to popular beliefs, and in either case divine favor might be obtained. Indeed, the imperial ambassador Ogier Ghiselin de Busbecq in the mid-sixteenth century reported, "I have known instances of Turks who had their children secretly baptised; their notion being that there must be some advantage in this rite, or otherwise it would never have been instituted."[180]

Examples of similar syncretic practices abound in the early modern Mediterranean.[181] During his 1553 mission, the Venetian diplomat Catarino Zeno visited the Orthodox monastery of Milesevo and reported witnessing both Muslims and Jews who came to hear prayers read by the monks and offered alms in return, often in greater numbers than Christian pilgrims. In Bosnia, Catholic monks "enjoyed a high reputation for exorcism of evil spirits, and they were often asked by individual Muslims or even the Ottoman authorities to perform the ritual."[182] In Spain, Muslims and Christians shared popular beliefs in Bible tales, "demons and angels, heaven and hell," and women from both religions shared in venerating Mary.[183]

As a counterpoint to its spiritual attractions, Galata drew many more Muslims "who wished to enjoy themselves there *a la franca.*" Evliya Çelebi reported that there were two hundred taverns and houses of debauchery in the city, concluding that "to say Galata is to say taverns—may God pardon us!" Despite his alarm, he seems to have known the area well and described its various wines and culinary offerings in detail.[184] A century earlier, Lâtifi described Galata as "the biggest tavern in the world."[185] Foreign travelers observed much the same about Galata's nightlife: Thévenot reported, "The Greeks have many cabarets in Galata which attract a good deal of the rabble of Constantinople." The popularity of these taverns led to their regular closure by the Ottomans in the difficult years from 1590 to 1640, as a reaction against and expiation for the sinfulness of the patrons. Evliya Çelebi reports that there was an Ottoman official specifically assigned to prevent riots and other troubles associated with the town's taverns.[186]

While Venetian patricians, merchants, and citizens might most often encounter Ottoman-Muslims at festivities, religious festivals, on the hunt, or in private salons, commoners met regularly in everyday settings, especially in commerce and industry. Particularly in the maritime industries, it was not at all uncommon for men of all sorts to work side by side. In 1596, for example, a list of forty-six carpenters who repaired a Venetian merchant ship included Slavs, Messinans, Genoese, Neapolitans, French, Romans, Greeks, Germans, Puglians, Corsicans,

Portuguese, Spaniards, Venetians, Rhodiots, and six Muslims. Caulkers working on the same ship made up an equally diverse group.[187] This mix was not uncommon, as several other account books register similar work crews, and non-Muslims were counted among the members of Constantinople's many guilds, especially those that traded and worked with European merchants. Muslim outfitters also provided for the needs of the Venetian ships that came to the port.[188] It was also very common for a Muslim *reis* to captain merchant ships on which non-Ottomans served.[189]

Another common meeting ground, which warrants further research, was the galleys, both Ottoman and European. In the case of the former, it appears that in 1611–13 "Moslems were in the minority on their own ships," with the majority of the crews being made up of Christians. In addition to these fields of encounter, individual Venetians might contract with Ottoman-Muslims to navigate the complexities of the Porte, and instances of Muslims serving Venetian merchants as *cernitori*, and the converse, were also not unheard of.[190]

Opportunities for encounters between the varied populations of Constantinople were numerous, regular and highly diverse. Observers may have divided the urban area into ethnic and religious quarters, but in fact Christians lived alongside Muslims in many parts of the city. Interactions at the commercial, political, social, and religious levels were experienced regularly in the varied world of greater Constantinople, and claims that geographically proximate groups lived within the same orbit but with their trajectories rarely crossing clearly obscure the more vibrant reality of this complex community. Muslims, Christians, Jews, Europeans, Ottomans, and Persians all lived and worked and celebrated together in the Ottoman capital of the sixteenth and seventeenth centuries. Their interactions may have flared during moments of stress, and in certain ways may have been characterized by misperception and conflict, but more common were the sorts of everyday exchanges described in this chapter.

This reality was made possible, at least in part, by the fact that individual and group identities in this period were not rigid or monochromatic; identity was more complex than a bipartite model of self and other. Behind labels such as Venetian or Ottoman were groups and individuals possessed of more ambiguous and adaptable identities. Individuals who interacted in Constantinople and other cities of the Mediterranean defined themselves along a spectrum of categories of identity which might include geographical, social, familial, gender, cultural, religious, political, and other factors. Venice's nation in Constantinople included Venetians born, Venetians made, non-Venetians, Greek-Venetians, and even Ottoman subjects. Venice's baili were Christian and Venetian, but they were also diplomats and gentlemen, and they were thus able to develop relationships with Ottoman-Muslims of similar standing based on their political and social identities. Muslim inhabitants of the city often shared similar confidence in the miraculous properties of places or individuals with their Christian neighbors, and they often interacted through work and trade and thus developed a shared sense of community based on profession. Identities based on regional provenance and familial relations were as important pieces of the puzzle of identity as faith or polity, perhaps even more so. Although religion and political affiliation were certainly key, it is overly simple to try to essentialize or reduce the complexity of early modern identities to a single category or two.

Individual and group identities were composites, constructed of concentric circles or multiple layers. Additionally, identity was more than the sum total of its various parts: it was malleable, instrumental, a dynamic process of negotiation rather than a static, essentialized object. When we perceive the Mediterranean world in these terms, and not in simple binary divisions that assume an inherent clash between civilizations, then the striking evidences of peace and coexistence between peoples of diverse religious and cultural backgrounds can be more readily understood, and may perhaps hold out some hope for our own troubled times.

Notes

ABBREVIATIONS
Archives

ACDF	Archivio Congregatio pro doctrina fidei, Rome
ASFi	Archivio di stato di Firenze
ASV	Archivio di stato di Venezia
Correr	Museo Correr, Venice
DSA	Dubrovnik State Archives
Marciana	Biblioteca Marciana, Venice
VatLib	Vatican Library, Rome

Sources

All archival sources are located in the ASV unless otherwise indicated.

APC	*Archivi propri—Costantinopoli*
AvCom	*Avogaria di comun*
BAC	*Bailo a Costantinopoli*
Barbaro	M. Barbaro, *Arbori de patritii veneti*
CancG	*Cancelliere grande*
CapiXLett	*Capi del consiglio di dieci—Lettere di ambasciatori*
CollRel	*Collegio—Relazioni*
DBI	*Dizionario biografico italiano*
DocTR	*Documenti turchi*
DonàR	*Donà delle Rose* (Correr)
EI	*Encyclopedia of Islam*, New Edition
Gregolin	*Miscellanea Gregolin*
InqStat	*Inquisitori di stato*
It VII	*MS. Italiano, classe VII* (Marciana)
LSTR	*Lettere e scritture turchesche*
NotAtti	*Notarile—Atti*
NotTest	*Notarile—Testamenti*
RubriCST	*Rubricarii di Costantinopoli*
SDC	*Senato dispacci—Costantinopoli*
SDCop	*Senato dispacci—Copie Moderne*

SDelC   Senato deliberazioni—Costantinopoli
SegMiste   Senato segreta materie miste notabili
SMar   Senato—Mar
VSM   V Savii alla mercanzia
XSeg   Consiglio di dieci—Deliberazioni segrete
XSavi   Dieci savii alle decime in Rialto

INTRODUCTION

1. Venetian sources invariably refer to the Ottoman capital as *Constantinople* instead of *Istanbul*. While *Istanbul* is preferred among Ottomanists, because the bulk of my archival sources are Venetian and the primary focus is on the Venetian community, I have chosen to adhere to the geographical terminology of the documentary record. On this, see Runciman, "Constantinople-Istanbul."

2. Rubiés, *Travel and Ethnology*, 354–57, 366; Elsner and Rubiés, *Voyages and Visions*, 46; Castellani, "Pietro Della Valle"; Grey, *Travels of Pietro della Valle*, 1:i–ix. See also Ciampi, *Pietro della Valle il Pellegrino*.

3. In early modern times this suburb was called *Galata* or *Pera* interchangeably; in this study, however, I have favored *Galata*, which contemporary Venetian sources often used, except when quoting from documents in which *Pera* is used. To further confuse the matter, the Vigne di Pera was the area outside the walled city of Galata/Pera stretching along the crest of the hill and was the location of all the ambassadorial residences. The Vigne di Pera and Galata/Pera were clearly distinct areas in contemporaries' minds. The modern quarters of Beyoğlu and Karaköy correspond to the same area as early modern Galata. Pistarino, "Genoese in Pera," 63, 82 n. 2; Lewis, *Istanbul and the Ottoman Empire* 128–29; Belin, *Histoire de la Latinité de Constantinople*, 125–27; Mantran, *Istanbul dans la seconde moitié du XVIIe siècle*, 76; Sandys, *Relation of a Journey*, 38; d'Alessio, *Relatione*, 1 n.1, 3.

4. Della Valle, *De' viaggi*, 20.

5. Ibid. See also, Boppe, *Journal et correspondance*, 28, 33, 41.

6. Breisach, *On the Future of History*, 141; Burke, *Varieties of Cultural History*, 191–206. On the now not-so-new cultural history, see Hunt, *The New Cultural History*. For an update, see Bonnell and Hunt, *Beyond the Cultural Turn*.

7. See Schwartz, "Introduction"; Greenblatt, *Marvelous Possessions*, 1–25; Pagden, *European Encounters*, 1–15; Rubiés, *Travel and Ethnology*, x–xviii.

8. Parker, *Early Modern Tales*, 1–29; Faroqhi, *Approaching Ottoman History*, 14.

9. Scholars have long recognized the importance of the Venetian archives for work on the Ottoman Empire. See Baschet, *La diplomatie vénitienne*, 228; Mantran, "Venise, centre d'informations," 1:112, 114–15; Gökbilgin, "Le relazioni veneto-turche," 277; Faroqhi, *Approaching Ottoman History*, 15, 66, 110; Faroqhi, "Before 1600," 103; Kafadar, "The Ottomans and Europe," 1:629; İnalcık, " Outline of Ottoman-Venetian Relations," 1:83.

10. Martin and Romano, "Introduction," 8, 20–21; Horodowich, "New Venice," 6–10; Arbel, "Roman Catholics," 74, 86.

11. Pullan, "The Inquisition," 212; Luigi Groto, *Lettere famigliari*, vol. 1 (Venice, 1616),

110, cited in Olivieri, "Tempo et historia delle famiglie," 168. See also Beck et al., *Venezia, centro di mediazione.*

12. Schwoebel, *The Shadow of the Crescent,* 179–81; Lucchetta, "L'oriente mediterraneo,"3:386–87. On Bellini and Carpaccio, see Brown, *Venetian Narrative Painting.*

13. McNeill, *Venice.* On the impact of Ottoman and Islamic society on Venetian culture, see Fabris, *Venezia: sapore d'Oriente;* Pedani-Fabris, "Presenze islamiche a Venezia"; Concina, *Dell'arabico;* Howard, *Venice and the East;* Fabris, "Influssi orientali nell'antica cucina veneziana."

14. Babinger, "Le vicende veneziane," 2:143; Kretschmayr, *Geschichte von Vendig,* 2:635.

15. Burckhardt, *Civilization of the Renaissance in Italy,* 74; Babinger, "Le vicende veneziane," 2:143; Vaughan, *Europe and the Turk.*

16. İnalcık, "The Ottoman State," 1:60–61, 342–43; İnalcık, "Ottoman Galata," 60–61; İnalcık, "Outline of Ottoman-Venetian Relations," 1:87–88; Ashtor, "Venetian Supremacy in Levantine Trade"; Braudel, *The Perspective of the World,* 118–24. In recent years, scholars have argued for a view of Ottoman conquests not driven by zeal for jihad but rather as a rational, politico-economic policy of expansion that sought to control international trade routes. The most compelling discussion is in Brummett, *Ottoman Seapower,* 1–20, and her "Competition and Coincidence," 29–52. See also İslamoğlu and Keyder, "Agenda for Ottoman History."

17. Faroqhi, "Before 1600," 91–93, 97.

18. Priuli, *I diarii.* See also Perocco, "Un male non pensato," 287–89; Tenenti, "Space and Time in the Venetian World," 29; Dursteler, "Reverberations"; Aricò, *Lettere sul nuovo mondo.*

19. Lane, *Venice,* 234.

20. McNeill, *Venice,* 125–26; "Contarini, Simone," *DBI,* 29:493–97; Finlay, "Fabius Maximus in Venice," 994–96, 1025–26; Coco and Manzonetto, *Baili veneziani,* 9; Preto, *Venezia e i turchi,* 28; Gilbert, *The Pope, His Banker, and Venice,* 116–17; Zele, "Aspetti delle legazioni ottomane," 259; Tenenti, "Space and Time in the Venetian World," 36.

21. Fabris, "Artisinat et culture," 60; Girolamo Aleandro to Pietro Carnesecchi, 1 January 1534, in *Nunziature di Venezia,* 1:150; Gleason, "Confronting New Realities," 169–80.

22. "Gio Carlo Scaramelli ricordi a se stesso," *It VII* 1640 (7983), cc. 2r–7v; Gleason, "Confronting New Realities," 178.

23. Finlay, "Al servizio del Sultano," 83, 89; McNeill, *Venice,* 136; Pedani-Fabris, *In nome del Gran Signore,* 109; Gleason, "Confronting New Realities," 174.

24. Gleason, "Confronting New Realities," 172–76.

25. İnalcık, "The Ottoman State," 1:344; Brummett, "Competition and Coincidence"; Lane, "Venetian Shipping" and "The Mediterranean Spice Trade." See also Luzzatto, "La decadenza di Venezia"; Wake, "Europe's Pepper and Spice Imports"; Lybyer, "Ottoman Turks and the Routes of Oriental Trade," 577–88.

26. "Relatione . . . di Antonio Diedo," in S. Ljubić, *Commissiones et relationes Venetae* (Zagreb: Monumenta Spectantia Historiam Slavorum Meridionalim, 1880), 9:10, 3, cited in Kafadar, "A Death in Venice," 203–4; *SDCop,* reg. 15, c. 267–71, 17 Feb 1619 (MV), Almoro Nani to Senate. On Venice's dependence on Ottoman grain, see Aymard, *Venice, Raguse,* 125–41.

27. Nicholle, *Armies of the Ottoman Turks*, 37; Hale and Mallett, *Military Organization*, 317–19, 367–80.

28. Pius II, *Memoirs*, 139; Valensi, *Birth of the Despot*, 20; Schwoebel, *Shadow of the Crescent*, 179–80; Finlay, "Prophecy and Politics in Istanbul," 10–11.

29. Lane, *Venice*, 246, 393–94; Paruta, "Discorso sulla neutralità," in *Opere politiche*, 1:381–99. For a revealing discourse presented in the Senate after 1550 on Venice's position vis-à-vis the Ottomans, see *DonàR*, b. 397, no. 47.

30. The first of these titles has been especially popular; recent works include Daniel, *Islam and the West*; Lewis, *Islam and the West*; Esposito, *Islam and the West*; Chejne, *Islam and the West*; Hitti, *Islam and the West*. See also Vaughan, *Europe and the Turk*; Preto, *Venezia e i turchi*.

31. Darling, "Rethinking Europe and the Islamic World," 232.

32. Huntington, "Clash of Civilizations"; see also Wheatcroft, *Infidels*; Lewis, *What Went Wrong*; Lewis, *The Crisis of Islam*.

33. Lewis, *Cultures in Conflict*, 12–14; Bulliet, *Islamo-Christian Civilization*, 7; Bisaha, *Creating East and West*, 44–50; Vitkus, "Early Modern Orientalism," 208–9.

34. Kafadar, *Between Two Worlds*, 20–22; see also Lewis, "Some Reflections," 111; Raymond, "The Ottoman Conquest," 84; İnalcık, "Biases in Studying Ottoman History," 7–10.

35. Braude and Lewis, "Introduction," 1:2–4; Lewis, *Cultures in Conflict*, 44–5; Lewis, *Islam and the West*, 174, 179, 182; Moacanin, "Some Remarks on the Supposed Tolerance," 209–15; Akarli, *The Long Peace*.

36. Braude and Lewis, "Introduction," 1:16–17; Kafadar, *Between Two Worlds*, 20–21; Mantran, "L'Empire ottoman," 189; McNeill, "The Ottoman Empire in World History," 34.

37. Schwoebel, *Shadow of the Crescent*, ix; Maxime Rodinson, *Europe and the Mystique of Islam*, 9.

38. The quote is found in Kafadar, "The Ottomans and Europe," 1:589; see also Mantran, "L'Empire ottoman," 192. On the Vatican's position, see "Saying No to Turkey"; Said, *Covering Islam*.

39. Zinkeisen, *Geschichte des osmanischen Reiches*; Iorga, *Geschichte des osmanischen Reiches*; Vaughan, *Europe and the Turk*; Coles, *Ottoman Impact on Europe*; Gibb and Bowen, *Islamic Society and the West*. For a good survey of Ottoman historical writing, see Kreiser, "Clio's Poor Relation," 24–43. For the most recent entry in this tradition, see Goody, *Islam in Europe*.

40. Rouillard, *The Turk in French History*; Chew, *The Crescent and the Rose*; Southern, *Western Views of Islam*; Daniel, *Islam and the West*; Schwoebel, *Shadow of the Crescent*; Preto, *Venezia e i turchi*. See also Libby, "Venetian Views of the Ottoman Empire"; Shaw and Heywood, *English and Continental Views*.

41. Bisaha, *Creating East and West*; Blanks and Frassetto, *Western Views of Islam*; Setton, *Western Hostility to Islam*; Beck, *From the Rising of the Sun*.

42. An excellent recent overview of the historiography of image is Blanks, "Western Views of Islam."

43. Lewis, *Islam and the West*, 73, 83; Setton, "Lutheranism and the Turkish Peril," 143, 151, 153, 163 n. 11. Margolin, "Erasme et la Guerre Contre les Turcs"; Daniel, *Islam and the*

West, 281–83; Baumer, "England, the Turk, and the Common Corps," 27–28; Matar, *Turks, Moors, and Englishmen;* Kafé, "Le mythe Turc et son déclin," 191–92.

44. Wolf, *Europe and the People without History,* 3–7; Schwartz, "Introduction," 6–7; Breisach, *On the Future of History,* 144–45, 152–53; Burke, *Varieties of Cultural History,* 186–87, 201–6.

45. Rodinson, *Europe and the Mystique of Islam,* 8; Blanks, "Western Views of Islam," 40–41.

46. Valensi, *Birth of the Despot,* 56. See also Setton's *Western Hostility to Islam* and Kafé, "Le mythe Turc et son déclin."

47. Rodinson, *Europe and the Mystique of Islam,* 38–43; Darling, "Rethinking Europe and the Islamic World," 230; Dotson, "Perceptions of the East," 185–86; Rubiés, "Travel Writing as a Genre," 22; Rubiés, "Instructions for Travellers," 144, 148–50; Kamps and Singh, *Travel Knowledge,* 37.

48. Setton, *Western Hostility to Islam,* 47–53; Rodinson, *Europe and the Mystique of Islam,* 23–40; Rouillard, *The Turk in French History.*

49. Elliott, *The Old World and The New,* 12–14; Trevor-Roper, "A Case of Coexistence," 173; Setton, *Western Hostility to Islam,* 46; Dursteler, "Reverberations." Göllner's monumental study, *Turcica,* suggests the increase in both interest and information: he found approximately one thousand publications on the Ottoman Empire for the first half of the sixteenth century and 2,500 for the second half. Valensi, *Birth of the Despot,* 111 n.118.

50. Not all scholars have embraced this view of the *relazioni.* Carter, "Ambassadors of Early Modern Europe," 279–80; Benzoni, "A proposito dei baili veneziani," 72–76; Benzoni, "Ranke's Favorite Source," 57; Benzoni, "A proposito della fonte prediletta di Ranke"; Tenenti, "Profilo di un conflitto secolare," 12–15; Preto, "Le relazioni dei baili veneziani," 129–30; Preto, *Venezia e i turchi,* 100.

51. Sahlins, *Boundaries;* Greene, *A Shared World;* McKee, *Uncommon Dominion;* Prestholdt, "Portuguese Conceptual Categories," 383–406; Rubiés, *Travel and Ethnology;* also Vink, "Images and Ideologies."

52. Other recent examples of the growing literature on medieval and early modern identity include Davis, *Women on the Margins;* Canny and Pagden, *Colonial Identity in the Atlantic World;* Wolfe, *Changing Identities in Early Modern France;* Adams, *Bourgeois Identity in Early Modern France;* Smyth, *Medieval Europeans.*

53. Prestholdt, "Portuguese Conceptual Categories," 383–84, 399; Brummett, "Understanding Space"; see also Kafadar, "The Ottomans and Europe," 1:619–20; Vink, "Images and Ideologies," 82–87.

54. Bulliet, *Islamo-Christian Civilization,* 1–43; see also Alcalay, *After Jews and Arabs,* 3–13, 21; Darling, "Rethinking Europe and the Islamic World," 245.

55. Darling, "Rethinking Europe and the Islamic World," 246.

56. Breisach, *On the Future of History,* 144–45, 152–53; Brown, *Postmodernism for Historians,* 117–18.

57. Elliott, "A Europe of Composite Monarchies," 49, 70–71.

58. Della Valle, *De' Viaggi,* 20.

59. Armstrong, *Nations Before Nationalism*, 238; Lewis, *The Political Language of Islam*, 2–4.

60. On the ethnoreligious complications of the label *Turk*, see Kafadar, *Between Two Worlds*, 31; Said, *Covering Islam*, xx–xxxi. Lewis writes that within the Turkish Republic to this day it is a widely held opinion that the only authentic "Turks" are Muslims, all other non-Muslim inhabitants are characterized as "Turkish citizens." Lewis, *Islam and the West*, 143, 185. See also Erlap, "Turkey and the European Community," 1.

61. Vitkus, "Early Modern Orientalism," 213.

62. Lewis, *The Crisis of Islam*, xxii; Masters, "Trading Diasporas," 347–51, 357; Braude and Lewis, "Introduction," 1:27–8; Yapp, "Europe in the Turkish Mirror," 138–39.

63. Kafadar, *Between Two Worlds*, 19.

64. Donia and Fine, *Bosnia and Hercegovina*, 26.

65. McKee, *Uncommon Dominion*.

66. Hanlon, *Confession and Community*; Davis, *Society and Culture in Early Modern France*, 2, 7–9, 15–16; Ward, "Religious Diversity and Guild Unity," 77–97.

67. Zachariadou, "Co-Existence and Religion," 119–29. In Venice's Greek possessions, noble and commoner Venetian settlers intermarried with local Greeks, attended Orthodox mass, and were known "to baptise their children, to marry and to bury their dead in accordance with the Orthodox rite." A report from 1602 states that "there is no quarrel on matters of religion, since both communities live freely in their own rites, and the Greek notables and others of their rite often go to Latin churches to hear mass, and the Latins frequent the churches of the Orthodox. The clergy of both rites are respected by all." According to this observer, St. Francis was venerated by Orthodox and Catholic alike. Stergios G. Spanakes, *Mnemeia tes Kretikes historias* (Herakleion: Candia, 1940–76), 4:86–87, cited in Maltezou, "Historical and Social Context," 33–35.

68. Benzoni, *Venezia nell'età della controriforma*, 27; McNeill, *Venice*, 93.

69. The rhetoric used in attempts to shame Venice from its accommodating policy toward the Ottomans was turned on the French when they began to treat closely with the sultans. Spain, for example, referred to the French as the "turcs de Ponant." Quatrefages, "La perception gouvernementale espagnole," 72, 81; Poumarède, "Justifier l'injustifiable," 217–46.

70. İnalcık, "The Ottoman State," 1:373. On alliances with the Ottomans, see Vaughan, *Europe and the Turk*, 104–186; Lane, *Venice*, 235; İnalcık, "Turkish Impact on the Development of Modern Europe," 52–53; Babinger, "Le vicende veneziane," 2:143.

71. Vitkus, "Early Modern Orientalism," 212; Spitz, *The Protestant Reformation*, 330.

72. VatLib, *Urb. Lat.* 836, cc. 407r–v, "Relation di Mons. Pietro Cedolini Vescovo di Liesena dal present stato dell'Imperio Turchesco et molti particolari degni di consideratione"; Kafadar, "The Ottomans and Europe," 1:618–22; see also Kafadar, *Between Two Worlds*.

73. *SDC*, b. 19, cc. 132r–135r, 19 Apr 1584, Gianfrancesco Morosini to Senate; Vaughan, *Europe and the Turk*, 134–46; Setton, "Lutheranism and the Turkish Peril."

74. Della Valle, *De' viaggi*, 20.

75. Foster and Daniell, *Life of Busbecq*, 1:257; Blount, *Voyage into the Levant*, 5; Wood, "Mr. Harrie Cavendish," 24.

76. Hobsbawm, *Nations and Nationalism*, 3, 17–18; Gellner, *Nations and Nationalism*;

Anderson, *Imagined Communities;* see also Feldbæk, "Clash of Cultures in a Conglomerate State," 80; Chaudhuri, "Trade as a Cultural Phenomenon," 208.

77. Smith, *The Nation in History;* see also Smyth, *Medieval Europeans;* Moeglin, "Nation et nationalisme"; Forde, *Concepts of National Identity in the Middle Ages.* For a recent treatment of nation in the Middle Ages which challenges these views, see Geary, *The Myth of Nations.* For a particularly insightful treatment of identity and the myth of ethnicity in medieval Crete, see McKee, *Uncommon Dominion.*

78. Zernatto, "Nation: The History of a Word," 351–52; see also Benveniste, *Indo-European Language and Society,* 295–304. On the history of the word and concept of *nation* from classical times, see White, "What Is a Nationality," 6; Casevitz and Basset, *"Peuple, Nation, État,"* 153–59; James, *Nation Formation,* 9–14; le Guern, "Le mot *Nation,*" 161–67. For an occasionally insightful discussion of medieval and early modern ideas of nation, see Post, "Medieval and Renaissance Ideas of Nation," 3:318–24.

79. Dante, *Paradiso* 19.138, cited in Zernatto, "Nation: The History of a Word," 353; Hobsbawm, *Nations and Nationalism,* 15–17; Chabod, *L'idea di nazione,* 175–76. On Machiavelli's use of nation, compare, for example, 1:55 and 3:43 in *Discourses,* 243–48, 517–19. For a suggestive juxtaposition of uses of *nazione* to indicate both birthplace and *patria* in Goldoni, see Folena, *Vocabolario del veneziano,* 385.

80. Geary, *The Myth of Nations,* 41–62; Kibre, *The Nations in the Mediaeval Universities,* 3–5; Schulze, *States, Nations, and Nationalism,* 105–6; Zernatto, "Nation," 353–58; Coulton, "Nationalism in the Middle Ages," 10–11.

81. Tietze, *Counsel for Sultans,* 63; Naima, *Annals,* 1:125, 176, 279–81; Lewis, *Istanbul and the Ottoman Empire,* 96–100. See also Wells, *Literature of the Turks,* 76–77.

82. Lewis, *From Babel to Dragomans.* 25; Lewis, *The Political Language of Islam,* 38–42; Masters, "Trading Diasporas," 347–51; Heath, "Unholy Alliance," 304.

83. Kirshner, "Between Nature and Culture," 193.

84. *SDCop,* reg. 14, c. 10, 8 Sep 1618, Almoro Nani to Senate.

85. Chabod, *L'idea di nazione,* 46–47; Fishman, "Language and Ethnicity," 25; Mazzini, *The Duties of Man,* 55; Armstrong, *Nations before Nationalism,* 279; Cassia, "Religion, Politics, and Ethnicity in Cyprus," 20. A good example of the secondary nature of language in prenational times is Italy, where at unification in 1861 only 2.5 percent of the population could speak Italian, while the rest "inhabited a 'forest of dialect.' " Eley and Suny, "Introduction," 7.

86. Eley and Suny, "Introduction," 8; Feldbæk, "Clash of Cultures," 81; Bumbaca, "Schede per scolari francesi a Padova," 137–39.

87. Sahlins, *Boundaries,* 268.

88. Braude and Lewis, "Introduction," 1:27–28; Fishman, "Language and Ethnicity," 25. See also "Colloque sur la langue," 3:139–95.

89. On the lingua franca, see Cortelazzo, "Che cosa s'intendesse"; Wansbrough, *Lingua Franca in the Mediterranean.*

90. Chabod, *L'idea di nazione,* 175–81; Nicolay, *The Navigations into Turkie,* 130v–31v.

91. See Wilson, "Reflecting on the Turk"; Wilson, "Reproducing the Contours of Venetian Identity"; Newton, *The Dress of the Venetians,* 132–44; Hughes, "Earrings for Circumcision," 155–77.

92. Sandys, *Relation of a Journey*, 78; Sturdza, *Dictionnaire historique et généalogique*, 564.

93. Mundy, *Travels*, 26–27. Other examples of these costume books include *Life in Istanbul, 1588;* Bruyn, *Omnium;* Deserpz, *Recueil;* Sluperius, *Omnium;* Amman, *Gynaeceum . . .*; Bertelli, *Omnium.*

94. Faroqhi, *Subjects of the Sultans*, 110; Murphey, "Forms of Differentiation," 136–38. See also, generally, Hughes, "Sumptuary Law and Social Relations," 69–99.

95. Kibre, *The Nations in the Mediaeval Universities*, 3–5; Schulze, *States, Nations, and Nationalism*, 105–6; Zernatto, "Nation: The History of a Word," 353–56; Coulton, "Nationalism in the Middle Ages," 20; James, *Nation Formation*, 10–11

96. Chabod, *L'idea di nazione*, 175–81; de Groot, "The Dutch Nation in Istanbul," 137.

97. Elliott, "A Europe of Composite Monarchies," 58; Elliott, "Revolution and Continuity," 47–48.

98. Sahlins, *Boundaries*, 269.

99. Anderson, *Imagined Communities*, xi. For a reassessment of the composite state in light of recent events, see Elliott, "A Europe of Composite Monarchies."

100. On the legal and juridical status and privileges of the Venetian *stato da mar* in relation to the *dominante*, see Cozzi, *Repubblica di Venezia e stati italiani;* also Cozzi and Knapton, *Repubblica di Venezia nell'età moderna;* McNeill, *Venice*, 148–49; Tucci, "Psychology of the Venetian Merchant," 363; Martin and Romano, "Introduction," 7–8, 20–21.

101. Arbel, "Colonie d'oltremare," 5:979; Tenenti, "Space and Time in the Venetian World," 19.

102. Trebbi, "La cancelleria veneta," 76; Ventura, *Relazioni degli ambasciatori veneti*, 1:xxix.

103. Grubb, *Firstborn of Venice*, 172–74.

104. Elliott, "A Europe of Composite Monarchies," 48–71.

105. Berengo, *La società veneta*, 31. On this failure in general, see Grubb, "When Myths Lose Power," 74–78.

106. The classic treatment of the dissolution of the Venetian state in the War of the League of Cambrai is Ventura, *Nobiltà e popolo*, 121–87. See also Gilbert, *The Pope, His Banker, and Venice.*

107. Tenenti, "Space and Time in the Venetian World," 18–19.

108. Martines, *Power and Imagination*, 288.

109. Hill, *History of Cyprus*, 3:765–1040; Greene, "Ruling an Island," 199; Setton, *Venice, Austria, and the Turks*, 118–19; Goffman, *The Ottoman Empire and Early Modern Europe*, 154–58.

110. Blount, *Voyage into the Levant*, 60.

111. Argenti, *Diplomatic Archive of Chios*, 2:850–52; see also Goffman, *The Ottoman Empire and Early Modern Europe*, 151–54.

112. Cessi, *Storia della repubblica di Venezia*, 489–505; Arbel, "Colonie d'oltremare," 956–58; Vaughan, *Europe and the Turk*, 139; Rodinson, *Europe and the Mystique of Islam*, 35; Arbel, "Roman Catholics," 82. Two decades after Cambrai, the papal nuncio in France reported that the Venetian ambassador became very "nervous" at its mention because

Venice still feared greatly the threat of another combined European force against the city. Lestocquoy, *Correspondence des nonces*, 1:54.

113. *SDC*, b. 57, cc. 279v–280r, 13 Jun 1603, Francesco Contarini to Senate; Kunt, "Ethnic-Regional (*Cins*) Solidarity," 233–39. See also Kafadar, "The Ottomans and Europe," 1:604–5.

114. Elliott, "A Europe of Composite Monarchies," 51–52; Davis, "Boundaries and the Sense of Self," 53–63; Matthee, "Merchants in Safavid Iran," 264–65.

115. Armstrong, *Nations before Nationalism*, 6; Sahlins, *Boundaries*, 270–71. See also Anderson, *Imagined Communities;* Renan, "What Is a Nation," 42–55; Schulze, *States, Nations, and Nationalism,* 97; Galbraith, "Nationality and Language," 27–28.

116. Foster and Daniell, *Life of Busbecq*, 1:330; Dallam, "Diary," 79; Wood, *Mr. Harrie Cavendish*, 13.

117. Kirshner, "Between Nature and Culture," 179–203; Sahlins, *Unnaturally French*, 66–69.

118. Molho, "Ebrei e marrani," 2:1019–20; Cassia, "Religion, Politics, and Ethnicity in Cyprus," 21–24.

119. Bennassar and Bennassar, *Les chrétiens d'Allah;* Scaraffia, *Rinnegati;* Rostagno, *Mi faccio turco;* Benzoni, "Il «farsi turco.»"

120. *VSM, Risposte*, reg. 138, c. 121r; Tucci, "Psychology of the Venetian Merchant," 363–64. For a comparative view of early modern citizenship in France, see Sahlins, *Unnaturally French.*

121. Sahlins, *Boundaries*, xv.

122. Brummett, "Understanding Space," 4.

123. While scholars of the Ottoman Empire have rightly insisted on the richness and importance of Ottoman sources in writing Ottoman history, there has also been a recognition that Venetian archives contain unique sources that are essential to the study of the empire. See Kafadar, "Ottomans and Europe," 629; Baschet, *La diplomatie vénitienne*, 228; Mantran, "Venise, centre d'information sur les turcs," 112–15; Faroqhi, *Approaching Ottoman History*, 15, 66, 110; İnalcık, "An Outline of Ottoman-Venetian Relations," 83; Shaw, "Ottoman and Turkish Studies in the United States," 120; Lewis, "The Ottoman Archives."

124. Hanlon, *Confession and Community*, 8–11.

125. Greenblatt, *Marvelous Possessions*, 7; Bitterli, *Cultures in Conflict*, 7; Greenblatt, *Renaissance Self-Fashioning.*

126. Rubiés, "Travel Writing as a Genre," 8; Faroqhi, "Crisis and Change," 2:605.

CHAPTER 1. THE VENETIAN NATION IN CONSTANTINOPLE

1. Eliud Ashtor, "Venetian Supremacy in Levantine Trade"; Braudel, *The Perspective of the World*, 118–24.

2. Babinger, *Mehmed the Conqueror*, 255–66.

3. İnalcık, "The Ottoman State," 1:230–34, 262–64, 273, 342–43; İnalcık, "Ottoman Galata," 60–61; İnalcık, "Outline of Ottoman-Venetian Relations," 1:87–88.

4. Tucci, "Tra Venezia e mondo turco," 42; "Relazione di Simone Contarini," in Barozzi and Berchet, *Relazioni*, 1:235; d'Alessio, *Relatione*, 31.

5. Yerasimos and Bacqué-Grammont, "La résidence du baile de Venise à Balikpazari," 38–39; Schneider, and Nomidis, *Galata.*

6. This dating is much earlier than 1645 as proposed by Mantran, *Istanbul dans la seconde moitié du XVIIe siècle,* 38.

7. *SDC,* b. 122, cc. 374r–382r, 19 Jun 1641, Girolamo Trevisan to Senate; *DonàR,* b. 23, cc. 66r–67r.

8. Della Valle, *De' viaggi,* 1:183.

9. *SDC,* b. 74, c. 192v, 11 Jan 1612 (MV), Cristoforo Valier to Senate; Bertelè, *Il Palazzo degli Ambasciatori di Venezia,* 92–95.

10. *BAC,* b. 331-I, 2 Mar 1632.

11. Occasionally merchants might venture into the countryside to buy raw materials at a discount directly from the source, despite the physical dangers and Ottoman laws that forbade such activity. Goffman, *Izmir and the Levantine World,* 89, 143–44; Goffman, "Capitulations," 156; Mantran, *Istanbul au siècle de Soliman,* 186; *BAC,* b. 250, c. 10r, 1 Feb 1589 (MV), Command to Kadı of Galata and Emir Maetassigno.

12. Blochet, "Relation du voyage en Orient," 199; Harreld, *High Germans in the Low Countries,* 50–57.

13. *CapiXLett,* b. 1, no. 84, 23 Dec 1529, Leonin Servo to Senate.

14. *APC,* b. 8, cc. 249r–255r, 1595 (MV), "Processo contro un Dragomano."

15. *DonàR,* b. 23, c. 66r.

16. *SDC,* b. 41, cc. 475v–476r, 19 Aug 1595, Marco Venier to Senate; *SDC,* b. 61, c. 275v, 23 July 1605, Ottaviano Bon to Senate; Bertelè, *Il palazzo degli Ambasciatori di Venezia,* 149; d'Alessio, *Relatione,* 29–30.

17. *It VII* 1084 (8521), cc. 4r–v, 31 Dec 1636, Alvise Contarini to Senate; *SDelC,* f. 7, 17 Nov 1588, Senate to Bailo; *SDC,* b. 113, cc. 622r–634v, 16 Dec 1632, Giovanni Cappello to Senate; Bertelè, *Il palazzo degli Ambasciatori,* 131 n.46.

18. "Relazione di Paolo Contarini," in Albèri, *Relazioni,* 9:250; Simon, "I rappresentanti diplomatici veneziani," 57; *SDC,* b. 17, c. 429r, 9 Aug 1583, Gianfrancesco Morosini to Senate.

19. *DonàR,* b. 23, cc. 66r–67r; *It VII* 1084 (8521), c. 15r, 23 Jan 1636 (MV), Pietro Foscarini and Alvise Contarini to Senate; della Valle, *De' viaggi,* 1:184–87; Bertelè, *Il Palazzo degli Ambasciatori,* 50–52, 157–59.

20. Lane, *Venice,* 286–87. Some merchants in Alexandria also rented private homes. Ashtor, *Levant Trade,* 407.

21. On *bedestans* in the Ottoman Empire, see İnalcık, "The Hub of the City."

22. *BAC,* b. 339; *BAC,* b. 278, reg. 400, cc. 159r–160r, 22 Feb 1615 (MV). In the Byzantine era, the emperors provided a house for the bailo, one for his councillors, and a third to hold public property, as well as twenty-five houses available for the use of Venetian merchants. Diehl, "La colonie vénitienne," 95.

23. *SDC,* b. 43, cc. 224r–241r, 14–19 May, Copy of Trial; *BAC,* b. 265, reg. 374, cc. 72v–73r, 13 Mar 1586.

24. *Gregolin,* b. 12ter-I, 21 Jul 1590, Tullio Fabri in Candia to Antonio Paruta; ibid., 7 Sep 1590, Tullio Fabri in Venice to Antonio Paruta.

25. *Gregolin,* b. 6, 21 Jun 1524, Gianfrancesco Bragadin to Bailo; *CancG,* b. 14, 6 Apr

1575. The baili occuppied a prominent position in the highly symbolic order of Venice's grand ducal processions. Following the doge, his six counselors, the Procuratori di San Marco, the *savi grandi,* and the Council of Ten, came the five most important resident ambassadors in Venice's service, "Rome, Vienna, Madrid, Paris, and Constantinople." Muir, *Civic Ritual in Renaissance Venice,* 199.

26. Dursteler, "The *Bailo* in Constantinople."

27. On the mysterious death of Bailo Girolamo Lippomano, see Tormene, "Il bailaggio a Costantinopoli;" "Lorenzo Bernardo," *DBI,* 9:308–10; Preto, *I servizi secreti di Venezia,* 76–78.

28. Simon, "I rappresentanti diplomatici veneziani," 56. Bailo derives from *Baiulus* meaning *portatore;* in practice it also meant *reggitore* or *governatore* (see for example, Dante, *Paradiso* 6:73, where Octavian Augustus is described as *baiulo*). Pedani-Fabris, *In nome del Gran Signore,* 7; see also "Bāylōs," in *EI,* 1:1008.

29. Thomas, *Diplomatarium Veneto-Levantium* (Venice, 1880–89), 1:103, cited in Villain-Gandossi, "Les attributions du Baile," 240; see also Diehl, "La colonie vénetienne," 114, 122–27.

30. There has been some debate on whether early Italian representatives such as the bailo were consuls or ambassadors, indeed the Venetian Senate itself in 1574 felt it necessary to legislate that baili were on equal footing with other ambassadors. By the end of the sixteenth century, however, the importance and status of the baili were clearly established. *SMar,* reg. 42, c. 113r, 5 Feb 1574 (MV); Mattingly, *Renaissance Diplomacy,* 58–59.

31. On the early history of the office of bailo under the Byzantines, see Nicol, *Byzantium and Venice,* 181–201, 289–91; Bertelè, *Il palazzo degli Ambasciatori,* 19–28; Robbert, "Rialto Businessmen"; Coco and Manzonetto, *Baili veneziani,* 13; Maltezou, *Ho thesmos tou en Kônstantinoupolei;* Maltezou, "Il quartiere veneziano di Costantinopoli"; Brown, "Venetians and the Venetian Quarter"; Diehl, "La colonie vénetienne"; Madden, *Enrico Dandolo,* 173–94.

32. Chojnacki, "Identity and Ideology in Renaissance Venice," 265; Gleason, "Confronting New Realities," 169–80.

33. Simon, "Les dépêches de Marin Cavalli," 1:268.

34. Lollino, *Vita del cavaliere Ottaviano Bon,* 8–9.

35. "Relazione di Daniele Barbarigo," in Albèri, *Relazioni,* 6:37–38.

36. "Relazione di Simone Contarini," in Barozzi and Berchet, *Relazioni,* 1:234.

37. Mattingly, *Renaissance Diplomacy,* 99; Preto, *I servizi secreti,* 197.

38. Preto, *I servizi secreti,* 484; Luca, "Alcuni 'confidenti' del bailaggio veneto."

39. Simon, "I rappresentanti diplomatici veneziani," 65; Simon, "Les dépêches de Marin Cavalli," 1, 303–5; de Zanche, *Tra Constantinopoli e Venezia.*

40. Burke, "Early Modern Venice," 393.

41. In 1586 this included subconsulates in Aleppo, Alexandria-Cairo, Izmir, Fochie, Mytilene and Anatolia, Chios, Gallipoli, Silivri, Palormo, and Rhodes. Simon, "I rappresentanti diplomatici veneziani," 57; Steensgaard, "Consuls and Nations in the Levant," 25–26; *SDelC,* f. 5, 4 Oct 1583, Senate to Bailo; *SMar,* reg. 55, c. 87v, 9 Nov 1594; *SDC,* b. 23, cc. 229r–239v, 16 Apr 1586, Lorenzo Bernardo to Senate; *BAC,* b. 268, reg. 381, c. 41r, 2 Aug 1592.

42. *XSeg,* f. 20, 26 Sep 1577.

43. *Senato Secreto Deliberazioni,* reg. 71, cc. 371–491, cited in Simon, "Les dépêches de Marin Cavalli," 2:159–63.

44. SDC, b. 60, c. 316v, 14 Feb 1604 (MV), Ottaviano Bon to Senate; see also "Relazione di Pietro Foscarini", in Barozzi and Berchet, *Relazioni,* 2:101.

45. For a sample, see *BAC,* b. 250–52, 374–75, and the collections *Lettere e scritture turchesche* and *Documenti turchi.* The latter collection has been minutely indexed in Pedani-Fabris, *Documenti turchi;* see also Faroqhi, "Venetian Presence in the Ottoman Empire."

46. *Gregolin,* b. 2, 17 Nov 1593, Alvise and Leonardo Sanudo in Venice to Marco Venier; *Gregolin,* b. 2, 27 Mar 1594, Alvise and Leonardo Sanudo in Venice to Marco Venier; Simon, "I rappresentanti diplomatici veneziani," 59, 62.

47. Tucci, "Tra Venezia e mondo turco," 45; Ashtor, *Levant Trade,* 411.

48. *BAC,* b. 295, c. 4v, 22 Feb 1596 (MV); "Relazione di Alvise Contarini," in Barozzi and Berchet, *Relazioni,* 1:331. On Venice's public health system, see Vanzan Marchini, *I mali e i rimedi,* 13–37, 65–102; see also Cipolla, *Fighting the Plague.*

49. Simon, "I rappresentanti diplomatici veneziani," 62; Faroqhi, "Venetian Presence in the Ottoman Empire," 363.

50. D'Alessio, *Relatione,* 73; Matteucci, *Un glorioso convento,* 358–62; d'Alessio, *Le couvent et l'eglise des Saints-Pierre-et-Paul,* 14–16.

51. Mun, "L'Établissement des Jesuites."

52. Simon, "I rappresentanti diplomatici veneziani,"62; *BAC,* b. 365-I, 3 Jun 1588. On this, see also Tenenti, "Gli schiavi di Venezia"; Davis, "Slave Redemption in Venice," 457; Davis, *Christian Slaves, Muslim Masters;* Rudt de Collenberg, *Esclavage et rançons.*

53. SDC, b. 15, c. 32r, 2 Apr 1581, Paolo Contarini to Senate; "Relazione di Daniele Barbarigo," in Albèri, *Relazioni,* 6:43; APC, b. 2, c. 13v, 29 Mar 1525, Piero Bragadin to Senate; *DocTR,* b. 4, no. 484, ca. 2 Oct 1542, Sultan to Doge; LSTR, b. 3, cc. 31r–v, 2 Nov 1574, Mehmed Paşa to Doge.

54. SMar, reg. 86, cc. 293r–294r, 3 Feb 1627 (MV); also SDelC, f. 10, 10 Aug 1604, in Pregadi.

55. DocTR, b. 4, 475, ca. 28 Mar 1542, Sultan to several *kadı* between Constantinople, and Ragusa and Bosnia; SDC, b. 66, c. 296r, 21 Sep 1608, Simone Contarini to Senate from San Niccolò del Lido; InqStat, b. 416, 14 Jul 1612, excerpt from letter from Bailo to Senate.

56. SMar, reg. 86, cc. 293r–294r, 3 Feb 1627 (MV); 10 Aug 1604, in Pregadi, SDelC, f. 10. In his manual of advice on the office of ambassador, Marino Cavalli listed the minimum *famiglia* of a "mediocre ambassador." This included "a majordomo, a steward, a waiter, two butlers, a stable master, four valets, a secretary, a cook and a scullery-boy, a mule-driver, a carriage driver, three stable-boys, a page." Bertelè, *Informatione,* 60.

57. For a comparison, the French ambassador's *famiglia* in 1605 included at least twenty-one, and perhaps as many as thirty-four, people. Among these were "a treasurer, a surgeon, a chef, a wine steward, a pastry chef, a falconer, an astrologer, a groom, and a Turkish dragoman"; Biron, *Ambassade en Turquie,* 1:16–19. The *famiglia* of the first Dutch ambassador to the Porte, Cornelis Haga, numbered twenty people including a painter, a clerk and a tailor, a messenger, majordomo, cellar master-butler, doorkeeper, cook and assistant cook, stableman, two valets, three dragomans and one apprentice dragoman, a

Turkish scribe, two janissaries, and a German apothecary. De Groot, "The Dutch Nation in Istanbul," 133–34.

58. "Relazione di Paolo Contarini," in Albèri, *Relazioni*, 9:250.

59. Bertelè, *Il palazzo degli Ambasciatori*, 121–24.

60. Sherley, "Discours of the Turkes," 14.

61. On the *cittadini*, the essential work is Zannini, *Burocrazia e burocrati*, 37–45; see also Grubb, "Elite Citizens," 339–56.

62. *SDC*, b. 75, c. 102r, 3 Apr 1613, Cristoforo Valier to Senate.

63. *SDelC*, f. 5, 16 Oct 1582, Senate to Baili; *CollRel*, b. 5, "Relazione di Cristoforo Valier."

64. Villain-Gandossi, "Les dépêches chiffrées," 64–66.

"Summary of letters sent . . . by Marco Venier:"

—1593 29 Jan, 3 letters; 12–13 Feb, 2 letters; 26–27 Feb, 5 letters

—1594 12 Mar, 2 letters; 13 Mar, 2 letters; 24–25 Mar, 4 letters; 26 Mar, 1 letter; 2–3 Apr, 2 letters; 15–16 Apr, 6 letters; 22 Apr, 2 letters; 3–4 May, 4 letters; 20–21 May, 3 letters; 6–8 June, 5 letters; 11–12 June, 2 letters; 16 June, 1 letter; 25–26 June, 3 letters; 1 July, 2 letters; 8 July, 2 letters; 22–23 July, 4 letters; 27 July, 2 letters.

From *SDC*, b. 39, c. 575r, 24 Jul 1594, Marco Venier to Senate.

65. *SDelC*, f. 9, 21 Feb 1597, Senate to Bailo; de Zanche, "Tra Costantinopoli e Venezia," 57–60.

66. Cited in Zannini, *Burocrazia e burocrati*, 157. Complaints by secretaries about the "fattiche dello scrivere" seem to have been common; see *SDCop*, reg. 12, cc. 105–6, 7 Oct 1597, Girolamo Cappello to Senate.

67. *CapiXLett*, b. 7, no. 45–47, no. 58, 2 Mar 1608; Davis, *Pursuit of Power*, 8.

68. *SMar*, reg. 44, cc. 175r–v, 12 Dec 1579.

69. For example, see *SDC*, b. 59, cc. 133r–139r, 18 May 1604, Gabriel Cavazza to Senate; "Bonrizzo, Alvise," *DBI*, 12:365–66.

70. *SDC*, b. 75, c. 1r, 9 Mar 1613, Gabriel Cavazza in Adrianopole to Senate; *SDC*, b. 21, c. 557r, 16 Aug 1585, Lorenzo Bernardo to Senate; *SDC*, b. 19, cc. 132r–135r, 19 Apr 1584, Gianfrancesco Morosini to Senate; *SDC*, b. 58, cc. 239v–244r, 2 Jan 1603 (MV), Francesco Contarini to Senate; *SDC*, b. 53, cc. 332r–336v, 12 Jul 1601, Agostino Nani to Senate; *SDC*, b. 50, c. 90r, 16 Oct 1599, Girolamo Cappello to Senate; *SDC*, b. 21, cc. 1r–5v, 12 Mar 1585, Gianfrancesco Morosini to Senate. See also, *SDC*, b. 17, cc. 421r–422v, 9 Aug 1583, Gianfrancesco Morosini to Senate; *InqStat*, b. 416, 15 Jul 1630.

71. *SMar*, reg. 60, c. 39r, 14 Jun 1600; Zannini, *Burocrazia e burocrati*, 187–88; *SMar*, reg. 86, cc. 68v–69r, 27 May 1627; *SMar*, reg. 61, c. 35v, 30 Jun 1601.

72. See Casini, "Realtà e simboli," 233–40.

73. *BAC*, b. 276, reg. 394, cc. 291v–292r, 24 Nov 1610; *BAC*, b. 276, reg. 397, c. 149v, 7 Mar 1613; *BAC*, b. 329, 4 Aug 1597, "Processo contro alcuno di haver portati contrabandi sopra la nave Martinella."

74. For an example of these financial records, see *DonàR*, b. 148, no. 3, "Memoriale di mano di Mr Cesare Ziliol suo ragionato nell'Ambasceria di Constantinople delle spese straordinarie"; *SMar*, reg. 48, cc. 141r–142r, 30 Jan 1587 (MV).

75. *Gregolin,* b. 12ter-I, 4 Jul 1590, Tulio Fabri in Gallipoli to Antonio Paruta; *SDelC,* f. 12, 4 Dec 1612, Senate to Bailo; *It VII* 1087 (8524), cc. 145r–146r, 20 Jun 1639, Alvise Contarini to Senate; *BAC,* b. 280, reg. 403, c. 116r, 7 Feb 1619 (MV).

76. *SDCop,* reg. 12, cc. 105–6, 7 Oct 1597, Girolamo Cappello to Senate; *SDCop,* reg. 13, c. 24, 13 Jan 1598 (MV), Girolamo Cappello to Senate; *SDC,* b. 55, c. 88r, 14 Apr 1602, Agostino Nani to Senate.

77. *It VII* 1084 (8521), cc. 14r–v, 31 Dec 1636, Alvise Contarini to Senate.

78. On the *medico di casa,* see Lucchetta, "Il medico del bailaggio di Costantinopoli."

79. Nicolay, *Navigations into Turkie,* 93r; *SDC,* b. 59, cc. 81r–v, 13 Apr 1604, Francesco Contarini to Senate; see also Lewis, *Jews of Islam,* 129–31; Levy, *The Sephardim in the Ottoman Empire,* 76–77; Murphey, "Jewish Contributions to Ottoman Medicine," 61–70.

80. The bibliography on Ashkenazi is by now quite extensive: see Arbel, *Trading Nations,* 87–94; "Ashkenazi, Solomon." On Israel Conegliano, another Jewish physician trained at Padua who moved easily between Venice and Constantinople, see Roth, *History of the Jews in Venice,* 190–91.

81. Biron, *Ambassade en Turquie,* 1:123; *APC,* b. 9, c. 2:1r, 2 Dec 1595, Leonardo Donà and Marco Venier to Senate; *SDelC,* f. 10, 3 June 1600; *SDC,* b. 31, c. 387r, 21 July 1590, Girolamo Lippomano to Senate. The tragic voyage of the Gradenigo party is minutely recounted in *SDC,* b. 49, cc. 410r–414r, 27 Aug 1599, Vicenzo Gradenigo to Senate; *SDC,* b. 50, cc. 32r–33v, 5 Sep 1599, Vincenzo Gradenigo to Senate; *SDC,* b. 51, c. 10v, 7 Mar 1600, Girolamo Cappello to Senate. See also Brown, "Il viaggio di Vicenzo Gradenigo."

82. Mantran, "Venise, centre d'informations sur les turcs," 113. Despite the ubiquity and importance of the dragomans in this period, little has been written about them. See for example Marghetitch, *Étude sur les fonctions des drogman;* Paladino, "Due dragomanni veneti a Costantinopoli"; Cunningham, "Dragomania"; Pippidi, "Sur quelques drogmans de Constantinople"; Infelise, "Gian Rinaldo Carli Senior."

83. Bertelè, *Informatione,* 85.

84. Finlay, "Al servizio del Sultano," 79; Benzoni, "A proposito dei baili veneziani," 76–77.

85. Bates, *Touring in 1600,* 49–50; Manlio Cortelazzo, "Che cosa s'intendesse per 'lingua franca,'" 108–10.

86. Simon, "Les dépêches de Marin Cavalli," 1:280.

87. "Relazione di Gianfrancesco Morosini," in Albèri, *Relazioni,* 9:318–20; Tormene, "Il bailaggio a Costantinopoli," 393–94; *DonàR,* b. 148, cc. 132r–v; *It VII* 1086 (8523), cc.174r–v, 28 Aug 1638, Alvise Contarini to Senate.

88. Cited in Preto, *Venezia e i turchi,* 101.

89. Gio Batta. Salvago, *Africa overo barberia.*

90. Bertelè, *Il palazzo degli ambasciatori,* 121–22; Paladino, "Due dragomanni veneti a Costantinopoli," 187–88; Simon, "Les dépêches de Marin Cavalli," 1:280–85.

91. "Un Bailo accusato di stregoneria," 360–66.

92. Matteucci, *Un glorioso convento,* 148, 153; Pippidi, *Hommes et idées,* 82–84, 137–51; Stancovich, *Biografia degli uomini,* 434; Sturdza, *Dictionnaire historique et généalogique,* 572–73, 579, 586, 590–93.

93. *APC,* b. 2, c. 20r, 18 Jul 1525, Piero Bragadin to Senate; *APC,* b. 18, 5: cc. 8v–9r,

16 Jun 1621, Giorgio Giustinian to Senate. These concerns were common among all European ambassadors to the Porte who had to rely on dragomans. Tongas, *Les relations de la France avec l'Empire Ottoman*, 19; Wood, "The English Embassy at Constantinople," 540.

94. *SDC*, b. 39, c. 55r, 24 Mar 1594 Marco Venier to Senate.

95. Lucchetta, "La scuola dei 'giovani di lingua' "; Mantran, "Venise, centre d'informations sur les turcs," 113; Pippidi, *Hommes et idées*, 157; Tuncel, "L'âge des drogmans," 367.

96. *VSM*-II, reg. 61, 21 Feb 1550 (MV), in Senate.

97. Lucchetta, "La scuola dei 'giovani di lingua,' " 25–30.

98. Bertelè, *Informatione*, 61.

99. Tormene, "Il bailaggio a Costantinopoli," 393–34; *SDC*, b. 16, c. 219r, 14 Oct 1582, Paolo Contarini to Senate; *DonàR*, b. 23, cc. 66r–67r; *It VII* 1086 (8523), c. 435r, 12 Feb 1638 (MV), Alvise Contarini to Senate.

100. *SDC*, b. 41, cc. 475v–476r, 19 Aug 1595, Marco Venier to Senate; *APC*, b. 9, cc. 40r–v, 12 Dec 1595, Leonardo Donà and Marco Venier to Senate; *DonàR*, b. 148, c. 24, no. 3 "Memoriale di mano di Mr Cesare Ziliol . . ."

101. Bertelè, *Informatione*, 61–63; Tormene, "Il bailaggio a Costantinopoli," 393–94. In the seventeenth century, in addition to the majordomo, a *maestro di stalla*, or master of the stall, is also mentioned; Cavalli also mentions a *canevaro*, or wine steward, which was unique to the embassies of Rome and Constantinople. Bertelè, *Informatione*, 61; Bertelè, *Il palazzo degli ambasciatori*, 143.

102. *BAC*, b. 316-I, 1585, 1586, 1587, "Libro di Commandamenti"; *BAC*, b. 272, reg. 387, c. 21v, 11 Oct 1600; *BAC*, b. 273, reg. 390, cc. 135r–136r, 26 Sep 1603; *BAC*, b. 274, reg. 391, cc. 227r–228v, 15 Mar 1606; *BAC*, b. 274, reg. 391, cc. 292v–293v, 3 Aug 1606; *BAC*, b. 275, reg. 393, c. 186v, 28 Nov 1607; *BAC*, b. 276, reg. 394, cc. 42v–43r, 6 Apr 1609; *BAC*, b. 277, reg. 397, c. 160r, 24 May 1613; *BAC*, b. 279, reg. 402, c. 50v, 22 Apr 1617; *BAC*, b. 329, 4 Aug 1597, "Processo contro alcuno di haver portati contrabandi sopra la nave Martinella"; *BAC*, b. 269, reg. 382, c. 182v, 26 Mar 1596; *BAC*, b. 280, reg. 404, cc. 52r–54v, 12 Aug 1622; *APC*, b. 8, cc. 245r–290v, 1595 (MV), "Processo contro un Dragomano"; *BAC*, b. 329, 20 Oct 1594, "Processo et sententia criminal contro Giacomo di Luca di Cypro, condennato anni cinque in una delle gallee di condannati"; *BAC*, b. 331-I, no. 3, 2 Mar 1632, "Filza Corrente . . . dell'Eccmo Cappello, 1629–32."

103. *XSeg*, f. 22, 8 Feb 1581 (MV), Council of Ten to Duke of Candia; *InqStat*, b. 416, 14 Jul 1612, excerpt from letter from Bailo to Senate; *SDC*, b. 16, c. 170r, 15 Sep 1582, Paolo Contarini to Senate; *SDC*, b. 43, cc. 236r–241r, 19 May 1596, Marco Venier to Senate; *SDC*, b. 47, cc. 125v–126v, 2 May 1598, Girolamo Cappello to Senate.

104. *BAC*, b. 268, reg. 381, c. 46r, 27 Sep 1592; *SDC*, b. 50, cc. 32r–33v, 5 Sep 1599, Vicenzo Gradenigo in Thessaloníki to Senate.

105. *SDC*, b. 32, cc. 72r–v, 15 Sep 1590, Girolamo Lippomano to Senate; Lucchetta, "Sulla ritrattistica veneziana in oriente," 114, 118, 121; Fabris, "Artisinat et culture 55, 57. For evidence of the degree to which artistic and material boundaries between East and West were permeable, see Jardine and Brotton, *Global Interests*.

106. *InqStat*, b. 433, 9 May 1590, Alvise Rizzo in Venice to Giancarlo Scaramelli; *BAC*, b. 263, reg. 372, cc. 13v–14r, 18 Aug 1580.

107. Nicolay, *Navigations into Turkie*, 76r–v; Hughes, *Shakespeare's Europe*, 54–55.

108. *BAC*, b. 284, reg. 411, c. 306r, 14 Aug 1636; Wood, "The English Embassy at Constantinople," 540; Eldem, Goffman, and Masters, *The Ottoman City between East and West*, 145. The term "pig" was a Muslim epithet reserved for Christians; Jews were derided as "apes"; Lewis, *Jews of Islam*, 33. On the *yasakçıs*, see Goffman, *Britons in the Ottoman Empire*, 17.

109. *Compilazione delle leggi*, b. 157, no. 347–349, 27 June 1556, in Pregadi; Bertelè, *Il palazzo degli Ambasciatori*, 142; *BAC*, b. 347, 6 Sep 1629; Hughes, *Shakespeare's Europe*, 54–55.

110. Nicolay, *Navigations into Turkie*, 76r–v.

111. *SDC*, b. 23, cc. 521r–522r, 19 Aug 1586, Lorenzo Bernardo to Senate.

112. *BAC*, b. 329, 12 Nov 1598, "Processo contro Zorzi Argiti." For another escape, see *CapiXLett*, b. 7, no. 132, 28 May 1622, Giorgio Giustinian to Council of Ten.

113. *SDC*, b. 21, c. 180r, 17 Apr 1585, Gianfrancesco Morosini to Senate; *BAC*, b. 368, c. 1618, "Commandamento diretto alli Cadi di Constantinopli e Galata"; Faroqhi, "Venetian Presence in the Ottoman Empire," 378.

114. D'Alessio, *Relatione*, 29–30.

115. *BAC*, b. 369, 25 Oct 1647; *SDCop*, reg. 17, cc. 80–89, 7 Dec 1621, Giorgio Giustinian to Senate.

116. "Relazione di Alvise Contarini," in Barozzi and Berchet, *Relazioni*, 1:331.

CHAPTER 2. THE MERCHANTS OF VENICE

1. *BAC*, b. 269, reg. 382, c. 10v, 1 Mar 1594.

2. Subacchi, "Italians in Antwerp," 73.

3. Bratchel, "Regulation and Group Consciousness," 585.

4. Steensgaard, "Consuls and Nations in the Levant," 15; Mauro, "Merchant Communities," 255, 266, 286.

5. While Tucci suggests that four of nineteen merchants convened in the Council of Twelve in 1594 might have been noble based on their surnames, the chancellery records (in which nobles were always identified with the title of either *Magnifico* or *Clarissimo*, while citizens and others were called *domino, signore,* or *mr*) show this figure to be much too high. Tucci, "Psychology of the Venetian Merchant," 348.

6. Iorga, "Contribuțiunĭ la istoria Munteniei," 102.

7. Tucci, *Mercanti, navi*, 95–96; Sapori, *The Italian Merchant in the Middle Ages*; Lane, *Andrea Barbarigo*; Lane, *Venice*, 48–54.

8. Lane, *Andrea Barbarigo*, 84; Lane, *Venice*, 119–52; Tucci, "Psychology of the Venetian Merchant," 347–48.

9. Girolamo Muzio, *Il gentilhuomo*, (Venice, 1571), 126–28, cited in Zannini, *Burocrazia e burocrati*, 69.

10. Sanudo, *Diarii*, 35:257 cited in Bertelè, *Il palazzo degli Ambasciatori;* 69; ibid., 133.

11. Livi, Sella, and Tucci, "Un probleme d'histoire," 312–13; Zannini, *Burocrazia e burocrati*, 252.

12. Muir, *Civic Ritual in Renaissance Venice*, 119–34.

13. Davis, *A Venetian Family and Its Fortune*, 32. Donà no doubt was dismayed by

attitudes such as that expressed by one patrician who preferred to travel to Constantinople by land "to liberate myself from the Sea, [which is] totally contrary and dangerous to my complexion," *SDC,* b. 21, c. 168r, 23 Apr 1584, Lorenzo Bernardo to Senate from Ragusa. A similar sentiment was expressed by Alvise Contarini who, in recommending several changes in Venetian maritime practice, admitted "I have very little knowledge both of the profession of merchant which I have never done, and of navigation which I have never experienced"; *It VII* 1085 (8522), cc. 222r–227v, 6 Feb 1637 (MV), Alvise Contarini to Senate.

14. This label comes from Frederic Lane's influential *Venice: A Maritime Republic,* which links Venice's decline to its *terraferma* expansion. For an occasionally insightful, though more often curiously hyperbolic review of Lane's work, see Cochrane and Kirshner, "Deconstructing Lane's Venice." A good survey of the historiography of Venetian decline is Grubb, "When Myths Lose Power," 60–72.

15. Gullino, "I patrizi veneziani," 2:410–12.

16. Burke, *Venice and Amsterdam,* 55; Gullino, "I patrizi veneziani," 421–22. In the *Giudici di petizion,* see for example, b. 5, no. 44, 30 Mar 1599; b. 5, no. 2, 22 Jun 1595; b. 5, no. 74, 1586, "Conto di Magnifico Mr Zorzi Badoer"; b. 6, no. 23, 1590; b. 6, no. 53, 1585–88, "Conto di Bernardo Agudi mio cugnato assegnato per Iacomo e Zuanne Baldi"; b. 7, no. 88, 30 Apr 1604.

17. *SMar,* b. 187, cited in Gullino, "I patrizi veneziani," 417–18; "Report on Venice attributed to the Spanish Ambassador Don Alonso della Cueva, Marquis of Bedmar," *British Library,* Addtl. ms. 5471, cc. 147–53, cited in Chambers, and Pullan, *Venice: A Documentary History,* 257–60.

18. Gullino, "I patrizi veneziani," 415; Lane, *Venice,* 384. Tucci, "Psychology of the Venetian Merchant," 356, paints a bleaker picture; he shows a drop between 1500 and 1603 in patrician requests for state shipbuilding loans from 72.72% to 10.72%. This ignores, however, ships patricians purchased from other Venetians and, even more importantly, ships purchased outside of Venice, which were then granted Venetian status by the Senate. The records of the V Savii contain a number of such investments: Francesco Morosini bought four, perhaps five, foreign ships over a four-year span near the end of the century; Benetto Dolfin in 1596 bought a ship constructed in Constantinople and had it armed in Venice. *VSM-I,* reg. 139, c. 146v, 9 Jun 1597; cc. 167v–168r, 27 Sep 1597; c. 135r, 27 Feb 1596 (MV).

19. Tucci, *Mercanti, navi,* 145–46, 154–55. Tenenti's data, 1592–1609, show 128 patricians insured and seventy insurers. For this period, 9.1% of the insured are noble, and 11.6% of the insurers. Gullino, "I patrizi veneziani," 418–21. On insurance rates, which might reach ten to fourteen percent each way, see Stefani, *L'assicurazione a Venezia,* 1:99.

20. Tucci, "Psychology of the Venetian Merchant," 354–55; Davis, *A Venetian Family,* 54–57; Queller, *Venetian Patriciate,* 113–71.

21. Tucci, "Psychology of the Venetian Merchant," 350; Livi, Sella, and Tucci, "Un probleme d'histoire," 313–17; Lane, *Andrea Barbarigo,* 11–15; Benzoni, "Tra centro e periferia," 98–99; see also Stella, "La crisi economica veneziana"; Woolf, "Venice and the Terraferma," 181–87.

22. Not all contemporaries believed, as did Priuli, that the turn to the *terraferma* was

negative. One cadre believed that only by establishing Venetian hegemony over Italy could the city command resources equal to those of the great empires that surrounded it. Priuli, *I diarii;* Lane, *Venice,* 247.

23. Tucci, "Psychology of the Venetian Merchant," 352. The literature on the decline of Venice is quite extensive; good starting points are Livi, Sella, Tucci, "Un probleme d'histoire," 289-317, and Tucci, "Un ciclo di affari," 124. See also Rapp, *Industry and Economic Decline;* Rapp, "The Unmaking of the Mediterranean Trade Hegemony," 523-24; Sella, *Commerci e industrie;* Sella, "L'economia," 651-711; Pullan, *Crisis and Change in the Venetian Economy;* Pagano de Devitiis, *English Merchants,* 182-83.

24. Gullino, "I patrizi veneziani," 414-15; Davis, *A Venetian Family,* 31.

25. On Barbarigo, see Barbaro, 2:152; *AvCom, Nascite,* reg. 4, c. 201; Gullino, "I patrizi veneziani," 414-18.

26. Contarini, *The Commonwealth and Government of Venice,* 133-34.

27. Tucci, "Psychology of the Venetian Merchant," 348; Tucci, "Tra Venezia e mondo turco," 38; Lane, *Andrea Barbarigo,* 13-14, 17-18, 29-31, 36; *InqStat,* b. 433, 13 Sep 1590, Giovanni Bragadin to Bailo.

28. *BAC,* b. 264, reg. 424, c. 17r, 5 Jul 1584; *SDC,* b. 39, cc. 1r-v, 12 Mar 1594, Marco Venier to Senate.

29. *BAC,* b. 266, reg. 375, c. 147v, 11 Jan 1589 (MV); *SDC,* b. 30, c. 378r, 20 Jan 1589 (MV), Giovanni Moro to Senate.

30. *SDC,* b. 39, cc. 1r-v, 12 Mar 1594, Marco Venier to Senate.

31. Lane, *Venice and History,* 36-40.

32. *SDC,* b. 31, cc. 237r, 348r, contains a number of letters of exchange that suggest the Bragadin trade network and family involvement in them; *BAC,* b. 266, reg. 376, cc. 14v-15r, 2 Apr 1588; *BAC,* b. 268, reg. 380, cc. 39r-v, 10 Jul 1593; *BAC,* b. 368, no. 66, "Libro di spese di vitto di Nave," 1595; *SDCop,* reg. 11, c. 75, 20 Oct 1596, Marco Venier to Senate.

33. *BAC,* b. 268, reg. 381, cc. 19r-v, 18 May 1592; *BAC,* b. 317, cc. 50v-51r, 2 Dec 1591; *InqStat,* b. 433, 13 Sep 1590, Giovanni Bragadin to Bailo; Gullino, "I patrizi veneziani," 414-15; *NotAtti,* Zuan Andrea Catti, reg. 3356, c. 232v-233v, 1985, cited in Stefani, *L'assicurazione a Venezia,* 1:267-68; *NotAtti,* Zuan Andrea Catti reg. 3367, c. 485v-486v, 1596, in ibid.

34. *SDCop,* reg. 11, c. 78, 21 Oct 1596, Marco Venier to Senate.

35. *SDC,* b. 31, c. 473v, 18 Aug 1590, Girolamo Lippomano to Senate; *SDC,* b. 23, c. 48r-v, 11 Jun 1586, Lorenzo Bernardo to Senate.

36. *BAC,* b. 266, reg. 376, c. 51r, 28 Jul 1589; Barbaro, 2:152-53; *BAC,* b. 268, reg. 381, c. 83v, 25 Jul 1593; *BAC,* b. 344, 1580-95, "Declarations of debts owed to Polo and Piero Bragadin"; *AvCom, Nascite,* reg. 4, c. 201.

37. *SDC,* b. 39, cc. 1r-v, 12 Mar 1594, Marco Venier to Senate; *BAC,* b. 295, cc. 19v-20r, 1 Jul 1597; *SDC,* b. 57, 439r-v, 2 Aug 1603, Francesco Contarini to Senate.

38. Agostino Gussoni di Andrea, for example, remained in Constantinople for a year to study Ottoman government as preparation for a career in public service. *SDC,* b. 52, b. 44v, 5 Oct 1600, Agostino Nani to Senate.

39. Gullino has proposed a suggestive explanation for patrician families' reluctance to send their sons to the Levant after 1550: for households that had titular land holdings, *commende,* and trusts, the objective was not acquisition but conservation of wealth. The

chief way to ensure this was "through the continuity of the family, and [sending a son to the Levante] constitute[d] perhaps an excessive and unjustified risk . . . Especially since trade could also be exercised in the *dominante*." Gullino, "I patrizi veneziani," 414.

40. Luca di Linda, *Le relationi et descrittioni universali et particolari del mondo* (Venice, 1672), 536, cited in Tucci, "Psychology of the Venetian Merchant," 359–60. The *cittadini* have only recently come to be the focus of serious historical study; see Zannini, *Burocrazia e burocrati;* Trebbi, "La cancelleria veneta"; Grubb, "Elite Citizens."

41. Kirshner, "Between Nature and Culture," 191–93, 203; Sahlins, *Unnaturally French,* 66–69.

42. Tucci, "Psychology of the Venetian Merchant," 360, Zannini, *Burocrazia e burocrati,* 92.

43. Grubb, "Elite Citizens," 339–56; Ventura, "Introduction," 1:xxix; Zannini, *Burocrazia e burocrati,* 23.

44. *Maggior Consiglio—Deliberazioni,* Liber Rocca (1552–65), cc. 4r–5r, cited in Chambers and Pullan, *Venice: A Documentary History,* 276–8; *VSM-*I, reg. 142, cc. 39v–41r, 17 Dec 1607; Kirshner, "Between Nature and Culture," 179–203. In the case of Venice, Braudel's description of "the indispensable immigrant" is exactly right. Braudel, *The Mediterranean,* 1:334.

45. Tucci, "Psychology of the Venetian Merchant," 360, 363; Molà and Mueller, "Essere straniero a Venezia," 846–47.

46. Zannini, *Burocrazia e burocrati,* 44–45, 101–2.

47. *VSM-*I, reg. 138, cc. 55v–56v, 2 Sep 1588. In response to Venice's deteriorating commercial position, in 1610 the V Savii proposed a number of reforms, including revamping the citizenship requirements. Their suggestions were intended to make commerce more accessible to noncitizens and thus strengthen Venetian commerce. *VSM-*I, reg. 142, c. 190r (misnumbered 186r–188r), 5 Jul 1610. On Venetian citizenship, see Tucci, "Psychology of the Venetian Merchant," 362–63; Arbel, *Trading Nations,* ix, 2–3; Zannini, *Burocrazia e burocrati,* 23; Pullan, *Rich and Poor in Renaissance Venice,* 99–108.

48. Sella, *Commerci e industrie,* 35; Tucci, "Psychology of the Venetian Merchant," 362–63; Molà and Mueller, "Essere straniero a Venezia," 840; Mueller, "Veneti facti privilegio," 172.

49. F. Miari, *Il nuovo patriziato veneto dopo la serrata del Maggior Consiglio e la guerra di Candia e Morea* (Venice, 1891), cited in Gullino, "I patrizi veneziani," 422–23.

50. *VSM-*I, reg. 135, cc. 136r–v, 6 Sep 1566; reg. 137, c. 135r, 11 Dec 1584; reg. 138, cc. 125r–v, 27 Aug 1590; reg. 139, cc. 74v–75r, 2 Sep 1595; reg. 139, c. 20r, 9 Sep 1593; reg. 140, c. 1r, 9 Mar 1598. See also Pinto, ed., *Viaggio di C. Federici e G. Balbi,* xxii.

51. Matto Bandello, *Le novelle* (Bari, 1918), 2:22, cited in Tucci, "Psychology of the Venetian Merchant," 363–64. On Bergamo's unique relationship with the *dominante,* see Benzoni, "Venezia e Bergamo."

52. *BAC,* b. 270, reg. 385, c. 140r, 15 Jun 1600. *VSM-*I, reg. 139, c. 20r, 9 Sep 1593; *SDC,* b. 53, cc. 332r–336v, 12 Jul 1601, Agostino Nani to Senate. Contrary to what Blumenkranz suggests, the Agazzi were not Jews. Blumenkranz, "Les Juifs dans le commerce maritime de Venise," 146.

53. *Gregolin,* b. 12ter-I, 14 Apr 1588, Agostino Agazzi in Angori to Antonio Paruta; *BAC,*

b. 285, reg. 413, 23 Oct 1637; *SDelC*, f. 12, n.d. [ca. Dec 1611], Bernardo Agazzi to Senate; *SDC*, b. 52, cc. 318r–319v, 14 Jan 1600 (MV), Bernardino Agazzi to Agostino Nani.

54. *BAC*, b. 269, reg. 382, cc. 152r–v, 25 Oct 1595; *BAC*, b. 270, reg. 384, cc. 35r–v, 18 Mar 1597; *BAC*, b. 270, reg. 384, c. 171v, 25 Mar 1598.

55. *BAC*, b. 269, reg. 382, c. 182v, 26 Mar 1596; Brulez, *Marchands flamands a Venise*, 1, no. 879, no. 1008; *SDC*, b. 52, cc. 69v–70v, 23 Oct 1600, Agostino Nani to Senate.

56. Tucci, "Psychology of the Venetian Merchant," 363–64; *SDC*, b. 43, cc. 398v–402v, 20 Aug 1596, Marco Venier to Senate; *VSM*-I, reg. 139, cc. 173r–v, 20 Nov 1597.

57. *BAC*, b. 275, reg. 392, cc. 69v–70r, 7 Jul 1606; *BAC*, b. 270, reg. 385, c. 109v, 31 Jan 1599 (MV); *BAC*, b. 270, reg. 385, c. 137v, 13 Jun 1600; *BAC*, b. 280, reg. 404, cc. 21r–23v, 23 Apr 1621; *BAC*, b. 317, cc. 16v–17r, 11 Jul 1598.

58. *SDC*, b. 51, cc. 87r–v, 7 Apr 1600, Girolamo Cappello to Senate.

59. *BAC*, b. 339, 11 Apr 1595, copy of contract between Ali Ağa and Bernardino Agazzi; *SDC*, b. 53, c. 14r, 3 Mar 1601; *BAC*, b. 368, no. 78, "Conto . . . della nave nominata Santa Maria et San Francesco a seguito al Signor Ali Ağa sino al tempo della rinonzia fatagli del suo"; *SDC*, b. 52, cc. 69v–70v, 23 Oct 1600, Agostino Nani to Senate.

60. *SDC*, b. 52, cc. 318r–319v, 14 Jan 1600 (MV), Bernardino Agazzi to Agostino Nani; cc. 368r–373r, 31 Jan 1600 (MV), Agostino Nani to Senate.

61. *SDC*, b. 52, cc. 326r–328v, 20 Jan 1600 (MV), Agostino Nani to Senate; cc. 42r–v, 5 Oct 1600, Agostino Nani to Senate.

62. *DonàR*, b. 351, IV, Santa Croce, 1624.

63. Tucci, "Psychology of the Venetian Merchant," 362–63.

64. "Relazione di Gianfrancesco Morosini," in Albèri, *Relazioni*, 9:311; Greene, "Commerce and the Ottoman Conquest of Kandiye," 99–100, 114.

65. Mauroeide, *Ho Hellenismos sto Galata*, 237–49.

66. For examples of the extent of Candiot contraband, see *BAC*, b. 272, reg. 387, cc. 79v–80v, 5 Feb 1600 (MV); *InqStat*, b. 416, 7 Aug 1592, Letter from Bailo.

67. Cited in Pippidi, *Hommes et idées*, 127; Arbel, "Colonie d'oltremare," 5:958. On the Cretan wine trade, see also Tucci, "Il commercio del vino," 183–206. Alberti, *Viaggio a Costantinopoli*, gives a nice account of one of these overland caravans to Poland.

68. *CollRel*, b. 4, cc. 76r–v, Relation of Lorenzo Bernardo; *BAC*, b. 272, reg. 387, cc. 117r–v, 13 Apr 1601; *SDC*, b. 58, cc. 115r–116r, 1 Aug 1603, Sultan to *kadıs* of Constantinople and Galata.

69. *BAC*, b. 268, reg. 381, c. 41r, 2 Aug 1592; *BAC*, b. 279, reg. 402, cc. 82v–83r, 28 Jun 1617. The closure of the Black Sea to Italian, particularly Venetian, trade has been the subject of some controversy. While earlier scholars dated this event to the early sixteenth century, Gilles Veinstein has recently posited that the route did not close until the 1590s. Venetian sources, however, make clear that while reduced, the Black Sea route was never entirely closed, especially not to Greek-Venetian subjects. Veinstein, "From the Italians to the Ottomans," 229; Issawi, "The Ottoman Empire in the European Economy," 107–17; Lane, *Venice*, 348. See also Berindei, "Les Vénitiens en Mer Noire"; Faroqhi, "Venetian Presence in the Ottoman Empire," 371.

70. "Relazione di Alvise Contarini," in Barozzi and Berchet, *Relazioni*, 1:411–12; Arbel, "Colonie d'oltremare," 958. Maltezou, "Historical and Social Context," 30–31.

71. *BAC*, b. 263, reg. 372, c. 149r, 26 Aug 1582; *BAC*, b. 265, reg. 374, c. 9r, 29 Jul 1585; Pippidi, *Hommes et idées*, 126. On Servo's reputation, see *CapiXLett*, b. 3, no. 16–20, 30 Aug 1563, Leonin Servo to Bailo; *CapiXLett*, b. 3, no. 267, 26 Feb 1570 (MV); *SDC*, b. 17, cc. 335r–v, 29 Jun 1583, Gianfrancesco Morosini to Senate.

72. *VSM-I*, reg. 141, cc. 41r–v, 9 May 1603, for example, contains a deliberation by the V Savii regarding the approval of foreign factors trading under the aegis of Venice (something already well under way). *VSM-I*, reg. 142, cc. 186r–188r, 5 July 1610; *VSM-I*, reg. 143, cc. 1v–2v, Aug 1610; also *SMar*, reg. 187, contains "Notta de tutti li Nobelli hanno negotio in Levante come nelli libri de doana delle 6% . . . ," which was written to combat Santorini's proposal by showing the continuing vitality of patrician commerce; Gullino, "I patrizi veneziani," 417–18.

73. *VSM-I*, reg. 139, cc. 137v–138r, 15 Mar 1597; *BAC*, b. 270, reg. 384, cc. 94r–v, 30 Aug 1597; *BAC*, b. 270, reg. 385, c. 176v, 20 Sep 1600; *VSM-I*, reg. 141, c. 89r, 26 May 1604; *DonàR*, IV, Santa Croce, 1624.

74. *VSM-I*, reg. 135, c. 119v, 19 Feb 1564 (MV).

75. *VSM-I*, reg. 139, c. 20r, 9 Sep 1593; reg. 135, cc. 136r–v, 6 Sep 1566.

76. DSA, *Lettere e commissioni di Levante*, b. 37 (1590–92), cc. 22r–23v, 29 Apr 1590, Rectors to Girolamo Pianella.

77. *BAC*, b. 267, reg. 377, c. 28v, 9 Sep 1590; *BAC*, b. 275, reg. 393, c. 82v, 20 Feb 1606 (MV); *InqStat*, b. 433, 22 Oct 1594, Bortolomio Bontempello del Cadore to Tulio Fabri; Brulez, *Marchands flamands*, I, no. 81.

78. *BAC*, b. 269, reg. 382, cc. 238v–239v, 16 Aug 1596; *BAC*, b. 270, reg. 384, cc. 25r–26r, 22 Feb 1596 (MV); *InqStat*, b. 433, 12 Mar 1595, Alvise and Lunardo Sanudo in Venice to Tulio Fabri in Pera; *Gregolin*, b. 2, 17 Nov 1593, Alvise and Lunardo Sanudo in Venice to Marco Venier; 27 Mar 1594, Alvise and Leonardo Sanudo in Venice to Marco Venier.

79. *SDC*, b. 31, cc. 193r–196r, 13 May 1590, Girolamo Lippomano to Senate from Cernizza.

80. Cited in Villain-Gandossi, "Les attributions du Baile," 242–24.

81. *SDC*, b. 31, cc. 193r–196r, 13 May 1590, Girolamo Lippomano to Senate from Cernizza.

82. *BAC*, b. 272, reg. 387, c. 118r, 24 Apr 1601; *BAC*, b. 280, reg. 404, cc. 199v–200r, 2 Mar 1624.

83. *BAC*, b. 273, reg. 389, cc. 12v–14r, 24 May 1603; *BAC*, b. 273, reg. 390, cc. 197r–v, 21 Jun 1604; *BAC*, b. 278, reg. 400, cc. 226v–227r, 11 Jul 1616; *BAC*, b. 278, reg. 398, c. 7r, 2 May 1612; *BAC*, b. 317, cc. 22v–23r, 24 Sep 1614; *SDC*, b. 76, cc. 93r–94r, 25 Sep 1613, Cristoforo Valier to Senate.

84. Soruro received another caravan containing eighteen cases of silk in 1610. *SDC*, b. 78, cc. 210r–211v, 21 Jan 1614 (MV), Cristoforo Valier to Senate; *SDC*, b. 69, c. 407r, 10 Jul 1610, Simone Contarini to Senate. We get some sense of Soruro's wealth, as well as the lifestyle of a successful Venetian merchant, from the inventory of his goods made on his death in 1624, which includes a table clock, a Turkish sword, a dagger, a rapier, five paintings, four house rugs, and a reliquary. *BAC*, b. 369, 19 Mar 1624. At his death an Ottoman official estimated his wealth at sixty thousand ducats, though this amount was declared highly exaggerated by the bailo, who estimated his worth at forty thousand thalers. *SDC*,

b. 98, cc. 362r–v, 22 Dec 1624, Giorgio Giustinian to Senate; c. 470r, 3 Feb 1624 (MV), Giorgio Giustinian to Senate.

85. *BAC*, b. 277, reg. 397, c. 213v, 20 Oct 1613; *BAC*, b. 279, reg. 401, c. 151v, 14 Dec 1618.

86. *VSM-I*, reg. 136, c. 64r, 27 Sep 1575; reg. 141, cc. 39r–v, 26 Apr 1603; reg. 141, c. 16v, 23 Aug 1602; reg. 139, cc. 169r–v, 21 Oct 1597; Vercellin, "Mercanti turchi a Venezia," 244–47.

87. *VSM-I*, reg. 141, cc. 182r–183r, 9 Sep 1606.

88. *SDC*, b. 98, cc. 362r–v, 22 Dec 1624, Giorgio Giustinian to Senate; *BAC*, b. 278, reg. 400, c. 171r; *BAC*, b. 279, reg. 401, c. 25r; see also *BAC*, b. 279, reg. 401, cc. 12r, 33v.

89. *SDC*, b. 93, c. 362r, 11 Jun 1622, Giorgio Giustinian to Senate. Another famous Ottoman subject who sat in the Council of Twelve in the first decades of the sixteenth century, was Alvise Gritti, illegitimate son of the doge Andrea Gritti. *APC*, b. 1, c. 1r, 28 May 1525, "Piero Bragadin, bailo, *Contabilità*, 1524–26."

90. *SDC*, b. 98, cc. 362r–v, 22 Dec 1624, Giorgio Giustinian to Senate; cc. 390r–291v, 5 Jan 1624 (MV), Giorgio Giustinian to Senate.

91. *SDC*, b. 43, cc. 390r–391r, 3 Aug 1596, Marco Venier to Senate. It is not entirely clear if the Ludovico, son of Pietro of Venice, who was Dutch consul in Cyprus for eighteen years just after 1600 and appears in Ottoman records, is the same as our Ludovici, described in Venetian documents as Ludovico di Ludovici *q*. Pietro da Venezia. *Başbakanlık Arşivi Kılavuzu*, Maliyeden müdevver, 6004, c. 21, 1031/1621–22, cited in Faroqhi, "Venetian Presence in the Ottoman Empire," 369; *BAC*, b. 269, reg. 382, cc. 56v–58r, 8 Feb 1595 (MV).

92. *VSM-I*, reg. 139, c. 142r, 19 Mar 1597; *SDCop*, reg. 11, c. 75, 20 Oct 1596, Marco Venier to Senate; *BAC*, b. 269, reg. 382, cc. 212v–213v, 15 Mar 1596; *BAC*, b. 269, reg. 382, c. 231v, 1 Aug 1596; *BAC*, b. 269, reg. 382, cc. 56v–58r, 8 Feb 1595 (MV).

93. *SDC*, b. 43, cc. 390r–391r, 3 Aug 1596, Marco Venier to Senate; *APC*, b. 8, cc. 245r–290v, 1595 (MV); *SDCop*, reg. 11, c. 78, 21 Oct 1596, Marco Venier to Senate.

94. *SDCop*, reg. 11, c. 76, 21 Oct 1596, Marco Venier to Senate; *BAC*, b. 269, reg. 382, cc. 238v–239v, 16 Aug 1596; cc. 241v–242r, 21 Aug 1596.

95. *BAC*, b. 269, reg. 382, cc. 242v–243r, 22 Aug 1596; cc. 244v–246r, 30 Aug 1596. The Venetians were convinced that it was a Jewish conspiracy that prevented them from settling the matter. See *BAC*, b. 269, reg. 382, cc. 252v–253v, 254v–256r 1 Sep and 3 Sep 1596.

96. *SDC*, b. 43, cc. 398v–402v, 20 Aug 1596, Marco Venier to Senate; *BAC*, b. 269, reg. 382, c. 282r, 9 Nov 1596.

97. On this same phenomenon of "substitution" among medieval merchants, see Reyerson, "Merchants of the Mediterranean," 7.

98. *SDCop*, reg. 11, c. 78, 21 Oct 1596, Marco Venier to Senate.

99. Cooperman, "Venetian Policy towards Levantine Jews," 67–68; Ravid, "The Legal Status of the Jewish Merchants of Venice," 274.

100. Kafadar, "A Death in Venice," 201–3.

101. The question of why non-Venetians would want to trade with the nation is more complex. In the case of Ludovici and others from areas that did not enjoy formal recognition in the Ottoman Empire, it was necessary to trade under the protection of a recognized

nation. The capitulations stipulated that this nation be the French, but merchants may have been attracted to the Venetian because of the strength of its institutions and the influence of its heads, particularly given the problems the French and English nations experienced in this period.

The question of Ottoman subjects in the nation is more elusive. As subjects of the sultan, the treaties extended them legal trading rights and privileges equivalent to those of Venetian merchants: they paid the same tariffs and enjoyed, in theory at least, the protection of Venetian institutions. Perhaps Ottoman subjects were drawn to the Venetian nation for similar reasons as their non-Ottoman co-commercialists. For more on this, see chapter 5 for a discussion of the Ottoman Piron family.

CHAPTER 3. THE UNOFFICIAL NATION

1. Gara, "In Search of Communities," 135; Subacchi, "Italians in Antwerp," 75–83; Beck, "Éléments sociaux et économiques," 762–63; Bratchel, "Alien Merchant Communities."

2. Paola Subacchi has shown that the situation among the Italian nations in Antwerp was similar; only about 30 percent of the Italians working in that city belonged to the official nation. "Below the top level of the community there were small and medium-size merchants, craftsmen, agents and intermediaries and, generally, a crowd of people involved in all sorts of jobs, trading and activities." Subacchi, "Italians in Antwerp," 78–83.

3. Weisser, *Crime and Punishment in Early Modern Europe,* 63–5. For examples of the use of banishment in the often anarchic Friuli, see Edward Muir's fine study, *Mad Blood Stirring,* 72–76. For a more general discussion of banishment in late medieval Italy, see Starn, *Contrary Commonwealth.*

4. Povolo, "Nella spirale della violenza," 21–51; Povolo, "Crimine e giustizia a Vicenza," 411–32; Povolo, "Aspetti e problemi dell'amministrazione," 153–258. Enrico Basaglia situates the rise in banishment somewhat earlier, in the 1520s. Basaglia, "Il banditismo nei rapporti di Venezia," 425; Basaglia, "Il controllo della criminalità," 65–78.

5. *Parte presa, Adì 4.*

6. *Terraferma* rectors, despite their requests, did not enjoy this privilege. Grubb, "Catalysts for Organized Violence," 391; Molmenti, *I banditi della Repubblica veneta,* 87.

7. *SDelC,* f. 10, 23 Dec 1581, Council of Ten to Bailo; Povolo, "Nella spirale della violenza," 31, 43–44.

8. *SDelC,* f. 11, 31 May 1608, Senate to Bailo; *XSeg,* f. 26, 22 May 1598, Council of Ten to Bailo. On *salvacondotti* in the *stato da mar,* see also *Parte presa, Adì 22; SDelC,* f. 11, 31 May 1608, Senate to Bailo; *BAC,* b. 285, reg. 413, cc. 169r–170r, 17 May 1639.

9. Muir suggests that *banditi* often applied to more than one Venetian magistracy in attempts to have their sentences reduced. An audience before the bailo in Constantinople, then, might have represented something of a court of last resort. Muir, *Mad Blood Stirring,* 76

10. Preto, *I servizi secreti,* 247, 476; Molmenti, *I banditi della Repubblica veneta,* 85; Arbel, "Colonie d'oltremare," 5:960. For an earlier period, James Grubb reports that in 1426 upward of 1 percent of Vicenza's population, approximately 1,200 persons, had been

banished for debts or violence. In 1450 the Senate estimated that 800 men from the same city had been banished for homicide alone. Grubb, *Firstborn of Venice*, 104; Grubb, "Catalysts for Organized Violence," 389–90.

11. Molmenti, *I banditi della Repubblica veneta*, 87, 115; Muir, *Mad Blood Stirring*, 75; Grubb, "Catalysts for Organized Violence," 391.

12. *BAC*, b. 317, cc. 14r–17r, "Rubrica del Libro Primo degli Atti . . . Giovanni Cappello . . . da primo febraro 1629 . . . a 21 febraro 1632"; cc. 10r–14v, "Rubrica del Libro degli Atti dell'Eccellente Signor Luigi Contarini . . . 1636–1640."

13. *XSeg*, f. 24, 12 May 1588; *SDelC*, f. 12, 14 Jul 1612, Senate to Bailo; *SDelC*, f. 13, 10 Mar 1614, in Council of Ten.

14. *BAC*, b. 277, reg. 396, cc. 67v–68r, 3 Aug 1611; cc. 48r–v, 19 Jun 1611; reg. 397, cc. 55r–v, 4 Jul 1612; *BAC*, b. 273, reg. 390, cc. 35r–36v, 20 Mar 1603.

15. *BAC*, b. 348, 11 Sep 1638; *BAC*, b. 279, reg. 402, cc. 198v–199r, 30 Aug 1618; *XSeg*, f. 24, 12 May 1588.

16. *BAC*, b. 277, reg. 396, cc. 67v–68r, 3 Aug 1611; *CollRel*, b. 81, "Relazione di Tommaso Priuli"; Grubb, "Catalysts for Organized Violence," 390. Venice was one of the first states to establish poor laws, in 1529, and this certainly had an impact on the number of individuals banished for debts and other financial reasons. Pullan, *Rich and Poor in Renaissance Venice*, 239–326; Weisser, *Crime and Punishment in Early Modern Europe*, 102.

17. *BAC*, b. 278, reg. 400, c. 136v, 11 Jan 1615 (MV); *BAC*, b. 279, reg. 402, 64v–65r, 23 May 1617.

18. *BAC*, b. 277, reg. 396, cc. 67v–68r, 3 Aug 1611; *BAC*, b. 278, reg. 400, cc. 111v–112r, 23 Oct 1615.

19. *SDelC*, f. 11, 31 May 1608, Senate to Bailo Contarini; *BAC*, b. 278, reg. 400, c. 44r, 18 May 1615; c. 136v, 11 Jan 1615 (MV).

20. *BAC*, b. 270, reg. 385, c. 1r, 22 Aug 1598; *BAC*, b. 277, reg. 396, c. 27r–v, 4 Mar 1611; Hale, "Men and Weapons," 11, 16, 21 n. 85.

21. A final option, rarely utilized, was that suggested in 1576 by the Council of Ten, who directed that if Marco Boldù, a Venetian patrician, banished for "enormous crimes" presented himself in Constantinople, the bailo was to "with cautious, secret and secure mode . . . have him removed from life, either by way of venom or as seemed best to him." Molmenti, *I banditi della Repubblica veneta*, 98.

22. *BAC*, b. 280, reg. 404, cc. 126v–127v, 9 Jun 1623.

23. *CollRel*, b. 4, c. 81v–84v, "Relazione di Lorenzo Bernardo."

24. *CapiXD*, b. 6, no. 163, 22 Jul 1595, Marco Venier to Council of Ten.

25. *SDC*, b. 17, cc. 300r–302v, 14 Jun 1583, Gianfrancesco Morosini to Senate.

26. *BAC*, b. 277, reg. 396, cc. 27r–v, 4 Mar 1611.

27. *CapiXD*, b. 6, no. 160, 20 May 1595, Marco Venier to Council of Ten.

28. *BAC*, b. 270, reg. 385, c. 117v, 29 Jan 1599 (MV); c. 22r, 20 Nov 1598; *BAC*, b. 272, reg. 387, cc. 125r–v, 16 May 1601; *BAC*, b. 280, reg. 404, cc. 163v–164r, 27 Sep 1623; *BAC*, b. 278, reg. 400, c. 44r, 18 May 1615.

29. "Relazione di Gianfrancesco Morosini," in Albèri, *Relazioni*, 9:315–16; *SDC*, b. 33, c. 191r, 18 May 1591, Camillo Stella to Girolamo Lippomano; Imber, *Ottoman Empire*, 293–94.

30. *CapiXD*, b. 1, no. 110, 11 Mar 1534, Nicolò Giustinian to Council of Ten; *CapiXD*, b. 1, no. 219, 8 Jul 1550, Bailo Venier to Council of Ten; *SDC*, b. 18, cc. 168r–v, Gianfrancesco Morosini to Senate, 1 Nov 1583.

31. *SDC*, b. 73, cc. 314r–v, 28 Jul 1612, Cristoforo Valier to Senate.

32. *BAC*, b. 110, n.d. [after 1636].

33. *CollRel*, b. 5, c. 13v, "Relazione di Antonio Tiepolo"; also "Relazione di Antonio Tiepolo," in Albèri, *Relazioni*, 6:146. "Relazione di Giovanni Moro," in ibid., 9:353–54. *Mariol* is a variation of the Venetian *mariuolo*, or lowlife. Boerio, *Dizionario del dialetto veneziano*, 399.

34. *SDC*, b. 70, c. 214r, 13 Nov 1610, Simone Contarini to Senate.

35. *BAC*, b. 278, reg. 400, c. 60v, 12 Jun 1615.

36. *CollRel*, b. 79, cc. 19r–v, "Relazione di Alvise Giustinian, *Proveditor Generale in Candia*."

37. *CollRel*, b. 81, "Relazione di Tommaso Priuli, *Capitano in Candia*, 1632."

38. "Relazione di Simone Contarini," in Barozzi and Berchet, *Relazioni*, 1:237–38.

39. *SDC*, b. 16, cc. 262r–v, 4 Dec 1582, Gianfrancesco Morosini to Senate.

40. *CollRel*, b. 79, cc. 54v–55r, "Relazione di Benetto Moro, *Proveditor Generale in Candia*"; "Relazione di Giovanni Moro," in Albèri, *Relazioni*, 9:353–54; *CollRel*, b. 5, c. 13v, "Relazione di Antonio Tiepolo."

41. *CapiXD*, b. 6, no. 109, 29 Sep 1590, Bailo to Council of Ten; Preto, *I servizi secreti*, 247; Simon, "Dépêches," 1:186; *SDC*, b. 77, cc. 91r–v, 17 Apr 1614, Cristoforo Valier to Senate.

42. *SDC*, b. 51, cc. 231r–v, 3 Jun 1600, Girolamo Cappello to Senate. On Venetian artists in Persia, see Lewis, *Muslim Discovery of Europe*, 244–45, 256.

43. *CapiXD*, b. 6, no. 125, 29 Oct 1591, Bailo to Council of Ten.

44. *CapiXD*, b. 6, no. 116, 13 Oct 1590, Bailo to Council of Ten; *BAC*, b. 277, reg. 396, cc. 87r–v, 29 Jun 1611; *SMar*, reg. 89, cc. 211v–212v, 4 Dec 1631; *SMar*, reg. 95, cc. 185r–v, 23 Sep 1637.

45. *BAC*, b. 268, reg. 380, cc. 47v–49r, 30 Aug and 5 Sep 1593; *BAC*, b. 268, reg. 380, c. 22r; *XSavi*, b. 164, no. 887, 27 Aug 1582; *XSeg*, f. 25, 20 Jul 1593.

46. Davis, *Christian Slaves, Muslim Masters*, 23.

47. "Relazione di Alvise Contarini," in Barozzi and Berchet, *Relazioni*, 1:415; İnalcık, "Servile Labor," 26, 50–51 n.45. D'Alessio, "La communauté de Constantinople," 311.

48. "Relazione di Gianfrancesco Morosini," in Albèri, *Relazioni*, 9:306; İnalcık, "Servile Labor," 47; Kunt, "Transformation of Zimmi into Askeri," 1:62.

49. *BAC*, b. 265, 1585–87, for example, contains many slave manumissions, whereas almost none appear in *BAC*, b. 270, 1598–1600, and *BAC*, b. 275, 1604–8. On Ottoman slaves in this period, see Vatin, *Les Ottomans et l'Occident*, 113–37.

50. Scaraffia, *Rinnegati*, 30; Fabris, "Hasan 'Il veneziano' tra Algeria," 55; Bono, *I corsari barbareschi*, 378–87. On Cervantes, see *Don Quixote*, book IV, chapters 12–14, for a suggestive account of a Christian returned from captivity in Algiers, certainly informed by the author's experience.

51. *CollRel*, b. 4, c. 11v, "Relazione di Lorenzo Bernardo."

52. "Relazione di Alvise Contarini," in Barozzi and Berchet, *Relazioni*, 1:415; İnalcık, "The Ottoman State," 1:284. Tongas, *Les relations de la France avec l'Empire Ottoman*, 75.

53. Tenenti, "Gli schiavi di Venezia," 55; *SDC*, b. 22, c. 279r, 8 Dec 1585, Lorenzo Bernardo to Senate; *SDC*, b. 23, c. 148r, 5 Apr 1586, Lorenzo Bernardo to Senate; *InqStat*, b. 433, 23 May 1590; *BAC*, b. 265, reg. 373, cc. 32r–33r, 28 Feb 1586.

54. *Atti F Alcaini*, b. 24, cc. 18r–23r, 25 Apr 1582, cited in Corrazol, "Varietà notarile," 6:776; *SDC*, b. 75, cc. 77r–80r, 25 Mar 1613, Cristoforo Valier to Senate, attached letter of Marcantonio Borisi; *VSM*, reg. I:61, 31 Mar 1599, V Savii to Senate; *SMar*, reg. 81, cc. 58v–59v, 16 May 1623; *SMar*, reg. 79, cc. 14r–v, 20 Mar 1621.

55. Davis, "Slave Redemption in Venice," 457. For representative lists of slaves, see *BAC*, b. 365, n. II; *BAC*, b. 365, n. I, 3 Jun 1588 in Pregadi.

56. *Commemoriali*, reg. 24, cc. 14r–21r; "Relazione di Alvise Contarini," in Barozzi and Berchet, *Relazioni*, 1:414; Fabris, "Un caso di pirateria veneziana," 100.

57. *SDC*, b. 41, cc. 266r–268v, 28 May 1595, Marco Venier to Senate.

58. *Provveditori sopra ospedali e luoghi pii*, b. 98, no. 13, cc. 4–14. Davis, "Slave Redemption in Venice," 456, 466; Davis, *Christian Slaves, Muslim Masters*, 149–72; "Relazione di Alvise Contarini," in Barozzi and Berchet, *Relazioni*, 1:331; *APC*, b. 6, c. 109r, 30 Sep 1569, Marcantonio Barbaro to Senate.

59. *BAC*, b. 365-II, no. 46, 3 Oct 1625; *SDC*, b. 37, cc. 169r–173r, 1 May 1593, Matteo Zane to Senate.

60. "Relazione di Andrea Gritti," in Albèri, *Relazioni*, 9:42–43; *SDC*, b. 16, cc. 269v–272r, 5 Dec 1582, Gianfrancesco Morosini to Senate; *BAC*, b. 263, reg. 372, c. 14r, 19 Aug 1580; cc. 13v–14r, 18 Aug 1580.

61. *SDC*, b. 41, c. 425v, 4 Aug 1595, Marco Venier to Senate.

62. "Relazione di Alvise Contarini," in Barozzi and Berchet, *Relazioni*, 1:415; *APC*, b. 8, cc. 245r–290v, 1595 (MV).

63. *SDC*, b. 38, cc. 11v–14r, 6 Sep 1593, Matteo Zane to Senate; *DocTR*, b. 4, no. 484, [ca. 2 Oct 1542], Sultan to Doge; *LSTR*, b. 3, cc. 31r–v, 2 Nov 1574, Mehmed Paşa to Doge.

64. Braudel, *The Mediterranean*, 1:887–89.

65. *SDC*, b. 81, c. 263r, 9 Jul 1616, Almoro Nani to Senate; *BAC*, b. 277, reg. 397, c. 277v, 2 May 1614.

66. *SMar*, reg. 60, c. 113r, 14 Oct 1600; *BAC*, b. 265, reg. 374, cc. 126r–v, 16 Aug 1586; Stefani, *L'Assicurazione a Venezia*, 1:86–90.

67. *SDC*, b. 22, c. 279r, 8 Dec 1585, Lorenzo Bernardo to Senate; *SDC*, b. 23, c. 148r, 5 Apr 1586, Lorenzo Bernardo to Senate.

68. Wratislaw, *Adventures*, 125–26; Faroqhi, "Venetian Presence in the Ottoman Empire," 598; İnalcık, "The Ottoman State," 1:284; İnalcık, "Servile Labor," 27–30.

69. *InqStat*, b. 433, 14 Jun 1590; copies of three letters 1588–89 from Pietro Cavazza, to his father Piero, 11 Dec 1588.

70. *VSM-I*, reg. 142, cc. 9v–10r, 25 Mar 1607; *VSM-I*, reg. 139, c. 159v, 22 Aug 1597; *VSM-I*, reg. 140, c. 27v, 28 Sep 1598.

71. *SDC*, b. 26, c. 394r, 18 Feb 1587 (MV), Giovanni Moro to Senate; *BAC*, b. 344, 26 Jan 1624 (MV); *SDC*, b. 36, c. 134r, 12 Oct 1592, Matteo Zane to Senate; d'Alessio, "La communauté de Constantinople," 311; d'Alessio, *Relatione*, 32–34.

72. İnalcık, "Servile Labor," 30.

73. Wratislaw, *Adventures,* 190.

74. Simon, "Dépêches," 1:280–81, 284–85.

75. *BAC,* b. 263, reg. 372, cc. 163v–164r, 3 and 8 Oct 1582; İnalcık, "Servile Labor," 48; *SDC,* b. 32, cc. 40v–41r, 2 Sep 1590, Girolamo Lippomano to Senate.

76. Arbel, "Roman Catholics," 73, 76.

77. Cessi, *Storia della repubblica di Venezia,* 5–55; also Lane, *Venice,* 4–8, 42–3; Diehl, *Une république patricienne,* 11–19. Queller, *The Fourth Crusade,* 149–52; Hill, *History of Cyprus,* 3:657–764.

78. For a discussion of Venice's *stato da mar,* see Benjamin Arbel's concise and informative "Colonie d'oltremare"; also Slot, *Archipelagus Turbatus;* and Miller, *Latins in the Levant,* 654, which provides a useful list of Venice's possessions and the dates they were acquired and lost.

79. The city of Candia was also known as Chandax or Kastro. Maltezou, "Historical and Social Context," 20; Greene, "Commerce and the Ottoman Conquest of Kandiye," 96. For the population figures, see Lassithiotakis, "L'Isola di Candia," 46; Arbel, "Colonie d'oltremare," 955; Staurakēs, *Statistikē tou plēthysmou tēs Krētēs,* 185–87.

80. Lane, *Venice,* 43, 70; Cessi, *Storia della repubblica di Venezia,* 206–7; Ashtor, *Levant Trade,* 386–87; Arbel, "Colonie d'oltremare," 956, 978; Arbel, "Riflessioni sul ruolo di Creta," 245–51.

81. Arbel, "Colonie d'oltremare," 956; McKee, *Uncommon Dominion,* 133–67; Maltezou, "Historical and Social Context," 26. For differing viewpoints on the early period of Venetian rule in Candia, see Borsari, *Il dominio veneziano a Creta;* Gallina, *Una società coloniale del Trecento.*

82. Arbel, "Colonie d'oltremare," 956–58, 964–79; Lane, *Venice,* 99; Lassithiotakis, "L'Isola di Candia," 56–58. For examples of this Hellenization process, see Maltezou, "Historical and Social Context," 29–35, which cites a Venetian official's report: "Among the noble Venetians, many are those who have no memory of their noble descent . . . who preserve nothing but their surname and their few remaining fiefs . . . They have completely forgotten the Italian language and, since there is no possibility of hearing mass according to the Latin rite in any of the island's villages, they are obliged, while staying in their village . . . to baptise their children, to marry and to bury their dead in accordance with the Orthodox rite and Greek customs. And these are the Venieri, Barbarigi, Morosini, Boni, Foscarini." For an examination of the Venice's symbolic colonization of Crete, see Georgopoulou, *Venice's Mediterranean Colonies,* 213–53.

83. Maltezou, "Historical and Social Context," 30–32. Embiricos, *La renaissance crétoise,* treats this period from a cultural viewpoint.

84. Maltezou, "Historical and Social Context," 41–3; Lassithiotakis, "L'Isola di Candia," 46–50; Panopoulou, "Oi technites tou naupegeion tou Chandaka." On the grain supply problems on Crete, see Gallina, *Una società coloniale del Trecento,* 137–38.

85. Maltezou, "Historical and Social Context," 41–43.

86. Calabi, "Gli stranieri e la città," 5:922; McNeill, *Venice,* 199; Geanakoplos, *Byzantine East and Latin West,* 147–64; Burke, "Your Humble and Devoted Servants," 10–16.

87. *CapiXD,* b. 6, no. 131, 22 Feb 1591 (MV), Bailo to Council of Ten; *DonàR,* b. 23,

c. 128v; "Relazione di Simone Contarini," in Barozzi and Berchet, *Relazioni*, 1:229. Evidence of Greek-Venetian assimilation can be found in *CapiXD*, b. 2, no. 15, 29 May 1551, Navagero to Council of Ten.

88. *BAC*, b. 347, 2 May 1627; *DonàR*, reg. 23, c. 128v; *SDC*, b. 15, c. 92v, 9 Jun 1581, Paolo Contarini to Senate; *CollRel*, b. 5, cc. 28r–v, "Relazione di Ottaviano Bon."

89. *BAC*, b. 264, reg. 424, cc. 70r–v, 20 Dec 1584.

90. *BAC*, b. 265, reg. 373, c. 4v, 30 June 1585; *BAC*, b. 264, reg. 424, c. 29r, 30 Jul 1584; *BAC*, b. 317, cc. 54v–55r, 25 Jan 1599 (MV).

91. "Relazione di Simone Contarini," in Barozzi and Berchet, *Relazioni*, 1:229.

92. "Lista di Tinotti e Candiotti habitanti in Costantinopoli e loro professioni," *BAC*, b. 347, 2 May 1627.

93. "Relazione di Gianfrancesco Morosini," in Albèri, *Relazioni*, 9:315–16; Soranzo, *L'Ottomanno*, 62–63; Mantran, "Arsenali di Istanbul," 104; Imber, *Ottoman Empire*, 293–94.

94. *BAC*, b. 276, reg. 394, cc. 190r–v, 6 Feb 1609 (MV); *BAC*, b. 268, reg. 381, c. 98v, 12 Oct 1593; *BAC*, b. 272, reg. 387, c. 154v; *BAC*, b. 265, reg. 373, cc. 56r–v, 12 Jul 1586.

95. Greene, *A Shared World*, 110–21; Tucci, "Il commercio del vino," 183–206; Arbel, "Riflessioni sul ruolo di Creta," 249–51. For a sense of the trade by Greek-Venetian subjects in Constantinople in the late sixteenth century, see the detailed tables in Mauroeide, *Ho Hellenismos sto Galata*, 177–249. On the popular trade in Crete's cheeses, see Jacoby, "Cretan Cheese," 49–68. Zante maintained a thriving trade in raisins, though mostly these were exported to England; Fusaro, *Uva passa*. On da Gama, see *Trevisan Manuscript*, Library of Congress, Mss. Med. & Ren., 26, c. 35r.

96. *CollRel*, b. 5, c. 18r. "Relazione di Giovanni Correr"; Soranzo, *L'Ottomanno*, 94.

97. *CollRel*, b. 79, c. 18r, "Relazione di Zuanne Mocenigo, *Proveditor Generale in Candia.*"

98. "Relazione di Gianfrancesco Morosini," in Albèri, *Relazioni*, 9:315–16; Greene, "Ruling an Island," 195.

99. *DonàR*, reg. 148, cc. 132r–v. On Venetian rule on Cyprus and the role of discontent among the Cypriots in the Ottoman conquest in 1571, see Hill, *History of Cyprus*, 3:765–1040. On similar events in the conquest of Crete, see Greene, "Ruling an Island," 199.

100. "Relazione di Alvise Contarini," in Barozzi and Berchet, *Relazioni*, 1:411–12; *CollRel*, b. 81, "Relazione di Tommaso Priuli, *Capitano in Candia.*"

101. *SDC*, b. 68, cc. 10r–v, 5 Sep 1609, Simone Contarini to Senate; *SDC*, b. 57, cc. 184r–v, 23 May 1603, Francesco Contarini to Senate.

102. *SDC*, b. 19, cc. 73r–76r, 20 Mar 1584, Gianfrancesco Morosini to Senate.

103. *BAC*, b. 272, reg. 387, cc. 79v–80v, 5 Feb 1600 (MV); *InqStat*, b. 416, 7 Aug 1592, Letter from Bailo.

104. *SDC*, b. 20, cc. 444v–445r, 7 Jan 1584 (MV), Gianfrancesco Morosini to Senate. On contraband on the island of Zante, see Fusaro, *Uva passa*, 61–65.

105. *BAC*, b. 250, 18, Jun 1615, Commandment from Sultan to Kadı of Gallipoli and the Castellans.

106. "Relazione di Gianfrancesco Morosini," in Albèri, *Relazioni*, 9:315–16.

107. *SDelC*, f. 11, 6 Feb 1606 (MV), Senate to Bailo; Greene, *A Shared World*, 147–53.

108. *SDelC*, f. 11, 17 Nov 1606, excerpt from letter of Bailo to Senate; *CollRel*, b. 5, cc. 28r–v, "Relazione di Ottaviano Bon."

109. *SDelC*, f. 11, 17 Jan 1606 (MV), Alvise Priuli formerly *Procuratore di Candia* to Senate; "Relazione di Simone Contarini," in Barozzi and Berchet, *Relazioni*, 1:175.

110. *CollRel*, b. 79, cc. 32r–33r, "Relazione di Zuanne Mocenigo, *Proveditor Generale di Candia*"; Panopoulou, "Oi technites tou naupegeion tou Chandaka," 176.

111. On the exhaustion of the Venetian timber industry and its impact on shipbuilding, see Lane, *Ships and Shipbuilders*, 217–33. For a challenge to this view, see Appuhn, "Inventing Nature."

112. Tucci, "I greci nella vita marittima veneziana," 244.

113. *CollRel*, b. 79, c. 38v, "Relazione di Alvise Giustinian, *Proveditor Generale in Candia*."

114. *BAC*, b. 265, reg. 373, cc. 56r–v, 12 Jul 1586.

115. *BAC*, b. 276, reg. 394, cc. 190r–v, 6 Feb 1609 (MV). This was not an isolated instance. Mantran writes that non-Muslims were present in certain guilds, especially those that traded with European merchants, such as wool and hides. Mantran, "Minoritaires, métiers et marchands étrangers," 130.

116. *BAC*, b. 295, cc. 1r–6r, Jan–Nov 1596 (MV).

117. *SDC*, b. 15, cc. 90r–92v, 9 Jun 1581, Paolo Contarini to Senate.

118. *SDC*, b. 67, cc. 7r–v, 11 Mar 1609, Simone Contarini to Senate.

119. *BAC*, b. 348, 2 Nov 1639.

120. *SDC*, b. 23, cc. 477r–479v, 24 June 1586, Lorenzo Bernardo to Senate. See also *SDC*, b. 58, cc. 115r–116r, 1 Aug 1603, Sultan to *kadı* of Constantinople and Galata; *SDC*, b. 57, 311r–v, 13 Jun 1603, Francesco Contarini to Senate; *SDelC*, f. 6, 2 Aug 1586, Senate to Bailo.

121. See below on this. *BAC*, b. 267, reg. 377, cc. 34v–35r, 11 Sep 1590; *BAC*, b. 280, reg. 404, c. 101r, 27 Feb 1623; *BAC*, b. 274, reg. 391, c. 101v, 29 Jun 1605. The word *Cernitore* (fellmonger) is a derivative of *cernir*, the Venetian form of the modern *cernere*, which means to choose, to separate, to value.

122. *CollRel*, b. 5, cc. 28r–v, "Relazione di Ottaviano Bon."

123. Ibid.

124. D'Alessio, *Relatione*, 55–56; "Visita apostolica a Costantinopoli," in Hofmann, *Il vicariato apostolico di Costantinopoli*, 52, 55–6.

125. *SDC*, b. 113, 622r–634v, 16 Dec 1632, Giovanni Cappello to Senate. On the patriarchal vicar, see d'Alessio, *Relatione*, 77–79; Trannoy, "La «nation latine» de Constantinople," 247. For an incomplete list of the patriachal vicars of this period, see Gauchat, *Hierarchia catholica*, 162 n.4.

126. Trannoy, "La «nation latine» de Constantinople," 252; d'Alessio, *Le couvent et l'eglise des Saints-Pierre-et-Paul*, 14–16; *SDC*, b. 113, cc. 85r–88r, 16 Apr 1632, Giovanni Cappello to Senate; Faroqhi, "Venetian Presence in the Ottoman Empire," 363.

127. *SDC*, b. 113, cc. 622r–634v, 16 Dec 1632, Giovanni Cappello to Senate.

128. *APC*, b. 18, 6:44v–45r, 28 Oct 1621, Giorgio Giustinian to Senate; *XSeg*, f. 34, 4 May 1620, Council of Ten to Bailo; *CapiXD*, b. 7, no. 116, 27 June 1620, Almoro Nani to Council of Ten; Frazee, *Catholics and Sultans*, 73.

129. *CapiXD*, b. 1, no. 101, 18 Apr 1533, Pietro Zen to Council of Ten; İnalcık, "The Ottoman State," 1:94.

130. *BAC*, b. 267, reg. 377, c. 19v, 25 Aug 1590; *BAC*, b. 264, reg. 425, c. 98r, 2 Aug 1583; *BAC*, b. 265, reg. 373, cc. 133v–134r, 14 Sep 1587; *BAC*, b. 285, reg. 413, cc. 33v–39v, May 1637.

131. *BAC*, b. 267, reg. 378, cc. 4r–v, 10 Jul 1590; *BAC*, b. 268, reg. 380, cc. 17v–18r, 14 Jul 1592.

132. *BAC*, b. 278, reg. 398, cc. 111r–v, 23 Jun 1611; Marino Sanudo, *I diarii*, 3:129, 131, 1356, 1491, 1554, 1634, cited in Davis, "Shipping and Spying," 103; Mantran, *Istanbul au siècle de Soliman*, 75. Compare with Ashtor, *Levant Trade*, 408–10, for the fifteenth century. *BAC*, b. 273, reg. 390, c. 180r, 27 Feb 1603 (MV).

133. *BAC*, b. 347, 29 May 1627; *BAC*, b. 279, reg. 401, cc. 188r–v, 14 Dec 1619. For another unofficial merchant, see *BAC*, b. 267, reg. 377, c. 85v, 27 Apr 1591.

134. *BAC*, b. 269, reg. 382, c. 188r, 12 Feb 1596; *BAC*, b. 295, c. 6v, 10 Jun 1597; *APC*, b. 8, cc. 245r–290v, 1595 (MV); *BAC*, b. 273, reg. 389, cc. 18r–v, 28 Jun 1603.

135. *BAC*, b. 275, reg. 393, c. 27v, 6 Oct 1606.

136. *BAC*, b. 274, reg. 391, cc. 91r–94r, 15 Jun 1605; *BAC*, b. 348, 29 Oct 1640; *BAC*, b. 273, reg. 390, cc. 65r–v, 7 May 1603.

137. A similar situation existed in the Italian nation of Antwerp between the official merchants and many unofficial members of the broader community who worked as agents and intermediaries in the nation's trade. Subacchi, "Italians in Antwerp," 84–85, 89–90.

138. *BAC*, b. 278, reg. 400, c. 164r, 26 Feb 1615 (MV); *BAC*, b. 273, reg. 390, cc. 135r–136r, 26 Sep 1603; *BAC*, b. 275, reg. 393, c. 53v, 30 Dec 1606; *BAC*, b. 277, reg. 397, cc. 200v–201r, 8 Aug 1613; *BAC*, b. 265, reg. 374, cc. 107v–108r, 22 Jun 1586; *BAC*, b. 268, reg. 381, c. 53v, 21 Nov 1592; *BAC*, b. 268, reg. 381, cc. 18r–v, 18 May 1592; *BAC*, b. 274, reg. 391, c. 101v, 29 Jun 1605.

139. *BAC*, b. 273, reg. 390, cc. 65r–v, 7 May 1603; *BAC*, b. 277, reg. 396, c. 45v, 7 Jun 1611; *BAC*, b. 278, reg. 400, cc. 214v–215r, 18 Jun 1616; *BAC*, b. 331-I, 1633; also *BAC*, b. 274, reg. 391, cc. 215v–216r, 25 Feb 1605 (MV). Revealing is a 1629 statement by the nation's *cernitori* regarding the protection of their trade, which they believed was being overrun by interlopers. *BAC*, b. 347, 3 Mar 1629.

140. *BAC*, b. 267, reg. 377, c. 58r, 15 Dec 1590; *BAC*, b. 273, reg. 389, cc. 55v–56r, 5 Aug 1604; *BAC*, b. 295, c. 12v, 26 Oct 1597; *BAC*, b. 273, reg. 390, cc. 93r–94r, 5 Jul 1603. A Bernardin Corniani appears in a 1624 census living in the Sestiere di San Marco in Sant'Anzolo. His family numbered six persons, including two servants and he had one gondola. *DonàR* 351. For another hereditary transfer, see *BAC*, b. 266, reg. 375, c. 64v, 18 Sep 1588; *BAC*, b. 274, reg. 391, cc. 28r–v, 12 Jan 1604 (MV); *BAC*, b. 339, no. 8, n.d., Command to *kadı* of Gallipoli; *BAC*, b. 317, cc. 79r–v, 4 Mar 1615. See Lorenzo's case in *BAC*, b. 329, 26 Nov 1603, "Processo ad instanza di Vidali contro Bernardin cernitor."

141. *BAC*, b. 270, reg. 384, cc. 43v–44r, 10 Apr 1597; *BAC*, b. 274, reg. 391, cc. 148v–149r, 6 Sep 1605; *BAC*, b. 264, reg. 425, c. 136r, 1 Dec 1583.

142. *BAC*, b. 280, reg. 404, c. 101r, 27 Feb 1623; *BAC*, b. 348, 18 Nov 1640 and 24 Nov 1640.

143. *BAC*, b. 279, reg. 402, cc. 73r–74r, 17 Jun 1617; *BAC*, b. 347, 29 May 1627.

144. *BAC*, b. 277, reg. 396, c. 28v, 10 Mar 1611; *BAC*, b. 273, reg. 390, cc. 172r–173v, 14 Feb 1603 (MV).

145. *BAC*, b. 269, reg. 382, cc. 86v–87v, 15 Feb 1594.

146. Ibid.; *BAC*, b. 329, 30 July 1599; *BAC*, b. 268, reg. 381, n.p., 13 Aug 1592; *BAC*, b. 269, reg. 382, cc. 86v–87v, 15 Feb 1594.

147. *BAC*, b. 277, reg. 396, cc. 37v–38v, 6 May 1611; *BAC*, b. 275, reg. 392, cc. 141r–142r, 12 Dec 1607; *BAC*, b. 329, 9 Jun 1603, "Esame sopra la persona di Bernardo di Giorgi Raguseo." An index, made in 1680, of materials which were contained in the archive of the bailate in Constantinople, mentions a "Processo circa Niccolo Gonale fatto Carazaro," but the document has not survived. *SegMiste*, b. 229, c. 173r.

148. Scott, "The Problem of Invisibility," 5–6.

149. *SDelC*, f. 8, 27 Jul 1592, Bailo to Senate; Pedani-Fabris, "Veneziani a Costantinopoli," 75.

150. *BAC*, b. 295, c. 6v, 10 Jun 1597; *BAC*, b. 266, reg. 375, cc. 73v–74r, 30 Aug 1588; *APC*, b. 8, cc. 245r–290v, 1595 (MV), "Processo contro un Dragomano."

151. *BAC*, b. 268, reg. 381, c. 109r, 14 Nov 1593; *BAC*, b. 279, reg. 402, c. 141v, 24 Jul 1617; *BAC*, b. 279, reg. 402, cc. 198v–199r, 30 Aug 1618; *BAC*, b. 281, reg. 406, cc. 8r–v, 2 Jun 1624.

152. *BAC*, b. 278, reg. 399, 22 Jan 1628; *BAC*, b. 278, reg. 400, c. 60v, 12 Jun 1615.

153. Bennassar and Bennassar, *Les chrétiens d'Allah*, 235; Mantran, *Istanbul au siècle de Soliman*, 168; Clissold, "Christian Renegades and Barbary Corsairs," 510.

154. *It VII* 1086 (8523), c. 290r, 28 Oct 1638; *SDCop*, reg. 15, c. 123, 9 Dec 1619, Almoro Nani to Senate; John Sanderson, London, to Martin Calthorpe, Norfolk, 16 Jan 1609, in Foster, *Travels of John Sanderson*, 2: 259–60; *SDC*, b. 66, c. 407r, 27 Nov 1608, Ottaviano Bon to Senate; Wood, "The English Embassy at Constantinople," 541; *It VII* 1086 (8523), c. 59r, 8 May 1638.

155. *BAC*, b. 278, reg. 399, n.p., 22 Jan 1628; n.p., 12 Jun 1628.

156. *SMar*, reg. 94, cc. 158r, 13 Aug 1636; *BAC*, b. 263, reg. 372, cc. 13v–14r, 18 Aug 1580.

157. *BAC*, b. 281, reg. 406, c. 13v, 26 Jun 1621; *BAC*, b. 279, reg. 402, cc. 64v–65r, 23 May 1617; *BAC*, b. 284, reg. 411, cc. 206r–v, 20 Jun 1635; *BAC*, b. 278, reg. 400, cc. 38v–39v, 10 May 1615.

158. *InqStat*, b. 416, 28 Sep 1621; *BAC*, b. 278, reg. 400 cc. 107r–v, 14 Oct 1615.

159. *BAC*, b. 275, reg. 393, cc. 28r–v, 6 Oct 1606.

160. Bratchel, "Regulation and Group Consciousness," 592–93. Examples of married merchants accompanied by their wives include *BAC*, b. 284, reg. 411, cc. 269v–271v, 3 Apr 1636; Mundy, *Travels*, 1:163–65; DSA, *Testamenta Notariae*, b. 49 (1592–95), c. 143r, 10 Nov 1593, "Testamentum Elizabetta uxoris Joseph de Albrici Merciarij Bergomensis."

161. *BAC*, b. 267, reg. 377, c. 33v, 14 Sep 1590; *VSM-I*, reg. 139, cc. 67r–v, 1 Dec 1575; *SDC*, b. 58, c. 15r, 6 Sep 1603, Francesco Contarini to Senate, includes letter from Vice Consul Santo Bissi in Smirne to Bailo, 6 Aug 1603; Finlay, "Crisis and Crusade," 59.

162. Ashtor, *Levant Trade*, 407–8; *SDC*, b. 39, cc. 7r–8r, 12 Mar 1594, Marco Venier to Senate.

163. Sandys, *Relation of a Journey*, 86.

164. Mantran, *Istanbul au siècle de Soliman*, 168; Kafadar, "The Ottomans and Europe," 1:605. A similar situation existed between Italian merchants and English concubines in London; Bratchel, "Regulation and Group Consciousness," 593.

165. *CollRel*, b. 5, 19r, "Relatione di Maffio Venier"; see also Leonardo Donà's description, *DonàR*, reg. 23, cc. 110v–111r. Also Wratislaw, *Adventures*, 79–80; Sandys, *Relation of a Journey*, 86.

166. ACDF, *Dubia diversa ab anno 1570 ad Annum 1668*, b. 10, 10 Oct 1630; Cassia, "Religion, Politics, and Ethnicity in Cyprus," 22–3; Boppe, *Journal et correspondance, de Gédoyn*, 130.

167. On Alvise see, Davis, "Shipping and Spying," 99; see also Finlay, "Al servizio del Sultano," 79; Kretschmayr, "Ludovico Gritti"; Kellenbenz, "Handelsverbindungen," 197–99; Olivieri, "Tempo et historia delle famiglie"; Decei, "Aloisio Gritti."

168. *DonàR*, reg. 23, cc. 110v–111r. Boppe, *Journal et correspondance*, 79 n. 1; Foster, *Travels of John Sanderson*, 10.

169. DSA, *Acta Sanctae Mariae Maioris*, b. 467/1, no. 16, 14 Feb 1593 (MV), Ambrogio Grillo to Bartolomeo Borgiani.

170. BAC, b. 263, reg. 371, cc. 42r–v, 17 Jul 1546.

171. Kafadar, "The Ottomans and Europe," 1:605.

172. BAC, b. 274, reg. 391, cc. 288r–289r, 26 Jul 1606.

173. SDC, b. 43, cc. 226r–241r, 19 May 1596, Marco Venier to Senate.

174. SDC, b. 57, cc. 167r–168v, 8 May 1603, Francesco Contarini to Senate.

175. SDC, b. 68, cc. 273v–274v, 1 Nov 1609, Simone Contarini to Senate.

176. Hammer, *Histoire*, 2:472; SDC, b. 43, c. 243r, 31 May 1596, Marco Venier to Senate.

177. Hughes, *Shakespeare's Europe*, 68.

178. *It VII* 1086 (8523), c. 92r, 5 Jun 1638, Alvise Contarini to Senate. Arranging for a commercial partner to be caught *in flagrante* with a Muslim woman was a strategy at least one Neapolitan in Galata arranged in order to cheat his partner. SDC, b. 71, 217r–221v, 28 May 1611, Simone Contarini to Senate, "Case against Vincenzo Marini da Matalone di Caserta, Kingdom of Naples."

179. Tucci, "Tra Venezia e mondo turco," 38; SDC, b. 98, cc. 362r–v, 22 Dec 1624, Giorgio Giustinian to Senate; also SDC, b. 19, cc. 77r–87r, 3 Apr 1584, Gianfrancesco Morosini to Senate; SDC, b. 16, cc. 308r–309r, 22 Dec 1582, Gianfrancesco Morosini to Senate.

180. SDC, b. 98, cc. 362r–v, 22 Dec 1624, Giorgio Giustinian to Senate; Daniele Barbarigo makes a similar assessment in *CollRel*, b. 4, "Relazione di Daniele Barbarigo."

181. D'Alessio, "La communauté de Constantinople," 311; Tongas, *Relations de la France avec l'Empire Ottoman*, 75.

182. Moryson, *An Itinerary*, 1:425; Bates, *Touring in 1600*, 182.

183. Tucci, "Tra Venezia e mondo turco," 45; "Relazione di Gianfrancesco Morosini," in Albèri, *Relazioni*, 9:257; *Gregolin*, b. 12 ter. I, 7 Sep 1590, Tulio Fabri in Venice to Antonio Paruta in Pera.

184. Yerasimos, *Les voyageurs dans l'Empire Ottoman*, 9–11; also Lucchetta, "Viaggiatori, geografi e racconti di viaggio," 201.

185. Contarini, *Diario del viaggio,* 11; *SDC,* b. 73, cc. 71r–v, 7 Apr 1612, Cristoforo Valier to Senate; see also "Relazione di Pietro Foscarini," in Barozzi and Berchet, *Relazioni,* 2:118–19.

186. *Coll.Rel,* b. 5, cc. 1r–v, "Memoria d'un viaggio fatto a Costantinopoli et di alcune cose notate a quella porta nella circoncisione di Sultan Ahmetto figliuolo di Sultan Amorath presente Imperatore de Turchi. L'anno MDLXXXII."

187. *SDC,* b. 52, c. 44v, 5 Oct 1600, Agostino Nani to Senate; *SDC,* b. 81, cc.194v–195r, 28 May 1616, Almoro Nani to Senate; de Callières, *Negotiating with Princes,* 48–49.

188. *SDC,* b. 14, cc. 155r–v, 2 Jul 1580, Paolo Contarini to Senate; *SDC,* b. 55, cc. 183r–v, 21 Jun 1602, Agostino Nani to Senate.

189. *SDC,* b. 39, cc. 1r–v, 12 Mar 1594, Marco Venier to Senate; *BAC,* b. 269, reg. 382, c. 8v, 25 Feb 1593 (MV).

190. See Mauroeide, *Ho Hellenismos sto Galata,* 177–249.

191. Lane, *Venice,* 348, 381–84, 415; *CapiXD,* b. 7, no. 78, 3 Apr 1610, Simone Contarini to Council of Ten, mentions only three sailors from Venice proper.

192. *BAC,* b. 347, 8 Mar 1629; *BAC,* b. 329, 20 Oct 1594, "Processo et sententia criminal contro Giacomo di Luca di Cypro, condannato anni cinque in una delle gallee di condannati."

193. *It VII* 1087 (8524), c. 325r, 10 Oct 1639, Alvise Contarini to Senate; *It VII* 1085 (8522), 222r–227v, 6 Feb 1637 (MV); Lane, *Venice,* 382.

194. *SDC,* b. 14, c. 106r, 16 Mar 1580, Giovanni Cappello to Senate.

195. Lane, *Andrea Barbarigo;* Lane, *Venice,* 344–45; Queller, *Venetian Patriciate,* 34–39.

196. *SDC,* b. 18, cc. 435r–v, 18 Feb 1583 (MV), Gianfrancesco Morosini to Council of Ten.

197. *SDC,* b. 15, c. 32r, 2 Apr 1581, Paolo Contarini to Senate; *APC,* b. 18, 8: 16v, 6 Jan 1621 (MV), Giorgio Giustinian to Senate. For another case of a captured patrician youth, see *SDC,* b. 58, cc. 239v–244r, 2 Jan 1603 (MV), Francesco Contarini to Senate.

198. *BAC,* b. 272, reg. 387, c. 153v, 2 Aug 1601.

199. *CapiXD,* b. 7, no. 22, 18 Sep 1604, Francesco Contarini to Council of Ten; *BAC,* b. 277, reg. 396, c. 175r, 24 Mar 1612.

200. *It VII* 1086 (8523), 104r–v, 3 July 1638, Alvise Contarini to Senate.

201. *BAC,* b. 331-I, 2 May 1630; *CapiXD,* b. 7, no. 78, 3 Apr 1610, Simone Contarini to Council of Ten.

CHAPTER 4. JEWS, RENEGADES, AND EARLY MODERN IDENTITY

1. Yerasimos, *Les voyageurs dans l'Empire Ottoman.*

2. Miliopoulos, "Relation d'un voyage," 128, 141.

3. Foster and Daniell, *Life of Busbecq,* 1:330; Sandys, *Relation of a Journey,* 78; Moryson, *An Itinerary,* 2:90–91. Also, Bertelè, *Il palazzo degli Ambasciatori,* 141 n.107; *Lettres anecdotes de Cyrille Lucar,* 69.

4. Dallam, "Diary," 79, 83–84; Matteucci, *Un glorioso convento,* 404–11; Finkel, "French Mercenaries," 466.

5. Letts, *Pilgrimage of Arnold von Harff,* 102; Foster and Daniell, *Life of Busbecq,* 1:157; "Missione al Patriarco di Alessandria," 1:303; Wood, *Mr. Harrie Cavendish,* 13.

6. Yerasimos, "À propos des *sürgün* de Karaman," 357.

7. Eldem, Goffman, and Masters, *The Ottoman City between East and West*, 11.

8. Armstrong, *Nations before Nationalism*, 6. Fishman, "Language and Ethnicity," 6.

9. Sahlins, *Boundaries*, 270–71. My thinking on this notion of fluid identity has been influenced by Benedict Anderson, whose ideas are rooted in the work of earlier scholars of the nation, such as Ernst Renan and V. H. Galbraith. Anderson, *Imagined Communities*; Renan, "What Is a Nation," 42–55; Schulze, *States, Nations, and Nationalism*, 97; Galbraith, "Nationality and Language," 113; Kafadar, *Between Two Worlds*, 27–28.

10. Kafadar, *Between Two Worlds*, 20–21; Fernandez, "Historians Tell Tales," 118, 120.

11. Goodblatt, *Jewish Life in Turkey*, 8, 13; Molho, "Ebrei e marrani," 2:1011–26.

12. On the divisions among the various Jewish nations in Venice, see Pullan, *Jews of Europe*, 149–52; Roth, *History of the Jews in Venice*, 39–71.

13. Rozen, *History of the Jewish Community in Istanbul*, 87–98; Bodian, *Hebrews of the Portuguese Nation*, 1–19.

14. Bodian, *Hebrews of the Portuguese Nation*, ix–xiii, 6–17.

15. Segre, "Sephardic Settlements," 114–15 n.5.

16. Pullan, "A Ship with Two Rudders," 36; Rozen, *History of the Jewish Community in Istanbul*, 92; Bodian, *Hebrews of the Portuguese Nation*, 13. See also Pullan, *Jews of Europe*, 201–42.

17. Molho, "Ebrei e marrani," 2:1019–20; Pullan, "A Ship with Two Rudders," 45. On Righetto, see also Zorattini, "Anrriquez Nunez," 291–307.

18. Pullan, "A Ship with Two Rudders," 37–38.

19. Calabi, "Gli stranieri e la città," 5:939; Molho, "Ebrei e marrani," 2:1019–20; Pullan, "A Ship with Two Rudders," 57 n.123.

20. Calimani, *Storia del ghetto*, 155–64. On the Duke of Naxos, see Roth, *Doña Gracia of the House of Nasi*; Roth, *The Duke of Naxos of the House of Nasi*; Pullan, *Jews of Europe*, 98–99, 179–80; Levy, *The Sephardim in the Ottoman Empire*, 32–34.

21. Goodblatt, *Jewish Life in Turkey*, 104 n.30, 180–81. On conversion, marriage, and divorce in the Ottoman courts, see Cassia, "Religion, Politics, and Ethnicity in Cyprus," 23–23; Jennings, "Divorce in the Ottoman Sharia Court of Cyprus," 155–67; Zorattini, "Jews, Crypto-Jews, and the Inquisition," 110–11.

22. *VSM*-I, reg. 143, cc. 15r–v, 5 Jan 1610 (MV); *VSM*-I, reg. 145, c. 58r, 26 Mar 1620. Venetian records from Constantinople also report on a number of Jewish renegades there, for example, *SDC*, b. 23, cc. 401r–v, 28 May 1586, Lorenzo Bernardo to Senate. For the case of another Marrano who returned to Judaism then reconverted to Christianity, see Roth, "The Strange Case of Hector Mendes Bravo."

23. McNeill, *Venice*, 214; Lewis, *Jews of Islam*, 146–47; Levy, *The Sephardim in the Ottoman Empire*, 84–89. The theme of Jewish conversion to Christianity appears throughout Shakespeare's *The Merchant of Venice*. See, for example, I.iii.78–79 and II.iii.19–21.

24. Pullan, "A Ship with Two Rudders," 37.

25. Ibid., 44–45; Zorattini, "Anrriquez Nunez," 301–4; Molho, "Ebrei e marrani,"

2:1019–20; Pullan, *Jews of Europe*, 151; Roth, *History of the Jews in Venice*, 184, 191; Ravid, "From Yellow to Red," 179–210; Hughes, "Earrings for Circumcision," 155–77.

26. Pullan, "A Ship with Two Rudders," 37, 46.

27. Zorattini, "Anrriquez Nunez," 304; Molho, "Ebrei e marrani," 2:1019–20. For a similar identic odyssey, see Bodian, *Hebrews of the Portuguese Nation*, 5.

28. Ravid, "A Tale of Three Cities," 138–62; Ravid, "The Legal Status of the Jewish Merchants of Venice," 274; Arbel, "Jews in International Trade," 75–79; Arbel, *Trading Nations*, ix, 2–3. See also Segre, "Sephardic Settlements," 112–37; Cooperman, "Venetian Policy towards Levantine Jews," 65–84.

29. On the general organization and standing of the Ottoman Empire's Jewish communities in the early modern era, see Rozen, *A History of the Jewish Community in Istanbul;* Shmuelevitz, *Jews of the Ottoman Empire.*

30. On the debate over the importance of Jewish trade to Venetian economic fortunes, see Arbel, "Jews in International Trade," 93–4; Arbel, *Trading Nations*, ix, 2–3, 26, 28; Tenenti, *Naufrages, corsairs et assurances maritimes à Venise*, 14; Roth, *History of the Jews in Venice*, 175–78; Roth, *History of the Jews of Italy*, 334; Blumenkranz, "Les Juifs dans le commerce maritime de Venise," 146–51; Tucci, "Tra Venezia e mondo turco," 41–42; Segre, "Sephardic Settlements," 124. An interesting contemporary Jewish perspective on the benefit of the Jews to the Venetian state can be found in Simone Luzzatto's famous apologetic *Discorso;* see Ravid, "How Profitable the Nation of the Jewes Are," 159–80. For a particularly ferocious Venetian attack on the Jewish role in the Levantine trade, see *SDC,* b. 51, cc. 101r–105r, 8 Apr 1600, Girolamo Cappello to Senate.

31. Arbel, "Jews in International Trade," 73–96; Nicolay, *Navigations into Turkie*, 130v–131v; *SDCop,* reg. 19, cc. 148–53, 27 Aug 1625, Giorgio Giustinian to Senate; also many letters from Ottaviano Bon on the matter of Jewish merchants in *APC,* b. 10. See also Schiavi, "Gli ebrei in Venezia," 493. For reservations on accepting the anecdotal evidence on the Jewish commercial position, see Baron, *Social and Religious History of the Jews*, 18: 236–46; also Cooperman, "Venetian Policy towards Levantine Jews," 70.

32. Maestro, *L'attività economica*, 71, cited in Arbel, *Trading Nations*, 26. Jewish exports from Ragusa, 1590–1645, included 1,602 bundles of camlets; 77,202 bales and 267,384 pieces of cordovans; 135,881 oxhides; and 4,872 other hides. Burdelez, "Role of Ragusan Jews," 192.

33. Mantran, "Minoritaires, métiers et marchands étrangers," 132; Pullan, *Rich and Poor in Renaissance Venice*, 101–3; Tucci, "Tra Venezia e mondo turco," 51. The converse, Jews trading under Christian names, was also widespread and in part was necessary to avoid corsairs who targeted Jewish and Muslim merchandise. *SDC,* b. 54, c. 5v, 8 Sep 1601, Agostino Nani to Senate; *BAC,* b. 276, reg. 395, cc. 59v–60v, 14 Jan 1610 (MV); *BAC,* b. 275, reg. 392, cc. 124v–125v, 18 June 1607.

34. Arbel, *Trading Nations*, 10–11, 18–19. For an angry patrician response to the growing Jewish presence and importance in the city, see *VSM-I,* reg. 141, cc. 78r–80v, 10 Feb 1603 (MV).

35. *SDC,* b. 69, c. 145v, 17 Apr 1610, Simone Contarini to Senate; cc. 251r–252r, 15 May 1610, Simone Contarini to Senate.

36. Wilson, "Reflecting on the Turk," 49–52. On the shifting tides of Venetian tolerance for Protestants, see Martin, *Venice's Hidden Enemies*, 135–39, 194–95, 228. For a discussion in the context of early modern France, see Benedict, "Un roi, une loi, deux fois," 65–93.

37. Molho, "Ebrei e marrani," 2:1026–36; Pullan, "A Ship with Two Rudders," 39, 44–45.

38. Jacoby, "Venice and the Venetian Jews," 34–35; Mantran, "Minoritaires, métiers et marchands étrangers," 127. Marranos might become citizens, as technically they were Christians, but this process could be labyrinthine and adversarial. See for example the case of Rui Lopes and Diego Rodriguez, *VSM*-I, reg. 141, cc. 71r–v, 16 Jan 1603 (MV). Contrast this with the situation in the Netherlands where Jews could purchase burghership, though they could not hold civil office and this status was not heritable. Ravid, "How Profitable the Nation of the Jewes Are," 169.

39. *SDC*, b. 69, c. 407r, 10 Jul 1610, Simone Contarini to Senate.

40. *BAC*, b. 267, reg. 378, cc. 4r–v, 10 Jul 1590; *BAC*, b. 265, reg. 374, cc. 126r–v, 16 Aug 1586.

41. Blochet, "Relation du voyage en Orient," 344; *BAC*, b. 266, reg. 375, c. 24r, 9 Apr 1588; *BAC*, b. 266, reg. 375, cc. 126r–v, 26 Jul 1589; *SDC*, b. 57, cc. 153r–v, 18 Apr 1603, Francesco Contarini to Senate; *BAC*, b. 264, reg. 425, c. 140r, 10 Dec 1583; *BAC*, b. 274, reg. 391, cc. 215v–216r, 25 Feb 1605 (MV).

42. *CapiXLett*, b. 5, no. 145, 16 Mar 1580, Gabriele Cavazza to Council of Ten; *BAC*, b. 344, 4 May 1622; *BAC*, b. 263, "Sententiarum Primus sub Clarissimo Domino Alexandro Contareno Bailo . . . 1545–46," cc. 15r–v, 6 Jan 1545 (MV).

43. *SDC*, b. 19, cc. 29r–30r, 6 Mar 1584, Gianfrancesco Morosini to Senate.

44. Zorattini, "Jews, Crypto-Jews, and the Inquisition," 104–5.

45. Ravid, "The Legal Status of the Jewish Merchants of Venice," 278; Ravid, "A Tale of Three Cities," 148–55. *BAC*, b. 339, n.d., Bailo to Sultan; *BAC*, b. 267, reg. 378, cc. 4r–v, 10 Jul 1590; *BAC*, b. 265, reg. 374, cc. 126r–v, 16 Aug 1586.

46. Arbel, *Trading Nations*, 78–86; *CapiXLett*, b. 3, no. 253–55, 23 Jan 1570 (MV); Roth, *Jews in Venice*, 92–4; Calimani, *Storia del ghetto*, 174–77. On Jews as subjects, see Lane, *Venice*, 300; Arbel, *Trading Nations*, 178, 180; Cooperman, "Venetian Policy towards Levantine Jews," 65, 77; Ravid, "A Tale of Three Cities," 150. Another Jew in the 1530s, Meir Maurogonato, was "treated as a Venetian citizen" because of the faithful service he and his family had given to Venice. Schiavi, "Gli ebrei in Venezia," 488.

47. "Relazione di Gianfrancesco Morosini," in Albèri, *Relazioni*, 9:316.

48. Burdelez, "The Role of Ragusan Jews," 193; *SDC*, b. 22, cc. 193r–v, 30 Oct 1585, Lorenzo Bernardo to Senate; *SDC*, b. 20, c. 60r, 18 Sep 1584, Gianfrancesco Morosini to Senate.

49. Cooperman, "Venetian Policy towards Levantine Jews," 76–77; Ravid, "The Legal Status of the Jewish Merchants of Venice," 275–57; *DocTR*, b. 9, no. 1064, 30 Aug 1594, "Istanza di Giacobbe Castiel al Collegio."

50. *SDC*, b. 51, c. 133r, 21 Apr 1600, Girolamo Cappello to Senate; *SDC*, b. 51, c. 348r, 15 Jul 1600, Davide Abudenti to Girolamo Cappello; *SDelC*, f. 10, 2 Sep 1600, Senate to Baili;

Ravid, "The Legal Status of the Jewish Merchants of Venice," 278; Arbel, "Jews in International Trade," 92.

51. *SDC*, b. 35, c. 408r, 11 July 1592, Matteo Zane to Senate.

52. *SDCop*, reg. 12, c. 40, 21 Sep 1597, Girolamo Cappello to Senate; Segre, "Sephardic Settlements," 127. On the role of Esperanza, and other similar confidants of the sultanas, see Levy, *The Sephardim in the Ottoman Empire*, 29–30; also Mordtmann, "Die jüdischen kira im Serai der Sultane." Shaw confuses Esperanza with Esther, another important Jewish *kira*, influential with the so-called Venetian sultana, Nūr Bānū. Shaw, *Jews of the Ottoman Empire*, 90–91. On this confusion, see Skilliter, "Letters of Nūr Bānū," 518.

53. *SDC*, b. 58, cc. 216v–217r, 20 Dec 1603, Ağa of Janissaries to Francesco Contarini.

54. The phrase comes from the title of the important book by Bartolomé Bennassar and Lucile Bennassar, *Les chrétiens d'Allah: l'histoire extraordinaire des renégats, XVIe–XVIIe siècles*. See also Scaraffia, *Rinnegati*, 4; Rostagno, *Mi faccio turco*; Benzoni, "Il «farsi turco»"; Kissling, "Das Renegatentum."

55. Bono, "Pascià e Raìs algerini," 199–200; Bennassar, "Conversion ou reniement," 1351.

56. Rostagno, *Mi faccio turco*, 27; Scaraffia, *Rinnegati*, 8; Bennassar, "Frontières religieuses entre islam et chrétienité," 71–72. Rostagno's statistics from the Roman Inquisition suggest clearly that the sixteenth century was a heyday of the renegades: in 1582, 32.3 percent of "spontaneous appearances" were for apostasy to Islam, in 1603, 14 percent; 1615, 8.9 percent; 1 percent in 1650; 3.5 percent in 1658; *Mi faccio turco*, 38. Bono describes the same decline, but dates its beginning later to 1650; Bono, "Pascià e Raìs algerini," 221.

57. Letts, *Pilgrimage of Arnold von Harff*, 108.

58. Diego de Häedo, *Topographia e Historia General de Argel* (Valladolid, 1612), cited in Bono, "Pascià e Raìs algerini," 201–5. Population statistics are found in Chandler and Fox, *3000 Years of Urban Growth*, 358.

59. Clissold, "Christian Renegades and Barbary Corsairs," 509. See also Davis, "Slave Redemption in Venice," 464.

60. Bennassar, "Conversion ou reniement," 1349–50.

61. Rostagno, *Mi faccio turco*, 63; della Valle, *De' viaggi*, 1:246.

62. Cited in Frazee, *Catholics and Sultans*, 95–96.

63. On Çigalazade Sinan Paşa, see *EI*, 2:33–35; Rinieri, *Clemente VIII e Sinan Bassà Cicala*; also "*Cicala*, Scipione" and "*Cicala*, Visconte" in *DBI*, 25:320–40, 25:340–46.

64. Scaraffia, *Rinnegati*, 3, 31; Wratislaw, *Adventures*, 54; Veinstein, "Sur les conversions à l'Islam," 164–65. On medieval Christian perceptions of the moral promiscuity of Islam, see Daniel, *Islam and the West*, 158–85.

65. Fabris, "Il Dottor Girolamo Fasaneo," 105; Scaraffia, *Rinnegati*, 4–5. These motives of conversion are similar to ones advanced by medieval writers to explain the inexplicable, Christian apostates to Islam. Rostagno, *Mi faccio turco*, 7.

66. Scaraffia, *Rinnegati*, 4–5. İnalcık has found that in Ottoman lands in the late sixteenth century increases in the poll tax caused mass conversions; "The Ottoman State," 1:69.

67. Bono, "Pascià e Raìs algerini," 200–201.

68. *It VII* 882 (8505), IX, cc. 37v–38r, "Descritione dell'Imperio Turchesco del Reverendissimo Monseigneur Maffio Veniero, Arcivescovo di Corfu"; Blount, *Voyage into the Levant*, 112–15.

69. Setton, "Lutheranism and the Turkish Peril," 161; Vaughan, *Europe and the Turk*, 112.

70. Bennassar and Bennassar, *Les chrétiens d'Allah*, 19.

71. Pullan, "The Conversion of Jews," 54.

72. Scaraffia, *Rinnegati*, 23, 153.

73. *BAC*, b. 339, 8 Jul 1606, Consul of Cairo to Bailo; for a similar case, see *SDC*, b. 49, cc. 2r–v, 1 Mar 1599, Girolamo Cappello to Senate; *SDC*, b. 54, cc. 154r–v, 15 Dec 1601, Agostino Nani to Senate; *SDC*, b. 54, c. 117r; *SDC*, b. 54, c. 175r, 28 Dec 1601, Agostino Nani to Senate. On Wilson's play, see Chew, *The Crescent and the Rose*, 153–55.

74. *SDC*, b. 53, cc. 352r–v, 10 Jul 1601, Sultan to paşa of Cairo.

75. Wratislaw, *Adventures*, 10–18, 109–10; *SDC*, b. 26, c. 192r, 1 Nov 1587, Giovanni Moro in Adrianople to Senate. Also de Groot, "The Dutch Nation in Istanbul," 133–34.

76. On Fasaneo, see Fabris, "Il Dottor Girolamo Fasaneo," 105–18. Fasaneo was harassed and threatened for years, and was eventually assassinated under the bailo's direction. "Relazione di Girolamo Cappello," in Barozzi and Berchet, *Relazioni*, 2:52–53; *SDC*, b. 113, cc. 388r–390r, 4 Sep 1632, Girolamo Cappello to Senate.

77. *XSeg*, f. 25, 18 June 1593, Council of Ten to Bailo; Parker, *The Military Revolution*, 120, 129, 174.

78. Finkel, "French Mercenaries," 451–71; Bennassar and Bennassar, *Les chrétiens d'Allah*, 228, 237–42, 250; Bennassar, "Conversion ou reniement," 1363–64; Setton, "Lutheranism and the Turkish Peril," 161. Naima records the defections of several important Christian military leaders in the Holy Roman emperor's armies; *Annals*, 1:104, 191.

79. Heyberger, "Se convertir à l'Islam," 134; Scaraffia, *Rinnegati*, 126, 144–45; Preto, *Venezia e i turchi*, 190.

80. Riggio, "Musulmani in Calabria."

81. *SDC*, b. 98, cc. 298r–v, 4 Dec 1624, Simone Contarini at Corfu to Senate.

82. *SDC*, b. 18, c. 172r, 12 Nov 1583, Gianfrancesco Morosini to Senate; *SDC*, b. 16, c. 102v, 23 Jun 1582, Paolo Contarini to Senate; *SDelC*, f. 5, 11 Aug 1582, Senate to Bailo and Ambassador; *DocTR*, b. 7, no. 927, ca 23 Mar 1584 in Venice, Declaration of Haci Ahmed Hac.

83. *LSTR*, b. 5, cc. 116r–117v, 10 Nov 1592, Grand Vizier to Doge; ASFi, *Mediceo*, b. 4274, c. 297r, n.d., Mustafa Bassa to Gran Duke; *APC*, b. 2, c. 2r, 27 Aug 1524, Piero Bragadin to Senate.

84. Naima, *Annals*, 1:422–23.

85. *It VII* 1085 (8522), cc. 119r–123r, 14 Aug 1637 Alvise Contarini to Senate; *SDelC*, f. 5, 23 Jul 1583, Letters from Metropolitan of Athens.

86. Donia and Fine, *Bosnia and Hercegovina*, 38–40.

87. *SDC*, b. 20, c. 541r, 19 Jan 1584 (MV), Gianfrancesco Morosini to Senate; *SDC*, b. 16, 181r, 29 Sep 1582, Paolo Contarini to Senate. On the relationship of the various sects and movement between them in Islam, see Renard, "Seven Doors to Islam."

88. *Responsa* IV-128, cited in Goodblatt, *Jewish Life in Turkey*, 180–81; *Responsa* IV-5, cited in ibid., 211 n.28; Pullan, "The Conversion of Jews," 53, 55, 57; Frazee, *Catholics and Sultans*, 75.

89. Veinstein, "Sur les conversions à l'Islam," 165.

90. Bennassar and Bennassar, *Les chrétiens d'Allah*, 19; Fabris, "Il Dottor Girolamo Fasaneo," 105; Blount, *Voyage into the Levant*, 112–15.

91. Bennassar, "Conversion ou reniement," 1361; Veinstein, "Sur les conversions à l'Islam," 165. Daniel discusses briefly a Murad Bey, captured at age seventeen, who converted initially without thought but after "acquired a true knowledge of [Islam's] discipline" and hoped that God would allow his "last hour to be spent in the same faith." After his recapture by Christians, he refused to return to his birth faith. Daniel, *Islam and the West*, 308; also ACDF, *Dubia diversa ab anno 1570 ad Annum 1668*, b. 3, no. 2, 20 Aug 1601.

92. *DonàR*, b. 23, cc. 109v–110r; *SDC*, b. 53, cc. 377v–378r, 30 Jul 1601, Agostino Nani to Senate; Pedani-Fabris, "Safiye's Household," 21–22.

93. Donia and Fine, *Bosnia and Hercegovina*, 44.

94. Zachariadou, "À propos du syncrétisme islamo-chrétien," 403.

95. Scaraffia, *Rinnegati*, 115–20; Rostagno, *Mi faccio turco*, 52. Also Audisio, "Renégats marseillais," 46–48.

96. Scaraffia, *Rinnegati*, 115–20; Bennassar, "Frontières religieuses entre islam et chrétienité," 75; Wratislaw, *Adventures*, 89–94.

97. Archivio della Curia Arcivescovile di Pisa, *Inquisizione*, atti dal 1625, cc. 590r–591r, 19 May 1627, cited in Rostagno, *Mi faccio turco*, 92–94; Scaraffia, *Rinnegati*, 115–20. There are examples too numerous to list in the Venetian records from Constantinople of renegades who returned to Christianity. For a sample, see *BAC*, b. 265, reg. 374, c. 26r, 26 Aug 1585; *BAC*, b. 273, reg. 390, cc. 214r–v, 18 Aug 1604; Alberti, *Viaggio a Costantinopoli*, 18–34.

98. Rostagno, *Mi faccio turco*, 19, 23; Scaraffia, *Rinnegati*, 103, 105–7; Fabris, "Un caso di pirateria veneziana," 105; *VSM-I*, reg. 142, cc. 9v–10r, 25 Mar 1607. Rostagno found only two instances of renegades actually being executed. Rostagno, *Mi faccio turco*, 34–5.

99. Fabris, "Artisinat et culture," 54.

100. Sherley, "Discours of the Turkes," Nixon, *The Three English Brothers; It VII* 882 (8505), IX, cc. 40v–41r, "Descritione dell'Imperio Turchesco del Reverendissimo Monseigneur Maffio Venier, Arcivescovo di Corfu."

101. "Relazione di Simone Contarini," in Barozzi and Berchet, *Relazioni*, 1:160–61. Maffio Venier wrote similarly: "The Turks by birth are so modest, are so regal, that the renegade soldiers are much more given to rape, thievery, homicides, cruelty . . . Natural Turks . . . are for the most part innocent persons, as perturbingly they are a mix of good and wicked men"; *CollRel*, b. 5, c. 22v, "Relatione di Maffio Venier"; also Soranzo, *L'Ottomanno*, 176–77.

102. Tietze, *Counsel for Sultans*, 74 n. 178; Clissold, "Christian Renegades and Barbary Corsairs," 515.

103. *VSM-I*, reg. 142, cc. 83v–84r, 18 Aug 1608; *VSM-I*, reg. 144, cc. 31r–v, 14 Feb 1614 (MV).

104. Venetian scribes usually attempted to italianize Ottoman names and words, with varying degrees of success. They seem to have had particular difficulty with Gazanfer Ağa; in Venetian reports his name is variously written as Giafer Aga, Giaffer Aga, Gasamfer Aga, Casafer Aga.

105. Hammer, *Histoire*, 2:199–201. For more recent discussions that perpetuate Hammer's misidentification, see Fleischer, *Bureaucrat*, 72; Kafadar, "Les troubles monétaires," 391; Schmidt, "The Egri-Campaign of 1596"; Peirce, *The Imperial Harem*, 12, 179.

106. *CollRel*, b. 4, cc. 32r–v, "Relazione di Lorenzo Bernardo"; "Relazione di Matteo Zane," in Albèri, *Relazioni*, 9:437–38; *SDC*, b. 18, c. 426r, 24 Jan 1583 (MV), Gianfrancesco Morosini to Senate. There is no record of a Michiel as Podestà in Budua in the mid-sixteenth century, though there is a Luca Michiel q. Donado who was elected *potestà et provisor romani* in 1556, though he apparently refused the office. *Segretario alle voci— Maggior Consiglio*, reg. 3, 130, 156.

107. *CollRel*, b. 4, "Relazione di Lorenzo Bernardo"; *SDelC*, f. 6, 29 Dec 1584; Peirce, *The Imperial Harem*, 12; Fleischer, *Bureaucrat*, 72; Pedani-Fabris, "Safiye's Household," 14–15. On both the physiological and psychological experience of eunuchs, see Penzer, *The Harēm*, 140–50.

108. Hammer, *Histoire*, 2:199–201; Lybyer, *Government of the Ottoman Empire*, 244; Fleischer, *Bureaucrat*, 72–3.

109. "Kapu Aghasi," *EI*, 4:570–71; Pedani-Fabris, *Documenti turchi*, lxv, lxviii; Peirce, *The Imperial Harem*, 12; Peachy, *Selaniki's History*, 241–22.

110. *CollRel*, b. 5, c. 18r, "Relazione di Ottaviano Bon."

111. *SDC*, b. 56, cc. 208r–211v, 9 Jan 1602 (MV), Francesco Contarini to Senate.

112. Kafadar, "Les troubles monetaires," 390–91.

113. Naima, *Annals*, 1:91–2; Schmidt, "The Egri-Campaign of 1596," 136–37; Pedani-Fabris, "Veneziani a Costantinopoli"; Pedani-Fabris, "Safiye's Household," 9–32. For examples of other viziers who rose and fell because of Gazanfer's support, see *SDC*, b. 32, cc. 264r–265r, *Kapıağası* to Grand Vizier; *SDC*, b. 47, c. 90r, 20 Apr 1598, Girolamo Cappello to Senate. Naima, *Annals*, 1:108–9, recounts the case of Hasan Paşa: the sultan had refused to remove him, but Gazanfer and the sultana maneuvered successfully to have him removed and strangled in the Seven Towers. On Gazanfer's influence in the court, see also Kortepeter, *Ottoman Imperialism*, 151, 160–61, 215.

114. Schmidt, *Mustafa 'Ali's Künhü'l-Ahbar*, 1–2; Schmidt, "The Egri-Campaign of 1596," 136–37; Fleischer, *Bureaucrat*, 170, 182–83; Hammer, *Histoire*, 2:199–201.

115. Hammer, *Histoire*, 2:199–201. The roots of this vision of the harem dominating the sultans are found among contemporaries: Agostino Nani reported, "the Queen and the *kapıağası* who rule this machine do not think of its duration but of carrying the time ahead, and preserving their lives from the furious impetuousness of the militia"; *SDC*, b. 54, c. 210r, 13 Jan 1601 (MV), Agostino Nani to Senate. For a recent and very different assessment of this period, see Peirce, *Imperial Harem*.

116. Naima, *Annals*, 1:212–14.

117. Foster, *Travels of John Sanderson*, 216 n.1; Hammer, *Histoire*, 2:303–4; *SDC*, b. 56, cc. 208r–211v, 9 Jan 1602 (MV), Francesco Contarini to Senate. Gazanfer's execution was widely reported and commented on: see Kortepeter, *Ottoman Imperialism*, 223.

118. *SDC*, b. 47, cc. 302r–303r, 25 Jul 1598, Girolamo Cappello to Senate; *CollRel*, b. 4, "Relazione di Lorenzo Bernardo"; *SDC*, b. 39, cc. 40v–42v, 24 Mar 1594, Marco Venier to Senate; *SDC*, b. 42, c. 373r, 26 Jan 1595, Marco Venier to Senate.

119. *SDC*, b. 52, cc. 296r–297r, Agostino Nani to Senate, 6 Jan 1600 (MV); "Relazione di Gianfrancesco Morosini," in Albèri, *Relazioni*, 9:298–99.

120. *CollRel*, b. 4, cc. 32r–v, "Relazione di Lorenzo Bernardo"; *CollRel*, b. 4, cc. n.n., "Relazione di Lorenzo Bernardo," 1590.

121. *SDC*, b. 37, cc. 30r–v, 14 Mar 1593, Matteo Zane to Senate.

122. *SDC*, b. 52, cc. 296r–297r, Agostino Nani to Senate, 6 Jan 1600 (MV). Naima relates an incident in which an opponent described Gazanfer Aga as a Frank by birth. Naima, *Annals*, 1:91–92. Renegades in general seem to have been sensitive to their public image vis-à-vis their native states. Çigalazade, for example, on whose seal was written "Champion of the faith on land and sea," was attacked by an enemy vizier who "called him an infidel of the Muslim law, because having been with his mother, who was already a Turk, and having her in his power, he did not bring her to Constantinople, as per the Muslim precept." The vizier tried to have the *kapudanpaşa* declared by the müfti an "infidel having gone against the Muhammedan religion in not conducting his mother here, who was already a Turk, and that he was no longer a Muslim, and that he needed again to return and become a Turk, and to raise the finger, which is the usual sign of renouncing." Even earlier, Süleyman's favorite İbrahim was detested by the military and civil bureaucrats because of his unorthodox rise to power and his supposed sympathy for Christianity, resulting in the sacking of his palace in 1525 by the janissaries while İbrahim was in Egypt putting down a revolt. Rinieri, *Clemente VIII e Sinan Bassà Cicala*, 20–31; *SDC*, b. 55, cc. 23r–27v, 13 Mar 1602, Agostino Nani to Senate; Hammer, *Histoire*, 2:321; Finlay, "Al servizio del Sultano," 81.

123. *SDC*, b. 51, c. 242r, 16 Jun 1600, Girolamo Cappello to Senate.

124. *SDelC*, f. 6, 29 Dec 1584; *SDelC*, f. 7, 15 Feb 1590 (MV); *SDC*, b. 32, c. 367v, 5 Jan 1590 (MV), Girolamo Lippomano to Senate; *SDC*, b. 39, cc. 8v–10v, 12 Mar 1594, Marco Venier to Senate; *Miscellanea atti diversi e manoscritti*, b. 96, cited in Fabris, "Un caso di pirateria veneziana," 104.

125. *SDC*, b. 51, cc. 120v–121r, 20 Apr 1600, Girolamo Cappello to Senate; *SDC*, b. 37, cc. 278r–v, 7 Jun 1593, Matteo Zane to Senate.

126. *SDC*, b. 40, c. 142r, note of *Kapıağası*.

127. *SDC*, b. 56, c. 169v, 5 Jan 1602 (MV), Francesco Contarini to Senate.

128. *SDC*, b. 51, cc. 120r–v, 20 Apr 1600, Girolamo Cappello to Senate.

129. *SDC*, b. 19, cc. 1r–v, 6 Mar 1584, Gianfrancesco Morosini to Senate; *SDC*, b. 20, cc. 16r–19r, 4 Sep 1584, Gianfrancesco Morosini to Senate.

130. On Hasan's youth and early career, and in general, see Fabris, "Hasan 'Il veneziano' tra Algeria," 51–66; Bono, *I corsari barbareschi*, 383–87; Haëdo, *Topographia et historia general de Argel*.

131. Tormene, "Il bailaggio a Costantinopoli," 409–10; Scaraffia, *Rinnegati*, 8; Stefani, *Viaggio a Costantinopoli*, 42 n.2; "Relazione di Giovanni Moro," in Albèri, *Relazioni*, 9:356–61; Bono, "Pascià e Raìs algerini," 213–15; Bertelè, *Il palazzo degli Ambasciatori*, 133 n.61; Davis, *Christian Slaves, Muslim Masters*, 28–29.

132. Cervantes, *Don Quixote*, 293–94; "Relazione di Giovanni Moro," in Albèri, *Relazioni*, 9:356–61. On Cervantes' dealings with Hasan, see Bono, *I corsari barbareschi*, 383–87.

133. Hess, *The Forgotten Frontier*, 104, 108, 123; "Relazione di Giovanni Moro," in Albèri, *Relazioni*, 9:356–61, 359; Hammer, *Histoire*, 2:252. On Hasan's short, but successful career as *kapudanpaşa*, see Braudel, *Mediterranean*, 2:1189–90, 1193, 1223–24.

134. Stefani, *Viaggio a Costantinopoli*, 42; *SDC*, b. 33, cc. 257r–260v, 26 Jun 1591, Lorenzo Bernardo to Senate. Early in his career, in 1577, it was reported that Hasan knew only twenty-five words in Turkish; *SDC*, b. 11, no. 30, 20 May 1577, cited in Fabris, "Hasan 'Il veneziano' tra Algeria," 54. Kunt has shown that while slaves learned Turkish, they did not forget their mother tongues; "Ethnic-Regional (*Cins*) Solidarity," 235.

135. *BAC*, b. 266, reg. 376, cc. 71v–72r, 24 May 1590; *BAC*, b. 267, reg. 379, cc. 84r–v, 28 Nov 1591; *SDC*, b. 33, c. 111, 2 Mar 1591, Girolamo Lippomano to Senate. See also Fabris, "Hasan 'Il veneziano' tra Algeria," 60.

136. *SDC*, b. 28, c. 262r, Dec 1588, Giovanni Moro to Senate; *SDC*, b. 33, c. 260r, 26 Jun 1591, Lorenzo Bernardo to Senate.

137. Tenenti, *Piracy and the Decline of Venice*, 29; *SDC*, b. 31, c. 93r, 28 Feb 1590, Hasan Paşa to Giovanni Moro; Fabris, "Hasan 'Il veneziano' tra Algeria," 59–60.

138. *DocTR*, b. 8, no. 1011, [ca. 25 Jun 1590], Kapudanpaşa Hasan to Doge; no. 1013, 25 Sep 1590, Kapudanpaşa Hasan to Senate.

139. *SDC*, b. 32, c. 367v, 5 Jan 1590 (MV), Girolamo Lippomano to Senate; *BAC*, b. 267, reg. 379, cc. 84r–v, 28 Nov 1591; Pedani-Fabris, "Safiye's Household," 21–22. Fabris indicates that Hasan also convinced a cousin, Livio Celesti, to leave two young sons and to work for him in North Africa, though it is not clear that Livio ever renounced his birth faith. Fabris, "Hasan 'Il veneziano' tra Algeria," 60–61.

140. Hammer, *Histoire*, 2:267.

141. Haëdo, *Topographia et historia general de Argel*, 150–68, 181–84, cited in Hess, *The Forgotten Frontier*, 178–79.

142. "Relazione di Giovanni Moro," Albèri, *Relazioni*, 9:356–61; [Cavazza], *Viaggio di un ambasciatore*, 75–77. Giovanni Moro reported that Hasan harbored deep feelings of injury regarding his social status in Venice, and indeed one motivation for his initial corsair activity against Venice was "so that Your Serenity would repent not having had that conception of him that, carried away by the pride of his nature, it appeared to him he deserved." Moro suggests that Hasan wished to have a patrician slave from Venice "so as to be able to glory in having as a slave someone who was born by nature a lord."

143. Pedani-Fabris, "Safiye's Household," 28; Pedani-Fabris, "Veneziani a Costantinopoli," 80.

144. "Relazione di Matteo Zane," in Albèri, *Relazioni*, 9:438; *SDC*, b. 28, cc. 442r–v, 28 Jan 1588 (MV), Giovanni Moro to Senate; *SDC*, b. 50, c. 240r, 10 Jan 1599 (MV), Girolamo Cappello and Vicenzo Gradenigo to Senate; Pedani-Fabris, "Safiye's Household," 22.

145. *SDCop*, reg. 11, c. 275, 15 Feb 1596 (MV), Girolamo Cappello to Senate; *SDC*, b. 39, cc. 8v–10v, 12 Mar 1594, Marco Venier to Senate.

146. *SDC*, b. 18, cc, 207r–v, 29 Nov 1583, Gianfrancesco Morosini to Senate; "Relazione di Giovanni Moro," Albèri, *Relazioni*, 9:361–62.

147. Kunt, "Ethnic-Regional (*Cins*) Solidarity," 233; Barkey, *Bandits and Bureaucrats*, 31.

148. Nicolay, *Navigations into Turkie*, 71r–v, cited in Frazee, *Catholics and Sultans*, 95–96.

149. Kunt, "Ethnic-Regional (*Cins*) Solidarity," 233–35; see also Murphey, "Forms of Differentiation," 142.

150. Faroqhi, "In Search of Ottoman History," 216; Kafadar, "The Ottomans and Europe," 1:604–5. See also İnalcık, *The Ottoman Empire*, 87; Findley, *Ottoman and Civil Officialdom*, 25.

151. Topkapï, *TPA*, E 9607, cited in Kunt, "Transformation of Zimmi into Askeri," 61–63.

152. Scaraffia, *Rinnegati*, 166, 173.

153. Andrić, *Bridge on the Drina*.

154. Donia and Fine, *Bosnia and Hercegovina*, 45–48; Kunt, "Ethnic-Regional (*Cins*) Solidarity," 234–35; Lesure, "Notes et documents," 129 n.19; Woodhead, *Ta 'līkī-zāde's şehnāme-i hümāyūn*, 35 n.15.

155. Schmidt, *Mustafa 'Ali's Künhü'l-Ahbar*, 55; Woodhead, *Ta 'līkī-zāde's şehnāme-i hümāyūn*, 21 n.21. Ali complained elsewhere that Sokullu had appointed "an unfriendly Infidel, called 'Knows-no-God,' . . . to the office of prefect of police" of Constantinople. Tietze, *Counsel for Sultans*, 36.

156. At news of the victory in Hungary, Bailo Pietro Zen erected a fountain in front of his house that flowed with wine in celebration. Finlay, "Al servizio del Sultano," 83.

157. "Ibrahim Pasha," *EI*, 3:998–99; Jenkins, *Ibrahim Pasha;* Clot, *Suleiman the Magnificent*, 47–71; Finlay, "Prophecy and Politics in Istanbul," 6–9; Coles, *The Ottoman Impact*, 42; Kafadar, "The Ottomans and Europe," 1:605, 619; Coco and Manzonetto, *Baili veneziani*, 31; "Relazione di Daniello de' Ludovisi," in Albèri, *Relazioni*, 3:12–13, 28–29.

158. Jenkins, *Ibrahim Pasha*, 50–51, 83; Finlay, "Prophecy and Politics," 8–9; Finlay, "Al servizio del Sultano," 83; "Relazione di Daniello de' Ludovisi," in Albèri, *Relazioni*, 3:12–13, 28–29; Sanudo, *Diarii*, 40:698, cited in Tucci, "Tra Venezia e mondo turco," 38; Lamansky, *Secrets d'état de Venise*, 2:772–91.

159. On İbrahim's fall, see Shaw, *History*, 98, 179. The blood spilled when İbrahim was killed was left on the walls for years as a reminder of the destiny of arrogant servants. Finlay, "Al servizio del Sultano," 81, 101. Kochu Bey, adviser to Murad IV, "the Turkish Montesquieu," in 1630 wrote a penetrating analysis of the factors leading up to the present troubled state of Ottoman affairs. He writes, "The trouble began when Sultan Suleyman in 929/1523 made *Ibrahim Pasha*, a palace favourite, Grand Vezir in defiance of the old system . . . The withdrawal of the Sultan and the denigration of the Grand Vezir left the way open to the pernicious regime of palace favourites-of women, eunuchs, hangers-on, speculators, intriguers, and self-seekers, men of every religion and none, without loyalty, integrity, or virtue of any kind." Cited in Lewis, "Ottoman Observers," 75–76.

160. Rouillard, *The Turk in French History*, 441–57, 546–71; see also Stajnova and Zaimova, "Le thème ottoman."

161. Scaraffia, *Rinnegati*, 122; Rinieri, *Clemente VIII e Sinan Bassà Cicala*, 36, 84–98.

162. *SDC*, b. 57, cc. 279v–280r, 13 Jun 1603, Francesco Contarini to Senate.

163. Salignac to Henry IV, 22 May 1606, in Biron, *Ambassade en Turquie*, 2:52.

164. *SDC*, b. 69, c. 1r, 2 Mar 1610, Simone Contarini to Senate; McNeill, *Venice*, 293.

165. Arbel, "Nūr Bānū," 255–56. On Nūr Bānū, see also Skilliter, "Letters of Nūr Bānū," 515–36; Spagni, "Una sultana veneziana"; Rossi, "La sultana."

CHAPTER 5. MERCHANTS, PATRICIANS, CITIZENS, AND
EARLY MODERN IDENTITY

1. Kafadar, "The Ottomans and Europe," 1:621; Clissold, "Christian Renegades and Barbary Corsairs," 508.

2. Goffman, *Izmir and the Levantine World*, 78.

3. *SDC*, b. 38, c. 98r, 15 Oct 1593, Matteo Zane to Senate; *SDC*, b. 32, c. 377r, 5 Jan 1590 (MV), Girolamo Lippomano to Senate; *VSM*-I, reg. 135, c. 119v, 19 Feb 1564 (MV); *BAC*, b. 268, reg. 380, cc. 60v–63v, 30 Sep 1593; *CapiXLett*, b. 5, no. 149, 2 June 1580, Gabriel Cavazza to Council of Ten. An inventory of Stanga's house is in *BAC*, b. 268, reg. 381, cc. 152r–156r, 22 Oct 1593.

4. *BAC*, b. 266, reg. 375, c. 167v, 27 Apr 1590; Preto, *I servizi secreti*, 251; Lesure, "Notes et documents (I)," 143–44; *CapiXLett Rettori*, b. 292, cc. 175r–177r, cited in ibid., 158.

5. *SDC*, b. 23, cc. 186v–187r, 12 Apr 1586, Lorenzo Bernardo to Senate; *SDC*, b. 39, cc. 7r–8r, 12 Mar 1594, Marco Venier to Senate.

6. Preto, *I servizi secreti*, 120; Hassiotis, "Venezia e i domini veneziani," 1:130–31 n.40; ASFi, *Mediceo*, b. 4274, 21 Jul 1592, Anonymous to Messer Pulidoro.

7. *BAC*, b. 273, reg. 390, c. 173v, 14 Feb 1603 (MV); *BAC*, b. 277, reg. 396, c. 37v, 6 May 1611; *CapiXLett*, b. 7, no. 99, 8 Sep 1612, Cristoforo Valier to Council of Ten.

8. *BAC*, b. 277, reg. 397, cc. 152r–v, 26 Mar 1613; *NotAtti*, Zuan Andrea and Gio Francesco Catti, reg. 3383, 1607, c. 290r–292v, cited in Stefani, *L'assicurazione a Venezia*, 2:341–44; de Groot, *The Ottoman Empire and the Dutch Republic*, 60, 303 n.38.

9. De Groot, "The Dutch Nation in Istanbul," 133, 135; de Groot, *The Ottoman Empire and the Dutch Republic*, 107, 112, 134–36, 303 n.38.

10. *BAC*, b. 268, reg. 380, c. 6r, 16 Mar 1592; DSA, *Acta Sanctae Mariae Maioris*, b. 467/1, no. 23, 6 May 1594, Edoardo Gagliano to Bartolomeo Borgiani.

11. *BAC*, b. 266, reg. 375, cc. 145r–146r, 27 Nov 1589; *BAC*, b. 270, reg. 384, cc. 99v–100r, 13 Sep 1597; *SDC*, b. 31, c. 237r, letters of exchange; *BAC*, b. 269, reg. 382, cc. 89v–90r, 30 Jun 1595; *BAC*, b. 279, reg. 401, cc. 22v–23r, 29 Jul 1615; *BAC*, b. 264, reg. 424, cc. 110r–v, 28 Mar 1585; *BAC*, b. 266, reg. 375, 27 Jun 1582, Gasparo di Bossis to Edoardo Gagliano; *BAC*, b. 267, reg. 379, c. 98r, 2 Jan 1591 (MV); *BAC*, b. 317, cc. 54r–v, 25 Jan 1599 (MV); *BAC*, b. 344, 13 Jul 1600; *SDC*, b. 32, c. 113r, 29 Sep 1590, Girolamo Lippomano to Senate.

12. Tucci, "Gli investimenti assicurativi a Venezia," 157–58; *NotAtti*, Zuan Andrea Catti, reg. 3359, 1588, cc. 476v–477v, cited in Stefani, *L'assicurazione a Venezia*, 1:258–59; Brulez, *Marchands flamands à Venise*, 1, no. 72; *SDC*, b. 52, c. 380r, 3 Feb 1600 (MV), Agostino Nani to Senate; *SDC*, b. 15, cc. 200v–201r, 14 Oct 1581, Paolo Contarini to Senate; *DonàR*, b. 217, cc. 46r–v, 7 Mar 1605; *VSM*-I, reg. 141, cc. 54r–v, 12 Aug 1603.

13. *AvCom*, b. 595, 12 Jan 1592; *XSavi*, b. 168, no. 470, 22 Aug 1582.

14. *VSM*-I, reg. 141, c. 40v, 7 May 1603; Pippidi, *Hommes et idées*, 59, 81; Iorga, "Contribuțiuni la istoria Munteniei," 10; *XSavi*, b. 167, no. 21, 13 Mar 1582; *XSavi*, b. 168, no. 470, 22 Aug 1582; *DonàR*, b. 351, IV Santa Croce.

15. *BAC*, b. 265, reg. 374, c. 47r, 25 Dec 1585.

16. *BAC*, b. 263, reg. 372, c. 149r, 26 Aug 1582; *BAC*, b. 274, reg. 391, c. 183v, 7 Jan 1605 (MV).

17. *BAC*, b. 263, reg. 372, c. 149r, 26 Aug 1582; *BAC*, b. 269, reg. 382, cc. 98v–99r, 13 Apr 1595; cc. 238v–239v, 16 Aug 1596; *BAC*, b. 270, reg. 384, c. 171v, 25 Mar 1598; *BAC*, b. 339, 18 May 1602, Command of Sultan to *kadı* of Constantinople and Galata; *BAC*, b. 265, reg. 374, c. 76v–77r, 20 Mar 1586.

18. *SDC*, b. 55, cc. 268v–269r, 17 Aug 1602, Agostino Nani to Senate; *BAC*, b. 271, reg. 386, cc. 66v–67r, 6 Feb 1602.

19. *BAC*, b. 317, cc. 53r–v, 18 Nov 1614; *BAC*, b. 277, reg. 397, cc. 298r–v, 19 Jun 1614; *BAC*, b. 348, 30 Mar 1640.

20. *BAC*, b. 317, cc. 65v–68v, 28 Jan 1592; *BAC*, b. 270, reg. 385, c. 156r, 2 Aug 1600; *BAC*, b. 265, reg. 374, c. 39v, 4 Nov 1585; *BAC*, b. 266, reg. 376, cc. 26r–27v, 20 Jun 1588; *BAC*, b. 265, reg. 374, cc. 72v–73r, 13 Mar 1586.

21. *BAC*, b. 264, reg. 424, c. 63r, 12 Nov 1584; *SDelC*, f. 10, 18 Apr 1603; d'Alessio, *Le couvent et l'eglise des Saints-Pierre-et-Paul*, 18.

22. *BAC*, b. 270, reg. 385, c. 90r, 2 Sep 1599; *BAC*, b. 270, reg. 384, c. 91r, 15 Aug 1597; Rinieri, *Clemente VIII*, 172, 178–79.

23. *SDC*, b. 49, c. 372v, 7 Aug 1599, Girolamo Cappello to Senate; *SDC*, b. 55, cc. 268v–269r, 17 Aug 1602, Agostino Nani to Senate.

24. *BAC*, b. 271, reg. 386, cc. 66v–67r, 6 Feb 1602; *SDCop*, reg. 9, 26 Jul 1592, Matteo Zane to Senate; *BAC*, b. 317, c. 53v; *BAC*, b. 317, "Protocollo 1598," c. 17v; *SDC*, b. 55, cc. 268v–269r, 17 Aug 1602, Agostino Nani to Senate.

25. Faroqhi, "Before 1600," 86; *BAC*, b. 263, reg. 371, "Fedi di Baylazzi, et cottimi sotto il baylazzo del Cl.mo m Alessandro Contarini Baylo Dig.mo," c. 1v, 7 Feb 1545 (MV).

26. *BAC*, b. 348, 30 Mar 1640. Libania's dowry is described in *BAC*, b. 277, reg. 397, cc. 298r–v, 19 Jun 1614. Mantran incorrectly describes Navon as "incontestably a Jew"; Mantran, *Istanbul dans la seconde moitié du XVIIe siècle*, 529.

27. *SDC*, b. 68, cc. 500r–v, 26 Dec 1609, Simone Contarini to Senate. Edoardo had already had a close relationship as early as 1600 with the French ambassador who tried to protect him. *SDC*, b. 52, c. 382r, 3 Feb 1600 (MV), Agostino Nani to Senate.

28. *InqStat*, b. 148, no. 39, 15 Dec 1622, Inquisitors to Giorgio Giustinian.

29. *BAC*, b. 265, reg. 373, 87v–89r, 13 Mar 1587; *BAC*, b. 266, reg. 376, cc. 26r–27v, 20 Jun 1588.

30. Gara, "In Search of Communities," 153–54.

31. *BAC*, b. 265, reg. 373, cc. 87v–89r, 13 Mar 1587; *BAC*, b. 267, reg. 377, c. 99r, 27 May 1591; *BAC*, b. 270, reg. 385, c. 156r, 2 Aug 1600.

32. *APC*, b. 18, 8, c. 16v, 6 Jan 1621 (MV), Giorgio Giustinian to Senate.

33. *DonàR*, b. 23, cc. 109v–110r; *SDC*, b. 53, cc. 377v–378r, 30 July 1601, Agostino Nani to Senate.

34. *SDC*, b. 17, cc. 1r–2v, 8 Mar 1583, Gianfrancesco Morosini to Council of Ten; "Relazione di Matteo Zane," in Albèri, *Relazioni*, 9:438; Pedani-Fabris, "Safiye's Household," 21–22; Pedani-Fabris, "Veneziani a Costantinopoli," 78–79.

35. *SMar*, reg. 84, cc. 29v–30r, 14 Mar 1626; *SDC*, b. 113, c. 328r, 7 Aug 1632, Girolamo

Cappello to Senate; *SDC*, b. 113, cc. 517r–v, 1 Nov 1632, Girolamo Cappello to Senate; *SDC*, b. 113, cc. 504r–507v, 20 Oct 1632, Girolamo Cappello to Senate.

36. *InqStat*, b. 417, 24 Feb 1633 (MV), Pietro Foscarini to Senate; *SDC*, b. 113, cc. 504r–507v, 20 Oct 1632, Girolamo Cappello to Senate.

37. Lesure, "Michel Černović," 137–38; *CapiXLett*, b. 3, no. 56, 13 May 1566, Vettore Bragadin to Council of Ten; Villain-Gandossi, "Les dépêches chiffrées," 77; *XSeg*, f. 20, 24 May 1578, Council of Ten to Bailo.

38. *BAC*, b. 278, reg. 400, c. 272r, 20 Sep 1616; *BAC*, b. 317, "1614–1615," c. 291, 20 Oct 1614; *BAC*, b. 280, reg. 403, c. 201r, 20 Sep 1620; *BAC*, b. 280, reg. 404, c. 12v, 31 May 1621; *SDC*, b. 93, cc. 179r–183v, 30 Apr 1622, Giorgio Giustinian to Senate.

39. *SDC*, b. 93, cc. 510r–v, 6 Aug 1622, Giorgio Giustinian to Senate; cc. 328r–339r, 11 Jun 1622, Giorgio Giustinian to Senate; *SDCop*, reg. 18, 44–46, Nov 1622, Zuanbattista Locadello to Vicelli. See also Levy, *The Sephardim in the Ottoman Empire*, 30; Baron, *Social and Religious History of the Jews*, 18:145–46.

40. *DocTR*, b. 12, no. 1285, 31 Aug 1622, Ducale to Grand Vizier; *SDC*, b. 96, cc. 89r–v, 17 Sep 1623, Giorgio Giustinian to Senate; *SDC*, b. 96, cc. 206r–v, 11 Nov 1623, Zuanbattista Locadello to Girolamo Locadello in Venice.

41. *SDC*, b. 96, cc. 89r–v, 17 Sep 1623, Giorgio Giustinian to Senate; *SDCop*, reg. 18, cc. 126–30, 15 Apr 1623, Giorgio Giustinian to Senate.

42. *SDC*, b. 96, cc. 149r–150r, 15 Oct 1623, Giorgio Giustinian to Senate; *SDC*, b. 113, cc. 504r–507v, 20 Oct 1632, Giovanni Cappello to Senate; *BAC*, b. 281, reg. 405, c. 2r, 4 Mar 1621.

43. Foster, *Travels of John Sanderson*, 13.

44. Blochet, "Relation du voyage en Orient," 362–63; Foster, *Travels of John Sanderson*, 10, 13; *BAC*, b. 268, reg. 380, c. 55r, 12 Oct 1593.

45. *BAC*, b. 267, reg. 378, cc. 34r–v, 17 Mar 1591; 30 Dec 1586, William Shales and John Sanderson at Cairo to John Bate in Constantinople, cited in Foster, *Travels of John Sanderson*, 137–39.

46. *BAC*, b. 265, reg. 373, cc. 92v–93r, 15 Apr 1587; *BAC*, b. 265, reg. 374, cc. 194v, 27 May 1587; *BAC*, b. 266, reg. 375, cc. 53v–58v, 4 Aug 1588; 30 May 1586, Edward Barton to John Sanderson in Egypt, cited in Foster, *Travels of John Sanderson*, 129 n. 4, 275–6; *SDC*, b. 39, cc. 245r–v, 4 May 1594, Marco Venier to Senate.

47. *SDC*, b. 26, c. 272r, 9 Dec 1587, Giovanni Moro to Senate.

48. *SMar*, reg. 84, 209r, 29 Aug 1626; *It VII* 1193 (8883), cc. 65r–v, 28 Oct 1638, Iseppo Fabris in Cyprus to Alvise Contarini; Sanudo, *Diarii*, 55:37, cited in Cozzi, *Repubblica di Venezia e stati italiani*, 128–29.

49. *It VII* 1086 (8523), c. 364v, 18 Dec 1638, Alvise Contarini to Senate.

50. *SDC*, b. 39, cc. 412r–413v, 20 Jun 1594, Marco Venier to Senate.

51. *BAC*, b. 267, reg. 377, c. 14v, 26 Jul 1590; *BAC*, b. 267, reg. 377, Nov 1590, "Conto della Heredità del q. Zuane de Michel Orese fatto dal Signor Paulo Mariani delegato dal Illustrissimo Signor Bailo."

52. *SDC*, b. 39, cc. 245r–v, 4 May 1594, Marco Venier to Senate; *SDC*, b. 39, cc. 412r–413v, 20 Jun 1594, Marco Venier to Senate.

53. On Spanish intelligence efforts in the eastern Mediterranean, see Hassiotis, "Venezia e i domini veneziani," 117–36.

54. *SDCop*, reg. 11, c. 203, 24 Dec 1596, Marco Venier to Senate; Foster, *Travels of John Sanderson*, 13, 61–62.

55. İnalcık, "Ottoman Galata," 23; Pistarino, "Genoese in Pera," 66.

56. Mitler, "Genoese in Galata," 75, 79; d'Alessio, *Relatione*, 25–26, 71–72; İnalcık, "Ottoman Galata," 23, 28, 30, 31. On the Magnifica Comunità and the history in general of the Latin-rite in Constantinople, see Belin, *Histoire de la Latinité de Constantinople*, 121–362. On the various versions of the actual treaty between Mehmed and the Perots, see d'Alessio, "Traité entre les Génois de Galata et Mehmet II," 161–74.

57. Sturdza, *Dictionnaire historique et généalogique*, 564; Bertelè, *Il palazzo degli Ambasciatori*, 141 n.107; Belin, *Histoire de la Latinité de Constantinople*, 180; Frazee, *Catholics and Sultans*, 72, 95; Tongas, *Relations de la France avec l'Empire Ottoman*, 75.

58. An ecclesiastical visitor in 1622 put the number of Roman Catholics, including merchants, at 590. "Visita apostolica a Costantinopoli," in Hofmann, *Il vicariato apostolico di Costantinopoli*, 48.

59. Pistarino, "The Genoese in Pera-Turkish Galata," 75, 81; Yerasimos, "Galata à travers les récits de voyage," 118–19. After the war of 1537, the Latin-rite community in Pera was rejuvenated to some degree by refugees from the Venetian territories conquered by the Ottomans. D'Alessio, "La communauté de Constantinople," 312.

60. Della Valle, *De' viaggi*, 1:53; Sandys, *Relation of a Journey*, 78; Bertelè, *Il palazzo degli Ambasciatori*, 141 n.107. Letter dated 20 Mar 1664, Constantinople, in Carayon, *Relations Inédites*, 101.

61. Yerasimos, "Galata à travers les récits de voyage," 120; d'Alessio, *Relatione*, 22 n.1; *BAC*, b. 266, reg. 375, cc. 146r–v, 28 Nov 1589; *SMar*, reg. 67, cc. 87v–88r, 6 Nov 1607; *It VII* 1087 (8524), cc. 319v–320v, 28 Sep 1639, Alvise Contarini to Senate; *SDC*, b. 57, cc. 310v–311r, 13 Jun 1603, Francesco Contarini to Senate; *SDC*, b. 93, c. 531r, 20 Aug 1624, Giorgio Giustinian to Senate; Lucchetta, "La scuola"; Lewis, *From Babel to Dragomans*, 21, 148.

62. Frazee, *Catholics and Sultans*, 80; Belin, *Histoire de la Latinité de Constantinople*, 351.

63. Nicolay, *Navigations*, 65v; d'Alessio, *Relatione*, 21; *BAC*, b. 348, 30 Mar 1640; *Inq-Stat*, b. 416, 15 Feb 1607, Ottaviano Bon to Inquisitors, attached letter from Ambrosio Grillo to Abbate Ufterducci in Rome.

64. Sturdza, *Dictionnaire historique et généalogique*, 564.

65. *BAC*, b. 264, reg. 425, cc. 64v–65v, 12 May 1583. See also Dursteler, "Education and Identity."

66. *CollRel*, b. 5, c. 19v, "Relatione di Maffio Venier."

67. For a list of Galata's Latin-rite churches and their income, see *SDelC*, f. 10, 18 Apr 1603, Perots to Francesco Contarini; Mitler, "Genoese in Galata," 87. A detailed description of these churches is contained in d'Alessio, *Relatione*; see also d'Alessio, "Recherches"; Belin, *Histoire de la Latinité de Constantinople*, 187–346.

68. D'Alessio, *Relatione*, 21.

69. *SDC*, b. 73, cc. 294r–296r, 13 Jul 1612, Cristoforo Valier to Senate.

70. *InqStat,* b. 433, 20 Sep 1590; also ACDF, *Scritture riferite,* b. 279, c. 346r, cited in Matteucci, *Un glorioso convento,* 45.

71. Trannoy, "La «nation latine» de Constantinople," 250–52.

72. Frazee, *Catholics and Sultans,* 94–98.

73. *SDelC,* f. 10, 18 Apr 1603, Perots to Bailo. See also, *It VII* 1087 (8524), cc. 39v–43r, 26 Mar 1639, Alvise Contarini to Ambassador Nani in Rome; *SDC,* b. 31, cc. 140r–v, 28 Apr 1590, Giovanni Moro to Senate; *SDC,* b. 32, cc. 171r–v, 18 Oct 1590, Girolamo Lippomano to Senate.

74. *It VII* 1087 (8524), cc. 315v–322v, 28 Sep 1639, Alvise Contarini to Senate. See also Sonyel, "The Protégé System," 56–58.

75. *CapiXLett,* b. 6, no. 117, 25 Oct 1590, Bailo to Council of Ten; also, *APC,* b. 2, c. 20r, 18 Jul 1525, Piero Bragadin to Senate.

76. *CollRel,* b. 4, cc. 83v–84v, "Relazione di Lorenzo Bernardo"; *CollRel,* b. 5, cc. 46v–47v, "Relazione di Antonio Tiepolo"; *XSeg,* f. 25, 3 Jun 1592, Council of Ten to Bailo. See also Lucchetta, "La scuola," 19–40.

77. Seni, "Les levantins d'Istanbul," 161–63.

78. Trannoy, "La «nation latine» de Constantinople," 252.

79. Frazee, *Catholics and Sultans,* 73; Gabriel de Mun, "L'Établissement des Jesuites," 165; Belin, *Histoire de la Latinité de Constantinople,* 237–49. For a Venetian report on the establishment of a Jesuit mission in Constantinople, see *SDC,* b. 68, c. 273r, 1 Nov 1609, Simone Contarini to Senate.

80. *SDC,* b. 96, c. 74r, 18 Sep 1623, Giorgio Giustinian to Senate; *RubriCST,* reg. D14, cc. 55r–v, 28 May 1623, Giorgio Giustinian to Senate. See also, *SDC,* b. 79, cc. 131r–132r, 18 Apr 1615, Almoro Nani and Cristoforo Valier to Senate; d'Alessio, *Relatione,* 49–50.

81. *SDC,* b. 66, cc. 39r–43r, 22 Mar 1608, Ottaviano Bon to Senate; *BAC,* b. 339, no. 18, 10 Feb 1615, Command of sultan to *kadı* of Constantinople; *SDC,* b. 17, cc. 214r–217r, 17 May 1583, Gianfrancesco Morosini to Senate; Goffman, "The Ottoman Role in Patterns of Commerce," 140.

82. D'Alessio, *Relatione,* 22–24; Sturdza, *Dictionnaire historique et généalogique,* 564.

83. *BAC,* b. 267, reg. 378, cc. 27r–28v, 29 Nov 1590; *SDC,* b. 57, c. 429v, 2 Aug 1603, Francesco Contarini to Senate; *BAC,* b. 285, reg. 414, cc. 32r–33r, 25 Jun 1636; *BAC,* b. 285, reg. 413, cc. 52v–53r, 29 Jul 1637; *BAC,* b. 278, reg. 398, c. 8r, 17 May 1612; *BAC,* b. 275, reg. 392, cc. 113r–v, 23 May 1607; *BAC,* b. 272, reg. 387, c. 137r, 28 Jun 1601; *BAC,* b. 273, reg. 390, cc. 215r–v, 20 Aug 1604. The Piron's ship is almost certainly the *Pirona,* which Tenenti records present in Venice in 1607 and belonging to an Antonio Pironida; Tenenti, *Naufrages, corsairs et assurances maritimes à Venise,* 498. The ship was eventually lost in a storm off Gallipoli, and the Casa Piron lost it and twenty thousand ducats. *It VII* 1087 (8524), cc. 315v–318r, 28 Sep 1639, Alvise Contarini to Senate.

84. *BAC,* b. 268, reg. 381, cc. 28r–v, 30 May 1592; *SDelC,* f. 10, 18 Apr 1603, Perots to Bailo; Archivio della Sacra Congregazione di Propaganda fide, *Scritture Riferite nelle congregazioni generali* 162, cc. 210r–v, cited in Matteucci, *Un glorioso convento,* 153; *BAC,* b. 285, reg. 413, cc. 52v–53r, 29 Jul 1637; *BAC,* b. 317, cc. 35v–36v, 25 Nov 1598.

85. *BAC,* b. 272, reg. 387, c. 14r, 6 Oct 1600; *BAC,* b. 278, reg. 400, c. 272r, 20 Sep 1616; *BAC,* b. 275, reg. 393, c. 59v, 10 Jan 1606 (MV); *BAC,* b. 284, reg. 411, c. 242r, 24 Nov 1635.

86. *BAC*, b. 278, reg. 400, c. 164r, 26 Feb 1615 (MV); *SDC*, b. 77, c. 249r, 9 Jun 1614, Cristoforo Valier to Senate; *BAC*, b. 280, reg. 403, c. 111v, 4 Dec 1619; *BAC*, b. 279, reg. 402, c. 8r, 2 Dec 1616; *APC*, b. 8, cc. 245r–290v, 1595 (MV).

87. *It VII* 1087 (8524), cc. 315v–318r, 28 Sep 1639, Alvise Contarini to Senate.

88. *BAC*, b. 317, cc. 35v–36v, 25 Nov 1598; *BAC*, b. 284, reg. 411, c. 293r, 2 Jul 1636.

89. *BAC*, b. 276, reg. 394, cc. 237r–v, 3 Jul 1610.

90. *DonàR*, b. 217, cc. 46r–v, 7 Mar 1605; *It VII* 1087 (8524), cc. 315v–318r, 28 Sep 1639, Alvise Contarini to Senate; *BAC*, b. 274, reg. 391, cc. 292v–293v, 3 Aug 1606.

91. *SDC*, b. 43, cc. 158v–159v, 27 Apr 1596, Marco Venier to Senate; *BAC*, b. 329, 4 Aug 1597.

92. *BAC*, b. 269, reg. 382, cc. 241v–242r, 21 Aug 1596; *BAC*, b. 267, reg. 379, cc. 61r–v, 3 Oct 1591; *SDC*, b. 37, c. 115r, 23 Apr 1593, Matteo Zane to Senate.

93. An interesting postscript is the request in 1615 of Stefano Piron for "the defense and protection [that Venice offers] to those that confess their devotion to the Most Serene Republic." In support of this request, he pointed to his dealings in Venice, his regular payment of the *cottimi*, and the fact that he had "never utilized Turkish justice with another subject [of Venice]." Stefano's motivation for this request is illuminating: he wanted "to free myself from diverse Turkish *avanie*, and from many travails." "Have a commandment created," Piron continues, "in which it is expressed and declared that I may be defended by Your Illustriousness and by every other most excellent Bailo from Turkish molestations and *avanie* in a just way, as are defended others in this land, servants of the household of the Most Excellent Baili, so that while enjoying this benefit and grace I may, with security that I will not be troubled in extraordinary matters by the Turks, continue and amplify my trade to the benefit of the customs of your Serenity and to the utility of this *cottimo*." *BAC*, b. 317, cc. 81v–82v, 9 Mar 1615.

CHAPTER 6. AN URBAN MIDDLE GROUND

1. Huntington, "Clash of Civilizations," 22–49.

2. See, for example, Levy, *Jews, Turks, Ottomans;* Cassia, "Religion, Politics, and Ethnicity in Cyprus," 3–28.

3. Brummett, "Understanding Space"; see also Kafadar, "The Ottomans and Europe," 1:619–20.

4. Fredrik Barth, *Ethnic Groups,* cited in Armstrong, *Nations before Nationalism,* 4–5. Duara, "Historicizing National Identity," summarizes ideas more fully developed in his *Rescuing History from the Nation.*

5. Benedict, "Un roi, une loi, deux fois," 84; Faroqhi, *Approaching Ottoman History,* 14. For a fascinating and suggestive study on the nature of coexistence and conflict in a modern society, see Varshney, *Ethnic Conflict and Civic Life.*

6. Mantran, *Istanbul dans la seconde moitié du XVIIe siècle,* 23.

7. Sherley, "Discours of the Turkes," 15.

8. Foster, *Travels of John Sanderson,* 82–83; *DonàR,* b. 23, cc. 110v, 166r; Rosaccio, *Viaggio,* 76v; "Relazione di Simone Contarini," in Barozzi and Berchet, *Relazioni,* 1:154.

9. Stoianovich, "Cities," 44–59; Mantran, *Istanbul au siècle de Soliman,* 63; Mantran,

Istanbul dans la seconde moitié du XVIIe siècle, 44–45. Barkan, "Essai sur les données statistiques," 9–36; "Istanbul," *EI,* 4: 224–48; İnalcık, "Servile Labor," 47 n.9.

10. Barkan, "Essai sur les données statistiques," 9–36; Mantran, *Istanbul dans la seconde moitié du XVIIe siècle,* 44–45.

11. Gerber, "Social and Economic Position of Women," 239; Lapidus, "Muslim Cities and Islamic Societies," 49–60; Von Grunebaum, *Islam,* 145–46.

12. J. S. Furnivall, *Colonial Policy and Practice* (New York, 1956), 304–5, cited in Braude and Lewis, "Introduction," 1:1.

13. Mantran, *Istanbul au siècle de Soliman,* 65.

14. Mantran, *Istanbul dans la seconde moitié du XVIIe siècle,* 74. Thévenot, *Voyage du Levant,* 65; Sandys, *Relation of a Journey,* 38.

15. Kafadar, "The Ottomans and Europe," 1:598; Coco and Manzonetto, *Baili veneziani,* 24.

16. Sandys, *Relation of a Journey,* 77; Matković, "Itinerario," 114; Mantran, "Minoritaires, métiers et marchands étrangers," 128–29; Nicolay, *Navigations,* 65r.

17. İnalcık, "Ottoman Galata," 30; Eldem, Goffman, and Masters, *The Ottoman City between East and West,* 149–50.

18. Mantran, *Istanbul dans la seconde moitié du XVIIe siècle,* 78–79; Mantran, *Istanbul au siècle de Soliman,* 26–7, 73–6, 167–68. Mantran is not alone in arguing for this paradigm of living in but not among: several historians have posited the same situation for Venice, including Preto, *Venezia e i turchi.*

19. İnalcık, "Ottoman Galata," 21, 27–31; d'Alessio, "La communauté de Constantinople," 310–11; d'Alessio, "Traité entre les Génois de Galata et Mehmed II," 161–75; Pistarino, "The Genoese in Pera," 64, 66.

20. Rozen, "Public Space," 337–38; Goffman, *Britons in the Ottoman Empire,* 35.

21. Matkovic, "Itinerario di Marc' Antonio Pigafetta," 113; de Groot, "The Dutch Nation in Istanbul," 131–33; *BAC,* b. 275, reg. 392, cc. 82v–83r, 15 Oct 1606.

22. Mantran, *Istanbul au siècle de Soliman,* 71–2; Evliya, *Narrative,* 1–2:53; *SDC,* b. 74, cc. 148r–v, 22 Dec 1612, Cristoforo Valier to Senate; d'Alessio, *Relatione,* 39–41.

23. İnalcık, "Ottoman Galata," 108; Lewis, *Istanbul,* 101; Mantran, "Règlements fiscaux ottomans," 238 n.68.

24. Mantran, *Istanbul dans la seconde moitié du XVIIe siècle,* 76; Pistarino, " Genoese in Pera," 82; Yerasimos, "Galata à travers les récits de voyage," 119–20, 128; İnalcık, "The Ottoman State," 1:274; Eldem, Goffman, and Masters, *The Ottoman City between East and West,* 151–52.

25. "Relazione di Giovanni Moro," in Albèri, *Relazioni,* 9:334; della Valle, *De' viaggi,* 1:53; d'Alessio, *Relatione,* 8.

26. Evliya, *Narrative,* 2:51; Stoianovich, "Cities," 68; Mantran, "Minoritaires, métiers et marchands," 128–29; Mantran, *Istanbul dans la seconde moitié du XVIIe siècle,* 75.

27. *SDC,* b. 81, c. 411r, 8 Sep 1616, Almoro Nani to Senate; d'Alessio, "La communauté de Constantinople," 311; d'Alessio, *Relatione,* 22–24, 32–34.

28. Heyd, "Jewish Communities," 309–12; Rozen, "Public Space," 336–37. See also Yerasimos, "La communauté juive."

29. Yerasimos, "Galata à travers les récits de voyage," 118–28; Yerasimos, "La communauté juive"; Rozen, "Public Space," 334.

30. *BAC*, b. 264, reg. 424, cc. 111r–v, 3 Jul 1584; *BAC*, b. 317, cc. 53r–v, 18 Nov 1614; *BAC*, b. 317, cc. 35v–36v, 25 Nov 1598.

31. *BAC*, b. 317, cc. 38v–42r, Oct–Nov 1591; *BAC*, b. 331-I, 24 Mar 1632.

32. Matteucci, *Un glorioso convento*, 403.

33. Rozen, "Public Space," 339–40; Thévenot, *Voyage du Levant*, 41–52; d'Arvieux, *Memoires*, 4:492, cited in Mantran, "Minoritaires, métiers et marchands étrangers," 129.

34. Matković, "Itinerario," 114; Yerasimos, "Galata à travers les récits de voyage," 126; de Groot, "The Dutch Nation in Istanbul," 134.

35. Biron, *Ambassade en Turquie*, 1:91. Mantran, *Istanbul dans la seconde moitié du XVIIe siècle*, 79; Lewis, *Istanbul*, 128–29.

36. The Venetian embassy was probably located at one time in the Jewish quarter of Galata, from at least 1533, and did not move to the Vigne di Pera until after 1577. Yerasimos, "Galata à travers les récits de voyage," 123–24.

37. *BAC*, b. 271, reg. 386, cc. 28v–29v, 9 Mar 1601; *SDC*, b. 50, cc. 32r–33v, 5 Sep 1599, Vicenzo Gradenigo in Thessaloníki to Senate.

38. *SDC*, b. 43, c. 114r, 24 Apr 1596, Marco Venier to Senate.

39. *SDC*, b. 42, cc. 71r–75v, 81r, 27 Sep 1595, Marco Venier to Senate. See also Bertelè, *Il palazzo degli Ambasciatori*, 130–31. The baili were not the only ones to experience difficulties with neighbors: Edward Barton moved the English embassy in 1594 "after a complaint deposed against him by the inhabitants of his quarter for *tapage nocturne*." Yerasimos, "Galata à travers les récits de voyage," 125.

40. Faroqhi, "The Venetian Presence in the Ottoman Empire," 346; see also Baron, *A Social and Religious History of the Jews*, 18:233–46.

41. Moryson, *Itinerary*, 4:122, 125; Lithgow, *Adventures*, 148, cited in Baron, *A Social and Religious History of the Jews*, 18:243; Correr, PD 740 c. 2, cited in Calabi, "Gli stranieri e la città," 5:933.

42. Heyd, *Histoire du commerce du Levant*, 2:349.

43. Gibb and Bowen, *Islamic Society and the West*, 1:308.

44. See, for example, Mantran, *Istanbul dans la seconde moitié du XVIIe siècle*, 448–52; Mantran, *Istanbul au siècle de Soliman*; Mantran, *Histoire d'Istanbul*; Mantran, "Minoritaires, métiers et marchands étrangers," 130–32.

45. Braude and Lewis, "Introduction," 1:9; Lewis, *Islam and the West*, 32. See Douglas, *Purity and Danger*. See also Stoianovich, "Cities," 79–80.

46. Lewis, *Islam and the West*, 49.

47. Braude, "Venture and Faith," 537; *SDC*, b. 18, c. 172r, 12 Nov 1583, Gianfrancesco Morosini to Senate; *SDelC*, f. 5, 11 Aug 1582, Senate to Bailo and Ambassador.

48. Heyd, *Histoire du Commerce du Levant*, 2:349; Mantran, *Istanbul au siècle de Soliman*, 31; Mantran, "Minoritaires, métiers et marchands étrangers," 128. Even the doyen of Ottoman historians, Halil İnalcık, supported this view in his earlier work, though more recently he has altered his position. See "Capital Formation in the Ottoman Empire," 112–13, 135–36.

49. Braude, "Venture and Faith," 540.

50. Kafadar, "When Coins Turned into Drops of Dew," 17; Kafadar, "A Death in Venice," 191; Faroqhi, "In Search of Ottoman History," 225–26.

51. Kafadar, "A Death in Venice," 210–12.

52. Masters, "Trading Diasporas," 346–47; Imhaus, *Le minoranze orientali a Venezia;* Fleet, *European and Islamic Trade,* 22; Brummett, *Ottoman Seapower,* Maria Pia Pedani-Fabris has similarly challenged the view that Muslims diplomats rarely traveled to Christian lands but rather used minority intermediaries, especially Jews. She has documented that most Ottoman representatives who appeared in Venice in the sixteenth century were Muslim. Pedani-Fabris, *In nome del Gran Signore,* viii, 23.

53. Matthee, "Merchants in Safavid Iran," 249–53.

54. Rodinson, *Europe and the Mystique of Islam,* 19–24, 40; Faroqhi, *Subjects of the Sultans,* 15–16.

55. See for example *BAC,* b. 347, "Scritture di Turchi da 7 May 1627 a 10 Oct 1629," which contains a list of a dozen Ottoman-Muslims and describes the nature of their transactions in Venice. Venice's notarial records are also important for the study of Veneto-Ottoman commerce. See for a sample *Notarile-Atti,* reg. 11913, c. 269, 24 Dec 1592; reg. 11914, c. 141, 16 Mar 1593; reg. 11915, c. 38, 28 Jan 1593 (MV); reg. 11915, c. 62, 14 Feb 1593 (MV); reg. 11915, c. 71–3, 14 Feb 1593 (MV); reg. 11915, c. 193, 2 May 1594; reg. 11915, c. 214, 16 May 1594; reg. 11917, c. 469, 9 Nov 1596; reg. 11921, c. 397, 20 Sep 1600; reg. 11927, c. 419, 16 June 1606; reg. 11928, c. 175, 17 Mar 1607; reg. 11928, c. 864, 28 Nov 1607; reg. 11929, c. 566, 27 Sep 1608; reg. 11932, c. 7, 1 Feb 1610 (MV); reg. 11933, cc. 547–8, 25 Aug 1611. I am grateful to Vittorio Mandelli for these citations.

56. Vercellin, "Mercanti turchi e sensali a Venezia," 45.

57. One Muslim merchant active in Venice in the late sixteenth century was referred to as Amza, Stamza, Camza, and Hamza Çavuş. See, for example, *BAC,* b. 269, reg. 382, cc. 44r–v, 11 Aug 1594; cc. 98v–99r, 13 Apr 1595; c. 112v, 14 Jun 1595; "Libro di citationi," 2 May 1596.

58. *BAC,* b. 264, reg. 425, cc. 94r–v, 23 Jul 1583.

59. Kafadar, "A Death in Venice," 201; Lane, *Venice,* 292–94.

60. On Lorenzo Girardi q. Antonio, from Val Brembana near Bergamo, see Pedani-Fabris, *In nome del Gran Signore,* 173; *XSavi,* b. 164, f. 974, 31 Aug 1582; *SMar,* reg. 42, c. 86v, 24 Nov 1574; *VSM-I,* reg. 135, cc. 136r–v, 6 Sep 1566; *LSTR,* b. 3, cc. 93r–94r, 28 Feb 1575, Sultan to Doge; *LSTR,* b. 3, cc. 105r–v, n.d., Lorenzo Girardi to V Savii. His testament is in *NotTest,* b. 1192, f. 417, 26 May 1596.

61. *BAC,* b. 264, reg. 425, cc. 132r–133v, 7 Feb 1583 (MV). The *hüccet* is registered in *BAC,* b. 264, reg. 425, cc. 167v–168r, 30 May 1584. For Mehmed's letter to Girardi, see *BAC,* b. 264, reg. 424, cc. 31r–32r, 14 Aug 1584.

62. *VSM-I,* reg. 138, cc. 17r–19r, 28 Sep 1587.

63. *VSM-I,* reg. 138, cc. 17r–19r, 28 Sep 1587; 98r–v ff. On Membrè, see Vercellin, "Mercanti turchi e sensali a Venezia," 73; Fabris, "Artisinat et culture," 59.

64. *BAC,* b. 279, reg. 401, cc. 29v–30v, 30 Sep 1615.

65. *SDCop,* reg. 16, cc. 31–33, 13 Jun 1620, Almoro Nani to Senate; *BAC,* b. 275, reg. 393, c. 24v, 28 Sep 1606; *SDCop,* reg 15, cc. 232–33, 4 Feb 1619 (MV), Almoro Nani to Senate.

66. *SDCop*, reg. 16, cc. 4–9, 14 Jun 1620, Almoro Nani to Senate; *SDCop*, reg. 16, c. 150, 9 Apr 1619, Almoro Nani to Senate; *SDC*, b. 53, c. 398r, 10 Aug 1601, Agostino Nani to Senate; *SDC*, b. 98, cc. 362r–v, 22 Dec 1624, Giorgio Giustinian to Senate.

67. *SDCop*, reg. 16, cc. 31–33, 13 Jun 1620, Almoro Nani to Senate; *APC*, b. 17, cc. 6r–v, 22 Aug 1620, Almoro Nani and Giorgio Giustinian to Senate.

68. Mantran, "Minoritaires, métiers et marchands étrangers," 134–35; Faroqhi, "In Search of Ottoman History," 225–26; Faroqhi, "Before 1600," 98–99; Kunt, "Derviş Mehmed Paşa," 209–11.

69. Kunt, "Derviş Mehmed Paşa," 202–5, 213; de Groot, *The Ottoman Empire and the Dutch Republic*, 196–97. See also Hanna, *Making Big Money in 1600*, 107–8.

70. Kafadar, "A Death in Venice," 193–4; Kafadar, "On the Purity and Corruption of the Janissaries," 273, 275–76.

71. İnalcık,"The Ottoman State," 1:182–84; see also İslamoğlu and Keyder, "Agenda for Ottoman History," 44; Faroqhi, *Subjects of the Sultans*, 49. On Ottoman attempts to control the grain trade, see Murphey, "Provisioning Istanbul," 217–28.

72. İslamoğlu and Keyder, "Agenda for Ottoman History," 41; della Valle, *De' viaggi*, 1:119. See also the letter in which Andrea Mocenigo arranges for several ships to take grain to Venice, "through a very important person at this court, and other Turks who are my friends." Clearly this deal was not sanctioned legally: "Important men themselves make the offers, and the secret proposals, to private merchants, their confidants. This is something that they would not do with the bailo nor with the ministers of that Illustrious State"; *CapiXLett*, b. 3, no. 33, 13 Jul 1564, Andrea Mocenigo to Council of Ten.

73. *APC*, b. 8, cc. 245r–290v, 1595 (MV); *SDC*, b. 58, c. 338v, 20 Dec 1603 Francesco Contarini to Senate; *SMar*, reg. 92, cc. 159v–160r, 16 Sep 1634; also *It VII* 1085 (8522), cc. 119r–123r, 3 Apr 1637, Alvise Contarini to Senate.

74. *BAC*, b. 317, 26 Mar 1614; *BAC*, b. 269, reg. 382, cc. 212v–213v, 15 Mar 1596; Pedani-Fabris, *In nome del Gran Signore*, 40, 85, 172–76; Veinstein, "Marchands Otto-mans," 714–19.

75. *BAC*, b. 269, reg. 382, cc. 44r–v, 11 Aug 1594; *BAC*, b. 269, reg. 383, cc. 4r–v, 6 Jul 1594; *BAC*, b. 269, reg. 382, cc. 21r–v, 14 Jan 1594 (MV); *BAC*, b. 270, reg. 384, cc. 95v–96r, 3 Sep 1597; *InqStat*, b. 433, 30 Nov 1594, Domenico Balsarini to Tulio Fabri; 2 Apr 1595, Domenico Balsarini to Tulio Fabri; Mauroeide, *Ho Hellenismos sto Galata*, 245.

76. *BAC*, b. 269, reg. 382, "Libro di citationi," 2 May 1596; *BAC*, b. 270, reg. 384, c. 91r, 15 Aug 1597.

77. *BAC*, b. 270, reg. 385, c. 137v, 13 Jun 1600; *BAC*, b. 270, reg. 383, c. 109v, 31 Jan 1599 (MV).

78. *CollRel*, b. 4, c. 27v, "Relazione di Lorenzo Bernardo." Peachy, *Selaniki's History*, 205. Hammer refers to a Dschaafer Pascha who was "Franc de naissance," and had been *beyler-beyi* in Cyprus three times; Hammer, *Histoire*, 2:324. This Ca'fer should not be confused with the eunuch Ca'fer Paşa, who died in 1590. *SDC*, b. 31, c. 69v, Giovanni Moro to Senate.

79. *SDC*, b. 58, c. 167r, 22 Nov 1603, Francesco Contarini to Senate. These positions were potentially very lucrative: Mustafa Ali reported that deposed *beylerbeyi* were bidding forty thousand gold pieces for governorships which returned only thirty thousand. They did so because they could collect 110 *yük* of *akçe* (a *yük* was equivalent to 100,000 coins, literally

a horse load) for the imperial treasury and 240 *yük* for themselves. Tietze, *Counsel for Sultans*, 65.

80. Naima, *Annals*, 1:321, 351; Peachy, *Selaniki's History*, 205, 366; on Cairo, see *APC*, b. 17, c. 17r, 22 Aug 1620, Almoro Nani and Giorgio Giustinian to Senate.

81. *BAC*, b. 269, reg. 382, cc. 164r–165v, 19 Dec 1595; *BAC*, b. 276, reg. 395, cc. 22v–23r, 13 Nov 1609; *BAC*, b. 271, reg. 386, cc. 17r–18r, 15 Jan 1600 (MV); *BAC*, b. 273, reg. 389, cc. 49r–50v, 18 Jun 1604.

82. *BAC*, b. 273, reg. 389, cc. 49r–50v, 18 Jun 1604. Cotton had been imported in significant quantities from Cyprus since the fourteenth century. Lane contends that until at least 1600 Venice had no competition in supplying cotton to Europe. Lane, *Venice*, 298; Luzzatto, *Storia economica di Venezia*, 47; see also the 1358 document cited in Lopez and Raymond, *Medieval Trade*, 129. While certainly Venice was a key figure in this trade, the involvement of Ca'fer suggests that Ottoman merchants were also actively involved. For other examples of Ottoman cotton trade, see *BAC*, b. 266, reg. 376, c. 49r, 3 Jul 1589; *BAC*, b. 278, reg. 398, cc. 23v–24r, 22 Oct 1612; also Erdoğru, "The Servants and Venetian Interest"; Faroqhi, "Notes on the Production of Cotton," 415. Hakluyt mentions that as early as 1511 and 1534 English merchants were bringing cotton from the Levant, and by 1587 large quantities were being imported directly to London for the fustian industry. Wood, *History of the Levant Company*, 74 n.2; Willan, "Some Aspects of English Trade," 407–9.

83. Faroqhi, "Textile Production in Rumeli," 65; Faroqhi, "Crisis and Change," 2:458.

84. *BAC*, b. 276, reg. 395, cc. 22v–23r, 13 Nov 1609; *BAC*, b. 275, reg. 392, c. 123v, 17 Aug 1607; *DocTR*, b. 9, no. 1099 (ca 1599), Ex-*beylerbeyi* of Cyprus Ca'fer to Doge; *DocTR*, b. 8, no. 941, [ca. 24 Dec 1584], Ca'fer Paşa to Doge.

85. *BAC*, b. 270, reg. 385, cc. 142r–v, 26 Jun 1600; *BAC*, b. 271, reg. 386, cc. 14r–15r, 15 Jan 1600 (MV); *BAC*, b. 269, reg. 382, c. 53v, 30 Dec 1595; *SDC*, b. 62, c. 209v, 30 Dec 1605, Ottaviano Bon to Senate.

86. Mauroeide, *Ho Hellenismos sto Galata*, 233.

87. *BAC*, b. 275, reg. 392, c. 123v, 17 Aug 1607; *BAC*, b. 276, reg. 395, cc. 22v–23r, 13 Nov 1609; *APC*, b. 17, c. 17r, 22 Aug 1620, Almoro Nani and Giorgio Giustinian to Senate. See also *SDCop*, reg. 16, c. 85, 14 Aug 1620, Almoro Nani and Giorgio Giustinian to Senate.

88. Another example may be found in *BAC*, b. 273, reg. 390, cc. 197r–v, 21 Jun 1604, a partnership between Hasan Çavuş and Mehemed, *kapıcıbaşı* of Mustafa Paşa, the ex-*beylerbeyi* of Cyprus, now *paşa* in Bosnia who traded in Venice through Mustafa's factors Emanuel and Francesco Negroponte.

89. İnalcık, *The Ottoman Empire*, 162.

90. *CapiXLett*, b. 3, no. 63, 20 Jul 1566, Jacopo Soranzo to Council of Ten; *VSM-I*, reg. 141, cc. 35r–v, 14 Mar 1603; *SDC*, b. 33, cc. 157r–158r, 4 May 1591, Girolamo Lippomano to Senate; Matar, *Turks, Moors, and Englishmen in the Age of Discovery*, 33; Matthee, "Merchants in Safavid Iran," 259, 264; Faroqhi, "Crisis and Change," 2:502–5.

91. *BAC*, b. 317, cc. 16v–17r, 11 Jul 1598; *SDelC*, f. 13, 7 Apr 1615, Senate to Almoro Nani.

92. *SDC*, b. 75, c. 217r, 20 May 1613, Cristoforo Valier to Senate; *SDelC*, f. 12, 7 Sep 1613, statement by V Savii; *SDelC*, f. 12, 19 Nov 1613, Senate to Bailo. On Derviş's mission, see Pedani-Fabris, *In nome del Gran Signore*, 174.

93. *SDC*, b. 32, c. 113r, 29 Sep 1590, Girolamo Lippomano to Senate.

94. A ship patron complained that goods were put on his ship by force, which belonged to the *paşa*, *çavuş*, and *emin*. *BAC*, b. 270, reg. 384, c. 62v, 12 Jun 1597.

95. *VSM-I*, reg. 143, cc. 166r–v, 17 Sep 1613; *VSM-I*, reg. 141, cc. 29r–v, 18 Dec 1602. On the development of the port of Spalato, see Paci, *La scala di Spalato*.

96. *SDelC*, f. 13, 14 Apr 1615, Senate to Bailo; *VSM-I*, reg. 145, cc. 119r–v, 28 Sep 1621. Other incidents are in *SMar*, reg. 83, cc. 71r v, 10 Jun 1623; *SDelC*, f. 9, 2 Mai 1595, *VSM-I*, reg. 144, cc. 171r–173r, 21 May 1618.

97. *VSM-I*, reg. 136, c. 34r, 20 Mar 1574; *SDC*, b. 66, cc. 197r–198r, 12 Jul 1608, Ottaviano Bon to Senate; *SDC*, b. 40, cc. 269r–v, 14 Oct 1594, Ca'fer Paşa to Marco Venier; *SDC*, b. 63, c. 393r, Ca'fer Paşa to Ottaviano Bon.

98. *SDC*, b. 53, c. 322r, 1 July 1601, Agostino Nani to Senate; *SDC*, b. 58, c. 40r, 27 Sep 1603, Francesco Contarini to Senate; *SDC*, b. 58, c. 167r, 22 Nov 1603, Francesco Contarini to Senate.

99. *BAC*, b. 276, reg. 394, cc. 113r–114r, 7 Aug 1609; Kafadar, "A Death in Venice," 195–97. See "Notta delle caravane venute da Venezia et del scosso fatto per tal conto," in *SDC*, b. 78, cc. 210r–212v, 21 Jan 1614 (MV), Cristoforo Valier to Senate.

100. İnalcık, "The Ottoman State," 1:345–47; MS 553, Ltr XX, Rafaello de' Medici to Filippo da Empoli and Antonio Bartoli in Pera, 24 Apr 1521, cited in Richards, *Florentine Merchants*, 226. Kate Fleet's research on Ottoman-Genoese trade suggests the presence of Muslim merchants trading "outside their own territories" in the fifteenth century as well. Fleet, *European and Islamic Trade*, 140.

101. Foster, *Travels of John Sanderson*, xxxiii–xxxiv n.1; Matar, *Turks, Moors, and Englishmen*, 5–6.

102. Veinstein, "Marchands Ottomans," 713–38.

103. Blount, *Voyage into the Levant*, 5.

104. Imhaus, *Le minoranze orientali a Venezia*, 559–60.

105. Kafadar, "A Death in Venice," 192; Arbel, "Jews in International Trade," 75–77. For a legislative example of the special treatment accorded Ottoman-Muslim merchants, see Stefani, *L'assicurazione a Venezia*, 1:305–7.

106. Brown, *Venetian Narrative Painting*, 196–215. On the impact of Ottoman and Muslim models on the Venetian cityscape and architecture, see Howard, *Venice and the East*.

107. Pedani-Fabris, *In nome del Gran Signore*, 203–9; Kafadar, "A Death in Venice," 199–201; also G. A. Quarti, *La guerra contro il Turco a Cipro e a Lepanto* (Venice, 1935), 345, cited in Lesure, "Notes et documents," 148.

108. "Relazione di Matteo Zane," in Albèri, *Relazioni*, 9:443; Bertelè, *Il palazzo degli Ambasciatori*, 135 n.74. Figures supporting Zane's estimates of the *cottimi* are in *Bilanci generali*, 365–68.

109. Kafadar, "A Death in Venice," 203; Vercellin, "Mercanti turchi e sensali," 61–63; *VSM-I*, reg. 137, c. 68r–v, 31 Jul 1582.

110. On the *Fondaco dei turchi*, see Preto, *Venezia e i turchi*, 130–33; Turan, "Venedik'te Türk Ticaret Merkezi"; Simonsfeld, *Der Fondaco dei Tedeschi*; Calabi, "Gli stranieri e la città," 934; Kafadar, "A Death in Venice," 200–203; Tucci, "Tra Venezia e mondo turco," 52, 55.

111. Kafadar, "A Death in Venice," 203; *VSM-I*, reg. 145, c. 58r, 26 Mar 1620. For other instances of Muslim convert brokers, see Pedani-Fabris, "Presenze islamiche," 16.

112. *XSeg*, f. 28, 23 Jan 1605 in Council of Ten; *SDelC*, f. 10, 26 Apr 1603, Senate to Bailo.

113. Two Venetian merchants were caught preparing to load merchandise on an Ottoman vessel "to the prejudice of Venetian ships," but when the ship was discovered to belong to Hamza Çavuş, the bailo stated they and all Venetian merchants could load the ship. *BAC*, b. 269, reg. 383, c. 38r, 6 Jul 1594; cc. 44r–v, 11 Aug 1594.

114. İnalcık,"The Ottoman State," 1:182–34; Aymard, *Venise, Raguse*, 165–68; Mauroeide, *Ho Hellenismos sto Galata*, 240–43; Belfanti, "Una città e la carestia."

115. *BAC*, b. 317, cc. 27r–v, 5 Oct 1591; cc. 50v–51r, 2 Dec 1591; cc. 53r–v, 10 Dec 1591; cc. 58v–59r, 10 Jan 1592; cc. 62v–63r, 23 Jan 1592; cc. 70v–71r, 30 Jan 1592. On Venetian grain trade and consumption, see Braudel, *The Mediterranean*, 1:594–604; McGowan, *Economic Life in Ottoman Europe*, 35; Benzoni, "Tra centro e periferia," 100; Lane, *Venice*, 306.

116. *BAC*, b. 285, reg. 413, cc. 1r–v, Jan 1636, translation of Ottoman document; *BAC*, b. 265, reg. 374, c. 24v, 1 Aug 1585; *BAC*, b. 265, reg. 373, cc. 13v–14r, 27 Sep 1585; *BAC*, b. 273, reg. 389, cc. 11v–12r, 29 Apr 1603.

117. *SDC*, b. 54, c. 5v, 8 Sep 1601, Agostino Nani to Senate; *SMar*, reg. 13, c. 91b ff., cited in Ashtor, *Levant Trade*, 398.

118. *BAC*, b. 267, reg. 379, cc. 61r–v, 3 Oct 1591; *InqStat*, b. 416, 12 Mar 1620, Excerpt from Letter of Bailo to Council of Ten; *BAC*, b. 331-I, 1 Sep 1636. See also *BAC*, b. 344, 21 Apr 1625. Suraiya Faroqhi describes a similar scene involving the adventurer Ludovico di Varthema in Mecca in 1503 in "Red Sea Trade," 92.

119. Braude, "Venture and Faith," 532. Goodblatt, *Jewish Life in Turkey*, 123–24.

120. Gerber, "Jewish Tax-Farmers," 144; Eliezer Bashan, "Jewish Moneylending," 62–63. Christian monasteries in Jerusalem in the seventeenth century preferred loans from Jews at 16 percent interest to Muslim ones at 20 or 30 percent; Bashan, "Jewish Moneylending," 72–73; *BAC*, b. 263, reg. 372, c. 1r, 21 Jun 1580; *BAC*, b. 268, reg. 380, cc. 10r–v, 27 Apr 1592.

121. *BAC*, b. 276, reg. 395, cc. 14v–15r, 8 May 1609; *BAC*, b. 329, c. 2r, n.d.; *BAC*, b. 276, reg. 395, c. 87r, 26 May 1611; *APC*, b. 17, cc. 6r–v, 22 Aug 1620, Almoro Nani and Giorgio Giustinian to Senate; *BAC*, b. 275, reg. 393, cc. 48r–v, 16 Dec 1606.

122. Achille Olivieri is unequivocal: he states that without the assistance and mediation of Jews "the penetration of the Porte by the Venetian merchants is impossible. Alongside every Venetian merchant appears a Jew who fulfills the function of intermediary, or of a privileged interlocutor in the court of Constantinople." Olivieri, "Mercanti e 'mondi,' " 153.

123. İnalcık,"The Ottoman State," 1:202; *BAC*, b. 274, reg. 391, cc. 148v–149r, 6 Sep 1605; *BAC*, b. 276, reg. 395, cc. 59v–60v, 14 Jan 1610 (MV).

124. *BAC*, b. 270, reg. 385, c. 109v, 31 Jan 1599 (MV). Not all brokers were members of minority communities: a certain Mehmed Petener, for example, served as broker along with a Jew in a transaction in which two Venetian merchants bought some spices from several Ottoman-Muslims. *BAC*, b. 263, reg. 372, c. 105r, 23 Jan 1581 (MV).

125. Mantran, "La navigation vénitienne," 377–78; Mantran, "Minoritaires, métiers et marchands étrangers," 131–32.

126. Veinstein, "Marchands Ottomans," 727.

127. Kafadar, "A Death in Venice," 211; Kafadar, "The Ottomans and Europe," 1:621.

128. Pedani-Fabris, *In nome del Gran Signore*, 14–15.

129. *SDC*, b. 20, cc. 286r–287v, 19 Dec 1584, Gianfrancesco Morosini to Senate; *SDC*, b. 26, c. 247r, 1 Dec 1587, Lorenzo Bernardo to Senate; *APC*, b. 10, c. 11, 30 Jan 1604, Ottaviano Bon to Senate; c. 97r, 15 Jan 1605 (MV).

130. Queller, "How to Succeed as an Ambassador," 667–71.

131. On the concept of friendship in late medieval and early modern society, see Kent, introduction to *Bartolommeo Cederini*, 10–12; Molho, "Cosimo de' Medici," 18–21; also Najemy, *Between Friends*, 21–22; Ganz, "Florentine Friendship."

132. "Relazione di Paolo Contarini," in Albèri, *Relazioni*, 9:213; *APC*, b. 17, c. 13r, 22 Aug 1620, Almoro Nani and Giorgio Giustinian to Senate.

133. "Relazione di Paolo Contarini," in Albèri, *Relazioni*, 9:231–32.

134. *SDC*, b. 60, cc. 288r–290r, 20 Jan 1604 (MV), Ottaviano Bon to Senate.

135. Rycaut, *Present State of the Ottoman Empire*, 90–91.

136. *It VII* 1086 (8523), c. 149v, 20 Aug 1638, Alvise Contarini to Senate; *SDC*, b. 113, cc. 264v–266r, 10 Jul 1632, Giovanni Cappello to Senate.

137. *SDC*, b. 73, cc. 32v–33r, 24 May 1612, Simone Contarini and Cristoforo Valier to Senate; *SDC*, b. 55, cc. 261r–v, 4 Aug 1602, Agostino Nani to Senate.

138. *SDC*, b. 79, cc. 35r–37v, 21 Mar 1615, Almoro Nani and Cristoforo Valier to Senate; della Valle, *De' viaggi*, 1:205.

139. *SDC*, b. 71, c. 7v, 5 Mar 1611, Simone Contarini to Senate.

140. Sanudo, *Diarii*, 33:266, 278–79, 309, cited in Preto, *Venezia e i turchi*, 123–24.

141. İnalcık, "The Ottoman State," 1:47–48, 76–77; Kettering, "Gift-Giving." For a contemporary Ottoman discussion of bribery and gift-giving, see Chelebi, *The Balance of Truth*, 124–27.

142. *SDC*, b. 79, cc. 35r–37v, 21 Mar 1615, Almoro Nani and Cristoforo Valier to Senate.

143. Zele, "Aspetti delle legazioni ottomane," 272–73; *It VII* 882 (8505), V, c. 1r, "Relazione di Gian Jacopo Caroldo, secretario di Andrea Gritti"; Finlay, "Al servizio del Sultano," 79; Valensi, *Birth of the Despot*, 18–19.

144. "Relazione di Simone Contarini," in Barozzi and Berchet, *Relazioni*, 1:137–39.

145. Contarini also corresponded with other Ottoman officials: see the letter from Mahmud Paşa thanking him for a coral crown, and sending as a gift a porcelain brooch. *DocTR*, b. 11, no. 1260, n.d. [before Jan 1620], Mahmud Paşa to Simone Contarini.

146. Naima, *Annals*, 1:465–66; "Khalil Pasha Kaysariyyeli," *EI*, 4:970-72.

147. "Khalil Pasha Kaysariyyeli," *EI*, 4:970-72; "Relazione di Matteo Zane," in Albèri, *Relazioni*, 9:433.

148. *SDC*, b. 77, 17 Jun 1614, Halil Paşa to Simone Contarini. See also *DocTR*, b. 12, no. 1277, n.d. [ca. May 1621], Halil Paşa to Simone Contarini.

149. *SDC*, b. 81, c. 197r, 28 May 1616, Halil Paşa to Simone Contarini; *DocTR*, b. 11, no. 1248, n.d. [ca. 16 Feb 1619], Halil Paşa to Doge.

150. *DocTR*, b. 10, no. 1208, 21 May 1617, Grand Vizier Halil Paşa to Doge; *SDCop*, reg. 14, cc. 90–92, 6 Dec 1618, Grand Vizier Halil Paşa to Almoro Nani; *XSeg*, f. 31, 10 Mar 1614, bundle of letters regarding Halil Paşa's dependent Mordecai Cressi; *SDC*, b. 71, cc. 187r–v, May 1611, Halil Paşa to Doge. See a similar letter to the Grand Duke of Tuscany seeking the freedom of a Mahmud Negri, *per buona amicitia*. ASFi, *Mediceo*, c. 260r, n.d., Halil Paşa to Grand Duke; *SDC*, b. 74, cc. 260r–v, 11 Feb 1612 (MV), Cristoforo Valier to Senate, included letter from Halil Paşa in Adrianople to Bailo; "Khalil Pasha Kaysariyyeli," *EI*, 4:970–72.

151. Lesure, "Notes et documents," 138–42; "Sokollu Mehmed Pasha," *EI*, 9:706–11; Bertelè, *Il palazzo degli Ambasciatori*, 137–38 n.88; Yriarte, *La vie d'un patrician de Venise*, 130–31. This portrait was misattributed to Veronese and Tintoretto; Pallucchini and Rossi, *Tintoretto*, 2:127–28.

152. *Album Amicorum*, KB Hss 135 K4, Royal Library, The Hague, cited in de Groot, "The Dutch Nation in Istanbul," 132–37; van Rappard, *Ernst Brinck*, 40–41.

153. Biron, *Ambassade en Turquie*, 1:97, 116; "Khalil Pasha Kaysariyyeli," *EI*, 4:970–72. The Chevalier d'Arvieux reported attending similar parties in Izmir at which French, English, Greek, and Ottoman guests ate, danced and conversed. Eldem, Goffman, and Masters, *The Ottoman City between East and West*, 103.

154. Brennan, *Travel Diary of Robert Bargrave*, 99–100; Goffman, *Britons in the Ottoman Empire*, 25.

155. *SDC*, b. 57, cc. 208r–v, 16 May 1603, Francesco Contarini to Senate. Perhaps this official was Sataci Hasan Paşa, former Bey of Rumelia and of Diyarbakir, whom Selaniki mentions became famous while serving the harem, due to his knowledge of astrology, astronomy, and geometry. Peachy, *Selaniki's History*, 185–86. Contarini also is recorded discussing ships and shipbuilding with the renegade *kapudanpaşa* Cigala. "Francesco Contarini," *DBI*, 28:165–72.

156. *SDC*, b. 32, c. 138v, 8 Oct 1590, Girolamo Lippomano to Senate.

157. "Relazione di Paolo Contarini," in Albèri, *Relazioni*, 9:231–32; *SDC*, b. 22, c. 25r, 5 Sep 1585, Lorenzo Bernardo to Senate.

158. *SDC*, b. 76, cc. 158r–159r, 25 Oct 1613, Cristoforo Valier to Senate.

159. Biron, *Ambassade en Turquie*, 1:110. In a similar vein, Francesco della Valle, secretary to Alvise Gritti, reported that "many, many times Süleyman and İbrahim came [to his gardens] in private clothing for amusement." Francesco della Valle, *Una breve narracione della grandezza, virtù, valore et della infelice morte dell'IIll.mo Signor Conte Alvoise Gritti, It VII* 122 (6211), cited in Olivieri, "Tempo et historia," 169–70.

160. *DonàR*, b. 23, cc. 66r–67r; *It VII* 1084 (8521), c. 15r, 23 Jan 1636 (MV), Pietro Foscarini and Alvise Contarini to Senate.

161. Pippidi, *Hommes et idées*, 153; Sanudo, *I diarii*, 36:117 and passim; Bertelè, *Il palazzo degli Ambasciatori*, 50–52. On Ottoman attendance at English parties, see Goffman, *Britons in the Ottoman Empire*, 26–28.

162. *APC*, b. 2, c. 4r, 13 Dec 1524, Piero Bragadin to Senate. Nicolay recorded similar visits to the French embassy; Nicolay, *Navigations*, 91r.

163. "Relazione di Paolo Contarini," in Albèri, *Relazioni*, 9:250. On this, see also Si-

mon, "I rappresentanti diplomatici veneziani," 57; Robert Leo Ferring, "The Accomplished Ambassador," 132–33, 154.

164. *SDC*, b. 23, c. 186r, 12 Apr 1586 Lorenzo Bernardo to Senate. Orembei received a monetary gift from Venice at the marriage of a daughter to defray his expenses. *SDC*, b. 25, c. 197r, 21 Apr 1587, Lorenzo Bernardo to Senate.

165. *SDC*, b. 32, cc. 4v–5r, 1 Sep 1590, Girolamo Lippomano to Senate; *APC*, b. 10, c. 158r, 20 Oct 1607, Ottaviano Bon to Senate; *SDC*, b. 79, c. 101r, 18 Apr 1615, Almoro Nani and Cristoforo Valier to Senate.

166. *SDC*, b. 29, c. 223r, 24 May 1589, Giovanni Moro to Senate.

167. *SDCop*, reg. 14, c. 131, 17 Jan 1618 (MV), Almoro Nani and Francesco Contarini to Senate.

168. Faroqhi, *Approaching Ottoman History*, 14.

169. D'Alessio, *Relatione*, 42. Also, G.B. Cervellini, "Relazioni da Costantinopoli."

170. All three Latin-rite churches in Constantinople in 1550 were transformed into mosques by 1640. In Galata, San Paolo was made a mosque in 1535, Santa Maria de Draperis in 1663, San Francesco in 1697, Santa Anna in 1697, and San Sebastiano and Santa Clara disappeared in the sixteenth and seventeenth centuries. Of fourteen mosques in Galata, four at least were originally Christian churches. Mordtmann, "Constantinople," 2:874–75; Pistarino, "Genoese in Pera," 64; *SDC*, b. 58, cc. 402r, 21 Feb 1603 (MV), Francesco Contarini to Senate; Mantran, *Istanbul au siècle de Soliman*, 65.

171. D'Alessio, *Relatione*, 81; Cervellini, "Relazioni da Costantinopoli," 43; Pacifique, *Le voyage de Perse*, 27–28; Ortayli, "La vie quotidienne," 134.

172. Tongas, *Les relations de la France avec l'Empire Ottoman*, 73–77; Bruno, "Ambassadeurs de France."

173. Cocchia, *Storia delle Missioni dei Cappuccini*, 1:66.

174. "Visita apostolica a Costantinopoli," in Hofmann, *Il vicariato apostolico*, 64.

175. D'Alessio, *Relatione*, 68–70; Matteucci, *Un glorioso convento*, 110–11; "Visita apostolica a Costantinopoli," in Hofmann, *Il vicariato apostolico*, 59–60.

176. D'Alessio, *Relatione*, 68–70.

177. Pacifique, *Le voyage de Perse*, 27–28; d'Alessio, *Relatione*, 74; also Belin, *Histoire de la Latinité de Constantinople*, 336–44.

178. Pacifique, *Le voyage de Perse*, 27–28.

179. D'Alessio, *Relatione*, 69. On Islamic saint veneration and pilgrimage to sites associated with them, see Meri, *The Cult of Saints*, 59–213.

180. Foster and Daniell, *Life of Busbecq*, 1:256; *It VII* 882 (8505), no. 9, cc. 34r–v, "Descritione dell'Imperio Turchesco del Reverendissimo Monseigneur Maffio Venier, Arcivescovo di Corfù."

181. Zachariadou, "À propos du syncrétisme islamo-chrétien," 395–403; Zachariadou "Co-Existence and Religion."

182. Lopasic, "Islamization of the Balkans," 176–77.

183. Perry, "Contested Identities," 182.

184. Mordtmann, "Constantinople," 2:874–75; Mantran, *Istanbul au siècle de Soliman*, 26–27; Evliya, *Narrative*, 1–2:53.

185. Lâtifî. *Éloge d'Istanbul*, 115–17.

186. Thévenot, *Voyage du Levant*, 65–66; Evliya, *Narrative*, 1–2:52. See also *BAC*, b. 374-I, no. 50; *SDC*, b. 59, c. 151v, 18 May 1604, Girolamo Cappello to Senate; *SDC*, b. 59, c. 5v, 9 Mar 1604, Francesco Contarini to Senate; *BAC*, b. 110, 8 Oct 1633, Bailo to the Corti.

187. *BAC*, b. 368, 12 Jan 1595 (MV). This evidence contradicts the assertion that guilds "tended to be dominated or even exclusively held by a certain ethno-religious element" in Eldem, Goffman, and Masters, *The Ottoman City between East and West*, 161–62.

188. *BAC*, b. 368, VI, 24 Mar 1596; also *BAC*, b. 368, no. 79 and 80, 1596; *BAC*, b. 368, no. 78. Çizakça has shown that there was a gradual shift among arsenal workers in Constantinople: in 1529–30 most were Muslims; by 1645 most workers were Greek. Çizakça, "Ottomans and the Mediterranean," 2:776, 784; Mantran, "Minoritaires, métiers et marchands étrangers," 130.

189. Mauroeide, *Ho Hellenismos sto Galata*, 240–43, 249.

190. Çizakça, "Ottomans and the Mediterranean," 2:786–87; *BAC*, b. 263, reg. 371, cc. 35v–36r, 17 Mar 1546; *BAC*, b. 273, reg. 390, cc. 65r–v, 7 May 1603.

Glossary

For additional information on these and other terms, see Bayerele, *Pashas, Begs, and Effendis.*

Acemioğlan (T)—Apprentice janissary, selected through the *devşirme.*

Ağa (T)—Signor, lord; honorary title usually applied to military commanders.

Ahidname (T)—Written pledge of privilege granted by sultan.

Akça (T)—Ottoman silver coin. "Asper" in English.

Avania (It)—Extraordinary levy imposed by state in emergency situations. *Avariz* in Turkish.

Bailo (Ve)—Venetian consul and ambassador in Constantinople.

Bedestan (T)—Covered market in which a city's chief merchants maintained shops.

Beylerbeyi (T)—Governor-general of Ottoman province (*beylerbeyilik*).

Çavuş (T)—Messenger, member of corps of couriers.

Cernitore (It)—Fellmonger.

Cottimo (It)—Duties charged on goods shipped both ways between Venice and Constantinople.

Defterdar (T)—Treasurer, director of finances.

Devşirme (T)—Levy of boys from Christian subject population of Ottoman Empire for military service.

Dhimmi (A)—Non-Muslim subject. Also *zimmi.*

Divan (T)—Sultan's imperial council, government.

Emin (T)—A trusted person, usually an official of the sultan. Also, an intermediate legal status between *dhimmi* and *harbi,* i.e., a trusted *harbi* who enjoys resident status.

Famiglia (It)—In its early modern usage in Constantinople, the household of the bailo, comprised of his secretaries, dragomans, and other servants, not his blood relations.

Fondaco (It)—A combined hotel and warehouse which grouped foreign merchants of specific nations together.

Giovane di lingua (Ve)—Apprentice dragoman.

Harac (T)—Head tax required of all non-Muslim Ottoman subjects.

Haracgüzar (T)—Non-Muslim Ottoman subject, required to pay *harac.*

Harbi (T)—Non-muslim, enemy.

Hüccet (T)—Legal document.

Kadı (T)—Judge.

Kapıağası (T)—Head of the white eunuchs.

Kapıcıbaşı (T)—Head of the corps of guards of the imperial palace.

Kapudanpaşa (T)—Admiral of Ottoman fleet.

Millet (T)—Minority religious community recognized by an Islamic state.

More veneto (L)—Venetian usage; refers to Venetian calendar year that began on March 1. Abbreviated MV.

Müteferrika (T)—Member of sultan's elite personal guard.

Nişancı (T)—Member of imperial council responsible for chancery.

Parte (Ve)—Law, deliberation.

Paşa (T)—Honorific title reserved for beylerbeyi and vizirs.

Perma (It)—Small oared boat used to cross between Constantinople and Galata.

Quondam (L)—Deceased, often used as "child of deceased . . ." Abbreviated q.

Salvacondotto (It)—Safe conduct.

Sancak (T)—An administrative subdivision of a *beylerbeyilik,* administered by a *sancak-beyi.* The basic military-administrative unit of the Ottoman Empire.

Signoria (Ve)—The core council of the Venetian government, comprising ten men— the doge, the ducal councillors, and the heads of the *Quarantia.*

Rasonato (It)—Accountant.

Sipahi (T)—Member of Ottoman cavalry. Plural: *sipāhī.*

Taife (T)—Similar to European concept of nation. See also *millet. Tā'ifa* in Arabic.

Voyvoda (Sl)—Slavic title for prince, especially puppet rulers of Ottoman-controlled Wallachia and Moldavia. Also an official responsible for maintaining peace in a district or city, such as Galata; usually Christian.

V Savii (Ve)—The Venetian board of trade charged with protecting and promoting commerce.

Works Cited

ARCHIVAL SOURCES

Dubrovnik
Dubrovnik State Archives (DSA)

Acta Sanctae Mariae Maioris, busta 467
Lettere di Levante, busta 37 (1590–92)
Testamenta Notariae, busta 49 (1592–95)

Rome
Archivio Congregatio pro doctrina fidei (ACDF)

Dubia diversa ab anno 1570 ad Annum 1668, bundles 3, 10, 13

Vatican Library (VatLib)

Urb. Lat., 836

Venice
Archivio di stato di Venezia (ASV)

Archivi propri degli ambasciatori—Costantinopoli, buste 1, 2, 6–10, 16–18
Avogaria di comun, buste 153, 157, 181, 185, 362–78, 440, 452, 559–62, 595, 3521
Avogaria di comun—Nascite, libro d'oro, passim
Bailo a Costantinopoli, buste 110, 250–52, 263–280, 284, 285, 295, 297, 313–17, 329, 331, 339, 344, 347, 348, 364, 365, 368, 369, 371, 374, 375, 387
Barbaro, M., *Arbori de' patritii veneti*
Cancelliere grande, buste 13, 14
Capi del consiglio di dieci—Lettere di ambasciatori, buste 1–7
Collegio—Relazioni, buste 4–6, 65, 74, 79, 81, 88
Commemoriali, reg. 24
Compilazione delle leggi, busta 157
Consiglio di dieci—Deliberazioni segrete, filze 20–42
Dieci savii alle decime in Rialto, passim
Documenti turchi, buste 1–12

Giudici di petizion, buste 3–8

Inquisitori di stato, buste 148, 416, 417, 433, 701

Lettere e scritture turchesche, buste 1–5, 7

Maggior consiglio—Deliberazioni, reg. 24

Miscellanea Gregolin, buste 2, 7, 12–15

Notarile—Atti, passim

Notarile—Testamenti, passim

Provveditori sopra ospedali e luoghi pii, busta 98

Rubricarii di Costantinopoli, reg. D14

Segretario alle voci—Maggior consiglio, reg. 3, 4

Senato deliberazioni—Costantinopoli, filze 5–14

Senato dispacci—Copie moderne, reg. 7–19

Senato dispacci—Costantinopoli, buste 14–23, 25–26, 28–34, 37, 39–43, 47, 49–71, 73–79, 81, 90, 93, 96, 98, 113

Senato—Mar, reg. 31, 37, 40, 42–97

Senato segreta materie miste notabili, busta 229

V Savii alla mercanzia, buste 23, 135–45, 492, 493

V Savii alla mercanzia—Nuova serie, buste 50, 61, 85

Biblioteca Marciana (Marciana)

Alvise Contarini, Lettere al Senato, It VII 1084–88 (8521–25)

Dispacci da Costantinopoli al Senato Veneto, It VII 378 (8167)

Francesco Girardo Autobiografia, It VII 183 (8161)

Giacomo Balsarini, Console a Scio, Lettere ad Alvise Contarini, It VII 1191 (8881)

Gio Carlo Scaramelli, Ricordi a se stesso—Discorso sulla pace con i Turchi, It VII 1640 (7983)

Lettere ad Alvise Contarini bailo a Costantinopoli, It VII 1194 (8354)

Lettere di consoli veneti nel Levante al bailo Alvise Contarini, It VII 1193 (8883)

Lettere di diversi ad Alvise Contarini, It VII 1179 (8878)

Relazioni di Turchia, ecc., It VII 882 (8505)

Relazioni diverse, It VII 934 (9013)

Simone Contarini, Lettere al Senato, It VII 1082 (9098)

Tabelle nominative e cronologiche dei segretari della cancelleria ducale, It VII 1667 (8459)

Museo Correr (Correr)

Cod Cicogna, 1971, 423

Cod Correr—*Donà delle Rose*, reg. 23, 148, 180, 217, 351

Cod. Sagredo, PD 5702

Washington, D.C.
Library of Congress

Trevisan Manuscript, Mss. Med. & Ren., 26, c. 35r.

PUBLISHED PRIMARY SOURCES

Albèri, Eugenio. *Relazioni degli ambasciatori veneti al senato durante il secolo decimosesto*. 3rd ser., vols. 1–3. Florence: Società editrice fiorentina, 1840–55.

Alberti, Tommaso. *Viaggio a Costantinopoli di Tommaso Alberti (1609–1621)*. Ed. Alberto Bacchi della Lega. Bologna: Romagnoli dall'acqua, 1889.

Amman, Jost. *Gynaeceum, sive Theatrum Mulierum . . . artificiossimis . . . figuris expressos . . . add. octostichis Franc. Modii*. Frankfurt: Feyrabend, 1586.

Argenti, Philip P., ed. *Diplomatic Archive of Chios, 1577–1841*. Vol. 2. Cambridge: Cambridge University Press, 1954.

Barozzi, Niccolò, and Guglielmo Berchet, eds. *Le relazioni degli stati europei lette al senato dagli ambasciatori veneziani nel secolo decimosettimo. Turchia—Parte I–II*. Venice: P. Naratovich, 1871–72.

Bertelè, Tommaso, ed. *Informatione dell'offitio dell'ambasciatore di Marino de Cavalli il vecchio, MDL*. Florence: Olschki editore, 1935.

Bertelli, Ferdinando. *Omnium fere gentium nostrae aetatis habitus, nunquam ante hac aediti*. Venice: F. Bertelli, 1563.

Bilanci generali della repubblica di Venezia. 2nd ser., vol. 1, bk. 1. Venice: R. commissione per la pubblicazione dei documenti finanziari della repubblica di Venezia, 1912.

Biron, Théodore de Gontaut. *Ambassade en Turquie de Jean de Gontaut Biron Baron de Salignac, 1605 à 1610*. Vol. 1–2. Paris: Honoré Champion Éditeur, 1888–89.

Blochet, E. "Relation du voyage en Orient de Carlier de Pinon (1579)." *Revue de l'Orient latin* 12 (1909–11): 112–203, 327–421.

Blount, Henry. *A Voyage into the Levant . . . with particular observations concerning the moderne condition of the Turks, and other people under that empire*. 2nd ed. London: Andrew Crooke, 1636. Reprint, Amsterdam: Norwood Theatrum Orbis Terrarum, 1977.

Boppe, A., ed. *Journal et correspondance de Gédoyn 'Le Turc' consul de France à Alep, 1623–1625*. Paris: Typographie Plon-Nourrit et Cie, 1909.

Brennan, Michael, ed. *Travel Diary of Robert Bargrave, Levant Merchant, 1647–1656*. London: Hakluyt, 1999.

Brulez, Wilfrid, ed. *Marchands flamands à Venise, (1568–1605)*. Vol. 1–2. Rome-Bruxelles: L'Institut historique belge de Rome, 1965.

Bruyn, Abraham de. *Omnium pene Europae, Asiae, Aphricae Atque americae gentium habitus—Habits de diverses nations de l'Europe, l'Asie, Afrique, et amerique—Trachtenbuch der Furnembsten Nationen und Volcker kleydungen beyde Manns und Weybs personen in Europa, Asie, Africa und America*. Antwerp: Joos de Bosscher excudit, [c. 1610].

Carayon, Auguste, ed. *Relations inédites des missions de la compagnie de Jésus a Constantinople et dans le Levant*. Poitiers: Henri Oudain, 1864.

[Cavazza, Gabriele]. *Viaggio di un ambasciatore veneziano da Venezia a Costantinopoli nel 1591*. Venice: Fratelli Visentini, 1886.

Cervantes, Miguel de. *The First Part of the Delightful History of the Most Ingenious Knight Don Quixote of the Mancha*. Trans. Thomas Shelton. New York: P. F. Collier & Son, 1937.

Chambers, David, and Brian Pullan, eds. *Venice: A Documentary History*. Oxford: Blackwell, 1992.

Chelebi, Kātib. *The Balance of Truth*. Trans. G. L. Lewis. London: George Allen and Unwin, 1957.

Contarini, Gasper. *The Commonwealth and Government of Venice*. London: John Windet, 1599. Reprint, Amsterdam: Theatrum Orbis Terrarum, 1969.

Contarini, P. *Diario del viaggio da Venezia a Costantinopoli di M. Paolo Contarini che andava bailo per la repubblica veneta alla porta ottomana nel 1580*. Ed. Girolamo Olivieri. Venice: Teresa Gattei, 1856.

d'Alessio, E. Dalleggio. *Relatione dello stato della cristianità di Pera e Costantinopoli obediente al sommo pontefice romano*. Constantinople: Edizioni Rizzo & Son, 1925.

Dallam, Thomas. "The Diary of Master Thomas Dallam, 1599–1600." In *Early Voyages and Travels in the Levant*, ed. J. Theodore Bent. London: Hakluyt Society, 1893.

Davis, James C. *Pursuit of Power*. New York: Harper, 1970.

de Callières, Monsieur. *On the Manner of Negotiating with Princes; On the Uses of Diplomacy; the Choice of Ministers and Envoys; and the Personal Qualities Necessary for Success in Missions Abroad*. Trans. A. F. Whyte. Notre Dame, IN: University of Notre Dame Press, 1963.

della Valle, Pietro. *De' viaggi di Pietro Della Valle il Pellegrino. Descritti da lui medesimo in lettere familiari. Parte prima cioè La Turchia*. Rome: Vitale Mascardi, 1650.

Deserpz, Francois. *Recueil de la diversité des habits qui sont de present en usaige tant es pays d'Europe, Asie, Affrique et Illes sauvages, le tout fait apres le naturel*. Paris: Richard Breton, 1562.

Evliya Efendi. *Narrative of Travels in Europe, Asia, and Africa in the Seventeenth Century by Evliya Efendi*. Trans. Joseph von Hammer. Vol. 1–2. London: William H. Allen, 1846.

Foster, Charles Thornton, and F. H. Blackburne Daniell, eds. *The Life and Letters of Ogier Ghiselin de Busbecq*. London: C. Kegan Paul, 1881.

Foster, William, ed. *The Travels of John Sanderson in the Levant, 1584–1602; with His Autobiography and Selections from His Correspondence*. London: Hakluyt Society, 1931.

Grey, Edward, ed., *The Travels of Pietro della Valle in India*. Vol. 1. London: Hakluyt, 1892. Reprint, New Delhi: AES, 1991.

Hofmann, G. *Il vicariato apostolico di Costantinopoli 1453–1830*. Rome: Pont. Institutum Orientalium Studiorum, 1935.

Hughes, Charles. *Shakespeare's Europe: Unpublished Chapters of Fynes Moryson's Itinerary*. London: Sherratt & Hughes, 1903.

Lamansky, Vladimir. *Secrets d'état de Venise*. Vol. 2. Saint Petersburg: Imprimerie de l'Académie Impériale des Sciences, 1884. Reprint, New York: Burt Franklin, 1968.

Lâtifî. *Éloge d'Istanbul suivi du traité d l'incentive anonyme*. Trans. and ed. Stéphane Yerasimos. Arles: Acts Sud-Sinbad, 2001.

Lestocquoy, J., ed. *Correspondence des nonces en France, Carpi et Ferrerio, 1535–1540*. Vol. 1, *Acta Nuntiature Gallicae*. Rome: Presses de l'université Gregorienne, 1961.

Lettres anecdotes de Cyrille Lucar Patriarche de Constantinople, et sa confession de foi, avec des remarques . . . Amsterdam: Chez l'Honorè et Chatelain, 1718.

Letts, Malcolm, ed. and trans. *The Pilgrimage of Arnold von Harff, Knight from Cologne, through Italy, Syria, Egypt, Arabia, Ethiopia, Nubia, Palestine, Turkey, France and Spain, which He Accomplished in the Years 1496 to 1499*. London: Hakluyt Society, 1946.

Life in Istanbul, 1588: Scenes from a Traveller's Picture Book. Oxford: Bodelian Library, 1977.

Lithgow, William. *The Totall Discourse of the Rare Adventures and Painfull Peregrinations of Long Nineteen Years Travayles from Scotland to the Most Famous Kingdoms in Europe, Asia and Africa*. London: Nicholas Okes, 1632. Reprint, Glasgow: J. MacLehose, 1906.

Lopez, Robert S., and Irving W. Raymond, *Medieval Trade in the Mediterranean World*. New York: Norton, n.d.

Machiavelli, Niccolò. *The Discourses*. Trans. Leslie J. Walker, ed. Bernard Crick. London: Penguin, 1970.

Matković, P. "Itinerario di Marc' Antonio Pigafetta." *Starine* 22 (1890): 70–194.

Mazzini, Joseph. *The Duties of Man and Other Essays*. New York: E. P. Dutton, 1929.

Miliopoulos, J. "Relation d'un voyage en Orient par J. Bordier." *Archeion Pontou* 6 (1935): 86–158.

Moryson, Fynes. *An Itinerary. Containing His Ten Yeeres Travell through the Twelve Dominions of Germany, Bohmerland, Sweitzerland, Netherland, Denmarke, Poland, Italy, Turkey, France, England, Scotland, and Ireland*. London: John Beale, 1617. Reprint, Glasgow: James MacLehose & Sons, 1907.

Mundy, Peter. *The Travels of Peter Mundy, in Europe and Asia, 1608–1667*. Ed. Richard Carnac Temple. Cambridge: Hakluyt Society, 1907.

Naima. *Annals of the Turkish Empire from 1591 to 1659 of the Christian Era*. Trans. Charles Fraser. London: Oriental Translation Fund of Great Britain and Ireland, 1832.

Nicolay, Nicholas de. *The Navigations into Turkie*. London: Thomas Dawson, 1585. Reprint, Amsterdam: Theatrum Orbis Terrarum, 1968.

Nixon, Anthony. *The Three English Brothers*. London: n.p., 1607. Reprint, Amsterdam: Theatrum Orbis Terrarum, 1970.

Nunziature di Venezia. Vol. 1. Ed. Francesco Gaeta. Rome: Istituto storico italiano per l'età moderna e contemporanea, 1958.

Parte presa nell'eccelso Conseglio di Dieci, 1620. Adì 4. Giugno. In materia de Banditi, Relegati, et altramente condannati dell'Istria, Dalmatia, Isole di Leuante, et Regno di Candia, gratiati da Rappresentanti publici. Venice: Antonio Pinelli, 1620.

Parte presa nell'eccelso Conseglio di Dieci, 1620. Adì 22. Aprile. In materia de Banditi Relegati, confinati, et altramente condannati, gratiati da Rappresentanti publici. Venice: Antonio Pinelli, 1620.

Paruta, Paolo. *Opere politiche*. Ed. C. Manzoni. Florence: Felice le Monnier, 1852.

Peachy, William Samuel. *A Year in Selaniki's History: 1593–4*. Bloomington: Indiana University Press, 1984.

Pinto, Olga, ed. *Viaggio di C. Federici e G. Balbi alle Indie orientali*. Vol. 4, in *Il Nuovo Ramusio*. Rome: Istituto poligrafico dello stato, 1962.

Pius II. *Memoirs of a Renaissance Pope: The Commentaries of Pius II*. Trans. Florence A. Gragg; ed. Leona C. Gabel. New York: Capricorn Books, 1959.

Priuli, Girolamo. *I diarii*. Ed. A. Segre and R. Cessi. Città del Castello-Bologna: Casa editrice S. Lapis, 1912–41.

Provins, P. Pacifique de. *Le voyage de Perse et Brève relation du voyage des îles de l'Amérique*. In

Bibliotheca Seraphico-Cappucina, Sectio Historica, vol. 3–4, ed. P. Godfrey de Paris and P. Hilaire de Wingene. Assisi: Collegio di San Lorenzo da Brindisi dei minori cappucini, 1939.

Rabbath, Antoine, ed. *Documents inédits pour servir à l'histoire du Christianisme en Orient (XVI–XIX siècle).* 2 vols. Paris: A. Picard et Fils, 1905–11.

Richards, Gertrude Randolph Bramlette, ed. *Florentine Merchants in the Age of the Medici: Letters and Documents from the Selfridge Collection of Medici Manuscripts.* Cambridge, MA: Harvard University Press, 1932.

Rosaccio, Giuseppe. *Viaggio da Venezia a Costantinopoli Per Mare, e per Terra, & insieme quello di Terra Santa.* In Venetia, appresso Giacomo Franco, 1598. Reprint, Mariano del Friuli: Edizioni della laguna, 1992.

Rycaut, Paul. *The Present State of the Ottoman Empire.* London: John Starkey & Henry Brome, 1668. Reprint, New York: Arno Press, 1971.

Salvago, Gio Batta. *"Africa overo barberia": relazione al doge di Venezia sulle reggenze di Algeri e di Tunisi del dragomanno Gio Batta Salvago (1625).* Ed. Alberto Sacerdoti. Padua: CEDAM, 1937.

Sandys, George. *A Relation of a Journey Begun Anno Domini 1610. Foure Bookes.* 3rd ed. London: Ro Allot, 1632.

Sanudo, Marino. *I diarii.* Venice: F. Visentini, 1879–1902. Reprint Bologna: Forni, 1969–70.

Schmidt, Jan, ed. and trans. *Mustafā ʿĀlī's Künhü'l-ahbār and Its Preface According to the Leiden Manuscript.* Leiden: Nederlands Historisch-Archaeologisch Instituut Te Istanbul, 1987.

Shakespeare, William. *The Merchant of Venice.* In *The Riverside Shakespeare.* Boston: Houghton-Mifflin, 1974.

Sherley, Thomas. *"Discours of the Turkes."* *Camden Miscellany* 16 (1936): 1–38.

Sluperius, Jacobus. *Omnium fere nostrae aetatis Nationum, Habitus et Effigies.* Antwerp: Joannes Bellerus, 1562.

Soranzo, Lazzaro. *L'Ottomanno.* 4th ed. Naples: Stamperia Porta Reale, 1600.

Stefani, Federico, ed. *Viaggio a Costantinopoli di Sier Lorenzo Bernardo per l'arresto del bailo Sier Girolamo Lippomano Cav., 1591 aprile.* In *Monumenti storici publicati dalla R. Deputazione veneta di storia patria. Serie 4—Miscellanea,* vol. 4. Venice: A spese della società, 1887.

Taeschner, Franz. *Alt-Stambuler Hof- und Volksleber, ein türkisches Miniaturenalbum aus dem 17. Jahrhundert.* Hannover: Orient-Buchhandlung Heinz LaFaire, 1925.

Thévenot, Jean. *Voyage du Levant.* Ed. Stéphane Yerasimos. Paris: François Maspero, 1980.

Tietze, Andreas, ed. *Mustafa Ali's Counsel for Sultans of 1581.* Vienna: Verlag der Österreichischen Akademie der Wissenschaften, 1979.

Trevisan, Angelo. *Lettere sul nuovo mondo. Granada 1501.* Ed. Angela Caracciolo Aricò. Venice: Albrizzi editore, 1993.

Wells, Charles, trans. *The Literature of the Turks: A Turkish Chrestomathy.* London: Bernard Quaritch, 1891.

Wood, A. C., ed. *"By Fox, His Servant. Mr. Harrie Cavendish His Journey to and From Constantinople 1589."* *Camden Miscellany* 17 (1940): 1–29.

Wratislaw, A. H., trans. *Adventures of Baron Wenceslas Wratislaw of Mitrowitz*. London: Bell & Daldy, 1862.

SECONDARY SOURCES

Adams, Christine. *Bourgeois Identity in Early Modern France: A Professional Family in Eighteenth-Century Bordeaux*. Philadelphia: University of Pennsylvania Press, 2000.

Akarli, Engin. *The Long Peace: Ottoman Lebanon, 1861–1920*. Berkeley: University of California Press, 1993.

Alcalay, Ammiel. *After Jews and Arabs: Remaking Levantine Culture*. Minneapolis: University of Minnesota Press, 1993.

Anderson, Benedict. *Imagined Communities*. Rev. ed. London: Verso, 1991.

Andrić, Ivo. *The Bridge on the Drina*. Chicago: University of Chicago Press, 1977.

Appuhn, Karl. "Inventing Nature: Forests and State Power in Renaissance Venice." *Journal of Modern History* 72 (2000): 861–89.

Arbel, Benjamin. "Colonie d'oltremare." In *Storia di Venezia*, ed. Alberto Tenenti and Ugo Tucci, vol. 5. Rome: Istituto della enciclopedia italiana Treccani, 1991.

———. "Jews in International Trade: The Emergence of the Levantines and Ponentines." In *The Jews of Early Modern Venice*, ed. Robert C. Davis and Benjamin Ravid. Baltimore: Johns Hopkins University Press, 2001.

———. "Nūr Bānū (c. 1530–1583): A Venetian Sultana?" *Turcica* 24 (1992): 241–59.

———. "Riflessioni sul ruolo di Creta nel commercio mediterraneo del Cinquecento." In *Venezia e Creta*, ed. Gherardo Ortalli. Venice: Istituto veneto di scienze, lettere ed arti, 1998.

———. "Roman Catholics and Greek Orthodox in the Early Modern Venetian State." In *The Three Religions*, ed. Nili Cohen and Andreas Heldrich. Munich: Utz, 2002.

———. *Trading Nations: Jews and Venetians in the Early Modern Eastern Mediterranean*. Leiden: Brill, 1995.

Armstrong, John A. *Nations before Nationalism*. Chapel Hill: University of North Carolina Press, 1982.

"Ashkenazi, Solomon." In *Encyclopaedia Judaica*, 3:731–33. Jerusalem: Macmillan, 1971.

Ashtor, Eliyahu. *Levant Trade in the Later Middle Ages*. Princeton: Princeton University Press, 1983.

———. "The Venetian Supremacy in Levantine Trade: Monopoly or Pre-colonialism?" *Journal of European Economic History* 3 (1974): 5–53.

Audisio, Gabriel. "Renégats marseillais (1591–1595)." *Renaissance and Reformation* 28, no. 3 (1992): 31–58.

Aymard, Maurice. *Venise, Raguse et le commerce du blé pendant la seconde moitié du XIVe siècle*. Paris: SEVPEN, 1966.

Babinger, Franz. *Mehmed the Conqueror and His Time*. Princeton: Princeton University Press, 1978.

———. "Le vicende veneziane nella lotta contro i Turchi durante il XV secolo." In *Storia della civiltà veneziana*, ed. Vittore Branca, vol. 2. Florence: Sansoni, 1979.

Barkan, Ömer Lütfi. "Essai sur les données statistiques des registres de recensement dans l'empire Ottoman." *Journal of the Economic and Social History of the Orient* 1 (1957): 9–36.

Barkey, Karen. *Bandits and Bureaucrats: The Ottoman Route to State Centralization.* Ithaca: Cornell University Press, 1994.

Baron, Salo Wittmayer. *A Social and Religious History of the Jews.* Vol. 18. 2nd ed. New York: Columbia University Press, 1983.

Basaglia, Enrico. "Il banditismo nei rapporti di Venezia con gli stati confinanti." In *Bande armate, banditi, banditismo e repressione di giustizia negli stati europei di antico regime,* ed. Gherardo Ortalli. Rome: Jouvence, 1986.

———. "Il controllo della criminalità nella repubblica di Venezia. Il secolo XVI: un momento di passaggio." In *Venezia e la terraferma attraverso le relazioni dei rettori.* Milan: A. Giuffrè editore, 1980.

Baschet, M. Armand. *La diplomatie Vénitienne.* Paris: Henri Plon, 1862.

Bashan, Eliezer. "Jewish Moneylending in Constantinople and Smyrna during the 17th–18th Centuries as Reflected in the British Levant Company's Archives." In *The Mediterranean and the Jews: Banking, Finance and International Trade (XVI–XVIII Centuries),* ed. Ariel Toaff and Simon Schwarzfuchs. Ramat Gan, Israel: Bar-Ilan University Press, 1989.

Bates, E. S. *Touring in 1600: A Study in the Development of Travel as a Means of Education.* Boston: Houghton, Mifflin, 1911.

Baumer, Franklin L. "England, the Turk, and the Common Corps of Christendom." *American Historical Review* 50 (1944–45): 26–48.

Bayerle, Gustav. *Pashas, Begs, and Effendis: A Historical Dictionary of Titles and Terms in the Ottoman Empire.* Istanbul: Isis Press, 1997.

Beck, Brandon H. *From the Rising of the Sun: English Images of the Ottoman Empire.* New York: P. Lang, 1987.

Beck, Colette. "Éléments sociaux et économiques de la vie des marchands génois à Anvers entre 1528 et 1555." *Revue du Nord* 64 (1982): 759–84.

Beck, Hans-Georg, et al. *Venezia, centro di mediazione tra oriente e occidente (secoli XV–XVI): aspetti e problemi.* Florence: Leo S. Olschki editore, 1977.

Belfanti, Carlo Marco. "Una città e la carestia: Mantova, 1590–92." *Annali della fondazione Luigi Einaudi* 16 (1982): 99–140.

Belin, M. A. *Histoire de la Latinité de Constantinople.* 2nd ed. Paris: Alphonse Picard et fils, 1894.

Benedict, Philip. "*Un roi, une loi, deux fois:* Parameters for the History of Catholic-Reformed Co-existence in France, 1555–1685." In *Tolerance and Intolerance in the European Reformation,* ed. Ole Peter Grell and Bob Scribner. Cambridge: Cambridge University Press, 1996.

Bennassar, Bartolomé. "Conversion ou reniement? Modalitiés d'une adhésion ambigué des chrétiens à l'Islam (XVIe–XVIIe siècles)." *Annales, ESC* 6 (1988): 1349–66.

———. "Frontières religieuses entre islam et chrétienté: l'expérience vécue par les 'Renégats.'" In *Les frontières religieuses en Europe du XVe au XVIIe siècle: actes du XXXIe Colloque international d'études humanistes,* ed. Alain Ducellier et al. Paris: J. Vrin, 1992.

Bennassar, Bartolomé, and Lucile Bennassar, *Les chrétiens d'Allah: l'histoire extraordinaire des renégats, XVIe–XVIIe siècles.* Paris: Perrin, 1989.

Benveniste, Emile. *Indo-European Language and Society*. Trans. Elizabeth Palmer. London: Faber & Faber, 1973.

Benzoni, Gino. "A proposito dei baili veneziani a Costantinopoli: qualche spunto, qualche osservazione." *Studi Veneziani* 30 (1995): 69–77.

———. "A proposito della fonte prediletta di Ranke, ossia le relazioni degli ambasciatori veneziani." *Studi veneziani* 16 (1988): 245–57.

———. "Il «farsi turco» ossia l'ombra del rinnegato." In *Venezia e i turchi: Scontri e confronti di due civiltà*. Milan: Electa, 1985.

———. "Ranke's Favorite Source." In *Leopold von Ranke and the Shaping of the Historical Discipline*, ed. Georg G. Iggers and James M. Powell. Syracuse: Syracuse University Press, 1990.

———. "Tra centro e periferia: il caso veneziano." In *Studi veneti offerti a Gaetano Cozzi*. Venice: Il Cardo, 1992.

———. "Venezia e Bergamo: implicanze di un dominio." *Studi Veneziani* 20 (1990): 15–58.

———. *Venezia nell'età della controriforma*. Milan: Mursia, 1973.

Berengo, Marino. *La società veneta alla fine del Settecento: Ricerche storiche*. Florence: Sansoni, 1956.

Berindei, Minhea. "Les Vénitiens en Mer Noire XVIe–XVIIe siècles: Nouveaux documents." *Cahiers des études russes et soviétiques* 30 (1989): 207–23.

Bertelè, Tommaso. *Il palazzo degli Ambasciatori di Venezia a Costantinopoli*. Bologna: Casa editrice Bologna, 1932.

Bisaha, Nancy. *Creating East and West: Renaissance Humanists and the Ottoman Turks*. Philadelphia: University of Pennsylvania Press, 2004.

Bitterli, Urs. *Cultures in Conflict: Encounters between European and non-European Cultures, 1492–1800*. Trans. Ritchie Robertson. Cambridge: Polity, 1989.

Blanks, David R. "Western Views of Islam in the Premodern Period: A Brief History of Past Approaches." In *Western Views of Islam in Medieval and Early Modern Europe: Perception of Other*, ed. David R. Blanks and Michael Frassetto. New York: St. Martin's Press, 1999.

Blumenkranz, Bernard. "Les Juifs dans le commerce maritime de Venise (1592–1609): A propos d'un livre récent." *Revue des études Juives*, 3rd ser., 2 (1961): 143–51.

Bodian, Miriam. *Hebrews of the Portuguese Nation: Conversos and Community in Early Modern Amsterdam*. Bloomington: Indiana University Press, 1997.

Boerio, Giuseppe. *Dizionario del dialetto veneziano*. Venice: Giovanni Cecchini editore, 1856. Reprint, Florence: Giunti, 1993.

Bonnell, Victoria E., and Lynn Hunt, eds. *Beyond the Cultural Turn: New Directions in the Study of Society and Culture*. Berkeley and Los Angeles: University of California Press, 1999.

Bono, Salvatore. *I corsari barbareschi*. Turin: ERI, 1964.

———. "Pascià e Raìs algerini di origine italiana." In *Algeria e Italia*, ed. R. H. Raniero. Milan: Marzorati, 1982.

Borsari, Silvano. *Il dominio veneziano a Creta nel XIII secolo*. Naples: F. Fiorentino, 1963.

Bratchel, M. E. "Alien Merchant Communities in Sixteenth-Century England: Community

Organisation and Social Mores." *Journal of Medieval and Renaissance Studies* 14 (1984): 39–62.

——. "Regulation and Group Consciousness in the Later History of London's Italian Merchant Colonies." *Journal of European Economic History* 9 (1980): 585–610.

Braude, Benjamin, and Bernard Lewis, "Introduction." In *Christians and Jews in the Ottoman Empire: The Functioning of a Plural Society*, ed. Benjamin Braude and Bernard Lewis, vol. 1. New York: Holmes & Meier, 1982.

——. "Venture and Faith in the Commercial Life of the Ottoman Balkans, 1500–1650." *International History Review* 7 (1985): 519–42.

Braudel, Fernand. *The Mediterranean and the Mediterranean World in the Age of Philip II*. 2 vols. New York: Harper, 1972.

——. *The Perspective of the World*. New York: Harper & Row, 1984.

Breisach, Ernst. *On the Future of History*. Chicago: University of Chicago Press, 2003.

Brown, Callum G. *Postmodernism for Historians*. Harlow, UK: Pearson-Longman, 2005.

Brown, Horatio F. "Venetians and the Venetian Quarter in Constantinople to the Close of the Twelfth Century." *Journal of Hellenic Studies* 40 (1920): 68–88.

——. "Il viaggio di Vicenzo Gradenigo, Bailo, da Venezia a Costantinopoli 1599." In *Scritti storici in memoria di Giovanni Monticolo*, ed. C. Cipolla et al. Venice: Carlo Ferrari, 1922.

Brown, Patricia Fortini. *Venetian Narrative Painting in the Age of Carpaccio*. New Haven: Yale University Press, 1988.

Brummett, Palmira. "Competition and Coincidence: Venetian Trading Interests and Ottoman Expansion in the Early Sixteenth-Century Levant." *New Perspectives on Turkey* 5–6 (1991): 29–52.

——. *Ottoman Seapower and Levantine Diplomacy in the Age of Discovery*. Albany: State University of New York Press, 1994.

——. "Understanding Space: Regions and Empires." Paper presented at the annual meeting of the Middle East Studies Association of North America, Phoenix, AZ, 19–22 November 1994.

Bruno, P. "Ambassadeurs de France et capucins français a Constantinople au XVIIe siècle d'après le journal du P. Thomas de Paris." *Études franciscaines* 29 (1913): 232–59.

Bulliet, Richard W. *The Case for Islamo-Christian Civilization*. New York: Columbia University Press, 2004.

Bumbaca, A. Delazari. "Schede per scolari francesi a Padova." *Quaderni per la storia dell'università di Padova* (1970): 137–144.

Burckhardt, Jacob *The Civilization of the Renaissance in Italy*. New York: Modern Library, 1954.

Burdelez, Ivana. "The Role of Ragusan Jews in the History of the Mediterranean Countries." In *Jews, Christians, and Muslims in the Mediterranean World after 1492*, ed. Alisa Meyuhas Ginio. London: Frank Cass, 1992.

Burke, Ersie. " 'Your Humble and Devoted Servants': Greco-Venetian Views of the Serenissima." In "Street Noises, Civic Spaces and Urban Identities in Italian Renaissance Cities," ed. F. W. Kent. Special issue, *Monash Publications in History* 34 (2000): 10–16.

Burke, Peter. "Early Modern Venice as a Center of Information and Communication." In

Venice Reconsidered, ed. John Martin and Dennis Romano. Baltimore: Johns Hopkins University Press, 2000.

———. *Varieties of Cultural History.* Ithaca: Cornell University Press, 1997.

———. *Venice and Amsterdam: A Study of Seventeenth-Century Elites.* 2nd ed. Cambridge: Polity Press, 1994.

Calabi, Donatella. "Gli stranieri e la città." In *Storia di Venezia,* ed. Alberto Tenenti and Ugo Tucci, vol. 5. Rome: Istituto della enciclopedia italiana Treccani, 1991.

Calimani, Riccardo. *Storia del ghetto di Venezia.* Milan: Rusconi, 1985.

Canny, Nicholas, and Anthony Pagden, eds. *Colonial Identity in the Atlantic World: 1500–1800.* Princeton: Princeton University Press, 1987.

Carter, C. H. "The Ambassadors of Early Modern Europe." In *From the Renaissance to the Counter-Reformation: Essays in Honor of Garrett Mattingly,* ed. Charles H. Carter. New York: Random House, 1965.

Casevitz, Michel, and Louis Basset, "*Peuple, Nation, État* en Grec ancien." In *Les mots de la nation,* ed. Sylvianne Rémi-Giraud and Pierre Rètat. Lyons: Presses universitaires de Lyon, 1996.

Casini, Matteo. "Realtà e simboli del cancellier grande veneziano in età moderna (secc. XVI–XVII)." *Studi veneziani* 22 (1991): 195–251.

Cassia, Paul Saint. "Religion, Politics, and Ethnicity in Cyprus during the Turkocratia (1571–1878)." *Archives Européennes de Sociologie* 27 (1986): 3–28.

Castellani, Aldo. "Dal diario inedito di Pietro Della Valle." *Miscellanea di storia delle esplorazioni* 21 (1996): 153–214.

Cervellini, G. B. "Relazioni da Costantinopoli del Vicario Patriarcale Angelo Petricca (1636–1639)," *Bessarione* 28 (1912): 15–53.

Cessi, Roberto. *Storia della repubblica di Venezia.* Florence: Giunti Martello, 1981.

Chabod, Federico. *L'idea di nazione.* Rome-Bari: Laterza, 1996.

Chandler, Tertius, and Gerald Fox. *3000 Years of Urban Growth.* New York: Academic Press, 1972.

Chaudhuri, K. N. "Trade as a Cultural Phenomenon." In *Clashes of Cultures: Essays in Honour of Niels Steensgaard,* ed. Jens Christian V. Johansen, Erling Ladewig Petersen, and Henrik Stevnsborg. Odense: Odense University Press, 1992.

Chejne, Anwar G. *Islam and the West: The Moriscos, a Cultural and Social History.* Albany: State University of New York Press, 1983.

Chew, Samuel C. *The Crescent and the Rose: Islam and England during the Renaissance.* Oxford: Oxford University Press, 1937.

Chojnacki, Stanley. "Identity and Ideology in Renaissance Venice: The Third Serrata." In *Venice Reconsidered: The History and Civilization of an Italian City-State, 1297–1797,* ed. John Martin and Dennis Romano. Baltimore: Johns Hopkins University Press, 2000.

Ciampi, Ignazio. *Della vita e delle opere di Pietro della Valle il Pellegrino.* Rome: Barbera, 1880.

Cipolla, Carlo. *Fighting the Plague in Seventeenth-Century Italy.* Madison: University of Wisconsin Press, 1981.

Çizakça, Murat. "Ottomans and the Mediterranean: An Analysis of the Ottoman Shipbuilding Industry as Reflected by the Arsenal Registers of Istanbul 1529–1650." In *Le genti del mare Mediterraneo,* ed. Rosalba Ragosta, vol. 2. Naples: Pironti, 1982.

Clissold, Stephen. "Christian Renegades and Barbary Corsairs." *History Today* 26 (1976): 508–15.

Clot, André. *Suleiman the Magnificent: The Man, His Life, His Epoch.* London: Saqi Books, 1992.

Cochrane, Eric, and Julius Kirshner. "Deconstructing Lane's Venice." *Journal of Modern History* 47 (1973): 321–34.

Cocchia, Rocco. *Storia delle Missioni dei Cappuccini.* Vol. 1. Paris: P. Lethielleux, 1867.

Coco, Carla, and Flora Manzonetto. *Baili veneziani alla sublime porta: storia e caratteristiche dell'ambasciata veneta a Costantinopoli.* Venice: Stamperia di Venezia, 1985.

Coles, Paul. *The Ottoman Impact on Europe.* London: Thames & Hudson, 1968.

"Colloque sur la langue comme expression de l'identité culturelle et comme instrument de communication entre les cultures." In *La langue: identité et communication,* vol. 3. Paris: UNESCO, 1986.

Concina, Ennio. *Dell'arabico: a Venezia tra Rinascimento e oriente.* Venice: Marsilio, 1994.

Cooperman, Bernard Dov. "Venetian Policy towards Levantine Jews in Its Broader Italian Context." In *Gli ebrei e Venezia, secoli XIV–XVIII,* ed. G. Cozzi. Milan: Edizioni comunità, 1987.

Corrazol, Gigi. "Varietà notarile: scorci di vita economica e sociale." In *Storia di Venezia,* ed. Gaetano Cozzi and Paolo Prodi, vol. 6. Rome: Istituto della enciclopedia italiana, 1994.

Cortelazzo, Manlio. "Che cosa s'intendesse per 'lingua franca'." *Lingua nostra* 26 (1965): 108–10.

Coulton, G. C. "Nationalism in the Middle Ages." *Cambridge Historical Journal* 5 (1935): 15–40.

Cozzi, Gaetano. *Repubblica di Venezia e stati italiani.* Turin: Einaudi, 1982.

Cozzi, Gaetano, and Michael Knapton. *La Repubblica di Venezia nell'età moderna: dalla guerra di Chioggia al 1517.* Turin: UTET, 1986.

Cunningham, Allan. "Dragomania: The Dragomans of the British Embassy in Turkey." *Middle Eastern Affairs,* no. 2, ed. A. Hourani. *St Anthony's Papers* 11 (1961): 81–100.

d'Alessio, E. Daleggio. "La communauté de Constantinople au lendemain de la conquête ottomane." *Échos d'orient* 36 (1937): 309–17.

———. *Le couvent et l'eglise des Saints-Pierre-et-Paul a Galata.* Istanbul: Milli Nesriyat Yurdu, 1935.

———. "Recherches sur l'histoire de la latinité de Constantinople (suite)." *Échos d'orient* 25 (1926): 21–41.

———. "Traité entre les Génois de Galata et Mehmet II." *Échos d'orient* 39 (1940): 161–75.

da Mosto, Andrea. *L'Archivio di stato di Venezia.* Vol. 1. Rome: Biblioteca d'arte editrice, 1937.

Daniel, Norman. *Islam and the West: The Making of an Image.* Rev. ed. Oxford: Oneworld, 1993.

Darling, Linda. "Rethinking Europe and the Islamic World in the Age of Exploration." *Journal of Early Modern History* 2 (1998): 221–46.

Davis, James C. "Shipping and Spying in the Early Career of a Venetian Doge, 1496–1502." *Studi Veneziani* 16 (1974): 97–108.

———. *A Venetian Family and Its Fortune, 1500–1900: The Donà and the Conservation of Their Wealth.* Philadelphia: American Philosophical Society, 1975.

Davis, Natalie Zemon. "Boundaries and the Sense of Self in Sixteenth-Century France." In *Reconstructing Individualism: Autonomy, Individuality, and the Self in Western Thought,* ed. Thomas C. Weller et al. Stanford: Stanford University Press, 1986.

———. *Society and Culture in Early Modern France.* Stanford: Stanford University Press, 1975.

———. *Women on the Margins: Three Seventeenth-Century Lives.* Cambridge, MA: Harvard University Press, 1995.

Davis, Robert C. *Christian Slaves, Muslim Masters: White Slavery in the Mediterranean, the Barbary Coast, and Italy, 1500–1800.* New York: Palgrave, 2003.

———. "Slave Redemption in Venice, 1585–1797." In *Venice Reconsidered: The History and Civilization of an Italian City-State, 1297–1797,* ed. John Martin and Dennis Romano. Baltimore: Johns Hopkins University Press, 2000.

Decei, Aurelio. "Aloisio Gritti în Slujba Sultanului Soliman Kanunî, După unele Documente Turceşti inedite (1533–1534)." *Studii si materiale de istorie medie* 7 (1974): 101–60.

de Groot, A. H. "The Dutch Nation in Istanbul 1600–1985: A Contribution to the Social History of Beyoğlu." *Anatolica* 14 (1987): 131–50.

———. *The Ottoman Empire and the Dutch Republic: A History of the Earliest Diplomatic Relations, 1610–1630.* Leiden: Nederlands Historisch-Archaeologisch Institut, 1978.

de Zanche, Luciano. "Tra Costantinopoli e Venezia: Dispacci di Stato e lettere di mercanti dal Basso Medioevo alla caduta della Serenissima." *Quaderni di storia postale* 25 (2000).

Diehl, Charles. "La colonie vénitienne à Constantinople à la fin du XIVe siècle." *Mélanges de l'École Française de Rome* 3 (1883): 90–131.

———. *Une république patricienne: Venise.* Paris: Ernest Flammarion, 1931.

Dispacci degli ambasciatori al senato. Rome: Ministero dell'interno, 1959.

Donia, Robert J., and John V. A. Fine Jr. *Bosnia and Hercegovina: A Tradition Betrayed.* New York: Columbia University Press, 1994.

Dotson, John. "Perceptions of the East in Fourteenth-Century Italian Merchant Manuals." In *Across the Mediterranean Frontiers: Trade, Politics, and Religion, 650–1450,* ed. Dionisius A. Agius and Ian Richard Netton. Turnhout: BREPOLS, 1997.

Douglas, Mary. *Purity and Danger.* London: Routledge & K. Paul, 1966.

Duara, Prasenjit. "Historicizing National Identity, or Who Imagines What and When." In *Becoming National,* ed. Geoff Eley and Ronald Grigor Suny. Oxford: Oxford University Press, 1996.

———. *Rescuing History from the Nation: Questioning Narratives of Modern China.* Chicago: University of Chicago Press, 1995.

Dursteler, Eric. "The *Bailo* in Constantinople: Crisis and Career in Venice's Early Modern Diplomatic Corps." *Mediterranean Historical Review* 16 (2001): 1–25.

———. "Education and Identity in Constantinople's Latin-rite Community, ca. 1600." *Renaissance Studies* 18 (2004): 287–303.

———. "Identity and Coexistence in the Eastern Mediterranean, ca. 1600: Venice and the Ottoman Empire." *New Perspectives on Turkey* 18 (1998): 113–30.

———. "Neighbors: Venetians and Ottomans in Early Modern Galata." In *Multicultural Europe and Cultural Exchange,* ed. James P. Helfers. Turnhout, Belgium: BREPOLS, 2005.

———. "Reverberations of the Voyages of Discovery in Venice, ca. 1501: The Trevisan Manuscript in the Library of Congress." *Mediterranean Studies* 9 (2001): 43–64.

Eldem, Edhem, Daniel Goffman, and Bruce Masters, *The Ottoman City between East and West: Aleppo, Izmir, and Istanbul*. Cambridge: Cambridge University Press, 1999.

Eley, Geoff, and Ronald Grigor Suny. "Introduction," in *Becoming National*. Oxford: Oxford University Press, 1996.

Elliott, J. H. "A Europe of Composite Monarchies." *Past and Present* 137 (1992): 48–71.

———. *The Old World and the New*. Cambridge: Cambridge University Press, 1970.

———. "Revolution and Continuity in Early Modern Europe." *Past and Present* 42 (1969): 35–56.

Elsner, Jás, and Joan P. Rubiés, eds. *Voyages and Visions: Towards a Cultural History of Travel*. London: Reaktion Books, 1999.

Embiricos, Alexandre. *La renaissance Crétoise. XVIe et XVIIe siècles*. Vol. 1: *La littérature*. Paris: Société d'Édition «Les Belles Lettres», 1960.

Encyclopedia of Islam. Ed. H. A. R. Gibbs, et al. New ed. Leiden: Brill, 1979–.

Erdoğru, M. Akif. "The Servants and Venetian Interest in Ottoman Cyprus in the Late Sixteenth and Early Seventeenth Centuries." *Quaderni di studi arabi* 5 (1997): S97–S120.

Erlap, Atila. "Turkey and the European Community: Forging New Identities along Old Lines." *New Perspectives on Turkey* 8 (1992): 1–14.

Esposito, John L. *Islam and the West*. Colchester, VT: St. Michael's College, 1991.

Fabris, Antonio. "Artisinat et culture: Recherches sur la production vénitienne et le marché ottoman au XVIe siècle." *Arab Historical Review for Ottoman Studies* 3–4 (1991): 51–60.

———. "Un caso di pirateria veneziana: la cattura della galea del Bey di Gerba (21 ottobre 1584)." *Quaderni di studi arabi* 8 (1990): 91–112.

———. "Il Dottor Girolamo Fasaneo, alias Receb." *Archivio veneto* 133 (1989): 105–18.

———. "Hasan 'Il veneziano' tra Algeria e Costantinopoli." *Quaderni di studi arabi*, 5 (1997): S51–S66.

———. "Influssi orientali nell'antica cucina veneziana." *Levante* 35 (1993): 21–28.

———. *Venezia: sapore di Oriente*. Venice: Centro Internazionale della Grafica, 1990.

Faroqhi, Suraiya. *Approaching Ottoman History: An Introduction to the Sources*. Cambridge: Cambridge University Press, 1999.

———. "Before 1600: Ottoman Attitudes towards Merchants from Latin Christendom." *Turcica* 34 (2002): 69–104.

———. "Crisis and Change, 1590–1699." In *An Economic and Social History of the Ottoman Empire*, ed. Halil İnalcık and Donald Quataert, vol. 2. Cambridge: Cambridge University Press, 1994.

———. "In Search of Ottoman History." *Journal of Peasant Studies* 18 (1991): 211–41.

———. "Notes on the Production of Cotton and Cotton Cloth in XVIth and XVIIth Century Anatolia." *Journal of European Economic History* 8 (1979): 405–17.

———. "Red Sea Trade and Communications Observed by Evliya Çelebi (1671–72)." *New Perspectives on Turkey* 5–6 (1991): 87–105.

———. *Subjects of the Sultans*. London: I. B. Tauris, 2000.

———. "Textile Production in Rumeli and the Arab Provinces: Geographical Distribution and Internal Trade (1560–1650)." *Journal of Ottoman Studies* 1 (1980): 61–82.

———. "The Venetian Presence in the Ottoman Empire (1600–1630)." *Journal of European Economic History* 15 (1986): 345–84.

Feldbæk, Ole. "Clash of Cultures in a Conglomerate State: Danes and Germans in 18th Century Denmark." In *Clashes of Cultures: Essays in Honour of Niels Steensgaard,* ed. Jens Christian V. Johansen, Erling Ladewig Petersen, and Henrik Stevnsborg. Odense: Odense University Press, 1992.

Fernandez, James. "Historians Tell Tales: Of Cartesian Cats and Gallic Cockfights." *Journal of Modern History* 60 (1988): 113–27.

Ferring, Robert Leo. "The Accomplished Ambassador by Christopher Varsevicius and Its Relation to Sixteenth Century Political Writings with a Translation of the Treatise from Latin." Ph.D. diss., Notre Dame University, 1959.

Findley, Carter V. *Ottoman and Civil Officialdom: A Social History.* Princeton: Princeton University Press, 1989.

Finkel, C. F. "French Mercenaries and the Ottoman State in the Sixteenth and Seventeenth Centuries: The Desertion of the Papa Garrison to the Ottomans in 1600." *Bulletin of the School of Oriental and African Studies* 55 (1992): 451–71.

Finlay, Robert. "Al servizio del Sultano: Venezia, i turchi e il mondo cristiano, 1523–1538." In *Renovatio Urbis,* ed. Manfredo Tafuri. Rome: Officina edizioni, 1984.

———. "Crisis and Crusade in the Mediterranean: Venice, Portugal, and the Cape Route to India (1498–1509)." *Studi veneziani* 28 (1994): 45–90.

———. "Fabius Maximus in Venice: Doge Andrea Gritti, the War of Cambrai, and the Rise of Habsburg Hegemony, 1509–1530." *Renaissance Quarterly* 53 (2000): 988–1031.

———. "Prophecy and Politics in Istanbul: Charles V, Sultan Suleyman, and the Habsburg Embassy of 1533–1534." *Journal of Early Modern History* 2 (1998): 1–31.

Fishman, J. A. "Language and Ethnicity." In *Language, Ethnicity and Intergroup Relations,* ed. Howard Giles. London: Academic Press, 1977.

Fleet, Kate. *European and Islamic Trade in the Early Ottoman State: The Merchants of Genoa and Turkey.* Cambridge: Cambridge University Press, 1999.

Fleischer, C. *Bureaucrat and Intellectual in the Ottoman Empire: The Historian Mustafa Âlī.* Princeton: Princeton University Press, 1986.

Folena, Gianfranco. *Vocabolario del veneziano di Carlo Goldoni.* Rome: Istituto della Enciclopedia italiana, 1993.

Forde, Simon, et al., eds. *Concepts of National Identity in the Middle Ages.* Leeds: University of Leeds, 1995.

Frazee, Charles. *Catholics and Sultans: The Church and the Ottoman Empire 1453–1923.* London: Cambridge University Press, 1983.

Fusaro, Maria. *Uva passa: una guerra commerciale tra Venezia e l'Inghilterra (1540–1640).* Venice: Il Cardo, 1996.

Galbraith, V. H. "Nationality and Language in Medieval England." *Transactions of the Royal Historical Society* 23 (1941): 113–28.

Gallina, Mario. *Una società coloniale del Trecento: Creta fra Venezia e Bisanzio.* Venice: Deputazione editrice, 1989.

Ganz, Margery A. "Florentine Friendship: Donato Acciaiuoli and Vespasiano da Bisticci." *Renaissance Quarterly* 43 (1990): 372–83.

Gara, Eleni. "In Search of Communities in Seventeenth-Century Ottoman Sources: The Case of the Kara Ferye District." *Turcica* 30 (1998): 135–61.

Gauchat, Patritium. *Hierarchia catholica medii et recentioris aevi*. Vol. 4. Monasterii: Sumptibus et Typis Librariae Regensbergianae, 1935.

Geanakoplos, Deno J. *Byzantine East and Latin West: Two Worlds of Christendom in Middle Ages and Renaissance*. Oxford: Blackwell, 1966. Reprint, Hamden, CT: Archon Press, 1976.

Geary, Patrick J. *The Myth of Nations: The Medieval Origins of Europe*. Princeton: Princeton University Press, 2002.

Gellner, Ernst. *Nationalism*. New York: New York University Press, 1997.

———. *Nations and Nationalism*. Ithaca: Cornell University Press, 1983.

Georgopoulou, Maria. *Venice's Mediterranean Colonies: Architecture and Urbanism*. Cambridge: Cambridge University Press, 2001.

Gerber, Haim. "Jewish Tax-Farmers in the Ottoman Empire in the Sixteenth and Seventeenth Centuries." *Journal of Turkish Studies* 10 (1986): 143–54.

———. "Social and Economic Position of Women in an Ottoman City, 1600–1700." *International Journal of Middle East Studies* 12 (1980): 231–44.

Giannetto, Francesco. "Il servizio di posta veneziano nella Roma di Paolo IV secondo i dispacci di Bernardo Navagero (1555–1558)." *Clio* 26 (1990): 123–38.

Gibb, H. A. R., and H. Bowen. *Islamic Society and the West*. 2 vols. London: Oxford University Press, 1950.

Gilbert, Felix. *The Pope, His Banker, and Venice*. Cambridge, MA: Harvard University Press, 1980.

Gleason, Elisabeth G. "Confronting New Realities: Venice and the Peace of Bologna, 1530." In *Venice Reconsidered: The History and Civilization of an Italian City-State, 1297–1797*, ed. John Martin and Dennis Romano. Baltimore: Johns Hopkins University Press, 2000.

Goffman, Daniel. *Britons in the Ottoman Empire, 1642–1660*. Seattle: University of Washington Press, 1998.

———. "The Capitulations and the Question of Authority in Levantine Trade, 1600–1650." *Journal of Turkish Studies* 10 (1986): 155–61.

———. *Izmir and the Levantine World, 1550–1650*. Seattle: University of Washington Press, 1990.

———. *The Ottoman Empire and Early Modern Europe*. Cambridge: Cambridge University Press, 2002.

———. "The Ottoman Role in Patterns of Commerce in Aleppo, Chios, Dubrovnik, and Istanbul (1600–1650)." In *Decision Making and Change in the Ottoman Empire*, ed. Caesar E. Farah. Kirksville, MO: Thomas Jefferson University Press, 1993.

Gökbilgin, Tayyib. "Le relazioni Veneto-Turche nell'etá di Solimano il Magnifico." *Il Veltro* 2–4 (1979): 265–88.

Göllner, C. *Turcica. Die europäischen türkendrucke des XVI jahrhunderts*. 2 vols. Bucharest: Editura Academiei, 1961, 1968.

Goodblatt, Morris S. *Jewish Life in Turkey in the XVIth Century: As Reflected in the Legal*

Writings of Samuel De Medina. New York: Jewish Theological Seminary of America, 5712 [1952].

Goody, Jack. *Islam in Europe.* Cambridge: Polity, 2004.

Greenblatt, Stephen. *Marvelous Possessions: The Wonder of the New World.* Chicago: University of Chicago Press, 1991.

———. *Renaissance Self-Fashioning: From More to Shakespeare.* Chicago: University of Chicago Press, 1980.

Greene, Molly. "Commerce and the Ottoman Conquest of Kandiye." *New Perspectives on Turkey* 10 (1994): 95–118.

———. "Ruling an Island without a Navy: A Comparative View of Venetian and Ottoman Crete." *Oriente Moderno* 20 (2001): 193–207.

———. *A Shared World: Christians and Muslims in the Early Modern Mediterranean.* Princeton: Princeton University Press, 2000.

Greenfeld, Liah. *Nationalism: Five Roads to Modernity.* Cambridge, MA: Harvard University Press, 1992.

Grubb, James S. "Catalysts for Organized Violence in the Early Venetian Territorial State." In *Bande armate, banditi, banditismo e repressione di giustizia negli stati europei di antico regime,* ed. Gherardo Ortalli. Rome: Jouvence, 1986.

———. "Elite Citizens." In *Venice Reconsidered: The History and Civilization of an Italian City-State, 1297–1797,* ed. John and Dennis Romano. Baltimore: Johns Hopkins University Press, 2000.

———. *Firstborn of Venice: Vicenza in the Early Renaissance State.* Baltimore: Johns Hopkins University Press, 1988.

———. "When Myths Lose Power: Four Decades of Venetian Historiography." *Journal of Modern History* 58 (1986): 43–94.

Gullino, Giuseppe. "I patrizi veneziani e la mercatura negli ultimi tre secoli della Repubblica." In *Mercanti e vita economica nella repubblica veneta (secoli XIII–XVIII),* ed. Giorgio Borelli, vol. 2. Verona: Banca popolare di Verona, 1985.

Haëdo, Diego de. *Topographia et historia general de Argel.* Madrid, 1927.

Hale, J. R. "Men and Weapons: The Fighting Potential of Sixteenth Century Venetian Galleys." In *War and Society: A Yearbook of Military History,* ed. Brian Bond and Ian Roy. London: Croom Helm, 1975.

Hale, J. R., and Michael Mallett. *The Military Organization of a Renaissance State: Venice c. 1400–1617.* Cambridge: Cambridge University Press, 1984.

Hammer, M. de. *Histoire de l'Empire Ottoman.* Trans. M. Dochez. 2 vols. Paris: Béthune et Plon, 1844.

Hanlon, Gregory. *Confession and Community in Seventeenth-Century France: Catholic and Protestant Coexistence in Aquitaine.* Philadelphia: University of Pennsylvania Press, 1993.

Hanna, Nelly. *Making Big Money in 1600: The Life and Times of Ismail Abu Taqiyya, Egyptian Merchant.* Syracuse: Syracuse University Press, 1998.

Harreld, Donald J. *High Germans in the Low Countries: German Merchants and Commerce in Golden Age Antwerp.* Leiden: Brill, 2004.

Hassiotis, Giovanni K. "Venezia e i domini veneziani tràmite di informazioni sui turchi per gli spagnoli nel sec. XVI." In *Venezia, centro di mediazione tra oriente e occidente (secoli XV–XVI): aspetti e problemi,* ed. Hans-Georg Beck, Manoussous Manoussacas, and Agostino Pertusi, vol. 1. Florence: Leo S. Olschki editore, 1977.

Heath, Michael. "Unholy Alliance: Valois and Ottomans." *Renaissance Studies* 3 (1989): 303–15

Hess, Andrew. *The Forgotten Frontier: A History of the Sixteenth-Century Ibero-African Frontier.* Chicago: University of Chicago Press, 1978.

Heyberger, Bernard. "Se convertir à l'Islam chez les Chrétiens de Syrie." *Dimensioni e problemi della ricerca storica* 2 (1996): 133–52.

Heyd, Uriel. "The Jewish Communities of Istanbul in the Seventeenth Century." *Oriens* 6 (1953): 299–314.

Heyd, Wilhelm. *Histoire du commerce du Levant au Moyen Âge.* 2 vols. Leipzig: Otto Harrassowitz, 1923.

Hill, George. *A History of Cyprus.* Vol. 3: *The Frankish Period, 1432–1571.* Cambridge: Cambridge University Press, 1972.

Hitti, Philip Khuri. *Islam and the West: A Historical Cultural Survey.* Princeton: Van Nostrand, 1962.

Hobsbawm, E. J. *Nations and Nationalism since 1870.* 2nd ed. Cambridge: Cambridge University Press, 1992.

Horodowich, Liz. "New Venice: Historians and Historiography in the 21st Century Lagoon." *History Compass* 2 (2004): 1–27.

Howard, Deborah. *Venice and the East: The Impact of the Islamic World on Venetian Architecture 1100–1500.* New Haven: Yale University Press, 2000.

Hughes, Diane Owen. "Earrings for Circumcision: Distinction and Purification in the Italian Renaissance City." In *Persons in Groups: Social Behavior as Identity Formation in Medieval and Renaissance Europe,* ed. Richard C. Trexler. Binghamton, NY: Medieval and Renaissance Texts and Studies, 1985.

———. "Sumptuary Law and Social Relations in Renaissance Italy." In *Disputes and Settlements: Law and Human Relations in the West,* ed. John Bossy. Cambridge: Cambridge University Press, 1983.

Hunt, Lynn, ed. *The New Cultural History.* Berkeley and Los Angeles: University of California Press, 1989.

Huntington, Samuel P. "The Clash of Civilizations?" *Foreign Affairs* 72 (summer 1993): 22–49.

Imber, Colin. *The Ottoman Empire, 1300–1650.* New York: Palgrave Macmillan, 2002.

Imhaus, Brunehild. *Le minoranze orientali a Venezia, 1300–1510.* Rome: Il veltro editrice, 1997.

İnalcık, Halil. "Biases in Studying Ottoman History." *Studies on Arab-Turkish Relations* 2 (1987): 7–10.

———. "Capital Formation in the Ottoman Empire." *Journal of Economic History* 29 (1969): 97–140.

———. "The Hub of the City: The Bedestan of Istanbul." *International Journal of Turkish Studies* 1 (1979–80): 1–17.

———. *The Ottoman Empire: The Classical Age.* London: Weidenfeld & Nicholson, 1973.

———. "Ottoman Galata, 1453–1553." In *Première Rencontre Internationale sur l'Empire Otto-man et la Turquie Moderne,* ed. Edhem Eldem. Istanbul: Éditions-Isis, 1991.

———. "The Ottoman State: Economy and Society, 1300–1600." In *An Economic and Social History of the Ottoman Empire: 1300–1600,* ed. Halil İnalcık and Donald Quataert, vol. 1. Cambridge: Cambridge University Press, 1994.

———. "An Outline of Ottoman-Venetian Relations." In *Venezia, centro di mediazione tra oriente e occidente (secoli xv–xvi): aspetti e problemi,* ed. Hans-Georg Beck, Manoussos Manoussacas, and Agostino Pertusi, vol. 1. Florence: Olschki editore, 1977.

———. "Servile Labor in the Ottoman Empire." in *The Mutual Effects of the Islamic and Judeo-Christian Worlds: The Eastern European Pattern,* ed. Abraham Ascher, Tibor Halasi-Kun, and Béla K. Király. Brooklyn: Brooklyn College Press, 1979.

———. "The Turkish Impact on the Development of Modern Europe." In *The Ottoman State and Its Place in World History,* ed. Kemal H. Karpat. Leiden: Brill, 1974.

Infelise, Mario. "Gian Rinaldo Carli Senior, dragomanno della repubblica." *Acta Histriae* 5 (1997): 189–98.

Iorga, Nicolae. "Contribuţiunĭ la istoria Muntenieĭ în a doua jumătate a secoluluĭ XVI–lea." *Analele academiei romane,* 2nd ser., 18 (1895–96): 1–112.

———. *Geschichte des osmanischen Reiches.* Gotha: F. Perthes, 1908–13.

İslamoğlu, Huri, and Çağlar Keyder. "Agenda for Ottoman History." *Review* 1 (1977): 31–55.

Issawi, Charles. "The Ottoman Empire in the European Economy, 1600–1914: Some Ob-servations and Many Questions." In *The Ottoman State and Its Place in World History,* ed. Kemal H. Karpat. Leiden: Brill, 1974.

Jacoby, David. "Cretan Cheese: A Neglected Aspect of Venetian Medieval Trade." In *Medieval and Renaissance Venice,* ed. Ellen E. Kittell and Thomas F. Madden. Urbana: University of Illinois Press, 1999.

———. "Venice and the Venetian Jews in the Eastern Mediterranean." In *Gli ebrei e Venezia, secoli XIV–XVIII,* ed G. Cozzi. Milan: Edizioni comunità, 1987.

James, Paul. *Nation Formation: Towards a Theory of Abstract Community.* London: Sage, 1996.

Jardine, Lisa, and Jerry Brotton. *Global Interests: Renaissance Art between East and West.* Ithaca: Cornell University Press, 2000.

Jenkins, Hester Donaldson. *Ibrahim Pasha: Grand Vizir of Suleiman the Magnificent.* New York: Columbia University, 1911.

Jennings, Ronald C. "Divorce in the Ottoman Sharia Court of Cyprus, 1580–1640." *Studia Islamica* 78 (1993): 155–67.

Kafadar, Cemal. *Between Two Worlds: The Construction of the Ottoman State.* Berkeley and Los Angeles: University of California Press, 1995.

———. "A Death in Venice (1575): Anatolian Muslim Merchants Trading in the Serenis-sima." *Journal of Turkish Studies* 10 (1986): 191–218.

———. "On the Purity and Corruption of the Janissaries." *Turkish Studies Bulletin* 15 (1991): 273–80.

——. "The Ottomans and Europe." In *Handbook of European History, 1400–1600,* ed. Thomas A. Brady, Jr., Heiko A. Oberman, and James D. Tracy, vol. 1. Leiden: Brill, 1994.

——. "Les troubles monétaires de la fin du XVIe siècle et la prise de conscience ottomane du déclin." *Annales: ESC* 46 (1991): 381–400.

——. "When Coins Turned into Drops of Dew and Bankers Became Robbers of Shadows: The Boundaries of Ottoman Economic Imagination at the End of the Sixteenth-Century." Ph.D diss., McGill University, 1986.

Kafé, Esther. "Le mythe Turc et son déclin dans les relations de voyage des Européens de la renaissance." *Oriens* 21–22 (1968–69): 159–95.

Kamps, Ivo, and Jyotsna G. Singh, eds. *Travel Knowledge: European "Discoveries" in the Early Modern Period.* New York: Palgrave, 2001.

Kellenbenz, Hermann. "Handelsverbindungen zwischen Mitteleuropa und Istanbul über Venedig in der ersten Hälfte de 16. Jahrhunderts." *Studi veneziani* 9 (1967): 193–99.

Kent, F.W. "Introduction." In *Bartolommeo Cederini and His Friends: Letters to an Obscure Florentine.* Florence: Olschki, 1991.

Kettering, Sharon. "Gift-Giving and Patronage in Early Modern France." *French History* 2 (1988): 131–51.

Kibre, Pearl. *The Nations in the Mediaeval Universities.* Cambridge, MA: Mediaeval Academy of America, 1948.

Kirshner, Julius. "Between Nature and Culture: An Opinion of Baldus of Perugia on Venetian Citizenship as Second Nature." *Journal of Medieval and Renaissance Studies* 9 (1979): 179–208.

Kissling, H. J. "Das Renegatentum in der Glanzeitt des Osmanischen Reiches." *Scientia* 55 (1961): 18–26.

Kortepeter, C. Max. *Ottoman Imperialism during the Reformation: Europe and the Caucasus.* New York: New York University Press, 1972.

Kreiser, Klaus. "Clio's Poor Relation: Betrachtungen zur osmanischen Historiographie von Hammer-Purgstall bis Stanford Shaw." *Weiner Beiträge zur Geschichte der Neuzeit* 10 (1983): 24–43.

Kretschmayr, Heinrich. *Geschichte von Vendig.* 2 vols. Gotha: F. A. Perthes, 1920.

——. "Ludovico Gritti, Eine Monographie." *Archiv für österreichische Geschichte* 83 (1897): 1–106.

Kunt, Metin I. "Derviş Mehmed Paşa, *Vezir* and Entrepreneur: A Study in Ottoman Political-Economic Theory and Practice." *Turcica* 9 (1987): 197–214.

——. "Ethnic-Regional (*Cins*) Solidarity in the Seventeenth-Century Ottoman Establishment." *International Journal of Middle East Studies* 5 (1974): 233–39.

——. "Transformation of Zimmi into Askeri." In *Christians and Jews in the Ottoman Empire: The Functioning of a Plural Society,* ed. Benjamin Braude and Bernard Lewis, vol. 1. New York: Holmes & Meier, 1982.

Lane, Frederic C. *Andrea Barbarigo: Merchant of Venice, 1418–49.* Baltimore: Johns Hopkins University Press, 1944.

——. "The Mediterranean Spice Trade: Further Evidence of Its Revival." In *Crisis and Change in the Venetian Economy,* ed. Brian Pullan. London: Methuen & Co., 1968.

———. *Ships and Shipbuilders of the Renaissance*. Baltimore: Johns Hopkins University Press, 1934.

———. "Venetian Shipping during the Commercial Revolution." In *Crisis and Change in the Venetian Economy*, ed. Brian Pullan. London: Methuen & Co., 1968.

———. *Venice: A Maritime Republic*. Baltimore: Johns Hopkins University Press, 1973.

———. *Venice and History: The Collected Papers of Frederic C. Lane*. Baltimore: Johns Hopkins Press, 1966.

Lapidus, Ira M. "Muslim Cities and Islamic Societies." In *Middle Eastern Cities*, ed. Ira M. Lapidus. Berkeley and Los Angeles: University of California Press, 1969.

Lassithiotakis, Michel. "'L'Isola di Candia, più d'ogn'altra lontana.'" In *Insularités ottomanes*, ed. Nicolas Vatin and Gilles Veinstein. Paris: Maisonneuve & Larose, 2004.

le Guern, Michel. "Le mot *Nation* dans les six premières éditions du *Dictionnaire de l'Académie*." In *Les mots de la nation*, ed. Sylvianne Rémi-Giraud and Pierre Rètat. Lyons: Presses universitaires de Lyon, 1996.

Lesure, Michel. "Michel Černović 'explorateur secretus' à Constantinople (1556–1563)." *Turcica* 15 (1983): 127–54.

———. "Notes et documents sur les relations vénéto-ottomanes 1570–1573." *Turcica* 4 (1972): 134–64; 8 (1976): 117–56.

Levy, Avigdor. *The Sephardim in the Ottoman Empire*. Princeton: Darwin Press, 1992.

———, ed. *Jews, Turks, Ottomans: A Shared History, Fifteenth Through the Twentieth Century*. Syracuse: Syracuse University Press, 2002.

Levy, Carl, ed. *Italian Regionalism: History, Identity, and Politics*. Oxford: Berg, 1996.

Lewis, Bernard. *The Crisis of Islam: Holy War and Unholy Terror*. New York: Random House, 2003.

———. *Cultures in Conflict: Christians, Muslims, and Jews in the Age of Discovery*. Oxford: Oxford University Press, 1995.

———. *From Babel to Dragomans: Interpreting the Middle East*. Oxford: Oxford University Press, 2004.

———. *Islam and the West*. Oxford: Oxford University Press, 1993.

———. *Istanbul and the Civilization of the Ottoman Empire*. Norman: University of Oklahoma Press, 1963.

———. *The Jews of Islam*. Princeton: Princeton University Press, 1984.

———. *The Muslim Discovery of Europe*. New York: Norton, 1982.

———. "The Ottoman Archives." *Archives* 4 (1960): 226–30.

———. "Ottoman Observers of Ottoman Decline." *Islamic Studies* 1 (1962): 71–87.

———. *The Political Language of Islam*. Chicago: University of Chicago Press, 1988.

———. "Some Reflections on the Decline of the Ottoman Empire." *Studia Islamica* 9 (1962): 111–27.

———. *What Went Wrong*. New York: HarperCollins, 2002.

Libby, Lester. "Venetian Views of the Ottoman Empire from the Peace of 1503 to the War of Cyprus." *Sixteenth Century Journal* 9 (1978): 101–26.

Livi, Carlo, Domenico Sella, and Ugo Tucci. "Un probleme d'histoire: la décadence economique de Venise." in *Aspetti e causa della decadenza economica veneziana nel secolo XVII*. Venice: Istituto per la collaborazione culturale, 1961.

Lollino, Luigi. *Vita del cavaliere Ottaviano Bon.* Venice: P. Naratovich, 1854.

Lopasic, Alexander. "Islamization of the Balkans with Special Reference to Bosnia." *Journal of Islamic Studies* 5 (1994): 163–86.

Luca, Cristian. "Alcuni 'confidenti' del bailaggio veneto di Costantinopoli nel Seicento." *Annuario dell'Istituto Romeno di Cultura e Ricerca Umanistica di Venezia* 5 (2003): 299–310.

Lucchetta, Francesca. "Il medico del bailaggio di Costantinopoli: fra terapie e politica (secc. XV–XVI)." *Quaderni di studi arabi* 5 (1997): S5–S50.

———. "La scuola dei 'giovani di lingua' veneti nei secoli XVI e XVII." *Quaderni di studi arabi* 7 (1989): 19–40.

———. "Sulla ritrattistica veneziana in oriente." *Quaderni di studi arabi* 8 (1990): 113–22.

Lucchetta, Giuliano. "L'oriente mediterraneo nella cultura di Venezia tra il 400 e il 500." In *Storia della cultura veneta,* ed. Girolamo Arnaldi and Manlio Pastore Stocchi, vol. 3, part 2: *Dal primo quattrocento al concilio di Trento.* Vicenza: Neri Pozza editore, 1984.

———. "Viaggiatori, geografi e racconti di viaggio dell'età barocca." In *Storia della cultura veneta,* ed. Girolamo Arnaldi and Manlio Pastore Stocchi, vol. 4, part 2: *Il 600.* Vicenza: Neri Pozza editore, 1984.

Luzzatto, Gino. "La decadenza di Venezia dopo le scoperte geografiche nella tradizione e nella realtà." *Archivio veneto,* 5th ser., 54–55 (1954): 162–81.

———. *Storia economica di Venezia dall'XI all'XVI secolo.* Venice: Marsilio editore, 1995.

Lybyer, Albert Howe. *The Government of the Ottoman Empire in the Time of Suleiman the Magnificent.* Cambridge, MA: Harvard University Press, 1913.

———. "The Ottoman Turks and the Routes of Oriental Trade." *English Historical Review* 120 (1915): 577–88.

Madden, Thomas F. *Enrico Dandolo and the Rise of Venice.* Baltimore: Johns Hopkins University Press, 2003.

Maltezou, Chryssa A. "The Historical and Social Context." In *Literature and Society in Renaissance Crete,* ed. David Holton. Cambridge: Cambridge University Press, 1991.

———. *Ho thesmos tou en Kônstantinoupolei Venetou vailou.* [Ο θεσμὸς τοῦ ἐν Κωνσταντινουπόλει Βενετοῦ Βαΐλου]. Athens: Ethnikon kai Kapodistriakon Panepistemion Athenon, Philosophike Schole, 1970.

———. "Il quartiere veneziano di Costantinopoli." *Thesaurimata* 15 (1978): 30–61.

Mantran, Robert. "Arsenali di Istanbul dal XV al XVII secolo: Qasim Pascia e Top-Hanè." In *Arsenali e città nell'occidente europeo,* ed. Ennio Concina. Rome: La nuova Italia scientifica, 1987.

———. "L'Empire ottoman: la vision européenne." *Studies on Turkish-Arab Relations* 1 (1986): 189–92.

———. *Histoire d'Istanbul.* N.p.: Fayard, 1996.

———. *Istanbul au siècle de Soliman le Magnifique.* Paris: Hachette, 1994.

———. *Istanbul dans la seconde moitié du XVIIe siècle.* Paris: Librairie Adrien Maisonneuve, 1962.

———. "Minoritaires, métiers et marchands étrangers à Istanbul aux XVIe et XVIIe siècles." In *L'Empire ottoman du XVIe au XVIIIe siècle: administration, économie, société.* London: Variorum Reprints, 1984.

———. "La navigation vénitienne et ses concurrentes en Méditerranée orientale aux XVIIe et XVIIIe siècles." In *Mediterraneo e Oceano Indiano, Atti del VI. Colloquio Internazionale di Storia Marittima, 1962. Fondazione Giorgio Cini.* Florence: Leo S. Olschiki, 1970.

———. "Règlements fiscaux ottomans: la police des marchés de Stamboul au début du XVIe siècle." *Cahiers de Tunisie* 14 (1956): 213–41.

———. "Venise, centre d'informations sur les turcs." In *Venezia, centro di mediazione tra oriente e occidente (secoli XV XVI): aspetti e problemi,* ed. Hans-Georg Beck, Manoussos Manoussacas, and Agostino Pertusi, vol. 1. Florence: Olschki editore, 1977.

Marghetitch, S. G. *Étude sur les fonctions des drogmans des missions diplomatiques ou consulaires en Turquie.* Constantinople: n.p., 1898. Reprint, Istanbul: Les Éditions Isis, 1993.

Margolin, Jean-Claude. "Erasme et la Guerre Contre les Turcs." *Il pensiero politico* 13 (1980): 3–38.

Martin, John. *Venice's Hidden Enemies: Italian Heretics in a Renaissance City.* Berkeley and Los Angeles: University of California Press, 1993.

Martin, John, and Dennis Romano. "Introduction." In *Venice Reconsidered: The History and Civilization of an Italian City-State, 1297–1797,* ed. John Martin and Dennis Romano. Baltimore: Johns Hopkins University Press, 2000.

Martines, Lauro. *Power and Imagination: City-States in Renaissance Italy.* Baltimore: Johns Hopkins University Press, 1988.

Masters, Bruce. "Trading Diasporas and 'Nations': The Genesis of National Identities in Ottoman Aleppo." *International History Review* 9 (1987): 345–67

Matar, Nabil. *Turks, Moors, and Englishmen in the Age of Discovery.* New York: Columbia University Press, 1999.

Matteucci, P. Gualberto. *Un glorioso convento francescano sulle rive del Bosforo: il San Francesco di Galata in Costantinopoli—c. 1230–1697.* Florence: Edizioni studi francescani, 1967.

Matthee, Rudi. "Merchants in Safavid Iran: Participants and Perceptions." *Journal of Early Modern History* 4 (2000): 233–68.

Mattingly, Garrett. *Renaissance Diplomacy.* London: Butler & Tanner, 1963.

Mauro, Frédéric. "Merchant Communities, 1350–1750." In *The Rise of Merchant Empires: Long Distance Trade in the Early Modern World, 1350–1750,* ed. James D. Tracy. Cambridge: Cambridge University Press, 1990.

Mauroeide, Phane. *Ho Hellenismos sto Galata (1453–1600). [Ο Ελληνισμός στο Γαλατα (1453–1600)].* N.p.: Ioannina, 1992.

McGowan, Bruce. *Economic Life in Ottoman Europe: Taxation, Trade, and the Struggle for Land, 1600–1800.* London: Cambridge University Press, 1981.

McKee, Sally. *Uncommon Dominion: Venetian Crete and the Myth of Ethnic Purity.* Philadelphia: University of Pennsylvania Press, 2000.

McNeill, William H. "The Ottoman Empire in World History." In *The Ottoman State and Its Place in World History,* ed. Kemal H. Karpat. Leiden: Brill, 1974.

———. *Venice: The Hinge of Europe, 1081–1797.* Chicago: University of Chicago Press, 1974.

Meri, Josef W. *The Cult of Saints among Muslims and Jews in Medieval Syria.* Oxford: Oxford University Press, 2002.

Miller, William. *The Latins in the Levant: A History of Frankish Greece (1204–1566)*. London: John Murray, 1908. Reprint, Cambridge: Speculum Historiale, 1964.

Mitler, Louis. "The Genoese in Galata: 1453–1682." *Journal of Middle East Studies* 10 (1979): 71–91.

Moacanin, Nenad. "Some Remarks on the Supposed Tolerance towards *dhimmis*." *Südost-forschungen* 48 (1989): 209–15.

Moeglin, Jean-Marie. "Nation et nationalisme du Moyen Âge à l'Époque moderne (France-Allemagne)." *Revue historique* 301 (1999): 537–53.

Molà, Luca, and Rheinhold C. Mueller. "Essere straniero a Venezia nel tardo Medioevo: accoglienza e rifiuto nei privilegi di cittadinanza e nelle sentenze criminali." In *Le migrazioni in Europa secc. XIII–XVIII*, ed. Simonetta Cavaciocchi. [Florence]: Le Monnier, 1994.

Molho, Anthony. "Cosimo de' Medici: *Pater Patriae* or *Padrino?*" *Stanford Italian Review* 1 (1979): 5–33.

———. "Ebrei e marrani fra Italia e Levante ottomano." In *Storia d'Italia—Annali*, vol. 11: *Gli ebrei in Italia*, ed. Corrado Vivanti. Turin: Giulio Einaudi editore, 1997.

Molmenti, Pompeo. *I banditi della Repubblica veneta*. 2nd ed. Florence: n.p., 1898. Reprint, Vittorio Veneto: Dario de Bastiani, 1989.

Mordtmann, J. H. "Constantinople." In *E. J. Brill's First Encyclopedia of Islam 1913–1936*, ed. M. Th. Houtsma et al., vol. 2. Leiden: Brill, 1913–38. Reprint, Leiden: Brill, 1987.

———. "Die jüdischen kira im Serai der Sultane." *Mitteilungen des Seminars für orientalischen Sprachen* 32 (1929): 1–38.

Mueller, Rheinhold C. "*Veneti facti privilegio:* les étrangers naturalisés à Venise entre XIVe et XVIe siècle." In *Les Étrangers dans la Ville: Minorités et espace urbain du bas Moyen Âge à l'époque moderne*, ed. Jaques Bottin and Donatella Calabi. Paris: Éditions de la Maison des sciences de l'homme, 1999.

Muir, Edward. *Civic Ritual in Renaissance Venice*. Princeton: Princeton University Press, 1981.

———. *Mad Blood Stirring: Vendetta and Factions in Friuli during the Renaissance*. Baltimore: Johns Hopkins University Press, 1993.

Mun, Gabriel de. "L'Établissement des Jesuites a Constantinople sous le regne d'Achmet 1er (1603–1617)." *Revue des questions historiques* 74 (1903): 163–72.

Murphey, Rhoads. "Forms of Differentiation and Expressions of Individuality in Ottoman Society." *Turcica* 34 (2002): 135–70.

———. "Jewish Contributions to Ottoman Medicine." In *Jews, Turks, Ottomans: A Shared History, Fifteenth through the Twentieth Century*, ed. Avigdor Levy. Syracuse: Syracuse University Press, 2002.

———. "Provisioning Istanbul: The State and Subsistence in the Early Modern Middle East." *Food and Foodways* 2 (1988): 217–63.

Najemy, John M. *Between Friends: Discourses of Power and Desire in the Machiavelli-Vettori Letters of 1513–1515*. Princeton: Princeton University Press, 1993.

Neff, Mary. "A Citizen in the Service of the Patrician State: The Career of Zaccaria de' Freschi." *Studi veneziani* 5 (1981): 33–61.

Newton, Stella Mary. *The Dress of the Venetians, 1495–1525*. Aldershot, UK: Scolar Press, 1988.

Nicholle, David. *Armies of the Ottoman Turks, 1300–1774*. London: Osprey, 1983.

Nicol, Donald M. *Byzantium and Venice: A Study in Diplomatic and Cultural Relations*. Cambridge: Cambridge University Press, 1988.

Norwich, John Julius. *A History of Venice*. London: Penguin, 1982.

Olivieri, Achille. "Mercanti e 'mondi': a Venezia, nel '500." *Studi veneziani* 7 (1983). 143–59.

———. "Tempo et historia delle famiglie a Venezia nel '500: le mitologie mediterranee fra i Gritti, i Cavalli, gli Oddo." *Studi Veneziani* 29 (1995): 167–92.

Ortalli, Gherardo, ed. *Venezia e Creta*. Venice: Istituto Veneto di Scienze, Lettere ed Arti, 1998.

Ortayli, Ilber. "La vie quotidienne des missions étrangeres à Galata." In *Première Rencontre Internationale sur l'Empire Ottoman et la Turquie Moderne*, ed. Edhem Eldem. Istanbul: Éditions-Isis, 1991.

Paci, Renzo. *La scala di Spalato e il commercio veneziano nei Balcani fra cinque e seicento*. Venice: Deputazione di storia patria per le venezie, 1971.

Pagano de Devitiis, Gigliola. *English Merchants in Seventeenth-Century Italy*. Cambridge: Cambridge University Press, 1997.

Pagden, Anthony. *European Encounters with the New World*. New Haven: Yale University Press, 1993.

Paladino, Giuseppe. "Due dragomanni veneti a Costantinopoli (Tommaso Tarsia e Gian Rinaldo Carli)." *Nuovo archivio veneto*, 2nd ser., 33 (1917): 183–200.

Pallucchini, Rodolfo, and Paola Rossi. *Tintoretto: Le opere sacre e profane*. 2 vols. Milan: Electa, 1982.

Panopoulou, Angeliki. "Oi technites tou naupegeion tou Chandaka kai ton Chanion kata to 16o kai 17o aiona [Οι Τεχνίτες των Ναυπηγείων του Χανδάκα και των Χανιών κατά το 16ο και 17ο Αιώνα]." *Krētikē hestia* 4, no. 3 (1989–90): 173–94.

Parker, Geoffrey. *The Military Revolution: Military Innovation and the Rise of the West, 1500–1800*. 2nd ed. Cambridge: Cambridge University Press, 1996.

Parker, Kenneth, ed. *Early Modern Tales of Orient*. London: Routledge, 1999.

Pecchioli, Renzo. *Dal «mito» di Venezia all'«ideologia americana»: itinerari e modelli della storiografia sul repubblicanesimo dell'età moderna*. Venice: Marsilio editori, 1983.

Pedani-Fabris, Maria Pia. *Documenti turchi dell'archivio di stato di Venezia*. Rome: Ministero per i beni culturali e ambientali, 1994.

———. *In nome del Gran Signore*. Venice: Deputazione editrice, 1994.

———. "Presenze islamiche a Venezia." *Levante* 35 (1993): 13–20.

———. "Safiye's Household and Venetian Diplomacy." *Turcica* 32 (2000): 9–32.

———. "Veneziani a Costantinopoli alla fine del XVI secolo." *Quaderni di studi arabi* 5 (1997): S67–S84.

Peirce, Leslie P. *The Imperial Harem: Women and Sovereignty in the Ottoman Empire*. Oxford: Oxford University Press, 1993.

Penzer, N. M. *The Harēm*. Philadelphia: J. B. Lippincott, n.d.

Perocco, Daria. "'Un male non pensato': Pietro Bembo e la scoperta dell'america." In *L'impatto della scoperta dell'America nella cultura veneziana, Atti del I Convegno Colombiano*, ed. A. Caracciolo Aricò. Rome: Bulzoni editore, 1990.

Perry, Mary Elizabeth. "Contested Identities: The Morisca Visionary Beatriz de Robles." In *Women in the Inquisition: Spain and the New World*, ed. Mary Giles. Baltimore: Johns Hopkins University Press, 1999.

Pippidi, Andrei. *Hommes et idées du Sud-Est européen à l'aube de l'âge moderne.* Bucharest: Editura Academiei, 1980.

Pippidi, D. "Sur quelques drogmans de Constantinople au XVIIe siècle." *Revue historique du sud-est européen* 10 (1972): 227–54.

Pistarino, Geo. "The Genoese in Pera—Turkish Galata." *Mediterranean Historical Review* 1 (1986): 63–85.

Post, Gaines. "Medieval and Renaissance Ideas of Nation." In *Dictionary of the History of Ideas: Studies of Selected Pivotal Ideas*, ed. Philip P. Wiener, vol. 3. New York: Charles Scribner's Sons, 1973.

Poumarède, Gérard. "Justifier l'injustifiable: l'Alliance Turque au miroir de la chrétienté (XVIe–XVIIe siècles)." *Revue d'histoire diplomatique* 111 (1997): 217–46.

Povolo, Claudio. "Aspetti e problemi dell'amministrazione della giustizia penale nella Repubblica di Venezia. Secoli XVI–XVII." In *Stato, società e giustizia nella Repubblica di Venezia nei secoli XV–XVIII*, ed. Gaetano Cozzi. Rome: Jouvence, 1981.

———. "Crimine e giustizia a Vicenza. Secoli XVI–XVII. Fonti e problematiche per l'approfondimento di una ricerca sui rapporti politico-giudiziari tra Venezia e la terraferma." In *Venezia e la terraferma attraverso le relazioni dei rettori*. Milan: A. Giuffrè editore, 1980.

———. "Nella spirale della violenza. Cronologia, intensità e diffusione del banditismo nella terraferma veneta (1550–1610)." In *Bande armate, banditi, banditismo e repressione di giustizia negli stati europei di antico regime*, ed. Gherardo Ortalli. Rome: Jouvence, 1986.

Prestholdt, Jeremy. "Portuguese Conceptual Categories and the 'Other' Encounter on the Swahili Coast." *Journal of Asian and African Studies* 36 (2001): 383–406.

Preto, Paolo. "Le relazioni dei baili veneziani a Costantinopoli." *Il Veltro* 2–4 (1979): 125–31.

———. *I servizi secreti di Venezia.* Milan: Il Saggiatore, 1994.

———. *Venezia e i turchi.* Florence: Sansoni, 1975.

Pullan, Brian. "The Conversion of Jews: The Style of Italy." *Bulletin of the John Rylands Library of Manchester* 70 (1988): 53–70.

———. "The Inquisition and the Jews of Venice: The Case of Gaspare Ribeiro, 1580–81." *Bulletin of the John Rylands Library of Manchester* 62 (1979): 207–31.

———. *The Jews of Europe and the Inquisition of Venice, 1550–1670.* London: I. B. Tauris, 1983.

———. *Rich and Poor in Renaissance Venice.* Cambridge, MA: Harvard University Press, 1971.

———. "'A Ship with Two Rudders': 'Righetto Marrano' and the Inquisition in Venice." *The Historical Journal* 20 (1977): 25–58.

———, ed. *Crisis and Change in the Venetian Economy in the Sixteenth and Seventeenth Centuries.* London: Metheun, 1968.

Quatrefages, René. "La perception gouvernementale espagnole de l'alliance franco-turque au XVIe siècle." *Revue internationale d'histoire militaire* 68 (1987): 71–84.

Queller, Donald E. "The Development of Ambassadorial Relazioni." In *Renaissance Venice*, ed. J. R. Hale. London: Faber & Faber, 1973.

——. *The Fourth Crusade: The Conquest of Constantinople, 1201–1204*. Philadelphia: University of Pennsylvania Press, 1977.

——. "How to Succeed as an Ambassador: A Sixteenth-Century Venetian Document." *Studia Gratiana* 15 (1972): 653–71.

——. *The Venetian Patriciate*. Urbana: University of Illinois Press, 1986.

Ranke, Leopold. *The Ottoman and Spanish Empires in the Sixteenth and Seventeenth Centuries*. Trans. Walter K. Kelly. London: Whitaker & Co., 1843. Reprint, New York: AMS, 1975.

Rapp, Richard. *Industry and Economic Decline in Seventeenth-Century Venice*. Cambridge, MA: Harvard University Press, 1976.

——. "The Unmaking of the Mediterranean Trade Hegemony: International Trade Rivalry and the Commercial Revolution." *Journal of Economic History* 25 (1975): 499–525.

Ravid, Benjamin. "From Yellow to Red: On the Distinguishing Head-Covering of the Jews of Venice." *Jewish History* 6 (1992): 179–210.

——. " 'How Profitable the Nation of the Jewes Are': *The Humble Addresses* of Menasseh ben Israel and the *Discorso* of Simone Luzzatto." In *Mystics, Philosophers, and Politicians*, ed. Jehuda Reinharz, Daniel Swetschinski, and Kalman P. Bland. Durham: Duke University Press, 1982.

——. "The Legal Status of the Jewish Merchants of Venice, 1541–1638." *Journal of Economic History* 35 (1975): 274–79.

——. "A Tale of Three Cities and Their *Raison d'État*: Ancona, Venice, Livorno, and the Competition for Jewish Merchants in the Sixteenth Century." In *Jews, Christians, and Muslims in the Mediterranean World after 1492*, ed. Alisa Meyuhas Ginio. London: Frank Cass, 1992.

Raymond, André. "The Ottoman Conquest and Development of the Great Arab Towns." *International Journal of Turkish Studies* 1 (1979–80): 84–101.

Renan, Ernst. "What Is a Nation?" In *Becoming National*, ed. Geoff Eley and Ronald Grigor Suny. Oxford: Oxford University Press, 1996.

Renard, John. "Seven Doors to Islam." Ph.D. diss., University of California, 1996.

Reyerson, Katherine L. "The Merchants of the Mediterranean: Merchants as Strangers." In *The Stranger in Medieval Society*, ed. F.R.P. Akehurts and Stephanie Cain Van D'Elden. Minneapolis: University of Minnesota Press, 1997.

Riggio, Achille. "Musulmani in Calabria convertiti al cristianesimo." *Archivio storico per la Calabria e Lucania* (1949): 45–59.

Rinieri, P. Ilario. *Clemente VIII e Sinan Bassà Cicala*. Rome: Civiltà cattolica, 1898.

Robbert, Louise Buenger. "Rialto Businessmen in Constantinople." *Dumbarton Oaks Papers* 49 (1995): 43–58.

Rodinson, Maxime. *Europe and the Mystique of Islam*. Trans. Roger Venius. Seattle: University of Washington Press, 1987.

Rossi, Ettore. "La sultana Nūr Bānū (Cecilia Venier-Baffo) moglie di Selīm II (1566–1574) e madre di Murād III (1574–1595)." *Oriente moderno* 33 (1953): 433–41.

Rostagno, Lucia. *Mi faccio turco: esperienze ed immagini dell'Islam nell'Italia moderna*. Rome: Istituto per l'oriente C. A. Nallino, 1983.

Roth, Cecil. *Doña Gracia of the House of Nasi*. Philadelphia: Jewish Publication Society, 1977.

———. *The Duke of Naxos of the House of Nasi*. Philadelphia: Jewish Publication Society, 1948.

———. *History of the Jews in Venice*. New York: Schocken Books, 1930.

———. *History of the Jews of Italy*. Philadelphia: Jewish Publication Society of America, 1946.

———. "The Strange Case of Hector Mendes Bravo." *Hebrew Union College Annual* 18 (1944): 221–45.

Rouillard, Clarence Dana. *The Turk in French History, Thought and Literature*. Paris: Boivin & Co., n.d.

Rozen, Minna. *A History of the Jewish Community in Istanbul: The Formative Years, 1453–1566*. Leiden: Brill, 2002.

———. "Public Space and Private Space among the Jews of Istanbul in the Sixteenth and Seventeenth Centuries." *Turcica* 30 (1998): 331–46.

Rubiés, Joan-Pau. "Instructions for Travellers: Teaching the Eye to See." *History and Anthropology* 9 (1996): 139–90.

———. *Travel and Ethnology in the Renaissance: South India through European Eyes, 1250–1625*. Cambridge: Cambridge University Press, 2000.

———. "Travel Writing as a Genre: Facts, Fictions, and the Invention of a Scientific Discourse in Early Modern Europe." *Journeys* 1 (2000): 5–35.

Rudt de Collenberg, W. H. *Esclavage et rançons des chrétiens en Méditerranée (1570–1600)*. Paris: Le Léopard d'or, 1987.

Runciman, Steven. "Constantinople-Istanbul." *Revue des études sud-est européennes* 7 (1969): 205–8.

Sahlins, Peter. *Boundaries: The Making of France and Spain in the Pyrenees*. Berkeley and Los Angeles: University of California Press, 1989.

———. *Unnaturally French: Foreign Citizens in the Old Regime and After*. Ithaca: Cornell University Press, 2004.

Said, Edward W. *Covering Islam: How the Media and the Experts Determine How We See the Rest of the World*. New York: Pantheon, 1981.

———. *Orientalism*. New York: Vintage Books, 1979.

Sapori, Armando. *The Italian Merchant in the Middle Ages*. New York: Norton, 1970.

"Saying No to Turkey." *New York Times*, August 15, 2004.

Scaraffia, Lucetta. *Rinnegati: Per una storia dell'identità occidentale*. Rome: Laterza, 1993.

Schiavi, Luigi Arnaldo. "Gli ebrei in Venezia e nelle sue colonie." *Nuova antologia* 47 (1893): 487–519.

Schmidt, Jan. "The Egri-Campaign of 1596; Military History and the Problem of Sources." In *Habsburgisch-osmanische Beziehungen*. Vienna: Verlag des Verbandes der wissenschaftlichen Gesellschaften Österreichs, 1985.

Schneider, A. M., and M. Is. Nomidis. *Galata, topographisch-archäologischer Plan mit erläuterndem Text*. Istanbul: N.p., 1944.

Schulze, Hagen. *States, Nations, and Nationalism: From the Middle Ages to the Present*. Trans. William E. Yuill. Oxford: Blackwell, 1996.

Schwartz, Stuart B. "Introduction." In *Implicit Understandings*, ed. Stuart B. Schwartz. Cambridge: Cambridge University Press, 1994.

Schwoebel, Robert. *The Shadow of the Crescent: The Renaissance Image of the Turk*. New York: St. Martins Press, 1969.

Scott, Joan Wallach. "The Problem of Invisibility." In *Retrieving Women's History: Changing Perceptions of the Role of Women in Politics and Society*, ed. S. Jay Kleinberg. Oxford: Berg/UNESCO, 1988.

Segre, Renata. "Sephardic Settlements in Sixteenth-Century Italy: A Historical and Geographical Survey." In *Jews, Christians, and Muslims in the Mediterranean World after 1492*, ed. Alisa Meyuhas Ginio. London: Frank Cass, 1992.

Sella, Domenico. *Commerci e industrie a Venezia nel secolo XVII*. Venice: Fondazione Cini, 1961.

———. "L'economia." In *Storia di Venezia*, ed. Gaetano Cozzi and Paolo Prodi, vol. 6. Rome: Istituto della enciclopedia italiana, 1994.

Seni, Nora. "Les levantins d'Istanbul à travers les récits des voyageurs du XIXe siècle." In *Première Rencontre Internationale sur l'Empire Ottoman et la Turquie Moderne*, ed. Edhem Eldem. Istanbul: Éditions-Isis, 1991.

Setton, Kenneth M. "Lutheranism and the Turkish Peril." *Balkan Studies* 3 (1962): 133–68.

———. *Venice, Austria, and the Turks in the Seventeenth Century*. Philadelphia: American Philosophical Society, 1991.

———. *Western Hostility to Islam and Prophecies of Turkish Doom*. Philadelphia: American Philosophical Society, 1992.

Shaw, Ezel Kural, and C. J. Heywood. *English and Continental Views of the Ottoman Empire, 1500–1800*. Berkeley and Los Angeles: University of California Press, 1972.

Shaw, Stanford. *History of the Ottoman Empire and Modern Turkey: Empire of the Gazis*. Vol. 1. Cambridge: Cambridge University Press, 1976.

———. *The Jews of the Ottoman Empire and the Turkish Republic*. New York: New York University Press, 1991.

———. "Ottoman and Turkish Studies in the United States." In *The Ottoman State and Its Place in World History*, ed. Kemal H. Karpat. Leiden: Brill, 1974.

Shmuelevitz, Aryeh. *The Jews of the Ottoman Empire in the Late Fifteenth and the Sixteenth Centuries*. Leiden: Brill, 1984.

Simon, Bruno. "Les dépêches de Marin Cavalli bayle a Constantinople (1558–1560)." Ph.D. diss., École des hautes études en sciences sociales, n.d.

———. "I rappresentanti diplomatici veneziani a Costantinopoli." In *Venezia e i turchi: scontri e confronti di due civiltà*. Milan: Electa editrice, 1985.

———. "La vie quotidienne a Costantinople d'apres les dépêches des envoyes vénitiens (1540–1566)." *Arab Historical Review for Ottoman Studies* 9–10 (1994): 201–7.

Simonsfeld, Henry. *Der Fondaco dei Tedeschi in Venedig und die deutsch-venetianischen Handelsbeziehungen*. 2 vols. Stuttgart: Neudruck der Ausg. (Cotta), 1887; Reprint, Aalen: Scientia-Verlag, 1968.

Skilliter, S. A. "The Letters of the Venetian 'Sultana' Nūr Bānū and Her Kira to Venice." In *Studia turcologica memoriae Alexii Bombaci Dicata*, ed. Aldo Gallotta and Ugo Marazzi. Naples: Istituto universitario orientale, 1982.

Slot, B. J. *Archipelagus Turbatus: les Cyclades entre colonisation latine et occupation ottomane c.*

1500–1718. 2 vols. Istanbul: Nederlands Historisch-Archaeologisch Instituut te Istanbul, 1982.

Smith, Anthony D. *The Nation in History: Historiographical Debates about Ethnicity and Nationalism.* Hanover: University Press of New England, 2000.

Smyth, Alfred P., ed. *Medieval Europeans: Studies in Ethnic Identity and National Perspectives in Medieval Europe.* London: Macmillan, 1999.

Sonyel, Salahi R. "The Protégé System in the Ottoman Empire." *Journal of Islamic Studies* 2 (1991): 56–66.

Southern, R. W. *Western Views of Islam in the Middle Ages.* Cambridge, MA: Harvard University Press, 1962.

Spagni, Emilio. "Una sultana veneziana." *Nuovo archivio veneto* 19 (1900): 241–348.

Spitz, Lewis W. *The Protestant Reformation, 1517–1559.* New York: Harper & Row, 1985.

Stajnova, Mihaila, and Raja Zaimova. "Le thème ottoman dans le théâtre de l'europe occidentale du XVIIe." *Études balkaniques* 20 (1984): 95–103.

Stancovich, Don Pietro. *Biografia degli uomini distinti dell'Istria.* Capodistria: Carlo Priora tipografo editore, 1888.

Starn, Randolph. *Contrary Commonwealth: The Theme of Exile in Medieval and Renaissance Italy.* Berkeley and Los Angeles: University of California Press, 1982.

Staurakēs, Nikolaos. *Statistikē tou plēthysmou tēs Krētēs.* [Στατιστική του Πληθυσμού της Κρήτης.] Athens: Typographer Palingenesia, 1890.

Steensgaard, Niels. "Consuls and Nations in the Levant from 1570–1650." *Scandinavian Economic History Review* 15 (1967): 13–53.

Stefani, Giuseppe, ed. *L'assicurazione a Venezia: dalle origini alla fine della Serenissima.* 2 vols. Trieste: Assicurazioni Generali di Trieste e Venezia, 1956.

Stella, Aldo. "La crisi economica veneziana della seconda metá del secolo XVI." *Archivio Veneto,* 5th ser., 58–59 (1956): 17–69.

Stoianovich, Traian. "Cities, Capital Accumulation, and the Ottoman Balkan Command Economy, 1500–1800." In *Cities and the Rise of States in Europe, a.d. 1000 to 1800,* ed. Charles Tilly and Wim P. Blockmans. Boulder: Westview Press, 1994.

Sturdza, Mihail-Dimitri. *Dictionnaire historique et généalogique des grandes familles de Grèce, d'Albanie et de Constantinople.* Paris: Chez l'auteur, 1983.

Subacchi, Paola. "Italians in Antwerp in the Second Half of the Sixteenth Century." In *Minderheden in Westeuropese steden (16de–20ste eeuw),* ed. Hugo Soly and Alfons K. L. Thijs. Brussels: Institut historique belge de Rome, 1995.

Tenenti, Alberto. *Naufrages, corsairs et assurances maritimes à Venise, 1592–1609.* Paris: SEVPEN, 1959.

———. *Piracy and the Decline of Venice, 1580–1615.* Berkeley and Los Angeles: University of California Press, 1967.

———. "Profilo di un conflitto secolare." In *Venezia e i turchi: scontri e confronti di due civiltà.* Milan: Electa, 1985.

———. "Gli schiavi di Venezia alla fine del Cinquecento." *Rivista storica italiana* 67 (1955): 52–69.

———. "The Sense of Space and Time in the Venetian World of the Fifteenth and Sixteenth Centuries." In *Renaissance Venice,* ed. J. R. Hale. London: Faber & Faber, 1973.

Tongas, Gérard. *Les relations de la France avec l'Empire Ottoman durant la première moitié du XVIIe siècle et l'Ambassade a Constantinople de Phillippe de Harlay, Comte de Césy (1619–1640)*. Toulouse: Imprimerie F. Boisseau, 1942.

Tormene, P. Augusto. "Il bailaggio a Costantinopoli di Girolamo Lippomano e la sua tragica fine." *Nuovo archivio veneto*, n. s., 3, t. 6 (1903): 375–431; 4, t. 7 (1904): 66–125, 288–333; 4, t. 8 (1904): 127–61.

Trannoy, A. "La «nation latine» de Constantinople." *Échos d'orient* 11 (1912): 246–56.

Trebbi, Giuseppe. "La cancelleria veneta nei secoli XVI e XVII." *Annali della fondazione Luigi Einaudi* 14 (1980): 65–125.

Trevor-Roper, H. R. "A Case of Coexistence: Christendom and the Turks." In *Historical Essays*. New York: Harper & Row, 1957.

Tucci, Ugo. "Il commercio del vino nell'economia cretese." In *Venezia e Creta*, ed. Gherardo Ortalli. Venice: Istituto veneto di scienze, lettere ed arti, 1998.

———. "I greci nella vita marittima veneziana." In *I greci a Venezia*, ed. Maria Francesca Tiepolo and Eurigio Tonetti. Venice: Istituto veneto di scienze, lettere ed arti, 2002.

———. *Mercanti, navi, monete nel Cinquecento veneziano*. Bologna: Il Mulino, 1981.

———. "The Psychology of the Venetian Merchant in the Sixteenth Century." In *Renaissance Venice*, ed. J. R. Hale. London: Faber & Faber, 1973.

———. "Tra Venezia e mondo turco: i mercanti." In *Venezia e i turchi: scontri e confronti di due civiltà*. Milan: Electa, 1985.

Tuncel, Bedrettin. "L'âge des drogmans." In *Istanbul à la jonction des cultures balkaniques, méditeranéennes, slaves et orientales, aux XVIe–XIXe siècles*. Bucharest: ΑΙΕSEE, 1977.

Turan, Şerafettin. "Venedik'te Türk Ticaret Merkezi." *Belleten* 32 (1968): 247–83.

"Un Bailo accusato di stregoneria." *Nuovo archivio veneto* 34 (1887): 359–66.

Valensi, Lucette. *The Birth of the Despot: Venice and the Sublime Porte*. Ithaca: Cornell University Press, 1993.

van Rappard, Frans Alexander Ridder. *Ernst Brinck, eerst secretaris van het nederlandsche gezantschap te Konstantinopel, later burgemeester van Harderwijk*. Utrecht: Kemink & Zoon, 1868.

Vanzan Marchini, Nelli-Elena. *I mali e i rimedi della serenissima*. Vicenza: Pozza, 1995.

Varshney, Ashutosh. *Ethnic Conflict and Civic Life: Hindus and Muslims in India*. New Haven: Yale University Press, 2002.

Vatin, Nicolas. *Les Ottomans et l'Occident (XVe–XVIe siècles)*. Istanbul: Isis Press, 2001.

Vaughan, Dorothy M. *Europe and the Turk: A Pattern of Alliances, 1350–1700*. Liverpool: University Press, 1954. Reprint, New York: AMS Press, 1976.

Veinstein, Gilles. "From the Italians to the Ottomans: The Case of the Northern Black Sea Coast in the Sixteenth Century." *Mediterranean Historical Review* 1 (1986): 221–37.

———. "Marchands Ottomans en Pologne-Lituanie et en Moscovie sous le règne de Soliman le Magnifique." *Cahiers du monde russe* 35 (1994): 713–38.

———. "Sur les conversions à l'Islam dans les Balkans Ottomans avant le XIXe siècle." *Dimensioni e problemi della ricerca storica* 2 (1996): 153–67.

Ventura, Angelo. "Introduction." In *Relazioni degli ambasciatori veneti al senato*. Vol. 1. Rome: Laterza, 1976.

———. *Nobiltà e popolo nella società veneta del Quattrocento e Cinquecento*. Rome: Laterza, 1964. Reprint, Milan: Edizioni Unicopoli, 1993.

Vercellin, Giorgio. "Mercanti turchi e sensali a Venezia." *Studi veneziani* 9 (1980): 45–78.
———. "Mercanti turchi a Venezia alla fine del Cinquecento." *Il Veltro* 23 (1979): 243–76.
Villain-Gandossi, Christiane. "Les attributions du Baile de Constantinople dans le fonction-nement des Échelles du Levant au XVIe siècle." *Recueils de la Societé Jean Bodin* 33, part 2 (1972): 227–44.
———. "Les dépêches chiffrées de Vettore Bragadin, baile de Constantinople (12 juillet 1564–15 juin 1566)." *Turcica* 1–2 (1978): 52–106.
Vink, Markus P. M. "Images and Ideologies of Dutch–South Asian Contact: Cross-Cultural Encounters between the Nayaka State of Madurai and the Dutch East India Company in the Seventeenth Century." *Itinerario* 21 (1997): 82–123.
Vitkus, Daniel J. "Early Modern Orientalism: Representations of Islam in Sixteenth- and Seventeenth-Century Europe." In *Western Views of Islam in Medieval and Early Modern Europe: Perception of Other,* ed. David R. Blanks and Michael Frassetto. New York: St. Martin's Press, 1999.
Von Grunebaum, G. E. *Islam: Essays in the Nature and Growth of a Cultural Tradition.* 2nd ed. London: Routledge & Kegan Paul, 1961.
Wake, C. H. H. "The Changing Pattern of Europe's Pepper and Spice Imports, ca. 1400–1700." *Journal of European Economic History* 8 (1979): 361–403.
Wansbrough, J. E. *Lingua Franca in the Mediterranean.* Richmond, UK: Curzon Press, 1996.
Ward, Joseph P. "Religious Diversity and Guild Unity in Early Modern London." In *Religion and the English People 1500–1640: New Voices, New Perspectives,* ed. Eric Josef Carlson. Kirksville, MO: Thomas Jefferson University Press, 1998.
Weisser, Michael R. *Crime and Punishment in Early Modern Europe.* Atlantic Highlands, NJ: Humanities Press, 1979.
Wheatcroft, Andrew. *Infidels.* New York: Random House 2004.
White, Philip. "What Is a Nationality?" *Canadian Review of Studies in Nationalism* 12 (1985): 1–23.
Willan, Thomas S. "Some Aspects of English Trade with the Levant in the Sixteenth Century." *English Historical Review* 70 (1955): 399–410.
Wilson, Bronwen. "Reflecting on the Turk in Late Sixteenth-Century Venetian Portrait Books." *Word and Image* 19 (2003): 38–58.
———. "Reproducing the Contours of Venetian Identity in Sixteenth-Century Costume Books." *Studies in Iconography* 25 (2004): 1–54.
Wolf, Eric. *Europe and the People without History.* Berkeley and Los Angeles: University of California Press, 1982.
Wolfe, Michael. *Changing Identities in Early Modern France.* Durham: Duke University Press, 1997.
Wood, A. C. "The English Embassy at Constantinople." *English Historical Review* 40 (1925): 533–61.
———. *A History of the Levant Company.* Oxford: Oxford University Press, 1935. Reprint, London: Frank Cass, 1964.
Woodhead, Christine. *Ta 'līkī-zāde's şehnāme-i hümāyūn: A History of the Ottoman Campaign into Hungary 1593–94.* Berlin: Klaus Schwarz Verlag, 1983.
Woolf, S. J. "Venice and the Terraferma: Problems of the Change from Commercial to

Landed Activities." In *Crisis and Change in the Venetian Economy*, ed. Brian Pullan. London: Methuen & Co., 1968.

Yapp, M. E. "Europe in the Turkish Mirror." *Past and Present* 137 (1992): 134–55.

Yerasimos, Stéphane. "À propos des *sürgün* de Karaman à Istanbul au XVIe siècle." In *Syncrétismes et hérésies dans l'Orient seldjoukide et ottoman (XIVe–XVIIIe siècle)*, ed. Gilles Veinstein. Paris: Peeters, 2005.

———. "La communauté juive d'Istanbul à la fin du XVIe siècle." *Turcica* 27 (1995): 101–33.

———. "Galata à travers les récits de voyage (1453–1600)." In *Première rencontre internationale sur l'Empire Ottoman et la Turquie moderne*, ed. Eldem Edhem. Istanbul: Isis, 1991.

———. *Les voyageurs dans l'empire ottoman (XIVe–XVIe siècles)*. Ankara: Imprimerie de la société turque d'histoire, 1991.

Yerasimos, Stéphane, and Jean-Louis Bacqué-Grammont. "La résidence du baile de Venise à Balikpazari. Essai de localisation," *Anatolia Moderna* 6 (1992): 1–11.

Yriarte, Charles. *La vie d'un patricien de Venise au 16e siècle*. Paris: E. Plon & Co., 1874.

Zachariadou, Elizabeth A. "À propos du syncrétisme islamo-chrétien dans les territoires ottomans." In *Syncrétismes et hérésies dans l'Orient seldjoukide et ottoman (XIVe–XVIIIe siècle)*, ed. Gilles Veinstein. Paris: Peeters, 2005.

———. "Co-Existence and Religion." *Archivium Ottomanicum* 15 (1997): 119–29.

Zannini, Andrea. *Burocrazia e burocrati a Venezia in età moderna: i cittadini originari (sec. XVI–XVIII)*. Venice: Istituto veneto di scienze, lettere ed arti, 1993.

Zele, Walter. "Aspetti delle legazioni ottomane nei Diarii di Marino Sanudo." *Studi veneziani* 18 (1989): 241–84.

Zernatto, Guido. "Nation: The History of a Word." *Review of Politics* 6 (1944): 351–66.

Zinkeisen, Johann Wilhelm. *Geschichte des osmanischen Reiches in Europa*. Hamburg: F. Perthes, 1840–63.

Zorattini, Pier Cesar Ioly. "Anrriquez Nunez alias Abraham alias Righetto: A Marrano Caught between the S. Uffizio of Venice and the Inquisition of Lisbon." In *The Mediterranean and the Jews: Banking, Finance, and International Trade (XVI–XVIII Centuries)*, ed. Ariel Toaff and Simon Schwarzfuchs. Ramat Gan, Israel: Bar-Ilan University Press, 1989.

———. "Jews, Crypto-Jews, and the Inquisition." In *The Jews of Early Modern Venice*, ed. Robert C. Davis and Benjamin Ravid. Baltimore: Johns Hopkins University Press, 2001.

Index

Mocenigo, Giovanni, 82

Moldavia, 138

Moliére, 179

money-lending, 171–72, 242n120

morality, 35, 65, 96, 97, 154, 170, 218n178

Moro, Giandomenico, 67

Moro, Giovanni, Bailo, 52, 68, 115, 155, 180

Morosini, Alvise, 64

Morosini, Gianfrancesco, Bailo, 70, 82, 100, 110, 116, 121, 122–23, 174

Moryson, Fynes, 96–97, 104, 158–59

Mundy, Peter, 15

Murad III, Sultan, 129

Murad Paşa, 172

Muslims, 51, 91, 143, 149, 153, 155, 156, 157, 158, 165, 171–72; as merchants, 26, 47, 51, 58, 59, 92, 148, 160, 161, 171–72. See also Islam

Mustafa Ali, 13, 119, 120, 127

Mustafa Bey, 51, 166

Muzio, Girolamo, 43

Nabi, 13

Naima, 13, 116, 120–21, 163, 165

Nani, Agostino, Bailo, 51–52, 122, 135, 175

Nani, Almoro, Bailo, 14, 69, 89, 175, 176, 180

Nasi, Joseph, 111

Nassuf Paşa, 166

Navon, Tommaso, 157

Naxos, Duchy of, 108, 111, 139

Nicolay, Nicholas de, 126, 154

Ni'matallah, 117

notary, 27, 30, 33, 34, 110, 145

Nūr Bānū, 129

Ömer Ağa, 125

Orembi, 180

Ottoman Empire, 3, 12, 35, 75–76, 86, 132, 148, 149; approaches to, 7–10, 20, 153; and bailo, 28, 38; Christians in, 11, 12, 31; commercial motives of, 189n16; concept of nation in, 13–14; and conflicts with Muslim powers, 12; and Crete/Candia, 80, 82; and Europe, 6–9, 12; expansion of, 23; and Greek-Venetian subjects, 86; industry in, 62, 66; Jews in, 12; language in, 14, 35; law in, 12, 38, 75; religious identity in, 11; and renegades, 130; and Rome/papacy, 144; and slaves, 72, 75; society in, 130, 132; and stato da mar, 79; taxation by, 86; tol-

erance toward minorities by, 7; and trade, 24; and unofficial nation, 62; and Venetian Empire, 3–6, 4–6, 12, 20–21, 23–24, 28, 29, 62, 78, 79, 151

Ottoman officials/state, 46, 56, 58, 59, 95–97, 101, 111, 112, 132, 133, 135–36, 138–39, 148; and banditi, 65; and devşirme, 126; and dragomans, 36; and Galata, 155; and Gazanfer Ağa as, 120–21; and Greek-Venetian tax evasion, 83; and Jews, 109–10; and slaves, 75; and trade, 162–69, 173

Ottomans, 39, 51, 126, 134, 154, 155, 160; at bailate, 27; and slavery, 73–74, 94; social and personal relationships of, 173–80

Ottoman subjects, 123, 147; and bailo, 30; dragomans as, 36, 39; European trade with, 159; and Jews, 110, 111; as merchants, 52, 131, 208n101; Perots as, 142, 145, 146, 149–50; Pirons as, 147; as protected merchants, 55–57, 58; in Venetian military, 5

Parker, Geoffrey, 115

Passi, David, 87, 111, 129

paternalism, 69, 93, 97, 100, 101

patriarchal vicar, 88–89, 137, 143, 144

patricians, 16, 17, 32, 44, 45–46, 48, 59, 119, 133, 147; as banditi, 65; and conversion, 137; in Council of Twelve, 41, 202n5; and cursus honorum, 31, 45–46; in government service, 44; identity of, 136–41, 149; Jewish agents of, 108–9; as merchants, 42–47, 49–50, 52, 60, 203n18; sons of, 47, 100, 204n39; as travelers, 98–99

Peçevi, 163

Pedani-Fabris, Maria Pia, 164, 238n52

Pera, 188n3. See also Galata; Vigne de Pera

Perots, 141–49, 156

Pesaro, 111

Pianella, Girolamo, 41, 42, 55–56, 57, 58, 60

Pigafetta, Antonio, 154, 157

piracy, 79, 84–85. See also corsairs

Piron, Antonio, 147, 148, 149

Piron, Niccolò, 147, 148

Piron, Stefano, 147, 235n93

Piron (Perone) family, 147–49

Pisani, Cecilia, 95

Pisani, Francesco, 101

Pius II, 6